Persian-English
English-Persian
Learner's Dictionary

Persian-English
English-Persian
Learner's Dictionary
A Dictionary for English Speakers
Studying Persian (Farsi/Dari)

by

Yavar Dehghani

IBEX Publishers
Bethesda, Maryland

Persian-English / English-Persian Learner's Dictionary
by Yavar Dehghani

Manufactured in the United States of America

The paper used in this book meets the minimum requirements of the American National Standard for Information Services – Permanence of Paper for Printed Library Materials, ANSI Z39.48 1984

IBEX Publishers, Inc.
Post Office Box 30087
Bethesda, Maryland 20824 USA
Telephone: 301-718-8188
Facsimile: 301-907-8707
www.ibexpublishers.com

Library of Congress Cataloging-in-Publication Information

Dehghani, Yavar.
Persian-English English-Persian learner's dictionary : a dictionary for English speakers studying Persian (Farsi/Dari) / by Yavar Dehghani.
p. cm.
English and Persian.
ISBN 1588140342 (alk. paper)
1. Persian Language—Dictionaries--English. 2. English Language—Dictionaries--Persian. I. Title

PK6379 .D443 2006
491/.55321—dc22
2006041755

Table of Contents

Preface

The increasing popularity of the study of Persian (also known as Farsi, Tajiki or Dari) in the English speaking world has created a need for a bi-directional Persian-English dictionary geared towards English speakers who are learning Persian.

I have been teaching Persian as a primary and foreign language both in Iran and Australia for many years. I always felt the need for such a dictionary, especially when I began to work as the Head of the Persian Department in the ADF School of Languages in Australia. I also knew that, in other English speaking countries, there were other Persian instructors and students who needed such a dictionary. Individuals who had used my Persian phrasebook also requested such a dictionary. Many students, although eager to use other reference works, found it difficult to read the Persian alphabet. This dictionary is compiled using a simple transliteration and not the Persian script.

The *Persian-English/English-Persian Learner's Dictionary* addresses a variety of audiences:
- English speaking students of Persian.
- English speakers who are seeking to communicate with Persian speakers.
- Children of Iranians, Afghans and Tajiks outside their homeland who wish to learn their mother language.
- Persian speakers who wish to learn English.

Although there are other Persian-English dictionaries, they are written for those for whom Persian is the first language, do not have transliteration, and are not as useful for non-native speakers.

The *Persian-English /English-Persian Learner's Dictionary* is also unique in several ways:
- **Bi-directional:** This is the first and only Persian-English / English-Persian dictionary in one volume which features both transliteration and Persian script.
- **Alphabet:** The alphabet used in Persian is completely different from the English, which can be a major barrier in the early stages of learning the language. This dictionary provides a simple transliteration of the Persian word along with its equivalent in the Persian alphabet.
- **Alphabetical order:** In this dictionary, the alphabetical order in the Persian-English section is based on the English spelling (with kh «خ», ch «چ» and sh «ش» as separate letters). This makes finding a word easy for the user who is not familiar with the Persian alphabet. In this method, they would be able to find the transliteration as quick as the English word and they can match it with the equivalent word in the script. So this dictionary is the first one which can be used by those

who are not comfortable with the Persian script. That is, when they hear a word like *khâb* they can refer to the dictionary immediately and find the meaning 'sleep' and if they are interested, they can look at the Persian equivalent خواب in front of it.

- **Correct use of words:** This dictionary gives synonyms in various contexts allowing the student to easily choose the correct meaning.

- **Linguistically oriented:** This dictionary gives grammatical suggestions on synonyms. The student will be able to choose one meaning over another using these hints rather than guessing and using an awkward meaning for a given text. It also gives the present tense form for the verbs which is different from the infinitive form (as a dictionary entry). This is especially helpful in using verb forms for non-native speakers. For example, the verb *to burn* in the dictionary is as an infinitive form *sukhtan*. When the infinitive marker *an* is taken off, the verb becomes past tense form *sukht*. However, the present tense form is different, *suz*, and a non-native speaker can not guess this by looking at the past tense form. Thus, giving this form in the dictionary makes it easier to make present tense forms grammatically correct. So the entry is like this: *sukhtan (suz)*.

- **Entries:** Approximately 18,000 entries covering both day-to-day and more specialized vocabulary.

Introduction

Persian is a member of the Indo-Iranian language group which itself is a member of the Indo-European language family. The major Iranian languages are Persian, Pashtu, Kurdish, Gilaki and Baluchi. Persian is the official language of Iran, Afghanistan (along with Pashtu) and Tajikistan. In addition, Persian is also spoken by a significant number of speakers in neighboring countries (Iraq, United Arab Emirates, Bahrain, Oman and Yemen). There are also large Persian speaking immigrant communities in North America, Western Europe and Australia

The history of the Persian language is divided into three major periods. Old Persian was spoken from beginning of the Achæmenid Empire (around 550 BC) until the conquest of Persia by Alexander. Middle Persian was spoken from 330 BC until the fall of the Sassanid dynasty (around seventh century). After the introduction of Islam in Iran, Persian was suppressed and Arabic became the official language. Two centuries later Modern Persian emerged and a slightly modified Arabic script was adopted for writing the language. Also, because of the Arab-Islamic influence many Arabic loan words entered the language.

The characters which we have used for the transliteration of Persian vowels and consonants in this dictionary, together with their sounds are as follow:

Vowels

The vowel system in Persian is simple and consists of six vowels:

a	as the 'a' in *ask* and *fast*
e	as the 'e' in *get* and *fell*
i	as the 'i' in *fit* and *pitch*
o	as the 'a' in *ball* or the 'o' in *mole*
u	as the 'u' in *rule* and *push*
â	as the 'o' in *top* or 'a' in *father*

Most Persian consonants are pronounced similar to their English counterparts:

b	as the 'b' in *boy*
ch	as the 'ch' in *cheese*
d	as the 'd' in *door*
f	as the 'f' in *feet*

j	as the 'j' in *jar*
m	as the 'm' in *me*
n	as the 'n' in *net*
s	as the 's' in *sin*
sh	as the 'sh' in *she*
t	as the 't' in *toy*
v	as the 'v' in *vest*
y	as the 'y' in *yes*
z	as the 'z' in *zip*

There are three consonants in Persian which do not exist in English. These are:

kh — as the 'ch' in the Scottish *loch*. It is pronounced at the back of the mouth, when the root of tongue makes a smooth contact with the end of the palate.

q — a guttural sound like a heavy French 'r', which is also pronounced at the back of the mouth, when the root of tongue makes a sudden contact with the end of the palate

zh — as the 'zh' in *Zhivago* or the 'g' in *mirage*

' — a glottal stop, which is pronounced in the throat and marks a break in the flow of speech.

The following consonants are slightly different from their English counterparts:

l — is pronounced in the front of the mouth, so it is similar to the 'l' in *life*, but not the 'l' in *role*.

k — is similar to the English 'k' before or after 'â, u, o' but it is palatalized before or after 'a, e, i' which is similar to the 'ck' in *backyard*.

r — similar to a trilled 'r' in English, but never silent or diphthongized.

h — as in the 'h' in *hit*. It is never silent.

g — like 'k' has two forms: it is like the 'g' in *got* before or after 'â, o, u', and similar to the 'g' in *get* before or after 'a, e, i.'

All Persian consonants can be doubled where they are always pronounced distinctly as in 'hot tea' but not in 'kettle.'

The pronunciation of Persian is easy and straightforward. Unlike in English, there is a consistency between pronunciation and spelling most of the time. Stress is generally on the last syllable of the word, as in e.g. *nânevâyi* 'bakery'. However, the stress on proper names is on the first syllable, as in e.g. *dâriyush* 'Darius'.

Words with Variant Meanings

Choosing a meaning out of two or more for a word in a bilingual dictionary is usually challenging, because the user does not know exactly which meaning is suitable for that particular word in a particular text. However, there are methods to help narrow the possibilities.

One way is to grammatically categorize the meaning of the English word. For example, if we specify noun, verb, and adjective forms of a word with their related meaning, it will help the reader to decide which meaning is best for that specific word form. That is why, in the English-Persian part of the dictionary, when necessary, we indicate in parenthesis in front of English words which meaning of the word is suitable for a specific grammatical category. For example, we separate the two different meanings of *about* in Persian by noting that one is an adverb (e.g. *about two kilos*) and the other is a preposition (e.g. *about him*). Otherwise, the non-native speaker would choose one for another by chance and the meaning can be completely wrong.

about   (adv) *taqriban* تقریباً   (pre) *dar morede* در مورد

Another way to distinguish different meanings in Persian is using the related meaning in English. For example, there are different meanings for the word *date* in English. By giving the different English equivalents of this word, we make it easier for the reader to choose the correct meaning.

date (appointment)   *qarâr* قرار

date (edible)   *khormâ* خرما

date (time)   *târikh* تاریخ

There are also English words which have several meanings in Persian, and there are no syntactically and semantically related hints for choosing one over the others. However, one of these words is more commonly used. This form is marked with (c). For example, there are different meanings for the word 'death' but one is used more often, which is *marg*.

death   *rehlat* رحلت   *mot* موت   (c) *marg* مرگ   *fot* فوت   *ajal* اجل

Simple and Compound Verbs in Persian

In Persian, there are two types of verbs: simple verbs which are one-word verbs and compound verbs. The common simple verbs are as follows:

Present	Past	Meaning
âvar	âvard	'bring'
âviz	âvikht	'hang'
ây	âmad	'come'
band	bast	'close, tie'
bar	bord	'take'
bin	did	'see'
bor	borid	'cut'
dah	dâd	'give'
dân	dânest	'understand'
dav	david	'run'
forush	forukht	'sell'
gir	gereft	'get, take'
guy	goft	'tell'
ist	istâd	'stand'
kan	kand	'dig'
kâr	kâsht	'plant'
kesh	keshid	'pull, draw'
kon	kard	'do'
kosh	kosht	'kill'
mân	mând	'stay'
mir	mord	'die'
nevis	nevesht	'write'
neshin	neshast	'sit'
par	parid	'fly, jump'
paz	pokht	'cook'
raqs	raqsid	'dance'
ras	rasid	'reach, arrive'
rav	raft	'go'
riz	rikht	'pour'
shav	shod	'become'
sâz	sâkht	'make, build'
shur	shost	'wash'
suz	sukht	'burn'
tavân	tavânest	'can'
khâb	khâbid	'sleep'

khâh	khâst	'want'
khar	kharid	'buy'
dâr	dâsht	'have'
pors	porsid	'ask'
chin	chid	'pick'
bardâr	bardâsht	'pick up'
gozâr	gozâsht	'put'
khân	khând	'read, sing'
shenâs	shenâkht	'know'
zan	zad	'hit'

Most Persian verbs are compound. These verbs consist of at least two words: a noun or an adjective which comes before a simple verb like *kon* 'do'. Some examples are:

COMPOUND VERB	MEANING
kon	**'do'**
bâzi mikonam	'I play'
bâz mikonam	'I close'
tamâm mikonam	'I finish'
qabul mikonam	'I accept'
kâr mikonam	'I work'
dah	**'give'**
neshân midaham	'I show'
ejâze midaham	'I let'
javâb midaham	'I answer'
zan	**'hit'**
dast mizanam	'I touch'
zang mizanam	'I ring'
hads mizanam	'I guess'
shav	**'become'**
rad mishavam	'I fail'
qabul mishavam	'I pass'
khaste mishavam	'I get tired'

For changing the Person and Number of the verb, the suffixes are attached only to the second part, and not on the first part, as in:

man   asb   savâr   mi   shav   am
I ride the horse

However, you cannot say:

man   asb   mi   savâr   am

Present and Past Tense

To form a verb in the present tense in Persian, we take the root verb (for example, *rav* 'to go') and add *mi* at the beginning and add the person suffix (for example, *am*) at the end. Unlike in English, the verb suffixes for different persons in Persian are different. So, the verb *rav* 'go' would have different forms as in here:

I go	*mi*	*rav*	*am*
You go	*mi*	*rav*	*i*
He/she/it goes	*mi*	*rav*	*ad*
We go	*mi*	*rav*	*im*
You go (plural/polite)	*mi*	*rav*	*id*
They go	*mi*	*rav*	*and*

As you see, the verb (*rav*) takes different suffixes (*am, i, ad, im, id, and*) for different persons. This suffix is in fact a sign of the subject on the verb.

However, the dictionary entry of a verb is in the infinitive form, e.g. *raftan* 'to go.' If we take the infinitive marker *an* out, the rest would be a past tense form, *raft* 'went.' Thus, the past and present forms of verbs are different in Persian and to help the reader we give the present form of the verb as well.

Abbreviations

These abbreviations are used in this dictionary:

(adj)	adjective
(adv)	adverb
(c)	common
(imp)	imperative
(inf)	informal
(n)	noun
(pre)	preposition
(v)	verb

Acknowledgements

During the compilation of this dictionary, my wife, Mojgan, who has also been teaching Persian for several years, helped me with typing, proofreading, and providing different equivalents for Persian or English entries. I should thank her for the hard work, support and encouragement.

I should also thanks my colleagues in the ADF School of Languages from whom I learned many things in teaching LOTE. Mr. Bruce Murray, the Director of Studies, Mr. David Deck, Mr. Simon Williams, Dr. Usnan Budiman, Mr. Mike Gretton and Mrs. Hilda Mils.

My appreciation goes to my Iranian friends in Melbourne who provided me with the first hand native speaker resources, especially Mr. Shahram Aminzadeh who gave me useful advice on software programs.

I would like my dear friends Dr. Darioush Salehi, Mr. Emil Gad and Mr. John Saliba for their continuous support and encouragement.

My thank goes to all my students in Persian courses at the ADF School of Languages, RMIT University and Centre for Adult Education who inspired me to write this dictionary.

Finally, I would like to dedicate this dictionary to my two year old daughter, Persia. I hope this dictionary and my other books on Persian will be an inspiration for her to learn and retain her cultural roots as an Australian citizen with an Iranian background.

— Yavar Dehghani

a

abacus *chortke* چرتکه

abandoned *matruk* متروک

abbreviated *mokhaffaf* مخفف

abbreviation *alâmate ekhtesâri* علامت اختصاری

ability *tavânâyi* توانایی

abject *zalil* ذلیل

able *qâder* قادر

abnormal *nâhanjâr* ناهنجار (c) *qeyre addi* غیر عادی

abolish (v) *elqâ' kardan* الغاء کردن

abolished *mansukh* منسوخ

abolition *elqâ'* الغاء

abortion *kurtâzh* کورتاژ (c) *seqt* سقط

about (adv) *taqriban* تقریبا (pre) *dar morede* در مورد

above *bâlâye* بالای

above-mentioned *nâmborde* نامبرده

abroad *khâreje* خارجه (c) *khârej* خارج *farang* فرنگ

abscess *domal* دمل

absence *qiyâb* غیاب (c) *qeybat* غیبت

absent minded *bikhiyâl* بی خیال

absent *qâyeb* غایب

absolute *motlaq* مطلق

absolutely *motlaqan* مطلقا

absorb (v) *jazb kardan* جذب کردن

absorbed *majzub* مجذوب

absorption *jazb* جذب

abstention *momtane'* ممتنع

abstract *kholâse* خلاصه

absurd (c) *mozakhraf* مزخرف *mohmal* مهمل

academy *âmuzeshgâh* آموزشگاه (c) *farhangestân* فرهنگستان *madrase* مدرسه

acanthus *kangar* کنگر

accent *lahje* لهجه

accept (v) *paziroftan (pazir)* پذیرفتن (پذیر)

acceptance *qabuli* قبولی (c) *paziresh* پذیرش

accepted *maqbul* مقبول

access *dastrasi* دسترسی

accident *sânehe* سانحه (c) *tasâdof* تصادف *hâdese* حادثه *pish âmad* پیشامد

accidentally *tasâdofan* تصادفا

accidents *havâdes* حوادث

according to *tebqe* طبق

account *hesâb* حساب

accountable *mas'ul* مسئول

accountant *hesâb dâr* حساب دار

accounting for *tojih* توجیه

accumulation *tarâkom* تراکم

accusation (c) *tohmat* تهمت *ettehâm* اتهام

accusative *maf'uli* مفعولی

accuse *mottaham kardan* متهم کردن

accused *mottaham* متهم

ace *âs* آس (c) *tak khâl* تک خال

ache (n) *dard* درد (v) *dard kardan* درد کردن

acne *jush* جوش

acquaintance *âshenâ* آشنا

acquitted *mobarrâ* مبرا

acrobatics *band bâzi* بند بازی

act (c) *amal* عمل *eqdâm* اقدام

action (c) *amal* عمل *fa'âliyat* فعاليت *eqdâm* اقدام

active *fa'âl* فعال

activity *fa'âliyat* فعاليت

actor (c) *bâzigar* بازيگر *honarpishe* هنرپيشه

acute *hâd* حاد

adapt (v) *eqtebâs kardan* اقتباس كردن

adaptation *eqtebâs* اقتباس

add (v) *jam' kardan* جمع كردن (v) *ezâfe kardan* اضافه كردن

added *mozâf* مضاف

addicted *mo'tâd* معتاد

addiction *e'tiyâd* اعتياد

addition *jam'* جمع

address *âdres* آدرس

addressee *mokhâteb* مخاطب

adequacy *kefâyat* كفايت

adhesive tape *navâr chasb* نوارچسب

adhesive *chasbnâk* چسبناک

adjacent *moshref* مشرف

adjective *sefat* صفت

adjusting *tanzim* تنظيم

administer (v) *edâre kardan* اداره كردن

administration *edâre* اداره

admiral *daryâsâlâr* درياسالار

admission *paziresh* پذيرش

admit (v) *paziroftan (pazir)* پذيرفتن (پذير)

adolescence *nojavâni* نوجوانى

adolescent *nojavân* نوجوان

adopted child *farzand khânde* فرزند خوانده

adult *bozorgsâl* بزرگسال

adulterer *zenâkâr* زناكار

adultery *zenâ* زنا

advanced *motaraqqi* مترقى (c) *pishrafte* پيشرفته

advancement *pishravi* پيشروى

advantage *emtiyâz* امتياز

adventure (c) *mâjarâ* ماجرا *sargozasht* سرگذشت

adventurous *mâjarâju* ماجراجو

adverb *qeyd* قيد

adverse *motezâd* متضاد

advertise (v) *âgahi kardan* آگهى كردن

advertisement *âgahi* آگهى

advice *nasihat* نصيحت *pand* پند *moshâvere* مشاوره *sefâresh* سفارش (c) *tosiye* توصيه

advise (v) *nasihat kardan* نصيحت كردن

advisor *moshâver* مشاور

aerial *ânten* آنتن

aeroplane *havâpeymâ* هواپيما

affairs *umur* امور

affect (v) *asar gozâshtan* اثر گذاشتن

affected *mobtalâ* مبتلا

affection *mehr* مهر *âtefe* عاطفه (c) *mohabbat* محبت *mehrebâni* مهربانى

affectionate *mohabbat amiz* محبت آميز (c) *mehrebân* مهربان

afternoon tea *asrâne* عصرانه

afternoon *asr* عصر

afterwards (c) ba'dan بعدا sepas سپس

again (c) dobâre دوباره mojaddad مجدد

against bar aleyh بر علیه barkhelâf برخلاف aleyh علیه (c) moqâbel مقابل

agate aqiq عقیق

age senn سن

aged sâlmand سالمند sâlkhorde سالخورده (c) mosen مسن

agency âzhâns آژانس (c) bongâh بنگاه namâyandegi نمایندگی

agent kârgozâr کارگزار âmel عامل onsor عنصر (c) ma'mur مامور namâyande نماینده

aggravation tashdid تشدید

aggression dast andâzi دست اندازی dast derâzi دست درازی parkhâsh پرخاش

aggressive parkhashgar پرخاشگر motajâvez متجاوز

agile châbok چابک (c) ferz فرز

agitated âshofte آشفته

ago qabl قبل

agony (c) dard درد ranj رنج

agree movâfeq موافق

agreement movâfeqat موافقت ahd عهد (c) tavâfoq توافق qarâr قرار konterât کنترات mo'âhede معاهده

agriculture (c) keshâvarzi کشاورزی zerâ'at زراعت

aid komak کمک

ailment neqâhat نقاهت

aim marâm مرام maqsud مقصود (c) hadaf هدف

aiming neshâne ravi نشانه روی

air havâ هوا

aircraft carrier nâve havâpeymâbar ناو هواپیمابر

airport forudgâh فرودگاه

alas afsus افسوس

album âlbom آلبوم

alcohol alkol الکل

alcoholic drink mashrub مشروب

alert khabardâr خبردار

algae khaze خزه jolbak جلبک

alien qaribe غریبه (c) bigâne بیگانه ajnabi اجنبی

alike mosâvi مساوی

alimony nafaqe نفقه

alive (n) zende زنده

all hame همه

allergy hassâsiyat حساسیت

alley (c) kuche کوچه kuy کوی

alliance (c) ettehâd اتحاد e'telâf اعتلاف

Allies mottafeqin متفقین

allocation jire جیره

allowance kharji خرجی

alloy âlyâzh آلیاژ

almond bâdâm بادام

almost taqriban تقریبا

alms zakât زکات

alone tanhâ تنها

alphabet alefbâ الفبا

also niz نیز (c) ham هم

alteration taqyiyr تغییر

alternation tanâvob تناوب

although agarche اگرچه

altitude ertefâ' ارتفاع

altogether jam'an جمعا (c) ruye ham rafte روی هم رفته

always hamishe همیشه

amateur qeyre herfeyi غیر حرفه ای

amazed heyrân حیران (c) mât مات

amazement boht بهت

amazing ta'ajjob âvar تعجب آور

ambassador safir سفیر

ambiguity ebhâm ابهام

ambiguous mobham مبهم

ambition jâhtalabi جاه طلبی

ambitious boland parvâz بلند پرواز

ambulance âmbulâns آمبولانس

ambush (c) kamin کمین shabikhun شبیخون

amen âmin آمین

amendment tarmim ترمیم

ammunitions (c) mohemmât مهمات taslihât تسلیحات

amnesia farâmushi فراموشی

amnesty amân امان

among (c) beyn بین miyân میان

amount mablaq مبلغ (c) meqdâr مقدار mizân میزان

amphibious dozist دوزیست

amplitude dâmane دامنه

amputation qat' قطع

anaemia kam khuni کمخونی

analogy qiyâs قیاس

analysis tajziye تجزیه tahlil تحلیل

anarchist harjo marj talab هرج و مرج طلب

ancestors (c) ajdâd اجداد niyâkân نیاکان

ancestral nasabi نسبی

anchor langar لنگر

anchorage langargâh لنگرگاه

anchovy koli mâhi ماهیکولی

ancient kohan کهن (c) qadimi قدیمی

and va و

anemometer bâdsanj باد سنج

angel (c) fereshte فرشته malak ملک

anger (c) asabâniyat عصبانیت khashm خشم

angle zel' ضلع (c) gushe گوشه konj کنج

angry khashmgin خشمگین (c) asabâni عصبانی qazabnâk غضبناک

animal (c) heyvân حیوان jânavar جانور

animate jândar جاندار

animosity kine کینه doshmani دشمنی

annex zamime ضمیمه

annihilation fanâ فنا

anniversary sâlgard سالگرد sâlruz سالروز

annos makhraj مخرج

announcement âgahi آگهی ettelâ'iyye اطلاعیه

announcer guyande گوینده

annoyance (c) ranjesh رنجش kodurat کدورت

annoyed delkhor دلخور ranjide رنجیده

annual sâliyâne سالیانه

annum (f) sâl سال

anonymous *gomnâm* گمنام
another (pre) *qeyr* غیر *digari*
دیگری *digar* دیگر
answer (c) *javâb* جواب *pâsokh*
پاسخ (v) *javâb dâdan* جواب دادن
ant *murche* مورچه
antecedent *sâbeqe* سابقه
antenna *ânten* آنتن
anthology *jong* جنگ
anthrax *siyâh zakhm* سیاه زخم
anthropology *mardom shenâsi*
مردم شناسی
antibiotics *ântibiyutik* آنتی بیوتیک
antibody *pâdtan* پادتن
anticipation *pish bini* پیش بینی
antidote *noshdâru* نوشدارو
pâdzahr پادزهر
antifreeze *zedde yakh* ضد یخ
antique *atiqe* عتیقه
antiquity *qedmat* قدمت
anus (c) *maq'ad* مقعد (inf) *kun*
کون *mâtaht* ماتحت
anxiety *ezterâb* اضطراب
anxious *moztareb* مضطرب
apologise (v) *ozr khâstan* عذر
خواستن
apology *ozr khâhi* عذر خواهی
ma'zerat معذرت *puzesh* پوزش
apostate *mortad* مرتد
apostle *havvâri* حواری
apparatus *dastgâh* دستگاه
apparent *namâyân* نمایان
apparently *zâheran* ظاهرا
appeal *farjâm* فرجام
appear (v) *barâmadan* برآمدن

appearance *zâher* ظاهر *qiyâfe*
قیافه
appeasement *deljuyi* دلجویی
appendix (annex) *zamime* ضمیمه
appendix (organ) *âpândis* آپاندیس
appetite *eshtehâ* اشتها
apple *sib* سیب
applicant *motaqâzi* متقاضی
dâvtalab داوطلب
application (for job) *taqâzâ* تقاضا
application (c) *kârbord* کاربرد
este'mâl استعمال
appointed *mansub* منصوب
appointment (c) *qarâr* قرار
entesâb انتصاب
appreciation *qadrdâni* قدردانی
apprehension *daqdaqe* دغدغه
apprentice *no âmuz* نو آموز
shâgerd شاگرد (c) *kârâmuz* کارآموز
apprenticeship *shâgerdi* شاگردی
appropriate *monâseb* مناسب
appropriateness *monâsebat*
مناسبت
approval *pasand* پسند (c) *tasvib*
تصویب
approve (v) *pasandidan (pasand)*
پسندیدن (پسند)
approximately *taqriban* تقریبا
apricot *zardâlu* زردآلو
April *âvril* آوریل
apron *pish band* پیش بند
aqueous *âbzi* آبزی
Arab *abrab* عرب
arbitration *miyânji gari* میانجی گری
arbitrator *miyânji* میانجی

arc *kamân* کمان

arch (c) *tâq* طاق *qos* قوس
gonbad گنبد

archaeologist *bâstânshenâs*
باستان شناس

archaeology *bâstânishenâsi* باستان
شناسی

archaic *kohan* کهن

architect *me'mâr* معمار

architecture *me'mâri* معماری

archives *ârshiv* آرشیو
(c) *bâyegâni* بایگانی

are (v) *hastand* هستند

area (c) *mantaqe* منطقه *mahdude*
ناحیه *nâhiye* محدوده

arena *arse* عرصه

Argentina *ârzhântin* آرژانتین

argue (v) *estedlâl kardan*
استدلال کردن (v) *da'vâ kardan*
دلیل (v) *dalil âvardan* دعوا کردن
آوردن

argument *estedlâl* استدلال *bahs*
دعوا *da'vâ* بحث

aristocrats *ashrâf* اشراف

arm *bâzu* بازو

armaments *taslihât* تسلیحات

armed *mosallahâne* مسلحانه
mosallah مسلح

Armenian *armani* ارمنی

armlet *bâzuband* بازوبند

armour *zereh* زره

armoured (adj) *zerehi* زرهی
(n) *zerehpush* زره پوش

armour-piercing *zerehshekan* زره
شکن

arms *selâh* سلاح *aslahe* اسلحه
jang afzâr جنگ افزار

army *sepâh* سپاه *lashkar* لشکر
(c) *artesh* ارتش

aroma *atr* عطر

aromatic *mo'attar* معطر

arrangement *tartib* ترتیب

arranging *tanzim* تنظیم

arrest *toqif* توقیف *jalb* جلب
bâzdâsht بازداشت (v) *bâzdâsht*
kardan بازداشت کردن

arrive (v) *rasidan (ras)* رسیدن (رس)

arrogant *mostakber* مستکبر
(c) *maqrur* مغرور *motakabber*
متکبر

arrow *tir* تیر

artery *sharayân* شریان *sorkhrag*
rag رگ سرخرگ

article (written) *maqâle* مقاله

artificial *sâkhtegi* ساختگی
(c) *masno'i* مصنوعی

artillery *tupkhâne* توپخانه

as if *engâr* انگار

as well *hamchenin* همچنین

as *chenânke* چنانکه

ash *khâkestar* خاکستر

ashamed *sarafkande* سرافکنده
sharmsâr شرمسار *khejel* خجل
(c) *sharmande* شرمنده

ashtray *zir sigâri* زیرسیگاری

Asia *âsiyâ* آسیا

ask (question) (v) *porsidan (pors)*
پرسیدن (پرس)

ask (request) (v) *khâstan (khâh)*
خواستن (خواه)

asparagus *mârchube* مارچوبه

aspect *janbe* جنبه
aspirin *âsperin* آسپرین
ass (inf) *kun* کون *maq'ad* مقعد
mâtaht ماتحت
assassin *âdam kosh* آدمکش
assault *hamle* حمله
assembly *majma'* مجمع *shurâ*
شورا *anjoman* انجمن
asset *mojudi* موجودی *manâl* منال
mâl مال (c) *dârâyi* دارایی
assign (v) *gomâshtan (gomâr)*
گماشتن (گمار)
assignment *taklif* تکلیف
ma'muriyat ماموریت
assistance *mosâ'edat* مساعدت
(c) *komak* کمک *madad* مدد
assistant (c) *dastyâr* دستیار
mo'âven معاون
associate *sharik* شریک
association *majma'* مجمع
anjoman انجمن
assorted *jur* جور
assume (v) *farz kardan* فرض کردن
assumption *hads* حدس *farz*
فرض
assured *delgarm* دلگرم
Assyrian *âsuri* آسوری
asterisk *setâre* ستاره
asthma *âsm* آسم
astonished *motahayyer* متحیر
astound *heyrân* حیران *mât* مات
astringent *efrite* عفریته
astrologer *monajjem* منجم
astrology *nojum* نجوم
astronaut *fazânavard* فضانورد

astronomer *setâre shenâs* ستاره
شناس *monajjem* منجم
astronomy *nojum* نجوم
asylum seeker *panâhande* پناهنده
asylum *panâhgâh* پناهگاه
at least *aqallan* اقلا *lâ aqal* لا اقل
at *dar* در
atheist *molhed* ملحد *bidin* بی دین
lâmazhab لامذهب
atmosphere *javv* جو
attached *mottasel* متصل
attachment (enclosed) *zamime*
ضمیمه *peyvast* پیوست
attachment *delbastegi* دلبستگی
attack *tahâjom* تهاجم *hamle* حمله
(v) *hamle kardan* حمله کردن
attempt *sa'y* سعی *kushesh* کوشش
attendance *hozur* حضور
attention (imp) *khabardâr* خبردار
tavajjoh توجه *e'tenâ* اعتنا
attentive *motavajjeh* متوجه
moltafet ملتفت
attorney *vakil* وکیل
attract (v) *majzub kardan*
مجذوب کردن
attracted *majzub* مجذوب
attraction *keshesh* کشش *jâzebe*
جاذبه
attractive (c) *jazzâb* جذاب *girâ*
گیرا
attribute *sefat* صفت
auction *mozâyede* مزایده *harrâj*
حراج (v) *harrâj kardan* حراج کردن
audience *hozzâr* حضار
audiometry *shenavâyi sanji* شنوایی
سنجی

audio-visual sam'i basari سمعی بصری

audit bâzdid بازدید (v) bâzdid kardan بازدید کردن

auditorium tâlâr تالار

August ut اوت

Austria otrish اتریش

author mo'allef مولف negârande نگارنده (c) nevisande نویسنده

authorities maqâmât مقامات

authority ekhtiyâr اختیار salâhiyat صلاحیت

authorization tanfiz تنفیذ

autocrat mostabed مستبد

automatic teller âber bank عابر بانک khodpardâz خودپرداز

automatic khodkâr خودکار

automatically khodbekhod خودبخود

autonomy khodmokhtâri خودمختاری

autopsy kâlbod shekâfi کالبد شکافی

autumn (c) pâyiyz پاییز khazân خزان

auxiliary komaki کمکی

availability dastrasi دسترسی

available farâham فراهم

avenue (street) khiyâbân خیابان

average miyângin میانگین motavasset متوسط

aversion tanaffor تنفر nefrat نفرت

avoid (v) ejtenâb kardan اجتناب کردن

avoidance ejtenâb اجتناب

awake bidâr بیدار

award jâyeze جایزه

aware khabardâr خبردار moltafet ملتفت (c) âgâh آگاه

axe tabar تبر

axis mehvar محور

axle mil میل

azure lâjavardi لاجوردی nili نیلی firuze فیروزه

b

baby *nini* نی نی (c) *nozâd* نوزاد
kudak کودک

bachelor degree *lisâns* لیسانس

bachelor *azab* عذب (c) *mojarrad* مجرد

back *aqab* عقب *posht* پشت

backbiting *qeybat* غیبت

backgammon *nard* نرد *takhte nard* تخته نرد

background *zamine* زمینه
pishine پیشینه

backing *poshtevâne* پشتوانه

backpack *kule poshti* کوله پشتی

bad luck *badbiyâri* بد بیاری

bad omen *shum* شوم

bad *bad* بد

badger *gurkan* گورکن

bag *kise* کیسه *kif* کیف

Baha'i *bahâyi* بهایی

Baha'ism *bahâyiyat* بهائیت

bail *zamânat* ضمانت

bailor *zâmen* ضامن

bait *to'me* طعمه

baker (c) *nânavâ* نانوا *shâter* شاطر

bakery *nânavâyi* نانوایی

balance (eqilibirum) *ta'âdol* تعادل

balance (money) *mojudi* موجودی

balcony *eyvân* ایوان

bald *kal* کل (c) *tâs* طاس *kachal* کچل *gar* گر

ball *tup* توپ

balloon *badkonak* بادکنک

ballot *ra'y* رای

banana *moz* موز

band *band* بند (c) *goruh* گروه
rubân روبان *navâr* نوار

bandage *bâdpichi* باند پیچی
pânsemân پانسمان

bandit *râhzan* راهزن

bank *bânk* بانک

bankruptcy *varshekastegi* ورشکستگی

banner *alam* علم *lavâ* لوا
(c) *parcham* پرچم

bar *mil* میل

barbequed *beryân* بریان

barber shop *ârâyeshgâh* آرایشگاه

barber *salmâni* سلمانی
(c) *ârâyeshgar* آرایشگر

barberry *zereshk* زرشک

bare *lokht* لخت

bargain *mo'âmele* معامله (v)
châne zadan چانه زدن

bark *'o'o kardan* عوعو کردن

barking *pârs* پارس *'o'o* عوعو

barley *jo* جو

barometer *feshârsanj* فشارسنج

barracks *pâdegân* پادگان

barrel *boshke* بشکه

barren *aqim* عقیم *bâyer* بایر

barrier *sadd* سد *mân'* مانع

base (military) *pâygâh* پایگاه

base *bonyâd* بنیاد *bon* بن *tah* ته
(c) *qâ'ede* قاعده

basement *zirzamin* زیرزمین

bases *mabâni* مبانی

bash (v) *kubidan (kub)* کوبیدن (کوب)

basic *asâsi* اساسی

basin *hoz* حوض

basis *zamine* زمینه *asâs* اساس
asl اصل *pâye* پایه

basket (c) *sabad* سبد *zanbil* زنبیل

basketball *basketbâl* بسکتبال

bass *bam* بم

bat *shappare* شب پره (c) *khoffâsh*
خفاش

bath *hammâm* حمام (v) *âbtani*
kardan آبتنی کردن

bathroom *dastshuyi* دستشویی

battery *bâtri* باطری

battle *razm* رزم *nabard* نبرد
mobâreze مبارزه (c) *jang* جنگ

battleship *razm nâv* رزمناو

bay *khalij* خلیج

bayonet *sarnize* سرنیزه

be able (v) *tavânestan (tavân)*
توانستن (توان)

be late (v) *dir kardan* دیر کردن

be (imp) *bâsh!* باش (v) *budan*
(hast) بودن (هست)

beach *daryâ kanâr* دریاکنار
(c) *sâhel* ساحل

bead *mohre* مهره

beak *menqâr* منقار

beam *parto* پرتو

bean *lubiyâ* لوبیا

bear *dobb* دب (c) *khers* خرس

beard *rish* ریش

bearded *rishu* ریشو

beast *heyvân* حیوان *jânavar* جانور
darande درنده *dad* دد

beat (v) *tapidan (tap)* تپیدن (تپ)
(v) *zadan (zan)* زدن (زن)

beaten *maqlub* مغلوب

beating *kotak* کتک

beautiful *qashang* قشنگ
khoshgel خوشگل *zibâ* زیبا

beauty *zibâyi* زیبایی

because *zirâ* زیرا (c) *chon* چون

become (v) *shodan (shav)* شدن
(شو)

bed sheet *malâfe* ملافه

bed *takhtkhab* تخت خواب *takht*
تخت

bedding *rakht khâb* رخت خواب

bedroom *otâq khâb* اتاق خواب

bee *zanbur* زنبور

beer *âbjo* آبجو

beet *choqondar* چغندر

before *qabl* قبل

beforehand *pish âpish* پیشاپیش
qablan قبلا

beg (v) *eltemâs kardan* التماس کردن
(v) *gedâyi kardan* گدایی کردن

beggar *gedâ* گدا

begging *gedâyi* گدایی *eltemâs*
التماس

begin (v) *âqâz kardan* آغاز کردن

beginner *no âmuz* نو آموز
mobtadi مبتدی

beginning *ebtedâ* ابتدا (c) *shoru'*
شروع *mabda'* مبدا *âqâz* آغاز

beginnings *avâyel* اوایل

behaviour (c) *raftâr* رفتار *kerdâr*
کردار

behind *aqab* عقب *posht* پشت
donbâl دنبال

belief *e'teqâd* اعتقاد *aqide* عقیده
bâvar باور *imân* ایمان

believe (v) *aqide dâshtan* عقیده داشتن (v) *bâvar kardan* باور کردن

believer *mo'taqed* معتقد *mo'men* مومن

bell *nâqus* ناقوس *zang* زنگ

belly *shekam* شکم

belonging *mota'alleq* متعلق

beloved *mahbub* محبوب

below *zir* زیر

belt pulley *falake* فلکه

belt *kamar band* کمربند

bench *nimkat* نیمکت

bend *monhani* منحنی *kham* خم (c) *pich* پیچ

beneath *zir* زیر

beneficiary *zinaf'* ذینفع

benefit *sud* سود *manfa'at* منفعت *estefâde* استفاده

benevolent *khayyer* خیر

bent *khamide* خمیده

bereaved *dâqdâr* داغدار

berry *tut* توت

beside *kenâr* کنار

best *behtarin* بهترین

bestowing *nesâr* نثار

bet *shart* شرط

betrayal *khiyânat* خیانت

betrayer *khâ'en* خائن

better *behtar* بهتر

betting *shartbandi* شرط بندی

between (c) *beyn* بین *miyân* میان

beverage *âshâmidani* آشامیدنی *nushâbe* نوشابه *nushidani* نوشیدنی

beware *nabâdâ* نبادا

beyond *mâfoq* مافوق

biased *moqrez* مغرض

bib *pish band* پیش بند

Bible *enjil* انجیل

bicycle *docharkhe* دوچرخه

bid *mozâyede* مزایده *shartbandi* شرط بندی

big *bozorg* بزرگ *dorosht* درشت

bilateral *dojânebe* دوجانبه

bilingual *dozabâne* دوزبانه

bill (e.g. phone bill) *surat hesab* صورت حساب

bill (legislative) *lâyehe* لایحه

bill (of a meal) *qabz* قبض

billion *milyârd* میلیارد

binoculars *durbin* دوربین

biography *sharhe hâl* شرح حال

biology *zistshenâsi* زیست شناسی

biopsy *nemune bardâri* نمونه برداری

bird *parande* پرنده

birds *parandegân* پرندگان

birth certificate *shenâsnâme* شناسنامه

birth *tavallod* تولد

bishop *osqof* اسقف

bite *gâz* گاز (v) *gâz gereftan* گازگرفتن

bitter *talkh* تلخ

bizarre *ajib* عجیب

black cherry *âlbâlu* آلبالو

black mulberry *shâhtut* شاه توت

black out *khâmushi* خاموشی

black *meshki* مشکی *siyâh* سیاه

blackboard *takhtesiyâh* تخته سیاه

blacksmith *âhangar* آهنگر

blade *tiq* تیغ
blame *sarzanesh* سرزنش
malâmat ملامت
blank *khâli* خالی *sefid* سفید
blanket *patu* پتو
blasphemy *kofr* کفر
bleating *ba'ba'* بع بع
blend (v) *âmikhtan (âmiz)*
(آمیختن)آمیز
bless you! *âfiyat bashe!* عافیت باشه
blessed *mobârak* مبارک
blessing *barakat* برکت *rahmat*
رحمت *feyz* فیض *ne'mat* نعمت
do'â دعا
blind (inf) *kur* کور (c) *nâbinâ* نابینا
roshandel روشندل
blindfold *cheshm baste* چشم بسته
blindly *kurkurâne* کورکورانه
blindness (inf) *kuri* کوری
(c) *nâbinâyi* نابینایی
blink (v) *cheshmak zadan* چشمک
زدن
blister *tâval* تاول
blitzing *qâfelgir* غافلگیر
blizzard *burân* بوران
bloating *nafkh* نفخ
block (buliding) *buluk* بلوک
blockage *sadd* سد
blocked *masdud* مسدود
blond *bur* بور
blood money *khun bahâ* خون بها
blood pressure *feshare khun* فشار
خون
blood sucker *khun âshâm* خون
آشام

blood thirsty *khun khâr* خون خوار
blood type *goruhe khuni* گروه خونی
blood *khun* خون
bloody *khunin* خونین (c) *khun*
âlud خون آلود
blossom (c) *shokufe* شکوفه
qonche غنچه
blouse *boluz* بلوز
blow nose (v) *fin kardan* فین کردن
blow up (v) *tarakidan (tarak)*
(ترک)ترکیدن
blow *fut* فوت (v) *bâd kardan*
باد کردن (v) *fut kardan* فوت کردن
(v) *damidam (dam)* (دم)دمیدن
blown up *monfajer* منفجر
blue *âbi* آبی
blunt (person) *rok* رک
blunt (thing) *kond* کند
bluntness *serâhat* صراحت
blurred *keder* کدر *târ* تار
boar *gorâz* گراز
board (c) *tâblo* تابلو *loh* لوح
takhte تخته
boarding house *pânsiyon* پانسیون
boast *lâf* لاف (v) *fakhr kardan*
لاف زدن (v) *lâf zadan* فخر کردن
(v) *nâzidan (nâz)* (ناز)نازیدن
boat *qâyeq* قایق
body (c) *badan* بدن *tan* تن
andâm اندام *jesm* جسم
bogyman *lulu* لولو
boil (v) *jushidan (jush)* جوشیدن
(جوش)
boiled *jushide* جوشیده
boiler *dig* دیگ

bold *jasur* جسور *natars* نترس *gostâkh* گستاخ

boldness *jasârat* جسارت

bomb *bomb* بمب

bombard (v) *bombârân kardan* بمباران کردن

bombardment *bombârân* بمباران

bomber *bombafkan* بمب افکن

bon voyage! *safar bekheyr* سفر بخیر

bond *gero* گرو *zamânat* ضمانت

bondsman *zâmen* ضامن

bone *ostekhân* استخوان

bonesetter *shekaste band* شکسته بند

bonnet *kâput* کاپوت

book seller *ketâb forush* کتاب فروش

book *ketâb* کتاب

bookbinding *sahhâfi* صحافی

bookcase *qafase* قفسه

booking *rezerv* رزرو

bookkeeper *hesâb dâr* حساب دار *daftardâr* دفتردار

booklet *ketâbche* کتابچه

bookshop *ketâb forushi* کتاب فروشی

boot *putin* پوتین *chakme* چکمه

booth *qorfe* غرفه *dakke* دکه

booty *qanimat* غنیمت

border *sarhadd* سرحد *marz* مرز

bored (c) *kasel* کسل *malul* ملول

boring *kasâlat âvar* کسالت آور *malâl angiz* ملال انگیز (c) *khaste konande* خسته کننده

born *motavalled* متولد

boss *ra'is* رئیس

both *har do* هر دو

bottle opener *dar bâz kon* در باز کن

bottle *botri* بطری

bottom *tah* ته

boundary *sarhadd* سرحد *marz* مرز

bouquet *daste gol* دسته گل

bow wow *'o'o* عوعو

bow *kamân* کمان *qos* قوس

bowing *sajde* سجده

bowl *tâs* طاس (c) *kâse* کاسه *piyâle* پیاله

box *ja'be* جعبه

boxer *moshtzan* مشت زن

boxing *boks* بوکس *moshtbâzi* مشت بازی

boy *pesar* پسر

boyfriend *dost pesar* دوست پسر

bra *sineband* سینه بند *korset* کرست

bracelet *alangu* النگو *bâzuband* بازوبند *dastband* دستبند

brain *maqz* مغز *mokh* مخ

brake *tormoz* ترمز

bran *sabus* سبوس

branch *sho'be* شعبه *shâkhe* شاخه

branching *enshe'âb* انشعاب

brand *model* مدل

brandy *konyâk* کنیاک

brass *berenj* برنج

brave *natars* نترس *rashid* رشید *delir* دلیر *delâvar* دلاور (c) *shojâ'* شجاع

bravery (c) shojâ'at شجاعت
shahâmat شهامت

bravo marhabâ مرحبا

brawl dâdo bidâd داد و بیداد

brazier manqal منقل

breach naqz نقض

bread nân نان

breadth arz عرض

break (v) shekastan (shekan)
شکستن (شکن)

breakfast (c) sobhâne صبحانه
nâshtâ ناشتا

breast pestân پستان (c) sine سینه
(inf) mame مه مه

breath nafas نفس

breathing tanaffos تنفس

breechblock galangedan گلنگدن

breed nezhâd نژاد

breeze nasim نسیم

bribe taker roshvekhâr رشوه خوار

bribe roshve رشوه (v) roshve
dâdan رشوه دادن

bribery roshve رشوه

brick âjor آجر

bridal chamber hejle حجله

bride arus عروس

bridge pol پل

bridle (c) mahâr مهار afsâr افسار
dahane دهانه lejâm لجام

brief mokhtasar مختصر kutâh کوتاه
kholâse خلاصه

briefcase kif کیف

brigade tip تیپ

brigadier general sartip سرتیپ

bright foruzân فروزان (c) roshan
روشن derakhshân درخشان

brightness roshanâyi روشنایی

brilliant (great) foqolâde فوق العاده

brimful labâlab لبالب

bring out (v) dar âvardan در آوردن

bring (v) âvardan (âvar) آوردن (آور)

bristle khâr خار

broad bean bâqelâ باقلا

broad pahn پهن

broadcast pakhsh پخش

broadcaster ferestande فرستنده

broad-shouldered chârshâne
چارشانه

broken (out of order) kharâb
خراب

broken (c) shekaste شکسته
gosikhte گسیخته

broker dallâl دلال

bronchus nâyzhe نایژه

brook juybâr جویبار

broom jâru جارو

broth âbgusht آبگوشت

brothel jende khâne جنده خانه
fâheshe khâne فاحشه خانه

brother barâdar برادر (inf)
dâdâsh داداش

brotherhood barâdari برادری

brown qahveyi قهوه ای

browned sorkh karde سرخ کرده
bereshte برشته

bruise kuftegi کوفتگی

bruised kufte کوفته

brunet sabze سبزه

brush one's teeth   (v) mesvâk zadan مسواک زدن
brush   bores برس   (v) bores zadan برس زدن
brutal   zâlem ظالم
bubble   hobâb حباب   kaf کف
bucket   satl سطل
bud   shokufe شکوفه   javâne جوانه   qonche غنچه
Buddhist   budâyi بودائی
buddy   rafiq رفیق
budget   budje بودجه
buffet   bufe بوفه
bug   hashare حشره
build   (v) sâkhtan (sâz) ساختن (ساز)   (v) dorost kardan درست کردن
builder   (c) bannâ بنا   sâzande سازنده
building   banâ بنا   emârat عمارت   (c) sâkhtemân ساختمان
built (body)   josse جثه
bulbils   piyâzche پیازچه
Bulgaria   bolqârestân بلغارستان
bulk (body)   josse جثه
bulky   qatur قطور
bull   gâv گاو
bullet   tir تیر   golule گلوله
bullion   shemsh شمش
bully   zurgu زورگو   gardan koloft گردن کلفت   qoldor قلدر
bump into   (v) barkhordan (bar khor) برخوردن (برخور)
bump   dast andâz دست انداز
bumper (car)   separ سپر
bunch   khushe خوشه   daste دسته

bundle   boqche بقچه
bunny   khargush خرگوش
burial   dafn دفن
buried   madfun مدفون
burn   sukhtegi سوختگی   (v) sukhtan (suz) سوختن (سوز)
burning   suzesh سوزش
burp   âroq آروغ   (v) âroq zadan آروغ زدن
burrow   naqb نقب
burst   (v) tarakidan (tarak) ترکیدن(ترک)
bury   (v) dafn kardan دفن کردن
bus station   terminâl ترمینال
bus   utubus اتوبوس
bush   jangal جنگل
business   (c) tejârat تجارت   bâzargâni بازرگانی   dâdo setad دادوستد
businessman   bâzâri بازاری   tâjer تاجر
bustard   nâmashru' نامشروع   zenâzâde زنازاده   harâmzâde حرامزاده
busy   sargarm سرگرم   sholuq شلوغ   mashqul مشغول
but   ammâ اما   vali ولی
butcher   qassâb قصاب
butler   nokar نوکر
butt   maq'ad مقعد   (inf) kun کون
butter   kare کره
butterfly   parvâne پروانه
button   dogme دگمه
buy   (v) kharidan (khar) خریدن (خر)
buyer   kharidâr خریدار

buying *kharid* خرید

by and large *montahâ* منتها

by means of *tavassot* توسط

by the way *zemnan* ضمناً

by *tavassot* توسط

bygone *gozashte* گذشته

by-way *birâhe* بیراهه

c

cabbage *kalam* كلم

cabinet (government) *kâbine* كابينه

cabinet *ganje* گنجه

cable *kâbl* كابل *sim* سيم

cafeteria *kâfe* كافه

cage *qafas* قفس

cake *keyk* كيك

calculate (v) *hesâb kardan* حساب كردن (v) *shomordan (shomâr)* شمردن (شمار)

calculation *hesâb* حساب *mohâsebe* محاسبه *shomâresh* شمارش

calendar *sâlnâme* سالنامه *taqvim* تقويم

calf *gusâle* گوساله

Caliph *khalife* خليفه

caliphate *khelâfat* خلافت

call to prayer *azân* اذان

called *mosum* موسوم

calligraphist *khattât* خطاط

calliper *pargâr* پرگار

callous *pine* پينه

calm down (v) *ârâm kardan* آرام كردن

calumet *chopoq* چپق

camel *shotor* شتر

camera *durbin* دوربين

camouflage *estetâr* استتار

camp *ordu* اردو (v) *châdor zadan* چادر زدن

camphor *kâfur* كافور

campus *mahavvate* محوطه

can (tin) *quti* قوطى

can opener *dar bâz kon* در باز كن

can (v) *tavânestan (tavân)* توانستن (توان)

canal *kânâl* كانال *majrâ* مجرا

canary *qanâri* قنارى

cancel (v) *bâtel kardan* باطل كردن (v) *laqv kardan* لغو كردن

cancellation (c) *laqv* لغو *faskh* فسخ

cancer *saratân* سرطان

candidate *kândid* كانديد *nâmzad* نامزد *dâvtalab* داوطلب

candidature *nâmzadi* نامزدى

candle *sham'* شمع

candy *shirini* شيرينى

cane (c) *asâ* عصا *chubdasti* چوبدستى

cannabis *shâhdâne* شاهدانه

canned food *konserv* كنسرو

cannon (military) *tup* توپ

cantaloupe *tâlebi* طالبى

cap (hat) *kolâh* كلاه

cap (lid) *dar* در

capability *orze* عرضه

capable *bâ orze* با عرضه

capacitor *khâzen* خازن

capacity *zarfiyyat* ظرفيت *gonjâyesh* گنجايش

cape (coastal) *damâqe* دماغه

capillary *muyrag* مويرگ

capital (asset) (c) *sarmâye* سرمايه *tankhâh* تنخواه

capital (main) (c) *sarmâye* سرمايه

capitalism *sarmâyedâri* سرمايه دارى

capitalist sarmâyedâr سرمایه دار

captain (army) sarvân سروان

captain (navy) nâkhodâ ناخدا

captivation taskhir تسخیر

captive asir اسیر

captivity esârat اسارت

capture (v) asir kardan اسیر کردن

car khodro خودرو mâshin ماشین otumobil اتومبیل

carat qirât قیراط

caravan (c) kârvân کاروان qâfele قافله

carcass janâze جنازه (c) jasad جسد lâshe لاشه

card kârt کارت

cardboard moqavvâ مقوا

care e'tenâ اعتنا movâzebat مواظبت (v) e'tenâ kardan اعتنا کردن

careful movâzeb مواظب

careless sahl angâr سهل انگار lâ ebâli لا ابالی

carelessly sarsari سرسری

caricature kârikâtor کاریکاتور

carnation mikhak میخک

carnivore gushtkhâr گوشت خوار

carotid artery shâhrag شاهرگ

carpenter najjar نجار

carpentry najjari نجاری

carpet farsh فرش

carriage kâleske کالسکه doroshke درشکه

carrier hâmel حامل nâqel ناقل

carrot havij هویج

carry (v) haml kardan حمل کردن

cart gâri گاری

cartilage qozruf غضروف

carton ja'be جعبه kârton کارتن

cartoon kârikâtor کاریکاتور

cartridge (military) feshang فشنگ

cartridge-shell puke پوکه

carving kandekâri کنده کاری

case (box) ja'be جعبه

case (client) mored مورد

case (frame) qâb قاب

case (grammar) hâlat حالت

cash register sanduq صندوق

cash naqd نقد

cashier sanduqdâr صندوق دار

casino qomârkhâne قمار خانه

Caspian khazar خزر

cassette navâr نوار

cast iron chodan چدن

cast qâleb قالب

castel (chess) rokh رخ

castel dezh دژ qal'e قلعه

casual movaqqat موقت

casualty sânehe سانحه talafât تلفات

cat gorbe گربه

catastrophe (c) fâje'e فاجعه mosibat مصیبت

catch (v) gereftan (gir) گرفتن (گیر)

category maqule مقوله

cathedral kelisâ کلیسا

catholic kâtolik کاتولیک

cattle galle گله

Caucasia qafqâz قفقاز

cause *mojeb* موجب *bâ'es* باعث
sabab سبب *ellat* علت (v) *bâ'es*
shodan باعث شدن
caution *ehtiyât* احتياط
cautious *mohtât* محتاط
cavalier *shovâliye* شواليه
cavalry (military) *savâre nezâm*
سواره نظام
cave *qâr* غار
caviar *khâviyâr* خاويار
cawing *qârqâr* قارقار
CD *sidi* سى دى
cease-fire *âtash bas* آتش بس
ceiling *saqf* سقف
celebrate (v) *jashn gereftan* جشن
گرفتن (v) *bargozâr kardan*
برگذار كردن
celebration *jashn* جشن
celery *karafs* كرفس
cell *sellul* سلول
cellar *zirzamin* زيرزمين
cement *simân* سيمان
cemetery *gurestân* گورستان
(c) *qabrestân* قبرستان
censorship *sânsor* سانسور
census *sarshomâri* سرشمارى
centimetre *sânt* سانت *sântimetr*
سانتيمتر
central (c) *markazi* مركزى *miyâni*
ميانى
centralised *motamarkez* متمركز
centralization *tamarkoz* تمركز
centre *markaz* مركز
century *sade* سده (c) *qarn* قرن
ceramic *serâmik* سراميك

cereals *qalle* غله
cerebellum *mokhche* مخچه
cerebrum *mokh* مخ
ceremony *âyin* آيين
certain *mosallam* مسلم *hatmi*
حتمى *motma'enn* مطمئن *qat'i*
قطعى
certainly *motma'ennan* مطمئنا
mosallaman مسلما *hatman* حتما
certificate *govâhi* گواهى
gavâhinâme گواهينامه
chain *zanjir* زنجير
chair *sandali* صندلى
chalk *gach* گچ
chamber *qorfe* غرفه *otâq* اتاق
champagne *shâmpâni* شامپانى
shâmpâyn شامپاين
champion *pahlavân* پهلوان
(c) *qahramân* قهرمان
championship *qahramâni* قهرمانى
chance *bakht* بخت
chandelier (c) *chelcherâq* چلچراغ
luster لوستر *sham'dân* شمعدان
change (coins) *khurd* خرد
change *taqyiyr* تغيير *tabdil* تبديل
avaz عوض (v) *avaz kardan*
عوض كردن
chanting *monâjât* مناجات
chaotic *maqshush* مغشوش
chapter *fasl* فصل
character *kheslat* خصلت
characteristics *khususiyyât*
خصوصيت
charge (legal) *ettehâm* اتهام
(v) *mahkum kardan* محكوم كردن
charged (legal) *mottaham* متهم

charity *sadaqe* صدقه *kheyrât* خيرات *ehsân* احسان *oqâf* اوقاف *kheyriyye* خيريه

charlatan *shârlâtân* شارلاتان *châkhân* چاخان *shayyâd* شياد *kallâsh* كلاش *nâto* ناتو

charm *afsun* افسون *jâdu* جادو *telesm* طلسم

charming *jazzâb* جذاب *delbar* دلبر

chart *nemudâr* نمودار

chase *ta'qib* تعقيب (v) *ta'qib kardan* تعقيب كردن

chastity *nâmus* ناموس

chat (v) *gap zadan* گپ زدن

chatting *gap zani* گپ زنى

cheap *arzân* ارزان

cheat *kolâh bardâr* كلاهبردار *hoqqe bâz* حقه باز (v) *gul zadan* گول زدن

cheater *motaqalleb* متقلب

cheating *taqallob* تقلب

check (bank) *chek* چک

check up *mo'âyene* معاينه

check (v) *chek kardan* چک كردن

checkmate *kishmât* كيش مات

cheek (inf) *lop* لپ *gune* گونه

cheerful *bashshâsh* بشاش

cheers! *be salamati* بسلامتى

cheese *panir* پنير

chemical *shimiyâyi* شيميايى

chemist *shimidân* شيمى دان

chemistry *shimi* شيمى

cherry *gilâs* گيلاس

chess *shatranj* شطرنج

chest (body) *sine* سينه

chest (box) *sanduq* صندوق

chew (v) *javidan (jav)* جويدن (جو)

chewing gum (c) *âdâms* آدامس *saqqez* سقز

chick *juje* جوجه

chicken kebab *juje kabâb* جوجه كباب

chicken *juje* جوجه *morq* مرغ

chickpea *nokhod* نخود

chicory *kâsni* كاسنى

chief (boss) *ra'is* رئيس

child (c) *bachche* بچه *kudak* كودک *khordsâl* خردسال *farzand* فرزند

childhood *kudaki* كودكى

childish *bachchegâne* بچگانه

Chile *shili* شيلى

chill (v) *châyiydan (chây)* چاييدن (چاى)

chilly *tond* تند

chime *nâqus* ناقوس

chimney *dudkesh* دودكش

chin *châne* چانه

China *chin* چين

chinaware *chini* چينى

Chinese *chini* چينى

chip-axe *tishe* تيشه

chiromancy *kafbini* كف بينى

chocolate *shokolât* شكلات

choose (v) *bargozidan (bar gozin)* برگزيدن

chosen *nokhbe* نخبه *bar gozide* برگزيده

Christian name esme kuchik اسم کوچک

Christian masihi مسیحی

Christianity masihiyat مسیحیت

chronic mozmen مزمن

chubby khepel خپل gushtâlu گوشتالو

church kelisâ کلیسا

cigarette butt tah sigâr ته سیگار

cigarettes sigâr سیگار

cilia mozhak مژک

cinema sinemâ سینما

cinematographer filmbardâr فیلم بردار

cinnamon dârchin دارچین

circle dâyere دایره

circuit madâr مدار

circular bakhshnâme بخشنامه

circulation (paper) tirâzh تیراژ

circulation jarayân جریان

circumcision khatne ختنه

circumference mohit محیط

circumstance chegunegi چگونگی hâlat حالت

circus sirk سیرک

citation eqtebâs اقتباس naqle qol نقل قول

citizen taba'e تبعه ahl اهل

citizens atbâ' اتباع

citizenship tâbe'iyat تابعیت

citrus fruits morakkabât مرکبات

city council shardâri شهرداری

city shahr شهر

civic madani مدنی

civil rights hoquqe madani حقوق مدنی

civilian shakhsi شخصی

civilised motamadden متمدن

civilization tamaddon تمدن

claimant modda'i مدعی

clairvoyant qeybgu غیبگو

clamp gire گیره

clan qabile قبیله tâyefe طایفه

clapping (v) dast zadan دست زدن

clash zado khord زدوخورد (v) barkhordan (bar khor) برخوردن (برخور)

class tabaqe طبقه

classification rade bandi رده بندی tabaqebandi طبقه بندی

classified mahramâne محرمانه serri سری

classroom kelâs کلاس

claw panje پنجه chang چنگ nâkhon ناخن changâl چنگال

clay gel گل

clean (c) tamiz تمیز pâk پاک pâkize پاکیزه

cleanliness nezâfat نظافت

clear sâf صاف

cleavage shekâf شکاف

cleft lip lab shekari لب شکری

cleft châk چاک

clergy faqih فقیه mo'ammam معمم sheykh شیخ âkhund آخوند mollâ ملا

clever zerang زرنگ (inf) nâqolâ ناقلا

cliché kelishe کلیشه

client arbâb ruju ارباب رجوع movakkel موکل moshtari مشتری

cliff sakhre صخره

climate âbohavâ آب و هوا

climb (v) bâlâ raftan بالا رفتن

clinic darmângâh درمانگاه matab مطب

clinical bâlini بالینی

clip gire گیره

cloak qabâ قبا shenel شنل

cloakroom rakht kan رختکن

clod kalukh کلوخ

clog (of blood) lakhte لخته

close (near) nazdik نزدیک

close (v) bastan (band) بستن (بند)

closed baste بسته

closet pastu پستو

clot lakhte لخته

cloth kohne کهنه

clothes hanger jâlebâsi جالباسی rakht âviz رخت آویز jârakhti جارختی

clothes (c) lebâs لباس rakht رخت

clothing pushâk پوشاک

cloud abr ابر

cloudy abri ابری

clown dalqak دلقک

club (stick) chomâq چماق

club bâshgâh باشگاه

clumsy bidasto pâ بی دست و پا shalakhte شلخته

cluster khushe خوشه

clutch (car) kelâj کلاج

coach (trainer) morabbi مربی

coagulated mon'aqed منعقد

coal zoqâl ذغال zoqâlsang ذغال سنگ

coalition e'telâf ائتلاف

coarse khashen خشن

coast karâne کرانه

coastal sâheli ساحلی

coaster qaltak غلتک

coat pâlto پالتو

cochlea halazun حلزون

cock khurus خروس

cockroach susk سوسک

coconut nârgil نارگیل

cocoon pile پیله

code kod کد

code ramz رمز

coefficient zarib ضریب

coffee qahve قهوه

coffin tâbut تابوت

cognomen laqab لقب

coil fanar فنر

coin sekke سکه

coincidence tasâdof تصادف

coincident mosâdef مصادف

cold (weather) sarmâ سرما

cold sarmâ khordegi سرما خوردگی zokâm ذکام

cold-blooded khunsard خونسرد

colic qolenj قولنج

collapse rizesh ریزش

collect (v) jam' kardan جمع کردن

collection âlbom آلبوم jam' âvari جمع آوری majmu'e مجموعه

college kâlej کالج dâneshkade دانشکده

colonel sarhang سرهنگ

colonization este'mâr استعمار

colonize (v) este'mâr kardan
استعمار کردن

colony mosta'mere مستعمره

color rang رنگ

coloration rang âmizi رنگ آمیزی

colored rangi رنگی

colt korre کره

column sotun ستون

coma eqmâ' اغما

comb shâne شانه

combat mobâreze مبارزه

combatant mobârez مبارز
razmande رزمنده

combination tarkib ترکیب

combustible sukhtani سوختنی

combustion sukht سوخت

come out (v) dar âmadan (dar ây)
در آمدن (در آیی)

come (v) âmadan (ây) آمدن (آی)

comedy komedi کمدی

comfort âsudegi آسودگی

comfortable râhat راحت âsude
آسوده

command farmân فرمان

commander (c) farmândeh فرمانده
sardâr سردار sarkarde سرکرده

commands avâmer اوامر

commence (c) eftetâh kardan
افتتاح کردن

commencement eftetâh افتتاح

commentary tafsir تفسیر

commentator mofasser مفسر

commerce tejârat تجارت
bâzargâni بازرگانی

commercial bâzâri بازاری tejâri
تجاری

commission komisiyon کمیسیون

commit a sin (v) gonâh kardan
گناه کردن

commitment ta'ahhod تعهد

committed mota'ahhed متعهد

commodities ajnâs اجناس

common motadâvel متداول
(c) moshtarak مشترک

commonwealth moshtarek
olmanâfe' مشترک المنافع

commotion (c) janjâl جنجال
alamshange الم شنگه

communist komonist کمونیست

community jâme'e جامعه

companion munes مونس

company (military) goruhân
گروهان

company (trade) sherkat شرکت

comparison (c) moqâyese مقایسه
tatbiq تطبیق

compass qotbnamâ قطب نما

compassion morovvat مروت
(c) mehrebâni مهربانی

compassionate delsuz دلسوز

compensate (v) jobrân kardan
جبران کردن

compensation jobrân جبران

competency salâhiyat صلاحیت

competent qâder قادر sâleh صالح
(c) lâyeq لایق

competition mosâbeqe مسابقه
reqâbat رقابت

compiling gerdâvari گردآوری

complain (v) gele kardan گله کردن
(v) shekâyat kardan شکایت کردن

complaint gele گله (c) shekâyat
شکایت shekve شکوه

complementary mokammel مکمل

complete kâmel کامل tamâm تمام

completion takmil تکمیل

complex (building) mojtame'
مجتمع

complex (psych.) oqde عقده

complicated boqranj بغرنج
(c) pichide پیچیده

complication âreze عارضه
pichidegi پیچیدگی

compliment ta'ârof تعارف

composer (musical) âhangsâz
آهنگ ساز

composition enshâ' انشا

compost kud کود

comprehension dark درک

comprehensive jâme' جامع

compressed feshorde فشرده

compromise (c) sâzesh سازش
mosâlehe مصالحه

compulsory ejbâri اجباری

computation mohâsebe محاسبه

concave moqa'arr مقعر

concentrated motamarkez متمرکز

concentration tamarkoz تمرکز

concept mafhum مفهوم

concert konsert کنسرت

conciliatory solhâmiz صلح آمیز

conclusion khâteme خاتمه

concrete simân سیمان

concurrent mosâdef مصادف

condemn (v) mahkum kardan
محکوم کردن

condemnation mahkumiyat
محکومیت

condemned mahkum محکوم

condensed feshorde فشرده

condenser khâzen خازن

condition (term) shart شرط

condition vaz' وضع

conditional mashrut مشروط
sharti شرطی

condolence tasliyat تسلیت

condom kâput کاپوت kândom
کاندوم

conduct raftâr رفتار

conductor (electrical) rasânâ
رسانا nâqel ناقل

cone makhrut مخروط

confectionary qannâdi قنادی

confess (v) e'terâf kardan
اعتراف کردن (v) eqrâr kardan اقرار
کردن

confession e'terâf اعتراف eqrâr
اقرار

confidant râzdâr رازدار mahram
محرم mo'tamed معتمد

confidence etminân اطمینان

confident delgarm دلگرم
motma'enn مطمئن

confidential mahramâne محرمانه
serri سری

confined mahdud محدود

confirmation tasvib تصویب
tasdiq تصدیق ta'yiyd تایید

conflict girodâr گیرودار
keshmakesh کشمکش

conformity motâbeqat مطابقت

confront (v) ruberu shodan روبرو شدن

confrontation moqâbele مقابله
movâjehe مواجهه

confused motashannej متشنج
sarâsime سراسیمه (c) gij گیج

congenital ersi ارثی mâdar zâdi مادرزادی

congestion tarâkom تراکم

congratulation tabrik تبریک

congregation jamâ'at جماعت

congress kongere کنگره

connected peyvaste پیوسته
mottasel متصل

connection ertebât ارتباط rabt ربط râbete رابطه

connections pârty پارتی

connector râbet رابط

conqueror fâteh فاتح

conscious (adj) âgâh آگاه (n) vejdân وجدان

consent qabul قبول movâfeqat موافقت

consequence natije نتیجه

conservation mohâfezat محافظت

conservative mohâfezekâr محافظه کار

consideration molâheze ملاحظه
re'âyat رعایت

consistency poshtkâr پشتکار

conspiracy tabâni تبانی dasise dasise توطئه tote'e دسیسه

constant mostamar مستمر

constellation manzume منظومه

constitution asâsnâme اساسنامه

constitutional mashrute مشروطه

constitutionalism mashrutiyat مشروطیت

construction (c) sâkhtemân ساختمان emârat عمارت

consul konsul کنسول

consulate general sarkonsul سرکنسول

consulate konsulgari کنسول گری

consult (v) mashvarat kardan مشورت کردن

consultation mashvarat مشورت
moshâvere مشاوره

consumption masraf مصرف

contact tamâs تماس

container zarf ظرف

contaminate (v) âlude kardan آلوده کردن

contaminated âlude آلوده

contemporary mo'âser معاصر

content mofâd مفاد

context matn متن

continence qenâ'at قناعت
khoddâri خودداری

continent qârre قاره

continually modâm مدام

continuation edâme ادامه

continue (v) edâme dâshtan ادامه داشتن

continuous past mâziye
estemrâri ماضی استمراری

continuous (c) *modâvem* مداوم
peyvaste پیوسته *momtad* ممتد
donbâledâr دنباله دار *mostamar*
مستمر

contraceptive *zedde hamelegi*
ضد حاملگی

contract *moqâte'e* مقاطعه
movâfeqat nâme موافقت نامه
konterât کنترات *peymân* پیمان
qarârdâd قرارداد *qabâle* قباله

contracted *monqabez* منقبض

contraction *enqebâz* انقباض

contractor *moqâte'e kâr* مقاطعه کار

contradiction *tazâd* تضاد
moqâyerat مغایرت *tanâgoz* تناقض

contradictory *naqiz* نقیض
moqâyer مغایر

contrary *barkhelâf* برخلاف

control *kontorol* کنترل

convenience *âsâyesh* آسایش

convent *deyr* دیر *some'e* صومعه

conventional *qarârdâdi* قراردادی

conversation *gofto shenud* گفت
و شنود *mohâvere* محاوره
(c) *goftegu* گفتگو *takallom* تکلم

converse *goftegu kardan*
گفتگو کردن

convex *mohaddab* محدب

convict *tabah kâr* تبهکار

convicted *mahkum* محکوم

conviction *mahkumiyat* محکومیت
hokm حکم

convoy (c) *kârvân* کاروان *qâfele*
قافله

convulsion *tashannoj* تشنج

cook *âshpaz* آشپز (v) *âshpazi*
kardan آشپزی کردن (v) *pokhtan*
پختن (پز) (*paz*)

cooked rice *polo* پلو

cooked *pokhte* پخته

cookie *koluche* کلوچه

cooking (c) *âshpazi* آشپزی
tabbâkhi طباخی

cool *khonak* خنک

cooperative *ta'âvoni* تعاونی

copper *mes* مس

copy (of books) *jeld* جلد *noskhe*
نسخه

copy *runevesht* رونوشت
sarmashq سرمشق

copying *runevisi* رونویسی

coral *marjân* مرجان

cord *târ* تار *zeh* زه *tanâb* طناب

cordial (psych.) *qalbi* قلبی

coriander *geshniz* گشنیز

cork *chub panbe* چوب پنبه

corn poppy *shaqâyeq* شقایق

corn *zorrat* ذرت *qalle* غله *balâl*
بلال

cornea *qarniye* قرنیه

corner *gushe* گوشه *konj* کنج

coronation *tâj gozâri* تاج گذاری

corporal *sarjukhe* سرجوخه

corpse (animals) *mordâr* مردار
lâshe لاشه

corpse (human) *janâze* جنازه
jasad جسد *meyyet* میت

correct *sahih* صحیح (v) *eslâh*
kardan اصلاح کردن (v) *dorost*
kardan درست کردن

correction tashih تصحیح eslâh اصلاح

correspondence nâme negâri نامه نگاری (c) mokâtebe مکاتبه

correspondent kârgozâr کارگزار (c) khabarnegâr خبرنگار

corridor dâlân دالان râhro راه رو

corrupt fâsed فاسد

corruption fasâd فساد

corset korset کرست

cosmos gity گیتی keyhân کیهان

cost kharj خرج qeymat قیمت

costly gerân گران

costume lebâs لباس

cottage kolbe کلبه

cotton (adj) nakhi نخی (n) panbe پنبه (adj) katâni کتانی

cough sorfe سرفه

council shurâ شورا

counselling nasihat نصیحت

counsellor moshâver مشاور

count (v) shomordan (shomâr) شمردن (شمار)

counter pish khân پیشخوان kontor کنتور (c) gishe گیشه

country (c) keshvar کشور marzobum مرزوبوم sarzamin سرزمین diyâr دیار سرزمین

coup kudetâ کودتا

couple zoj زوج

coupon kopon کوپن

courage (c) shojâ'at شجاعت jasârat جسارت jor'at جرات mardânegi مردانگی

courageous delâvar دلاور (c) shojâ' شجاع

court (legal) dâdgâh دادگاه

court (royal) darbâr دربار

court (sport) meydân میدان

court marshal mohâkemeye sahrâyi محاکمه صحرایی

courtyard hayât حیاط

cover (book) jeld جلد

cover rupush روپوش laffâfe لفافه (v) pushidan (push) پوشیدن (پوش)

covering hejâb حجاب pushesh پوشش

cow gâv گاو

coward tarsu ترسو nâmard نامرد

cowboy gâvcharân گاو چران

coy lavand لوند

coyness nâz ناز eshve عشوه

cozy denj دنج

crab kharchang خرچنگ

crack châk چاک tarak ترک darz درز (v) shekastan (shekan) شکستن (شکن) (v) tarakidan (tarak) ترکیدن (ترک)

cradle gahvâre گهواره

crafts sanâye'e dasti صنایع دستی

crafty makkar مکار

crag partgâh پرتگاه

crane (bird) dornâ درنا

crane (machine) jarasaqil جرثقیل

cranium jomjome جمجمه

crash soqut سقوط

crawl (v) khazidan (khaz) خزیدن (خز)

crazy khol خل divâne دیوانه

cream (diary) sarshir سرشیر khâme خامه

cream (medical) *kerem* کرم

crease *choruk* چروک

create (v) *âfaridan (âfarin)* آفریدن
(آفرین) (v) *ijâd kardan* ایجاد کردن

creation *khelqat* خلقت *ijâd* ایجاد
khâlq خلق

creator *khâleq* خالق

creature *makhluq* مخلوق *mojud*
موجود

creatures *mojudât* موجودات

credit card *kârte e'tebâri* کارت
اعتباری

credit transaction *nesye* نسیه

credit *e'tebâr* اعتبار

creditor *bestânkâr* بستانکار
talabkâr طلبکار

creek *nahr* نهر

creep *murmur* مورمور

crematory *kure* کوره

crest *tâj* تاج

crew *khadame* خدمه

crib *gahvâre* گهواره

cricket (insect) *jirjirak* جیرجیرک

crime *jenâyat* جنایت *jorm* جرم

criminal *jenâyi* جنایی *tabah kâr*
تبهکار *jâni* جانی *jenâyat kâr* جنایت
mojrem مجرم کار

crippled *shal* شل *chollaq* چلاق
lang لنگ

crisis *bohrân* بحران

crisp *tord* ترد

criterion *me'yâr* معیار *melâk* ملاک
zâbete ضابطه

critic *montaqed* منتقد

critical *bohrâni* بحرانی *hassâs*
حساس

criticism *enteqâd* انتقاد *eybjuyi*
عیبجویی

criticize (v) *enteqâd kardan*
انتقاد کردن (v) *irâd gereftan* ایراد
گرفتن

crocheting *qollâbduzi* قلاب‌دوزی

crockery *sofâl* سفال

crocodile *temsâh* تمساح

crop *hâsel* حاصل *mahsul* محصول

cross (n) *salib* صلیب
(v) *gozashtan (gozar)* (گذر) گذشتن

crossing *gozargâh* گذرگاه

crow *kalâq* کلاغ

crowd *ezdehâm* ازدحام

crowded *sholuq* شلوغ

crown *tâj* تاج

crowning *tâj gozâri* تاج گذاری

crucified *maslub* مصلوب

crude oil *nafte khâm* نفت خام

crude *khâm* خام

cruel *zâlem* ظالم *setamgar* ستمگر
birahm بیرحم *sangdel* سنگدل

cruelty *qasâvat* قساوت *setam* ستم
jor جور

cruise *safar* سفر

cruiser *razm nâv* رزمناو

crumpled *mochâle* مچاله

crusade *salibi* صلیبی

crushed *leh* له

crust *qeshr* قشر *puste* پوسته

cry (v) *ashk rikhtan* اشک ریختن
(v) *gerye kardan* گریه کردن (v) *jiq*
zadan جیغ زدن

crying *gerye* گریه

crypt *dakhme* دخمه

crystal *bulur* بلور

cube *moka'ab* مکعب

cubic *moka'ab* مکعب *hajmi* حجمی

cuckold *dayyus* دیوث *zanjalab* زنجلب *qoromsâq* قرمساق زن جلب

cucumber *khiyâr* خیار

cuddle *baqal* بغل (v) *baqal kardan* بغل کردن

cuddly *malus* ملوس

culmination *oj* اوج

cultivation *kesht* کشت

cultural *farhangi* فرهنگی

culture *farhang* فرهنگ

cuneiform *mikhi* میخی

cup *fenjân* فنجان

cupboard *ganje* گنجه

cupping *bâdkesh* بادکش

cure (c) *darmân* درمان *marham* مرحم *alâj* علاج *shafâ* شفا *châre* چاره *modâvâ* مداوا

curiosity *konjkâvi* کنجکاوی

curl (c) *fer* فر *tâb* تاب

curly *ferferi* فرفری

currency (money) *arz* ارز

currency *ravâj* رواج

current *râyej* رایج *jâri* جاری

currently *fe'lan* فعلاً

curse *la'nat* لعنت *nefrin* نفرین *doshnâm* دشنام

cursed *la'in* لعین *la'nati* لعنتی *mal'un* ملعون *telesm shode* طلسم‌شده

curtain *parde* پرده

curve *monhani* منحنی

curved *khamide* خمیده

cushion *poshti* پشتی *bâlesh* بالش

custody (arrest) *toqif* توقیف

custody (of a child) *hezânat* حضانت

custom *âyin* آیین *rasm* رسم

customary *râyej* رایج *marsum* مرسوم

customer *moshtari* مشتری

customs *gomrok* گمرک

cut one's hair (v) *eslâh kardan* اصلاح کردن

cut (v) *boridan (bor)* بریدن (بر)

cyanide *siyânor* سیانور

cycling *charkh savâri* چرخ سواری *dockarkhe savâri* دوچرخه سواری

cyclist *docharkhesavar* دوچرخه‌سوار

cyclone *gerdbâd* گردباد

cylinder *ostovâne* استوانه

cypress tree *sarv* سرو

Cyprus *qebres* قبرس

cystitis *kist* کیست

d

daffodil narges نرگس

dagger deshne دشنه qame قمه khanjar خنجر

daily ruzâne روزانه ruzmarre روزمره

dam sadd سد

damage latme لطمه gazand گزند (c) khesârat خسارت zâye'e ضایعه sadame صدمه qarâmat غرامت zarar ضرر

damaged âsib dide آسیب دیده

damn pedar sukhte پدرسوخته

damnation nefrin نفرین

damned la'in لعین la'nati لعنتی mal'un ملعون

damp martub مرطوب namnâk نمناک tar تر

dampness nam نم

dance (v) raqsidan (raqs) رقصیدن (رقص)

dancer raqqâs رقاص

dancing raqs رقص

dandelion qâsedak قاصدک

dandruff shure شوره

danger khatar خطر

dangerous khatarnâk خطرناک

daring jasur جسور

dark (color) tire تیره

dark (weather) târik تاریک

dark blue kabud کبود sormeyi سرمه ای

dark grey tusi طوسی

darkness (c) târiki تاریکی zolmat ظلمت

darkroom târik khâne تاریک خانه

darling mahbub محبوب aziz عزیز

dart nize نیزه

date (appointment) qarâr قرار

date (edible) khormâ خرما

date (time) târikh تاریخ

dated movarrakh مورخ

daughter dokhtar دختر

daughter-in-law arus عروس

dawn fajr فجر (c) sahar سحر

day ruz روز

daydreaming khiyâl bâfi خیالبافی

dazzled khire خیره

dead body na'sh نعش

dead drunk pâtil پاتیل kharmast خرمست

dead end bonbast بن بست

dead meyyet میت (c) morde مرده

deadline (c) mohlat مهلت mo'ed موعد

deadly margbâr مرگبار koshande کشنده

deaf (inf) kar کر nâshenavâ ناشنوا

deafness (inf) kari کری nâshenavâyi ناشنوایی

deal dâdo setad دادوستد mo'âmele معامله

dealer dallâl دلال

dear (c) aziz عزیز gerâmi گرامی

death rehlat رحلت mot موت (c) marg مرگ fot فوت ajal اجل

debate monâzere مناظره

debris âvâr آوار

debt deyn دین (c) bedehi بدهی qarz قرض

decade dahe دهه

decay fasâd فساد pusidegi
پوسیدگی (v) pusidan (pus) پوسیدن
(پوس) kerm khordegi کرم خوردگی

deceased (inf) morde مرده
marhum مرحوم faqid فقید
shâdravân شادروان

deceit (c) gul گول farib فریب
neyrang نیرنگ (v) gul zadan گول
زدن makr مکر

deceitful (c) faribande فریبنده
makkar مکار jalab جلب daqal
دغل

deceive (v) gomrâh kardan
گمراه کردن

December desâmr دسامبر

decency hayâ حیا

decent najib نجیب

deception gul گول farib فریب

decimal a'shâr اعشار

decision tasmim تصمیم

decisive qâte' قاطع

deck arshe عرشه

declaration ezhâriyye اظهاریه
bayâniye بیانیه

decline zavâl زوال enqerâz
انقراض

decomposition tajziye تجزیه

decoration tazyiyn تزیین

decrease kâhesh کاهش tanazzol
تنزل (v) kam shodan کم شدن

dedicate (v) ehdâ kardan اهدا کردن

dedication ehdâ اهدا

deduction kâhesh کاهش

deed kerdâr کردار

deep (c) amiq عمیق god گود
zharf ژرف

deer âhu آهو gavazn گوزن
jeyrân جیران

defeat shekast شکست

defeated maqlub مغلوب

defect naqs نقص

defective ma'yub معیوب nâqes
ناقص

defence modâfe'e مدافعه defâ' دفاع

defend (v) defâ' kardan دفاع کردن

defendant modâfe' مدافع

defender modâfe' مدافع

deficit kambud کمبود

define (v) ta'rif kardan تعریف کردن

definite motlaq مطلق mosallam
مسلم qat'i قطعی

definitely mosallaman مسلما
qat'an قطعا

definition ta'rif تعریف

deforestation jangal zodayi جنگل
زدایی

degradation khâri خواری

degree daraje درجه

delay ta'khir تاخیر mo'attali معطلی
(v) dir kardan دیر کردن

delegation hey'at هیئت

delete (v) hazf kardan حذف کردن

deletion hazf حذف

deliberate amdi عمدی

deliberation kankâsh کنکاش

delicacy zarâfat ظرافت

delicate zarif ظریف

delicious khoshmaze خوشمزه laziz
لذیذ

delight delkhoshi دلخوشی

delightful lezzat bakhsh لذت بخش

DELINEATION 48

delineation *khatkeshi* خط کشی
delinquent *bezehkâr* بزهکار
deliver (v) *rasândan (rasân)*
رساندن (رسان)
demand *taqâzâ* تقاضا
demise *dargozasht* درگذشت
democracy *demokrasi* دمکراسی
demolished *monhadem* منهدم
demolition *takhrib* تخریب
demon *div* دیو
demonstrations *tazâhorât* تظاهرات
râh peymâyi راهپیمایی
denial (c) *enkâr* انکار *hâshâ* حاشا
ketmân کتمان *takzib* تکذیب
denomination (sect) *ferqe* فرقه
denominator *makhraj* مخرج
density *qelzat* غلظت
dent *foruraftegi* فرورفتگی
dentist *dandânpezeshk* دندانپزشک
dandânsâz دندانساز
deny (v) *enkâr kardan* انکار کردن
depart (v) *harakat kardan*
حرکت کردن
department store *furushqahe*
zanjireyi فروشگاه زنجیره ای
departure *azimat* عزیمت
(v) *harakat kardan* حرکت کردن
(c) *harakat* حرکت
dependent *tâbe'* تابع
deposit (c) *bey'âne* بیعانه
seporde سپرده *amânat* امانت
(v) *gozâshtan (gozâr)* گذاشتن (گذار)
deposition *khal'* خلع
depressed *afsorde* افسرده
depression *afsordegi* افسردگی
deprivation *mahrumiyat* محرومیت

deprive (v) *mahrum kardan*
محروم کردن
deprived *mahrum* محروم
depth *omq* عمق
deputy *vakil* وکیل (c) *mo'âven*
nâyeb نایب معاون
description *tosif* توصیف *sharh*
tashrih تشریح شرح
desert dweller *sahrâneshin*
صحرانشین
desert *biyâbân* بیابان *sahrâ* صحرا
deserted *matruk* متروک
design *tarh* طرح *naqsh* نقش
designer *tarâh* طراح
desirable *delkhâh* دلخواه
desire *raqbat* رغبت *tamannâ* تمنا
shoq شوق *khâst* خواست *khâste*
خواسته
desk *miz* میز
despatch (v) *ferestâdan (ferest)*
فرستادن (فرست)
desperate *ma'yus* مایوس *nâ*
omid نا امید *darmânde* درمانده
despise *khâri* خواری
dessert *deser* دسر
destination *maqsad* مقصد
destiny *qadar* قدر *taqdir* تقدیر
falak فلک (c) *sarnevesht* سرنوشت
tâle' طالع *moqaddarât* مقدرات
destroy (v) *az beyn bordan* از بین
بردن
destroyer (military) *nâv shekan*
ناو شکن
destruction (c) *takhrib* تخریب
nâbudi نابودی *fanâ* فنا
destructive *mokharreb* مخرب

detailed *mashruh* مشروح
mofassal مفصل

detective *kârâgâh* کارآگاه

detention center *bâzdâshtgâh* بازداشتگاه

detention *bâzdâsht* بازداشت

deterioration *fasâd* فساد

determination *azm* عزم

development *tose'e* توسعه *roshd* رشد

deviation *enherâf* انحراف

device *abzâr* ابزار

devil *div* دیو *tâqut* طاغوت
ahriman اهریمن *eblis* ابلیس
sheytân شیطان

devoted *fadâkâr* فداکار *mokhles* مخلص

devotion *jân nesâri* جان نثاری *jân feshâni* جانفشانی *erâdat* ارادت

dew *shabnam* شبنم

dewlap *qabqab* غبغب

diabetic *diyabeti* دیابتی

diabolism *sheytanat* شیطنت

diagnosis *tashkhis* تشخیص

diagonal *orib* اریب

diagram *nemudâr* نمودار

dial tone *zang* زنگ

dialect *guyesh* گویش *lahje* لهجه

dialogue *gofto shenud* گفت وشنود
mohâvere محاوره *goftegu* گفتگو

diameter *qotr* قطر

diamond *almâs* الماس

diarrhoea *eshâl* اسهال

diary products *labaniyât* لبنیات

dice *tâs* طاس

dictation *dikte* دیکته *emlâ'* املا

dictator *mostabed* مستبد *diktâtor* دیکتاتور

dictatorship *estebdâd* استبداد

dictionary *diksheneri* دیکشنری
loqat nâme لغتنامه

die (v) *jân dâdan* جان دادن
(v) *mordan (mir)* مردن (میر)

difference *farq* فرق *tafâvot* تفاوت

different *motafâvet* متفاوت
mokhtalef مختلف

difficult *doshvâr* دشوار *moshkel* مشکل *sakht* سخت

difficulty *eshkâl* اشکال

dig (v) *hafr kardan* حفر کردن
(v) *kandan (kan)* کندن (کن)

digestion *govâresh* گوارش

digestive *govâreshi* گوارشی

digit *raqam* رقم *shomâre* شماره

dignity *sha'n* شان *sharaf* شرف

diligent *sakhtgir* سختگیر

diluted *raqiq* رقیق

dim *keder* کدر *tire* تیره

dimension *bo'd* بعد

dinner *shâm* شام

dinning room *nâhâr khori* ناهار خوری

diploma *govâhi* گواهی

diplopia *dobini* دوبینی

direct *bivâsete* بی واسطه
mostaqim مستقیم

direction (order) *dastur* دستور

direction *jahat* جهت *masir* مسیر
samt سمت *taraf* طرف

directly *mostaqiman* مستقیما

director (film)　kâr gardân کارگردان
director　mojri مجری　modir مدیر
directory　râh namâ راهنما
dirt　kesâfat کثافت
dirty　(c) kasif کثیف　nâpâk ناپاک
disabled　alil علیل
disagreement　mokhâlefat مخالفت
disappeared　nâpadid ناپدید
disappointed　ma'yus مایوس
delsard دلسرد
disaster　balâ بلا　mosibat مصیبت
fâje'e فاجعه
discharge　tarashshoh ترشح　daf'
دفع (v) daf' kardan دفع کردن
disciple　havvâri حواری
disciplinary　entezâmi انتظامی
discipline　enzebât انضباط
(v) adab kardan ادب کردن
disclose　(v) efshâ' kardan
افشا کردن
discomfort　nârâhati ناراحتی
disconnected　gosikhte گسیخته
discount　takhfif تخفیف
discover　(v) kashf kardan
کشف کردن
discoverer　kâshef کاشف
discovery　kashf کشف
discredit　âberu rizi آبروریزی
discrimination　farq فرق　tab'iz
تبعیض
discuss　(v) bahs kardan بحث کردن
(v) goftegu kardan گفتگو کردن
discussion　bahs بحث　mozâkere
مذاکره　mobâhese مباحثه
disease　bimâri بیماری　marizi
مریضی　maraz مرض

disgrace　âberu rizi آبروریزی
kheffat خفت　âr عار　nang ننگ
disgraced　sarafkande سرافکنده
sharmsâr شرمسار　(inf) keneft کنفت
disgraceful　sharmâvar شرم آور
nang âvar ننگ آور　nangin ننگین
disgusted　motanaffer متنفر
disgusting　nefrat angiz نفرت انگیز
dish washer　zarf shuyi ظرف شویی
dish　boshqâb بشقاب
disharmony　nefâq نفاق
dislocate　(v) dar raftan (dar rav)
در رفتن (در رو)
dislocation　dar raftegi در رفتگی
dismiss　(v) barkanâr kardan
برکنار کردن　(v) ekhrâj kardan
اخراج کردن
dismissal　ekhrâj اخراج　azl عزل
dismissed　morakhkhas مرخص
disobedience　nâfarmâni نافرمانی
sarpichi سرپیچی
disorder　ekhtelâl اختلال
disorganised　nâmorattab نامرتب
nâbesâmân نابسامان　mokhtall مختل
dispatch　e'zâm اعزام　ersâl ارسال
(v) e'zâm kardan اعزام کردن
dispersion　tafraqe تفرقه
disposition　fetrat فطرت
disproval　radd رد
dispute　goftegu گفتگو　monâzere
مناظره　monâqeshe مناقشه
mobâhese مباحثه
dissatisfied　nârâzi ناراضی
dissertation　pâyân nâme پایان نامه
dissolution　faskh فسخ　enhelâl
انحلال

dissolve (v) *hall kardan* حل کردن

distance *bo'd* بعد *masâfat* مسافت (c) *fâsele* فاصله

distillation *taqtir* تقطیر

distilled *moqattar* مقطر

distinct *shomorde* شمرده *moshakhkhas* مشخص

distinction *tashkhis* تشخیص

distortion *tahrif* تحریف

distress *nâchâri* ناچاری

distressed *parishân* پریشان (c)*kalâfe* کلافه

distribution *pakhsh* پخش *tozi'* توزیع *taqsim* تقسیم

distributor *tozi'konande* توزیع کننده

district *mahalle* محله *nâhiye* ناحیه

disturb (v) *âshofte kardan* آشفته کردن

disturbance *qoqâ* غوغا

disturbed *motashannej* متشنج *parishân* پریشان *âshofte* آشفته *maqshush* مغشوش *mokhtall* مختل

disunion *nefâq* نفاق

ditch *khandaq* خندق *godâl* گودال

diver *qavvâs* غواص

diverse *mokhtalef* مختلف *gunâgun* گوناگون *motanavve'* متنوع

diversion *enherâf* انحراف

diversity *tafâvot* تفاوت *tanavvo'* تنوع

divine *elâhi* الهی

diving *qavvâsi* غواصی

division *tozi'* توزیع *taqsim* تقسیم

divorce *talâq* طلاق

divorced *talâq gerefte* طلاق گرفته *motallaqe* مطلقه

dizziness *giji* گیجی *sargije* سرگیجه

dizzy *mang* منگ *gij* گیج

do (v) *anjâm dâdan* انجام دادن (v) (c) *kardan (kon)* کردن (کن) (v) *nemudan (nemâ)* نمودن (نما)

dock *eskele* اسکله

doctor *doktor* دکتر

doctrine *marâm nâme* مرامنامه

document *madrak* مدرک *sanad* سند

documentary *mostanad* مستند

dog *sag* سگ

dogberry *zoqâl akhte* ذغال اخته

doll *arusak* عروسک

domain *hite* حیطه *qalamro* قلمرو

dome *gonbad* گنبد

domestic (animals) *khânegi* خانگی *ahli* اهلی

domestic (e.g. flight) *dâkheli* داخلی

dominance *solte* سلطه *qalabe* غلبه *chiregi* چیرگی

dominant *mosallat* مسلط *qâleb* غالب

donkey *olâq* الاغ *khar* خر

door *dar* در

doorman *sarâydâr* سرایدار

dormitory *khâbgâh* خوابگاه

dossier *parvande* پرونده

dot *noqte* نقطه

double chin *qabqab* غبغب

double faced *doru* دورو

double minded *dodel* دودل

double *dogâne* دوگانه

DOUBT 52

doubt *tardid* تردید *shak* شک
zann ظن

doubtful *mashkuk* مشکوک

dough *khamir* خمیر

down *pâyiyn* پایین

downfall *zavâl* زوال *enqerâz*
انقراض

downhill *sarâziri* سرازیری
sarpâyiyni سرپایینی

dowry *mahr* مهر *mahriye* مهریه

dozen *dojin* دوجین

draft (finance) *safte* سفته *havâle*
حواله

draftsman *naqshe kesh* نقشه کش

drag (v) *keshidan (kesh)* کشیدن
(کش)

dragonfly *sanjâqak* سنجاقک

drain pipe *nâv dân* ناو دان

drainage *zehkeshi* زهکشی
fâzelâb فاضلاب

draught *khoshksâli* خشکسالی

draw *qor'e* قرعه (v) *keshidan*
(kesh) کشیدن (کش)

drawer *kesho* کشو

drawing *tarsim* ترسیم
(c) *naqqâshi* نقاشی

dreadful *khofnâk* خوفناک

dream (c) *khâb* خواب *royâ* رویا

dredging *lârubi* لاروبی

dress (c) *lebâs* لباس *pushâk*
پوشاک

dressing (food) *châshni* چاشنی

dressing room *rakht kan* رختکن

dried *khoshk* خشک

drill (practice) *tamrin* تمرین
mashq مشق

drill (tool) *mate* مته

drink (c) *nushâbe* نوشابه
nushidani نوشیدنی (v) *nushidan*
(nush) نوشیدن (نوش)
(v)(c) *khordan (khor)* خوردن (خور)

drinkable *nushidani* نوشیدنی

drinker (alcohol) (c) *mashrub*
مشروب خوار *khâr* *meykhâre* میخواره

drip *qatre* قطره (v) *chakidan*
(chak) چکیدن (چک)

dripping *chek chek* چک چک

drive (v)(c) *rânandegi kardan*
رانندگی کردن (v) *rândan (rân)* راندن
(ران)

driver *rânande* راننده

driving *rânandegi* رانندگی

drizzle *namnam* نم نم

drop *qatre* قطره *chekke* چکه

dropper *qatre chakân* قطره چکان

dropping *chek chek* چک چک

drug (medicine) *dâru* دارو

drugs (narcotics) *mavâdde*
mokhadder مواد مخدر

drum *tabl* طبل

drunk *mast* مست

drunkenness *masti* مستی

dry cleaner *utushuyi* اتوشویی
khoshkshuyi خشکشویی

dry *khoshk* خشک

dryness *khoshki* خشکی

dualist *moshrek* مشرک

dubbing *duble* دوبله

duck *morqâbi* مرغابی *ordak* اردک

dull (market) *kasâd* کساد

dull *keder* کدر *gerefte* گرفته

dumb (stupid)   kodan کودن
   pakhme پخمه
dumb   gong گنگ   (c) lâl لال
dummy (pacifier)   mame مه مه
dung   fazle فضله
duplicate   almosannâ المثنی
durability   davâm دوام
duration   tul طول   moddat مدت
during   heyn حین
dusk   qorub غروب
dust   gard گرد   qobâr غبار
   (v) gardgiri kardan گردگیری کردن
dustpan   khâk andâz خاک انداز
dusty   qobârâlud غبار آلود   khâk
   âlud خاک آلود
duty   taklif تکلیف
dwarf   kutule کوتوله
dynasty   dudmân دودمان   selsele
   سلسله   khânedân خاندان
dysentery   eshâl اسهال

E 54

e

each *har kodâm* هر کدام

eager *moshtâq* مشتاق

eagle *oqâb* عقاب

ear *gush* گوش

eardrum *somâkh* صماخ

early *zud* زود

earn (v) *dar âvardan* در آوردن

earning *dastmozd* دستمزد

earphone *gushi* گوشی

earring *gushvâre* گوشواره

earth (planet) *zamin* زمین

earth (soil) *khâk* خاک

earthquake *zamin larze* زمین لرزه *zelzele* زلزله

easiness *sohulat* سهولت

east *mashreq* مشرق *sharq* شرق

eastern *sharqi* شرقی

easy *âsân* آسان *sahl* سهل

eat (v) *khordan (khor)* خوردن (خور)

ecchymosis *khun mordegi* خون مردگی

echo *pezhvâk* پژواک *tanin* طنین

eclipse *kosuf* کسوف

ecology *mohite zist* محیط زیست

economy *eqtesâd* اقتصاد

edema *âmâs* آماس

edge *labe* لبه *tiqe* تیغه *kanâr* کنار

edible *khurâki* خوراکی

edition *châp* چاپ

editor *sardabir* سردبیر

editorial *sarmaqâle* سرمقاله

education *tahsil* تحصیل *âmuzesh* آموزش

eel *mârmâhi* مارماهی

effect *asar* اثر *ma'lul* معلول *ta'sir* تاثیر

effective *mo'asser* مؤثر

efficiency *kârâyi* کارآیی

efficient *mo'asser* موثر

effort *fa'âliyat* فعالیت *sa'y* سعی *talâsh* تلاش *kushesh* کوشش

egg (hen) *tokhme morq* تخم مرغ

egg *tokhm* تخم

eggplant *bâdemjân* بادمجان

Egypt *mesr* مصر

eight hundred *hashtsad* هشتصد

eight *hasht* هشت

eighteen *hijdah* هجده

eighteenth *hejdahom* هجدهم

eighty *hashtâd* هشتاد

either *yâ* یا

elaborate *mofassal* مفصل

elbow *ârenj* آرنج

elder *kadkhodâ* کدخدا

elect (v) *entekhâb kardan* انتخاب کردن

elected *montakhab* منتخب

election *entekhâb* انتخاب

electricity *barq* برق

electrocute (v) *barq gereftan* برق گرفتن

elegance *zibâyi* زیبایی *zarâfat* ظرافت

elegant *zarif* ظریف

elegist *nohekhân* نوحه خوان

elegy *nohe* نوحه *marsiye* مرثیه

element *onsor* عنصر

elementary *ebtedâyi* ابتدایی

elephant *fil* فیل
elevate (v) *afrâshtan (afrâz)* (افراز) افراشتن
elevated *mortafe'* مرتفع
elevator *âsânsor* آسانسور
eleven *yâzdah* یازده
eleventh *yâzdahom* یازدهم
eliminate (v) *hazf kardan* حذف کردن
elimination *elqâ'* الغاء *hazf* حذف
elm tree *nârvan* نارون
embankment *khâkriz* خاکریز
embarrassed *khejâlat zade* خجالت زده *khejel* خجل *sharmande* شرمنده
embarrassment *khejâlat* خجالت *sharmandegi* شرمندگی
embassy *sefârat* سفارت
embezzlement *ekhtelâs* اختلاس
embossed *monabbat* منبت
embossment *monabbat kâri* منبت کاری
embrace (v) *farâgereftan (farâgir)* فراگرفتن (فرا گیر)
embracing *khejâlat âvar* خجالت آور
embroidery *golduzi* گلدوزی
embryo *notfe* نطفه *janin* جنین
emeralds *zomorrod* زمرد
emotion *âtefe* عاطفه
emperor *emperâtor* امپراتور
emphasis *ta'kid* تاکید
emphasise (v) *ta'kid kardan* تاکیدکردن
empire *emperâtori* امپراتوری

employ (v) *estekhdâm kardan* استخدام کردن
employed *shâqel* شاغل
employee *kârmand* کارمند
employer *kârfarmâ* کارفرما
employment *estekhdâm* استخدام *shoql* شغل
empty *puch* پوچ *puk* پوک (c) *khâli* خالی
enamel *minâ* مینا
enamelwork *minâ kâri* مینا کاری
enclosure *hite* حیطه
encounter *moqâbele* مقابله *movâjehe* مواجهه
encouragement *tashviq* تشویق
end *khâteme* خاتمه *saranjâm* سرانجام *pâyân* پایان *entehâ* انتها (c) *âkhar* آخر (v) *tamâm shodan* تمام شدن
endowment *moqufât* موقوفات
endurance *tahammol* تحمل *tâqat* طاقت *esteqâmat* استقامت
enema *tanqiye* تنقیه
enemy *doshman* دشمن
energetic *fa'âl* فعال
energy *ramaq* رمق *enerezhi* انرژی
enforcement *ejrâ'* اجرا
engaged (fiancée) *nâmzad* نامزد
engaged *mashqul* مشغول
engagement *nâmzadi* نامزدی
engine *motor* موتور
engineer *mohandes* مهندس
engineering *mohandesi* مهندسی
England *ingilis* انگلیس
English *ingilisi* انگلیسی

engraving *hakkâki* حکاکی
qalamzani قلمزنی *kandekâri* کنده
کاری
enjoy *hazz kardan* حظ کردن
lezzat bordan لذت بردن
enjoyable *delchasb* دلچسب
enough *bas* بس *kâfi* کافی
enrolment *nâm nevisi* نام نویسی
entertaining *sargarm konande*
سرگرم کننده
entertainment *sargarmi* سرگرمی
enthusiasm *eshtiyâq* اشتیاق *zoq*
ذوق
enticing *faribande* فریبنده
entire *koll* کل *sartâsar* سرتاسر
entirely *kollan* کلا
entity *mâhiyat* ماهیت
entomologist *hashare shenâs*
حشره شناس
entrance *dahane* دهانه
entrenchment *sangarbandi*
سنگربندی
envelope *pâkat* پاکت
envious *hasud* حسود
environment *mohit* محیط
environmental *mohiti* محیطی
envoy *safir* سفیر *ferestâde* فرستاده
envy *hesâdat* حسادت
epicure *ayyâsh* عیاش
epidemic *shâye'* شایع
epilepsy *sar'* صرع
episodic *serial* سریال
equal *mosâvi* مساوی *barâbar* برابر
equality *barâbari* برابری *mosâvât*
مساوات *tasâvi* تساوی

equation *mo'âdele* معادله
equator *estevâ* استوا
equilibrium *movâzene* موازنه
ta'âdol تعادل
equipped *mojahhaz* مجهز
equivalent *mo'âdel* معادل
equivocal *mobham* مبهم
era *asr* عصر *ahd* عهد *dorân* دوران
zamân زمان
eradication *rishe kani* ریشه کنی
eraser *pâkkon* پاکن
erode (v) *farsudan (farsâ)* فرسودن
(فرسا)
eroded *farsude* فرسوده
erosion *farsâyesh* فرسایش
error *qalat* غلط *eshtebâh* اشتباه
eruption *favarân* فوران
escape *goriz* گریز *farâr* فرار
(v) *dar raftan (dar rav)* در رفتن
(در رو) (v) *gorikhtan (goriz)*
گریختن (گریز)
escapee *farâri* فراری *motavâri*
متواری
especially *khususan* خصوصا
makhsusan مخصوصا
espionage *jâsusi* جاسوسی
essay *maqâle* مقاله
essence *lobb* لب *johar* جوهر
zât ذات (c) *osâre* عصاره *mâhiyat*
ماهیت
essential *zaruri* ضروری *lâzem*
لازم
essentiality *lozum* لزوم
essentials *mabâni* مبانی
establish (v) *barqarâr kardan*
برقرار کردن

established *barqarâr* برقرار
dâyer دایر
establishment *ta'sis* تاسیس
esteemed *aziz* عزیز
estimate *takhmin* تخمین
barâvard برآورد
eternal *jâvid* جاوید *jâvedân* جاودان
eternity *abad* ابد
ethnic *nezhâdi* نژادی
ethnical *qomi* قومی
ethnicity *nezhâd* نژاد
etiquette *nazâkat* نزاکت
eulogy *maddâhi* مداحی *madh* مدح
euphoria *keyf* کیف
Europe *urupâ* اروپا
European *urupâyi* اروپایی
evacuation *takhliye* تخلیه
evaporation *tabkhir* تبخیر
Eve *havvâ* حوا
even (vs odd) *zoj* زوج
even *hattâ* حتی
evening *shab* شب
event *hâdese* حادثه *mâjarâ* ماجرا
pish âmad پیشامد *ettefâq* اتفاق
ruydâd رویداد
every day *har ruz* هر روز
every *hame* همه
everyone *hame* همه
evident *âshkâr* آشکار *ma'lum* معلوم
mashhud مشهود
evil *sharr* شر
evolution *takâmol* تکامل
ewe *mish* میش
ewer *âftâbe* آفتابه

exaggerate (v) *eqrâq kardan* اغراق کردن
exaggerated *mobâleqe âmiz* مبالغه آمیز
exaggeration *châkhân* چاخان
eqrâq اغراق *qolovv* غلو
mobâleqe مبالغه
exalted *mota'âl* متعال
exam *emtahân* امتحان *âzemun* آزمون
examination *mo'âyene* معاینه
âzemâyesh آزمایش
examine (medical) *mo'âyene kardan* معاینه کردن
examine (v) *âzemâyesh kardan* آزمایش کردن
example *mesâl* مثال
excavation *haffâri* حفاری *hafr* حفر
kâvosh کاوش
exceed (v) *charbidan (charb)* چربیدن (چرب)
excellency *janâb* جناب *hazrat* حضرت
excellent *âli* عالی *niku* نیکو
except *qeyr* غیر *bejoz* بجز *joz* جز
exception *estesnâ* استثنا
exchange (money) *arz* ارز
exchange *tabdil* تبدیل *tabâdol* تبادل
mo'âveze معاوضه
mobâdele مبادله (v) *ta'viz kardan* تعویض کردن
(v) *avaz kardan* عوض کردن
exciting *mohayyej* مهیج
exclusive *monhaser* منحصر
darbast دربست *enhesâri* انحصاری
excommunication *takfir* تکفیر

excrement *madfu'* مدفوع *fozulât* فضولات

excretion *tarashshoh* ترشح

excursion *siyâhat* سياحت *seyr* سير (c) *gardesh* گردش

excuse *ozr* عذر *bahâne* بهانه *dast âviz* دست آويز

excused *ma'zur* معذور *mo'âf* معاف

execute (do) (v) *ejrâ' kardan* اجرا كردن

execute (kill) (v) *e'dâm kardan* اعدام كردن

execution (killing) *tirbârân* تيرباران *e'dâm* اعدام

executioner *dezhkhim* دژخيم *jallâd* جلاد

executive *modir* مدير

exempt (v) *mo'âf kardan* معاف كردن *mo'âf* معاف

exemption *mo'âfiyat* معافيت

exercise *tamrin* تمرين

exhausted *bihâl* بى حال

exhaustion *tahlil* تحليل

exhibit *namâyesh gâh* نمايشگاه

exhumation *nabsh* نبش

exile *tab'id* تبعيد

existing *mojud* موجود

exit *khoruj* خروج

exorcist *jengir* جن گير

expansion *enbessat* انبساط *gostaresh* گسترش *tose'e* توسعه

expect (v) *entezâr dâshtan* انتظار داشتن

expectancy *tavaqqo'* توقع

expectant *montazer* منتظر

expectation *entezâr* انتظار

expel (v) *birun kardan* بيرون كردن

expense *kharj* خرج

expensive *gerân* گران

expensiveness *gerâni* گرانى

experience *tajrobe* تجربه

experienced (c) *bâ tajrobe* با تجربه *âzemude* آزموده *kârkoshte* كاركشته *kârdân* كاردان *sâbeqe dâr* سابقه دار

experiences *tajârob* تجارب

experimental *âzemâyeshi* آزمايشى *tajrobi* تجربى

expert *khebre* خبره *kârshenâs* كارشناس (c) *motakhasses* متخصص *mâher* ماهر

expertise *kârshenâsi* كارشناسى (c) *takhassos* تخصص

expired *monqazi* منقضى

explain (v) *bayân kardan* بيان كردن

explanation *sharh* شرح *tashrih* تشريح *tozih* توضيح *bayân* بيان

explicit *sarih* صريح

explode (v) *tarakidan (tarak)* تركيدن (ترك)

exploit (v) *bahrebardâri kardan* بهره بردارى كردن

exploitation *bahrekeshi* بهره كشى *estesmâr* استثمار *bahrebardâri* بهره بردارى

explosion *enfejâr* انفجار

explosive *monfajere* منفجره

exporter *sâder konande* صادر كننده

exports *sâderât* صادرات

expose (v) *fâsh kardan* فاش كردن

exposure *ma'raz* معرض

express (v) *bayân kardan* بيان كردن (v) *ezhâr kardan* اظهار كردن

expression *bayân* بیان

expression *ezhâr* اظهار   *ebârat* عبارت

expressive *guyâ* گویا

exquisite *nafis* نفیس

extended *momtad* ممتد   *keshide* کشیده

extension *gostaresh* گسترش
tose'e توسعه   *emtedâd* امتداد
tamdid تمدید

extensive *pahnâvar* پهناور

external *khâreji* خارجی

extinct (e.g.fire) *khâmush* خاموش

extinct (e.g.species) *monqarez*
منقرض

extinction *nâbudi* نابودی

extra *mozâ'af* مضاعف   *ezâfe* اضافه

extract *osâre* عصاره   (v) *estekhrâj*
kardan استخراج کردن

extraction *estekhrâj* استخراج

extraordinary *khâreq olâde* خارق
العاده

extravagance *esrâf* اصراف

extreme *montahâ* منتها

eye *cheshm* چشم

eyebrow *abru* ابرو

eyelash *mozhe* مژه

eyelid *pelk* پلک

f

fabric *pârche* پارچه

fabrication *ja'l* جعل

face to face *rudarru* رو در رو

face *chehre* چهره (c) *surat* صورت
ru رو *simâ* سیما

facilities *tashilât* تسهیلات

fact *haqiqat* حقیقت

faction *ferqe* فرقه

factor *âmel* عامل

factory *kârkhâne* کارخانه

facts *haqâyeq* حقایق

faculty *dâneshkade* دانشکده

fade (v) *pâlâsidan (palâs)* پلاسیدن
(پلاس)

faded *pazhmorde* پژمرده

fail (defeat) (v) *shekast khordan*
شکست خوردن

fail (exam) (v) *rad shodan* رد شدن

failure *shekast* شکست

fair (exhibition) *namâyesh gâh*
نمایشگاه

fair (just) *monsefâne* منصفانه *âdel*
عادل

fairy *pari* پری

faith *e'teqâd* اعتقاد *aqide* عقیده
imân ایمان *din* دین *mazhab* مذهب

faithful *mo'taqed* معتقد *mo'men*
مومن

fake *kâzeb* کاذب *qollâbi* قلابی

falcon *oqâb* عقاب *qush* قوش

fall (decrease) *nozul* نزول *soqut*
سقوط *oft* افت

fall (season) *pâyiyz* پاییز *khazân*
خزان

fall in love (v) *âsheq shodan* عاشق
شدن

fallacy *safsate* سفسطه

false *kâzeb* کاذب *nâdorost*
نادرست

falsification *taqallob* تقلب

fame *shohrat* شهرت

familial (kinship) *khânavâdegi*
خانوادگی *fâmily* فامیلی

familial (knowledge) *âshenâ* آشنا
balad بلد

familiarity *âshenâyi* آشنایی

family name *nâme fâmil* نام فامیل

family *fâmil* فامیل *khânevâr* خانوار
(c) *khânavâde* خانواده *âyele* عائله

famine *qahti* قحطی

famine-stricken *qahti zade* قحطی
زده

famous *mashhur* مشهور *ma'ruf*
معروف *nâmdâr* نامدار

fan (cooler) *panke* پنکه *bâdzan*
باد زن

fan (supporter) *tarafdâr* طرفدار

fanatic *mortaje'* مرتجع

fanatical *mota'asseb* متعصب

fancy *khiyâl* خیال

fantasy *takhayyol* تخیل

far *dur* دور

fare *kerâye* کرایه

farewell *khodâ hâfezi* خداحافظی
khodâ hâfez خداحافظ

farm (c) *mazre'e* مزرعه *keshtzâr*
کشتزار

farmer *barzegar* برزگر *dehqân*
دهقان (c) *keshâvarz* کشاورز
ra'yyat رعیت

farrier na'lband نعلبند

farsighted durandish دوراندیش

farsightedness durbini دوربینی

fart guz گوز (v) guzidan (guz) گوزیدن (گوز)

fascinated majzub مجذوب shifte شیفته

fashion mod مد

fast sari' سریع tond تند

fasten (v) bastan (band) بستن (بند)

fastidious nâzok nârenji نازک نارنجی

fasting ruze روزه

fat (oil) charbi چربی

fat (inf) khiki خیکی (c) châq چاق

fatal mohlek مهلک koshande کشنده

fatality margomir مرگ و میر

fate taqdir تقدیر sarnevesht سرنوشت

father in law pedar zan پدرزن pedar shohar پدر شوهر

father bâbâ بابا

father pedar پدر

fatherly pedarâne پدرانه

fatty charb چرب

fault eyb عیب taqsir تقصیر

faulty kharâb خراب ma'yub معیوب

fauna jândârân جانداران

favour mennat منت enâyat عنایت marhamat مرحمت (c) lotf لطف

favourite mahbub محبوب

fear (c) tars ترس bim بیم khof خوف

fearful bimnâk بیمناک

feasibility emkân امکان

feasible maqdur مقدور momken ممکن moyassar میسر shodani شدنی

feast eyd عید

feather par پر

features moshakhkhasât مشخصات

February fevriye فوریه

fee mablaq مبلغ qeymat قیمت

feeding taqziye تغذیه

feel (v) ehsâs kardan احساس کردن (v) hess kardan حس کردن

feeling hess حس ehsâs احساس

felt mâhut ماهوت namad نمد

female mo'annas مونث mâde ماده zanâne زنانه

feminine mâde ماده zanâne زنانه

fence narde نرده hesâr حصار chapar چپر parchin پرچین

fencing shamshir bâzi شمشیربازی

ferment mâye مایه

fermentation takhmir تخمیر

fern sarakhs سرخس

fertile bârvar بارور hâsel khiz حاصل خیز

fertilise (v) bârvar kardan بارورکردن

fertilization leqâh لقاح

fertilizer kud کود

festival jashnvare جشنواره jashn جشن eyd عید

few kam کم chand چند

few, a ba'zi بعضی

fewer kamtar کمتر

fiancée nâmzad نامزد

fiction khiyâli خیالی

field (court) meydân میدان
field (study) reshte رشته
field mazre'e مزرعه keshtzâr کشتزار
fifteen pânzdah پانزده
fifty panjâh پنجاه
fig anjir انجیر
fight razm رزم zado khord
زدوخورد da'vâ دعوا nabard نبرد
nezâ' نزاع (v) da'vâ kardan
دعوا کردن (v) jang kardan
درگیر (v) dargir shodan جنگ کردن
شدن
fighter jangande جنگنده jangju
جنگجو mobârez مبارز razmande
رزمنده
figure raqam رقم shekl شکل
file (record) parvande پرونده
file (tool) sohân سوهان
fill (v) por kardan پر کردن
fillet râste راسته mâhiche ماهیچه
fillip talangor تلنگر
film film فیلم
filtered tasfiye shode تصفیه شده
filth kesâfat کثافت cherk چرک
filthy kasif کثیف
filtration tasfiye تصفیه
final âkherin آخرین
fine (delicate) zarif ظریف
fine (penalty) jarime جریمه
finger snap beshkan بشکن
finger angosht انگشت
fingering dastmâli دستمالی
finish pâyân پایان
Finland fanlând فنلاند

fire (sack) (v) ekhrâj kardan
اخراج کردن
fire fighter âtash neshân آتش نشان
fire off (v) dar kardan (dar kon)
در کردن (در کن)
fire station âtash neshâni آتش
نشانی
fire worshiper âtash parast آتش
پرست
fire âtash suzi آتش سوزی âtash
آتش
firecracker taraqqe ترقه
fireplace bokhâri بخاری
fireproof nasuz نسوز
fireworks âtash bâzi آتشبازی
firm (company) sherkat شرکت
firm (strong) qâyem قایم
(c) mohkam محکم qors قرص
first ebtedâ ابتدا nakhost نخست
(n) avval اول (c) avvalin اولین
nakhostin نخستین
first-aid komakhâye avvaliyye
کمکهای اولیه
firstly avvalan اولا
fish mâhi ماهی
fisherman mâhigir ماهیگیر
fishery mâhigiri ماهیگیری
fissure sheyâr شیار
fist mosht مشت
fit (faint) tashannoj تشنج qash
غش
five hundred pânsad پانصد
five panj پنج
fixed sâbet ثابت
fizzle chos چس
flabby khiki خیکی sost سست

flaccid *lakht* لخت

flag *alam* علم *lavâ* لوا *beyraq* بيرق (c) *parcham* پرچم

flake *shure* شوره

flakes *barfak* برفک

flannel *kise* کيسه

flask *qomqome* قمقمه

flat (building) *âpârtemân* آپارتمان

flat (tyre) *panchar* پنچر

flat *sâf* صاف *mosattah* مسطح

flatterer *châplus* چاپلوس

flattery *tamalloq* تملق

flavour *maze* مزه *ta'm* طعم

flax *dâs* داس

flea *kak* کک

flight *parvâz* پرواز

flint *chakhmâq* چخماق

flirting *lâs* لاس

floating *shenâvar* شناور

flock *galle* گله

flood *seyl* سيل

floor (ground) *zamin* زمين *kaf* کف

floor (storey) *tabaqe* طبقه *martabe* مرتبه

florescent *mahtâbi* مهتابی

florist *gol forush* گل فروش

flour *ârd* آرد

flow (tide) *madd* مد

flower *gol* گل

flowerpot *goldân* گلدان

fluctuation *navasân* نوسان

flue *zokâm* ذکام *ânfulânzâ* آنفولانزا

fluency *ravâni* روانی

fluent *salis* سليس *ravân* روان

fluff *kork* کرک

fluid *sayyal* سيال (c) *mâye'* مايع

flute *ney* نی

fly (e.g. plane, birds) (v) *parvâz kadan* پرواز کردن

fly swat *magas kosh* مگس کش

fly *magas* مگس *pashe* پشه (v) *paridan (par)* پريدن (پر)

foam *kaf* کف

focus *kânun* کانون

fodder *olufe* علوفه

foetus *janin* جنين

fog *meh* مه

foggy *mehâlud* مه آلود

foil *zarvaraq* زرورق

folder *pushe* پوشه

follow (obey) (v) *peyravi kardan* پيروی کردن

follow (v) *donbâl kardan* دنبال کردن (v) *ta'qib kardan* تعقيب کردن

follower *tâbe'* تابع *morid* مريد *peyro* پيرو

following *ta'qib* تعقيب

fontanel *malâj* ملاج

food *khurâki* خوراکی *ta'âm* طعام (c) *qazâ* غذا *khurâk* خوراک

fool *ahmaq* احمق (v) *kalak zadan* کلک زدن

foot *pâ* پا

football player *futbâlist* فوتباليست

football *futbâl* فوتبال

footboy *pâdo* پادو

foothill *dâmane* دامنه

footpath *piyâde ro* پياده رو

footprint radde pâ رد پا

footstep qadam قدم

for barâye برای

forage olufe علوفه

forbearance cheshm pushi چشم پوشی

forbid (v) mamnu' kardan ممنوع کردن (v) man' kardan منع کردن

forbidden qadaqan غدغن mamnu' ممنوع

force (army) lashkar لشکر

force feshâr فشار zur زور niru نیرو

forearm sâ'ed ساعد

forecast pish bini پیش بینی

forehead jabin جبین (c) pishâni پیشانی shaqiqe شقیقه

foreign bigâne بیگانه

foreigner khâreji خارجی

foreman (c) sarkârgar سرکارگر mobâsher مباشر

foremost moqaddam مقدم

forerunner pishro پیشرو

forest jangal جنگل

forestalling pish dasti پیش دستی

forester jangalbân جنگلبان

forever hamishe همیشه

forge ja'l kardan جعل

forged taqallobi تقلبی

forgery ja'l جعل

forget (v) farâmush kardan فراموش کردن

forgive (v) afv kardan عفو کردن (v) bakhshidan (bakhsh) بخشیدن (بخش) (v) gozashtan (gozar) گذشتن (گذر)

forgiveness âmorzesh آمرزش maqferat مغفرت (c) afv عفو gozasht گذشت

fork changâl چنگال

form form فرم shekl شکل

formal rasmi رسمی

formality ta'ârof تعارف rasmiyyat رسمیت

formation tashkil تشکیل

former sâbeq سابق pishin پیشین (c) qabli قبلی

formula formul فرمول

fort dezh دژ qal'e قلعه

fortification taqviyat تقویت

fortunate khoshbakht خوشبخت

fortunately khoshbakhtâne خوشبختانه

fortune teller rammâl رمال (c) fâlbin فال بین tâle'bin طالع بین

fortune telling fâlgiri فال گیری

fortune (c) servat ثروت fâl فال

forty chehel چهل

foster (v) bozorg kardan بزرگ کردن

foster-child farzand e rezâ'i فرزند رضائی

foul play nâmardi نامردی nâru نارو

found (v) peyrizi kardan پی ریزی کردن

foundation (company) mo'assese موسسه

foundation *bonyâd* بنياد *mabnâ* مبنا *asâs* اساس *bonyân* بنيان *pey* پی

founder *mo'asses* موسس *bâni* بانی

founding *peyrizi* پی ریزی

fountain pen *khod nevis* خودنويس

fountain *favvâre* فواره

four *châhâr* چهار

fourteen *châhârdah* چهارده

fox *rubâh* روباه

fraction *kasr* کسر

fracture *shekastegi* شکستگی

fragile *shekanande* شکننده

fragment *khorde* خرده

fragrance *atr* عطر

frail *zarif* ظريف *nahif* نحيف

frame *qâb* قاب *chârchub* چارچوب *kâdr* کادر

France *farânese* فرانسه

frank *sarih* صريح *biparde* بی پرده *pust kande* پوست کنده (c) *rok* رک

frankness *serâhat* صراحت

freckle *lak* لک

freckles *kakomak* کک و مک

free (not bound) *âzâd* آزاد

free (of charge) *majjani* مجانی *mofti* مفتی (c) *râyegân* رايگان *moft* مفت

free (v) *âzâd kardan* آزاد کردن

freedom seeker *âzâdi khâh* آزادی خواه

freedom (c) *âzâdi* آزادی *rahâyi* رهايی

freely *âzâdâne* آزادانه

freemasonry *ferâmâsoneri* فراماسونری

freeway *bozorgrâh* بزرگراه

French *farânesavi* فرانسوی

frequency *basâmad* بسامد *ferekâns* فرکانس

frequently *qâleban* غالبا

fresh (c) *tâze* تازه *noras* نورس

friction *sâyesh* سايش *estekâk* اصطکاک

Friday *jom'e* جمعه

fried *sorkh karde* سرخ کرده

friend *âshenâ* آشنا (c) *dust* دوست *rafiq* رفيق

friendly *dustâne* دوستانه

friendship *dusti* دوستی

frigate *nâv* ناو

fright *tars* ترس

frog *qurbâqe* غورباغه

from *az* از

front *jelo* جلو *pish* پيش *moqâbel* مقابل

frontier *marz* مرز

frontline *jebhe* جبهه

frown *akhm* اخم

frozen *monjamed* منجمد

fruit *mive* ميوه

fruitful *samar bakhsh* ثمربخش

frying pan *mâhi tâbe* ماهی تابه *tâbe* تابه

fuck (v) *gâyiydan (gây)* گاييدن (گای)

fuel *sukht* سوخت

fuelling *sukhtgiri* سوختگيری

fugitive *farâri* فراری

fulfil (v) *anjâm dâdan* انجام دادن

fulfilment *anjâm* انجام

full (not hungery) *sir* سیر

full moon *badr* بدر

full *por* پر

fun *tafrih* تفریح

function *amalkard* عملکرد

funeral *tarhim* ترحیم *khâk sepâri*
خاک سپاری *khatm* ختم

fungus *qârch* قارچ

funnel *qif* قیف

funny (person) *shukh* شوخ

funny (thing) *khande dâr* خنده دار

fur *khaz* خز

furious *khashmgin* خشمگین
(c) *asabâni* عصبانی

furnace (c) *kure* کوره *tanur* تنور

furniture *asâs* اثاث *mobl* مبل

fussy *moshkel pasand* مشکل پسند

future *âyande* آینده

futurity *âkherat* آخرت

g

gable roof *shirvâni* شیروانی

gadfly *kharmagas* خرمگس

gain *manfa'at* منفعت

gait *gâm* گام

galaxy *kahkashân* کهکشان

gallery *negâr khâne* نگار خانه

gallows *dâr* دار

gamble *qomâr* قمار

game *mosâbeqe* مسابقه *bâzi* بازی

gap *shekâf* شکاف

garage (parking) *gârâzh* گاراژ

garage *mekâniki* مکانیکی *ta'mirgâh* تعمیر گاه

garbage man *supur* سپور

garbage *âshqâl* آشغال

garden *bâq* باغ

gardening *bâqbâni* باغبانی

gargling *qarqare* غرغره

garlic *sir* سیر

garment *rakht* رخت

gas *gâz* گاز

gasoline *gâzo'il* گازوئیل

gassy *gâzdâr* گازدار

gate *darvâze* دروازه

gather (v) *jam' kardan* جمع کردن

gathering *ejtemâ'* اجتماع

gathering *gerdâvari* گردآوری

gauge *kontor* کنتور

gauze *gâz* گاز

gazelle *jeyrân* جیران

gear (of a vehicle) *dande* دنده

gearbox *girboks* گیربکس

gender *jens* جنس

gene *zhen* ژن

genealogist *shajareshenâs* شجره شناس

genealogy *shajarenâme* شجره نامه *nasab* نسب

general (army rank) *zhenerâl* ژنرال

general *umumi* عمومی *kolli* کلی

generalisation *ta'mim* تعمیم

generation (offspring) *nasl* نسل

generation *tolid* تولید

generator *movalled* مولد

generosity *morovvat* مروت *sakhâvat* سخاوت *karam* کرم

generous *sakhâvat mand* سخاوتمند *javân mard* جوانمرد *bakhshande* بخشنده

genesis *peydâyesh* پیدایش

genital *tanâsoli* تناسلی

genius *nâbeqe* نابغه *tizhush* تیزهوش

gentle *molâyem* ملایم

gentleman *âqâ* آقا

genuine *asl* اصل

geology *zamin shenâsi* زمین شناسی

geranium *sham'dâni* شمعدانی

germ *mikrob* میکروب

Germany *âlmân* آلمان

gesture *zhest* ژست *eshâre* اشاره

get involved (v) *dargir shodan* درگیر شدن

get pregnant (v) *âbestan shodan* آبستن شدن

get up (v) *boland shodan* بلند شدن (v) *barkhâstan (bar khiz)* برخاستن (برخیز)

get (v) gereftan (gir) (گیر) گرفتن

ghost ruh روح

giant qul غول

giddiness giji گیجی

giddy mang منگ gij گیج

gift hedye هدیه mohebat موهبت
chesm roshani چشم روشنی tohfe
تحفه

gifted nâbeqe نابغه

ginger zanjabil زنجبیل

giraffe zarrâfe زرافه

girl dokhtar دختر

girlfriend dost dokhtar دوست دختر

girlish dokhtarâne دخترانه

gist lobb لب

give an injection (v) âmpul
zandan آمپول زدن

give lessons (v) dars dâdan درس
دادن

give up (v) enserâf dâdan انصراف
دادن

give (v) dâdan (dah) دادن (ده)

glad khoshhâl خوشحال shâd شاد

glance negâh نگاه

gland qodde غده

glass (cup) livân لیوان

glass blower shishegar شیشه گر

glass shishe شیشه

glasses eynak عینک

glaze lo'âb لعاب

glazed tile kâshi کاشی

glazier shishebor شیشه بر

glib tongued charb jabân چرب
زبان

global jahâni جهانی

globe kore کره

gloom zolmat ظلمت

gloomy (dark) târik تاریک

gloomy (upset) pakar پکر
deltang دلتنگ qamgin غمگین

glorious mojallal مجلل

glory obohhat ابهت jalâl جلال
sokuh شکوه

glottis châknây چاکنای

gloves dastkesh دستکش

glow (v) derakhshidan (derakhsh)
درخشیدن (درخش)

glue serish سریش (c) chasb چسب
(v) chasbidan (chasb) چسبیدن
(چسب)

gluttonous shekamu شکمو

go back (v) bargashtan (bargard)
برگشتن (برگرد)

go on a strike (v) e'tesâb kardan
اعتصاب کردن

go (v) raftan (rav) رفتن (رو)

goal (aim) hadaf هدف

goal (in football) gol گل

goalkeeper darvâzebân دروازه بان

goat boz بز

god willing enshâ'allâh انشا الله

God allâh الله izad ایزد rabb
رب parvardegâr پروردگار (c) khodâ
خدا khodâvand خداوند

goddess elâhe الهه

goitre (c) guvatr گواتر qambâd
غمباد

gold (c) talâ طلا zar زر

golden talayi طلایی

goldsmith zargar زرگر

golf golf گلف

gonorrheae *suzâk* سوزاک

good bye *khodâ hâfez* خداحافظ

good evening *shab bekheyr* شب بخیر

good morning *sobh bekheyr* صبح بخیر

good news (c) *mozhde* مژده *navid* نوید

good night *shab bekheyr* شب بخیر

good omen *shogun* شگون

good *kheyr* خیر (c) *khub* خوب

goods *ajnâs* اجناس *kâlâ* کالا

good-tempered *khosh akhlâq* خوش اخلاق

goose *qâz* غاز

gorge *darre* دره

gorilla *guril* گوریل

gossip *sokhanchini* سخن چینی

gout *neqres* نقرس

govern (v) *hokumat kardan* حکومت کردن

government *dolat* دولت

governor general *farmândâr* فرماندار

governor (c) *ostândâr* استاندار *hâkem* حاکم *hokmrân* حکمران *zamâmdâr* زمامدار

governor's office *farmândâri* فرمانداری

grade *kelâs* کلاس

gradual *tadriji* تدریجی

graduate *fâreqottahsil* فارغ التحصیل (v) *fâreqottahsil shodan* فارغ التحصیل شدن

graduation *fâreqottahsili* فارغ التحصیلی

graft *peyvand* پیوند

grain *qalle* غله *bazr* بذر *dâne* دانه

gram *geram* گرم

grammar *dastur* دستور

grandchild *nave* نوه

grandeur *azamat* عظمت

grandfather *pedar bozorg* پدربزرگ *jad* جد

grandmother *mâdar bozorg* مادر بزرگ

granite *khârâ* خارا

grapefruit *dârâbi* دارابی

grapes *angur* انگور

grappling *gelâviz* گل آویز

grasp (v) *chang zadan* چنگ زدن

grass *alaf* علف *chaman* چمن

grateful *haq shenâs* حق شناس *mamnun* ممنون *motashakker* متشکر

grater *rande* رنده

gratitude *qadrdâni* قدردانی *tashakkor* تشکر

grave digger *qabrkan* قبرکن

grave *madfan* مدفن (c) *qabr* قبر *gur* گور

gravel *sangrize* سنگریزه *rig* ریگ *shen* شن

gravelled road *shuse* شوسه

graveyard *gurestân* گورستان (v) *qabrestân* قبرستان

gravity *jâzebe* جاذبه

gray *khâkestari* خاکستری

graze (v) *charidan (char)* چریدن

grazer *charande* چرنده

grazing *charâ* چرا

grease *geris* گریس

great (c) *foqolâde* فوق العاده *kabir* کبیر

greed *hers* حرص *tama'* طمع

greedy *tama'kâr* طمع کار

green *sabz* سبز

greengrocer *sabzi forush* سبزی فروش

greenhouse *garmkhâne* گرمخانه

greeting *dorud* درود

grenade *nârenjak* نارنجک

grey *khakestari* خاکستری *jogandomi* جوگندمی

grief *anduh* اندوه

grievance *gele* گله *shekâyat* شکایت

grieving *mâtam* ماتم

grilled *beryân* بریان

grind *sâyiydan (sây)* ساییدن (سای)

grindstone *sonbâde* سنباده

groan *nâle* ناله (v) *nâlidan (nâl)* نالیدن (نال)

groats *balqur* بلغور

grocer *baqqâl* بقال

grocery *baqqâli* بقالی *khârobâr forushi* خوار و بار فروشی

groin *keshâle* کشاله

groom *dâmâd* داماد

groomsman *sâqdush* ساقدوش

groove *godi* گودی *sheyâr* شیار

ground *zamin* زمین

groundless *alaki* الکی *pâ dar havâ* پا در هوا *kashki* کشکی

group leader *sardaste* سردسته

group *goruh* گروه

grouping *dastebandi* دسته بندی

grow up (v) *bozorg shodan* بزرگ شدن

grow (v) *bozorg kardan* بزرگ کردن (v) *ruyiydan (ruy)* روییدن (روی)

grown up *bozorgsâl* بزرگسال *bozorg* بزرگ

growth *nashv* نشو *nomovv* نمو *roshd* رشد

grudge *lajâjat* لجاجت *qaraz* غرض *laj* لج

grumble *shekve* شکوه *qor* غر

guarantee *tazmin* تضمین

guaranty *zamânat* ضمانت

guard *qarâvol* قراول *keshik* کشیک *mohâfez* محافظ *gârd* گارد *negahbân* نگهبان *herâst* حراست *pâsebân* پاسبان

guardian *qayyem* قیم *sarparast* سرپرست

guardianship *kefâlat* کفالت *qeymumat* قیمومت

guarding *morâqebat* مراقبت *negahbâni* نگهبانی

guerilla *cherik* چریک

guess *hads* حدس *hads zadan* حدس زدن

guest house *mehmân khâne* مهمان خانه

guest *mehmân* مهمان

guidance *pand* پند

guide *balad* بلد (c) *râh namâ* راهنما (v) *ershâd kardan* ارشاد کردن

guiding *ershâd* ارشاد

guilt *taqsir* تقصیر *gonâh* گناه

guilty *mojrem* مجرم *moqasser* مقصر *gonâhkâr* گناه کار

guinea pig *khukcheye hendi* خوکچه هندی

guitar *gitâr* گیتار

gulf *khalij* خلیج

gum (chewing) *âdâms* آدامس

gum (teeth) *lase* لثه

gun *tofang* تفنگ

gunfire *tirandâzi* تیراندازی

gunpowder *bârut* باروت

gunstock *qondâq* قنداق

gustatory *chashâyi* چشایی

guts *del* دل

guy *yâru* یارو *pesar* پسر

gymnasium *zurkhâne* زورخانه

gymnastics *zhimnastik* ژیمناستیک

gypsy *koli* کولی *qorbati* غربتی

h

habit *âdat* عادت

habitable *âbâd* آباد

haemorrhage *khunrizi* خون ریزی

haemorrhoids *bavâsir* بواسیر

Hague *lâhe* لاهه

hail *tagarg* تگرگ

hair dressing *ârâyeshgâh* آرایشگاه

hair *mu* مو

haircut *eslâh* اصلاح

hairdresser *salmâni* سلمانی
(c) *ârâyeshgar* آرایشگر

hairpin *gire* گیره *sanjâq* سنجاق

hairy *pashmâlu* پشمالو

Hajjis *hojâj* حجاج

half brother *barâdarkhânde* برادر خوانده

half dead *nime jân* نیمه جان

half mast *nime afrâshte* نیمه افراشته

half verse *mesrâ'* مصرع

half (c) *nesf* نصف *nim* نیم *nime* نیمه

half-done *nesfe* نصفه

half-finished *nefekâre* نصفه کاره

hall *tâlâr* تالار *sâlon* سالن

halt *tavaqqof* توقف

ham *gushte khuk* گوشت خوک

hammer *chakkosh* چکش

hammock *gahvâre* گهواره *nanu* ننو

hamper *sabad* سبد *zanbil* زنبیل

hand (for watch, etc.) *aqrabe* عقربه

hand crafts *sanâye'e dasti* صنایع دستی

hand made *dasti* دستی

hand over *tahvil dâdan* تحویل دادن

hand sewn *dast duz* دست دوز

hand writing *dast khat* دست خط *khat* خط

hand *dast* دست

hand-cooked *dast pokht* دست پخت

handcuff *dastband* دستبند
(v) *dastband zadan* دستبند زدن

handful *mosht* مشت

handicap *ma'luliyat* معلولیت

handicapped *ma'lul* معلول

handkerchief *dastmâl* دستمال

handle *daste* دسته *qabze* قبضه *dastgire* دستگیره

handmade *dast sâz* دست ساز

handsome *khoshgel* خوشگل *khosh qiyâfe* خوش قیافه

hang out (v) *palakidan (palak)* پلکیدن (پلک)

hang (v) *âvikhtan (âviz)* آویختن (آویز)

happiness *delkhoshi* دلخوشی *shâdi* شادی (c) *khoshi* خوشی *sa'âdat* سعادت

happy (c) *khoshhâl* خوشحال *shâd* شاد *khosh* خوش

harass (v) *âzâr dâdan* آزار دادن

harassment *âzâr* آزار

harbour *langargâh* لنگرگاه *bandar* بندر

hard *doshvâr* دشوار *moshkel* مشکل *sakht* سخت

hardship *maziqe* مضیقه *mashaqqat* مشقت

hare *khargush* خرگوش

harelip *lab shekari* لب شکری

harem *haramsarâ* حرمسرا

harm *latme* لطمه *âsib* آسیب
sadame صدمه *ziyân* زیان
(c) *zarar* ضرر *latme zadan*
لطمه زدن

harmful *ziyânâvar* زیان آور
mozerr مضر

harness *mahâr* مهار

harp *chang* چنگ

harvest *dero* درو *bardâsht* برداشت
(v) *dero kardan* درو کردن

hashish *bang* بنگ *hashish* حشیش

hasp *cheft* چفت

hasty *dast pâche* دستپاچه *ajul*
عجول

hat *kolâh* کلاه

hatch *dariche* دریچه

hatred *kine* کینه

haunting dog *tâzi* تازی

have (v) *dâshtan (dâr)* داشتن (دار)

hawk *qush* قوش

hawker *doregard* دوره گرد
dastforush دست فروش

hay *kâh* کاه

hazelnut *fandoq* فندق

hazy *mehâlud* مه آلود

he *u* او *ân* آن

head (cheif) *ra'is* رئیس

head *ra's* راس *sar* سر *kalle* کله

headache *sardard* سردرد

headgear *khud* خود

heading *onvân* عنوان

headmaster *modir* مدیر

headphone *gushi* گوشی

headquarter *farmândehi* فرماندهی
qarârgâh قرارگاه *setâd* ستاد

head-stall *afsâr* افسار

health care *behdâsht* بهداشت

health (c) *salâmati* سلامتی *bonye*
بنیه *behdâsht* بهداشت

healthy *tandorost* تندرست
(c) *sâlem* سالم

hear (v) *shenidan (shenav)* شنیدن
(شنو)

hearing aid *sam'ak* سمعک

hearing *senavâyi* شنوایی

heart *qalb* قلب

heart-breaking *delkharâsh* دلخراش

heart-rending *jegarsuz* جگرسوز

heat *harârat* حرارت *garmâ* گرما
garmi گرمی

heaven *behesht* بهشت

heavy *sangin* سنگین

Hebrew *ebri* عبری

hedge *parchin* پرچین

heel *pâshne* پاشنه

height (altitude) *ertefâ'* ارتفاع

height (tallness) *qad* قد

hell *darak* درک *duzakh* دوزخ
(c) *jahannam* جهنم

hello (on the phone) *alo* الو

hello (c) *salâm* سلام *salâm*
aleykom سلام علیکم

helm *sokkân* سکان

helmet *kolâh* کلاه

helmsman *sokkândâr* سکاندار

help *komak* کمک *emddad* امداد
(v) *komak kardan* کمک کردن

helpless *nâchâr* ناچار *bichâre*
بیچاره

hemisphere *nimkore* نیمکره

hemp *kanaf* کنف

hempseed *shâhdâne* شاهدانه

hen *morq* مرغ

henna *hanâ* حنا

hepatitis *hipâtit* هپاتیت

her majesty *olyâhazrat* علیاحضرت

herald *châvosh* چاوش *jârchi*
جارچی

herb *alaf* علف *giyâh* گیاه

herd *galle* گله

here *injâ* اینجا

heritage *mirâs* میراث

hernia *fatq* فتق

hero *pahlavân* پهلوان
(c) *qahramân* قهرمان

heroin *heroin* هروئین

herpes *tabkhâl* تبخال

hesitation *ta'ammol* تأمل

hiccup *sekseke* سکسکه

hidden *qâyeb* غایب *nahân* نهان
penhân پنهان (c) *makhfi* مخفی

hide (v) *makhfi kardan* مخفی کردن

hide-and-seek *qâyem mushak*
قایم موشک

high school *dabirestân* دبیرستان

high *boland* بلند

highlander *kuhestâni* کوهستانی

highness *hazrat* حضرت

highway (c) *bozorgrâh* بزرگراه
shâhrâh شاهراه

hijack (v) *robudan (robây)* ربودن
(ربای)

hijacker *robâyande* رباینده

hiking *piyâde ravi* پیاده روی

hill *tappe* تپه

Hindu *hendu* هندو

hinge *lolâ* لولا

hint *eshâre* اشاره

hire *kerâye* کرایه *ejâre* اجاره
(v) *ajir kardan* اجیر کردن
(v) *kerâye kardan* کرایه کردن
(v) *ejâre kardan* اجاره کردن

historian *movarrekh* مورخ
târikhnevis تاریخ نویس

historical *târikhi* تاریخی

history *târikh* تاریخ

hit (v) *zadan (zan)* زدن (زن)

hive *kandu* کندو

hoarders *mohtaker* محتکر

hobby *sargarmi* سرگرمی

hold (v) *gereftan (gir)* گرفتن (گیر)

holding *negahdâri* نگهداری

hole *rozan* روزن (c) *surâkh* سوراخ
manfaz منفذ *châle* چاله

holiday *ta'til* تعطیل *ta'tili* تعطیلی

holidays *ta'tilat* تعطیلات

Holy Spirit *ruh olqodos* روح القدس

holy war *jahâd* جهاد

holy *moqaddas* مقدس

homage *bey'at* بیعت

home *manzel* منزل (c) *khâne* خانه
maskan مسکن

homeland *keshvar* کشور
marzobum مرزوبوم (c) *mihan* میهن

homeless (c) *bikhânemân* بی
خانمان *âvâre* آواره *bipanâh* بی پناه
darbedar دربدر

homework *mashq* مشق

homicide *âdam koshi* آدمکشی

homosexual *hamjes bâz* همجنس باز

honest *sâdeq* صادق

honesty *sedâqat* صداقت

honey *asal* عسل

honour *sharâfat* شرافت (c) *eftekhâr* افتخار *âberu* آبرو

honourable *sharif* شریف

honoured *sarafrâz* سرافراز

hoodlum *châgukesh* چاقو کش

hoof *som* سم

hook *changak* چنگک *qollâb* قلاب

hoop *chanbare* چنبره

hope *omid* امید

hopeful (c) *omidvâr* امیدوار *ârezumand* آرزومند

hopeless *nâ omid* نا امید *ma'yus* مایوس

horizon *ofoq* افق

horizontal *ofoqi* افقی

horn (animal's) *shâkh* شاخ

horn (of cars, etc.) *buq* بوق

horny *hashari* حشری

horrible *tarsnâk* ترسناک

horse riding *asb savari* اسب سواری

horse *asb* اسب

horsefly *kharmagas* خرمگس

horseshoe *na'l* نعل

hose *shelank* شلنگ

hospitable *mehmân dust* مهمان دوست

hospital (c) *bimârestân* بیمارستان *marizkhâne* مریضخانه

hospitalise (v) *bastari kardan* بستری کردن

hospitalised *bastari* بستری

hospitality *mehmân navâzi* مهمان نوازی *pazirâyi* پذیرایی

host *mizbân* میزبان

hostage *gerogân* گروگان

hostess (of airplane) *mehmân dâr* مهماندار

hostile *khasmâne* خصمانه

hostility *doshmani* دشمنی

hostility *khushunat* خشونت *khusumat* خصومت

hot *dâq* داغ

hotel *hotel* هتل

hour *sâ'at* ساعت

house *manzel* منزل (c) *khâne* خانه

household (c) *khânavâde* خانواده *khânemân* خانمان

housewife *kadbânu* کدبانو (c) *khâne dâr* خانه دار

how many *chand* چند

how much *cheqadr* چقدر

how *chegune* چگونه (c) *chetor* چطور

however *lâken* لاکن *beharhâl* بهرحال

Hubble bubble *qaliyân* قلیان

hue *rang* رنگ

hug (c) *baqal* بغل *âqush* آغوش (v) *baqal kardan* بغل کردن

huge *azim* عظیم (inf) *gonde* گنده

human resources *kârgozini* کارگزینی

human rights *hoquqe bashar* حقوق بشر

human bashar بشر   âdam آدم
ensân انسان

humanism mardomi مردمى

humanitarian bashardust
بشردوست no' dust نوعدوست

humanity ensâniyat انسانيت

humble forutan فروتن   motavâze'
متواضع

humid martub مرطوب

humidity nam نم

humiliation kheffat خفت
(c) tahqir تحقير

hump (camel) kuhân كوهان

hunch quz قوز

hundred sad صد

hunger gorosnegi گرسنگى

hungry (inf) goshne گشنه
gorosne گرسنه

hunt (c) shekâr شكار   seyd صيد

hunter sayyâd صياد   (c) shekârchi
شكارچى

hurricane gerdbâd گردباد

hurry ajale عجله   (v) ajale kardan
عجله كردن

husband shohar شوهر

hushed maskut مسكوت

hush-hush bisarosedâ بى سروصدا

hut kolbe كلبه   kapar كپر

hyacinth sonbol سنبل

hybrid dorage دورگه

hydrotherapy âb darmâni آب
درمانى

hyena kaftâr كفتار

hygienic behdâshti بهداشتى

hypocrites monâfeq منافق

hypocritical riyâkâr رياكار

hypothesis farziyye فرضيه

    I

i

I *man* من

ice cream *bastani* بستنی

ideal *ârmân* آرمان

identical *moshâbeh* مشابه

identification card *kârte shenâsâyi* کارت شناسایی

identity card *shenâsnâme* شناسنامه

ideology *maslak* مسلک

idiom *estelâh* اصطلاح

idleness *batâlat* بطالت

idol *bot* بت

if *agar* اگر

ignorance *jahl* جهل *jahâlat* جهالت (c) *nâdâni* نادانی

ignorant (c) *nâdân* نادان *jâhel* جاهل

ill *bimâr* بیمار (c) *mariz* مریض

illegal *qeyreqânuni* غیر قانونی

illegitimate *harâmzâde* حرامزاده *nâmashru'* نامشروع

illiteracy *bisavâdi* بی سوادی

illiterate *bisavâd* بی سواد

illness *kasâlat* کسالت (c) *bimâri* بیماری *marizi* مریضی *nâkhoshi* ناخوشی *maraz* مرض

illusion *tavahhom* توهم

illustration *tasvir* تصویر

image *aks* عکس

imaginary *khiyâli* خیالی

imagination *khiyâl* خیال *tasavvor* تصور *takhayyol* تخیل

imitation *taqlid* تقلید

immature *nâbâleq* نابالغ

immediately *biderang* بیدرنگ (c) *foran* فورا

immigrant *mohâjer* مهاجر

immigrate (v) *mohâjerat kardan* مهاجرت کردن

immigration *mohâjerat* مهاجرت

immoderation *efrât* افراط

immune *masun* مصون

immunity *masuniyat* مصونیت

impact *tamâs* تماس

impatient *ajul* عجول *bihosele* بی حوصله

impeach (v) *estizâh kardan* استیضاح کردن

impeachment *estizâh* استیضاح

imperative *amri* امری

imperfect *nâqes* ناقص

implied *zemni* ضمنی

importance *ahamiyat* اهمیت

important *mohemm* مهم

imposition *tahmil* تحمیل

impossible *mahâl* محال *qeyre momken* غیر ممکن

impostor *shayyâd* شیاد *hoqqe bâz* حقه باز

impotence *nâtavâni* ناتوانی *nâtavân* ناتوان

impression *asar* اثر *ta'sir* تاثیر

improper (c) *nâmonâseb* نامناسب *nâshâyeste* ناشایسته

improvement *pishraft* پیشرفت *behbud* بهبود

in accord *mosâ'ed* مساعد

in addition to *alâve bar* علاوه بر

in case *chenânche* چنانچه

in cash naqdi نقدی

in charge motasaddi متصدی mas'ul مسئول

in debt madyun مدیون

in secret makhfiyâne مخفیانه

in terms of bar hasb e بر حسب

in turn nobati نوبتی

in dar در (inf) tu تو

inappropriate nâbejâ نابجا (c) nâmonâseb نامناسب bijâ بی جا

inborn fetri فطری

incapable bi'orze بی عرضه

incident ettefâq اتفاق ruydâd رویداد

inclined ma'tuf معطوف

include (v) gonjândan (gonjân) گنجاندن (گنجان)

including (c) shâmel شامل mashmul مشمول

incognito gomnâm گمنام

incoherent bisaro tah بی سروته

income (c) darâmad درآمد dakhl دخل

incompatibility monâfât منافات

incompatible moqâyer مغایر

incompetent bi'orze بی عرضه

incomplete nâqes ناقص nâtamâm ناتمام

incomprehensible qyre qâbele fahm غیر قابل فهم

incongruous nâjur ناجور

inconvenience mozâhemat مزاحمت

incorrect qalat غلط nâdorost نادرست

increase afzâyesh افزایش ezdiyâd ازدیاد (v) ezâfe kardan اضافه کردن (v) afzâyesh dâshtan افزایش داشتن

incumbent shâqel شاغل

indebted bedehkâr بدهکار maqruz مقروض

indecent sharmâvar شرم آور nâpasand ناپسند jelf جلف rakik رکیک

indecision shak شک

indefinite nakare نکره

indemnity jobrân جبران (c) tâvân تاوان qarâmat غرامت

indented tu rafte تورفته

independence esteqlâl استقلال

independent mostaqell مستقل

index finger sabbâbe سبابه

index zarib ضریب fehrest فهرست

indicted mottaham متهم

indifferent bitafâvot بی تفاوت

indigenous bumi بومی

indigestion su'e hâzeme سوء هاضمه

indirect qeyre mostaqim غیر مستقیم

indispensable hatmi حتمی

individual nafar نفر shakhs شخص fard فرد (adj) fardi فردی

induction esteqrâ استقرا

industrial san'ati صنعتی

industry san'at صنعت

ineffective bikhâsiyat بی خاصیت

inequality nabarâbari نابرابری

inevitable nâgozir ناگزیر

inexpensive arzân ارزان

inexperience *nâshigari* ناشیگری

infant *khordsâl* خردسال

infected *ofuni* عفونی

infection *ofunat* عفونت

infectious *ofuni* عفونی

inferiority *heqârat* حقارت

infertile *nâzâ* نازا

infertility *nâzâyi* نازایی

infinite *nâmahdud* نامحدود

infinitive *masdar* مصدر

inflamed *moltaheb* ملتهب

inflammation *eltehâb* التهاب

inflation *tavarrom* تورم

influence *ta'sir* تاثیر *nofuz* نفوذ

influential *mo'asser* موثر

influenza *ânfulânzâ* آنفولانزا

inform (v) *âgâh kardan* آگاه کردن

informal *qeyre rasmi* غیر رسمی

information *ettelâ'ât* اطلاعات

informed *mottale'* مطلع

informer *khabarchin* خبرچین

infrastructure *zirbanâ* زیربنا

infringement *takhallof* تخلف

ingredient *joz'* جزء

inhabitant *ahl* اهل *sâken* ساکن

inherit (v) *ers bordan* ارث بردن

inheritance *ers* ارث

initial *avval* اول

initialling *pârâf* پاراف

injection *tazriq* تزریق

injured *âsib dide* آسیب دیده (c) *majruh* مجروح

injury *zakhm* زخم

injustice *setam* ستم *haq koshi* حق کشی (c) *zolm* ظلم

ink *johar* جوهر *morakkab* مرکب

inlaid work *khâtam kâri* خاتم کاری

inlaid *monabbat* منبت

inmate *zendâni* زندانی

inn *mosâferkhâne* مسافر خانه

innate *fetri* فطری *zâti* ذاتی

inner *daruni* درونی

innocent *ma'sum* معصوم *bigonâh* بیگناه

innovation *ebtekâr* ابتکار (c) no *âvari* نوآوری

innovator *mobtaker* مبتکر

insane *divâne* دیوانه

inscription *katibe* کتیبه

insect *hashare* حشره

insecticide *hashare kosh* حشره کش

insecure *nâ amn* نا امن

insertion *darj* درج

inside out *poshto ru* پشت و رو

inside *darun* درون *dâkhel* داخل (c) *tu* تو

insight *basirat* بصیرت *ma'refat* معرفت

insignia *neshân* نشان

insignificant *nâqâbel* ناقابل

insist (c) *esrâr kardan* اصرار کردن

insistence *ta'kid* تاکید *pâfeshâri* پافشاری

insomnia *bikhâbi* بی خوابی

inspect (v) *bâzdid kardan* بازدید کردن

inspector bâzpors بازپرس bâzras بازرس

inspiration (c) elhâm الهام sorush سروش

inspire (v) elhâm kardan الهام کردن

install (v) nasb kardan نصب کردن

installing nasb نصب

instalment qest قسط aqsât اقساط

instant daf'e دفعه lahze لحظه

instigation tahrik تحریک

instinct qarize غریزه fetrat فطرت

institute mo'assese موسسه sâzemân سازمان

instruct (v) âmuzesh dâdan آموزش دادن

instruction âmuzesh آموزش

instructive âmuzande آموزنده

instructor morabbi مربی

insulator âyeq عایق

insult ehânat اهانت (v) ehânat kardan اهانت کردن

insurance bime بیمه

insure (v) bime kardan بیمه کردن

intact sâlem سالم

integrate (v) edqâm kardan ادغام کردن

integration edqâm ادغام

intellectual roshanfekr روشنفکر

intelligence sho'ur شعور

intelligent bâhush با هوش

intense shadid شدید

intensification tashdid تشدید

intension maqsud مقصود qasd قصد

intensity sheddat شدت

intensive foshorde فشرده

intention maqsad مقصد niyyat نیت manzur منظور erâde اراده

intentional amdi عمدی qasdi قصدی

intercourse (c) âmizesh آمیزش moqârebat مقاربت jamâ' جماع

interest sud سود bahre بهره

interested alâqemand علاقمند

interesting jâleb جالب

interfere (v) dekhâlat kardan دخالت کردن

interference modâkhele مداخله dekhâlat دخالت

internal daruni درونی (c) dâkheli داخلی

international beynolmelali بین المللی

internship kârvarzi کارورزی

interpret (v) ta'bir kardan تعبیرکردن

interpretation tafsir تفسیر ta'bir تعبیر

interpreter motarjem مترجم

interrogate (v) bâzjuyi kardan بازجویی کردن

interrogation bâzkhâst بازخواست bâzporsi بازپرسی bâzjuyi بازجویی

interrogator bâzju بازجو

interruption qat' قطع

intersection châhâr râh چهار راه taqâto' تقاطع

interval fâsele فاصله

intervene (v) dekhâlat kardan دخالت کردن

intervention modâkhele مداخله

interview mosâhebe مصاحبه

intestine *rude* روده

intimate *khodemâni* خودمانی *samimi* صمیمی

intonation *tanin* طنین

intoxicated (c) *mast* مست (inf) *lul* لول

intoxication *masti* مستی

intransitive (g) *lâzem* لازم

intricacy *pichidegi* پیچیدگی

intricate *boqranj* بغرنج

introduce (v) *mo'arrefi kardan* معرفی کردن

introduction (person) *mo'arrefi* معرفی

introduction (preface) *moqaddame* مقدمه

intrusion *modâkhele* مداخله *dekhâlat* دخالت

invalid (handicapped) *ma'lul* معلول *alil* علیل

invasion *dast andâzi* دست اندازی *tâkhto tâz* تاخت و تاز (c) *tajâvoz* تجاوز

invent (v) *ekhterâ' kardan* اختراع کردن

invention *ekhterâ'* اختراع

inventor *mokhtare'* مخترع

invertebrates *bimohregân* بی مهرگان

investigation *rasidegi* رسیدگی *bâzjuyi* بازجویی *tahqiq* تحقیق

investigator *bâzju* بازجو

invincible *shekast nâpazir* شکست ناپذیر

invisible *nâmar'i* نامرئی

invitation *da'vat* دعوت

invite (v) *da'vat kardan* دعوت کردن

invoice *fâktor* فاکتور

involved *gereftâr* گرفتار

Iran *irân* ایران

Iranian *irâni* ایرانی

Iraq *arâq* عراق

Ireland *irland* ایرلند

iris (eye) *enabiye* عنبیه

iris (flower) *gole zanbaq* گل زنبق

iron (metal) *âhan* آهن

iron *utu* اطو

irrational *nâma'qul* نامعقول

irregular *nâmonazzam* نامنظم

irrelevant *birabt* بی ربط *nâmarbut* نامربوط

irrigate (v) *âbyâri kardan* آبیاری کردن

irrigation *âbyâri* آبیاری

irrigator *âbyâr* آبیار

is not (v) *nist* نیست

is (v) *ast* است (هست)

Islam *eslâm* اسلام

Islamic guard *pâsdâr* پاسدار

island *jazire* جزیره

islands *jazâyer* جزایر

isolated *mojazzâ* مجزا

issue *shomâre* شماره

issuing *sodur* صدور

it *ân* آن

itching *khâresh* خارش

itinerary *safarnâme* سفرنامه

ivory *âj* عاج

ivy *pichak* پیچک

J

82

j

jackal shoqâl شغال

jacket kot کت zhâkat ژاکت

jail habs حبس zendân زندان
(v) habs kardan حبس کردن

jailor zendânbân زندانبان

jam morabbâ مربا

janitor mostakhdem مستخدم
(c) sarâydâr سرایدار farrâsh فراش

January zhânviye ژانویه

Japan zhâpon ژاپن

Japanese zhâponi ژاپنی

jaw ârvâre آرواره (c) fakk فک

jealous hasud حسود bakhil بخیل

jealousy hasad حسد hesâdat
حسادت

jeans jin جین

jeep jip جیپ

jeopardy khatar خطر

Jesus isâ عیسی

Jew kalimi کلیمی juhud جهود

jeweller javâher furush جواهر فروش

jewellery javâherât جواهرات
javâher جواهر

Jewish priest kâhen کاهن

Jewish juhud جهود

jinn jenn جن

job shoql شغل kâr کار

jockey savârkâr سوارکار

join (v) peyvastan (peyvand)
پیوستن (پیوند)

joined mottasel متصل molhaq
ملحق

joint (organ) mafsal مفصل

joint (adj) to'am توام moshtarak
مشترک

joint-stock sahâmi سهامی

joke jok جوک shukhi شوخی
mezâh مزاح

journalism ruznâme negâri روزنامه
نگاری

journalist ruznâme negâr روزنامه
نگار

journey mosâferat مسافرت

joy sorur سرور neshât نشاط

judge dâdras دادرس (c) qâzi قاضی
dâvar داور

judgement qazâvat قضاوت

judicial qazâyi قضایی

juggler sho'bade bâz شعبده باز

juggling cheshm bandi چشم بندی

juice âbe mive آب میوه

juicy âbdâr آبدار

July zhu'ye ژوئیه

jump paresh پرش (v) paridan
پریدن (پر) (par)

jumper (sweater) poliver پلیور

junction dorâhi دوراهی

June zhu'an ژوئن

junk kherto pert خرت وپرت

Jupiter moshtari مشتری berjis
برجیس

just (adv) faqat فقط

just monsef منصف

justice ensâf انصاف (c) edâlat
عدالت adl عدل

justification tojih توجیه

justified movajjah موجه

justly adelâne عادلانه

k

kebab seller kabâbi کبابی

kebab kabâb کباب

keen moshtâq مشتاق râqeb راغب

keeper negahbân نگهبان

keeping negahdâri نگهداری

kerb jadval جدول

kerosene naft نفت

ketchup sos سوس

kettledrum dohol دهل naqqâre نقاره

key kelid کلید

keyboard safhe kelid صفحه کلید

kick lagad لگد (v) lagad zadan لگد زدن

kicking joftak جفتک

kid tefl طفل bachche بچه

kidding shukhi شوخی

kidnap (v) robudan (robây) ربودن (ربای) (v) dozdidan (dozd) دزدیدن (دزد)

kidney koliye کلیه (inf) qolve قلوه

kill (v) koshtan (kosh) کشتن (کش)

kilo kilo کیلو

kilometre kilometre کیلو متر

kin khishâvand خویشاوند nazdikân نزدیکان

kind (affectionate) mehrebân مهربان

kind qabil قبیل qesm قسم tor طور (c) no' نوع

kindergarten kudakestân کودکستان

king malek ملک shâhanshâh شاهنشاه (c) shâh شاه pâdeshâh پادشاه soltân سلطان pâdeshâh پادشاه

kingdom (c) saltanat سلطنت pâdeshâhi پادشاهی

kingship shâhi شاهی

kinship nesbat نسبت

kiosk dakke دکه

kiss buse بوسه (inf) mâch ماچ (v) busidan (bus) بوسیدن (بوس) (v) mâch kardan ماچ کردن

kitchen âshpazkhâne آشپزخانه

kite bâdbâdak بادبادک

knee zânu زانو

knife châqu چاقو kârd کارد

knob dastgire دستگیره

know (being familiar) (v) shenâkhtan (shenâs) شناختن (شناس)

know (knowledge) (v) dânestan (dân) دانستن (دان)

know (something) (v) balad budan بلد بودن

know how lemm لم

knowledge dânesh دانش ma'lumât معلومات (c) elm علم

known mo'ayyan معین

knucklebone game qâb bâzi قاب بازی

Koran reader qâri قاری

Koran qor'ân قرآن

Korea kore کره

Kurdish kord کرد

l

label *barchasb* برچسب
laboratory *âzemâyeshgâh* آزمایشگاه
labour work *kârgari* کارگری
labourer *amale* عمله *fa'le* فعله
(c) *kârgar* کارگر
lace *band e kafsh* بند کفش
lack *adam* عدم *feqdân* فقدان
ladder *nardebân* نردبان
ladle *malâqe* ملاقه *chomche* چمچه
lady *bânu* بانو *khâtun* خاتون
(c) *khânom* خانم
ladybird *kafsh duzak* کفشدوزک
lagoon *mordâb* مرداب
lake *daryâche* دریاچه
lamb *barre* بره
lamella *tiqe* تیغه
lamp *lâmp* لامپ
lancet *nishtar* نیشتر
land (property) *zamin* زمین
land (soil) *khâk* خاک
land (vs. sea) *khoshki* خشکی
land (v) *forud âmadan* فرود آمدن
landing *forud* فرود
landlord (c) *sâhebkhâne* صاحب خانه *mojer* موجر
landscape *durnamâ* دورنما
(c) *manzare* منظره
lane (alley) *kuche* کوچه
lane (line) *khat* خط
lantern *fânus* فانوس
large (c) *bozorg* بزرگ *dorosht* درشت
(inf) *gonde* گنده

lark *chakâvak* چکاوک
larynx *hanjare* حنجره
lash *shallâq* شلاق
last (e.g.last one) *âkhar* آخر
last (previous) *gozashte* گذشته
last night *dishab* دیشب
last year *pârsâl* پارسال
latch *cheft* چفت
late (recent) *akhir* اخیر
late *dirvaqt* دیر وقت (c) *dir* دیر
latent *nahofte* نهفته
later on *ba'dan* بعدا
latest *âkherin* آخرین
laugh (v) *khandidan (khand)* خندیدن (خند)
laughter *khande* خنده
launderette *mashine lebasshuyi* ماشین لباس شویی
laundry *rakht shuyi* رخت شویی
lava *godâze* گدازه
lavatory *mostarâh* مستراح
(c) *tuvâlet* توالت
law *qânun* قانون
lawful *shar'e* شرعی
lawn mower *chaman zan* چمن زن
lawn *chaman* چمن
lawyer *hoquq dân* حقوقدان *vakil* وکیل
laxative *molayyen* ملین *mos-hel* مسهل
layer *tabaqe* طبقه *lâye* لایه
laziness *tanbali* تنبلی
lazy *tanbal* تنبل
lead *sorb* سرب

leader pishvâ پیشوا (c) rahbar
رهبر

leadership emâmat امامت
(c) rahbari رهبری

leaf barg برگ

league jâme varzeshi جام ورزشی

leak nasht نشت (v) chekke
kardan چکه کردن

leaking chekke چکه

lean lokhm لخم

leaning lam لم

leap year kabise کبیسه

learn (v) âmukhtan (âmuz)
(آموختن)آموز) (v) âmuzesh didan
آموزش دیدن (v)(c) yâdgereftan
یاد گرفتن (یاد گیر) (yâdgir) dars
درس خواندن khândan

lease kerâye کرایه ejâre اجاره
(v) kerâye kardan کرایه کردن

leash qallâde قلاده

least kamtarin کمترین

leather charm چرم

Lebanese lobnâni لبنانی

Lebanon lobnân لبنان

lectern teribun تریبون

lecture (c) sokhanrâni سخنرانی
notq نطق

lecturer sokhanrân سخنران
modarres مدرس

leech kane کنه

leek tare تره

left handed chap dast چپ دست

left chap چپ

leftist chapgerâ چپگرا

leftover tah mande ته مانده pas
mânde پس مانده

left-wing jenahe chap جناح چپ

leg (inf) leng لنگ sâq ساق

legacy mirâs میراث ers ارث

legal qânuni قانونی

legislation qânun gozâri قانون
گذاری

legitimacy haqqâniyat حقانیت

legitimate child halâl zâde حلال
زاده

legitimate masru' مشروع

leisure farâqat فراغت

lemon limu لیمو

lender vâmdahande وام دهنده

length derâzâ درازا (c) tul طول

lens adasi عدسی

lentil adas عدس

leopard palang پلنگ

leprosy jozâm جذام khore خوره

less kam کم

lesser kamtar کمتر

lesson dars درس

let off (v) dar kardan (dar kon)
در کردن (در کن)

let (v) gozâshtan (gozâr) گذاشتن
(گذار)

lethal mohlek مهلک koshande
کشنده

letter (of alphabet) harf حرف

letter nâme نامه

lettuce kâhu کاهو

level sath سطح

lever ahrom اهرم

lewd obâsh اوباش

liability bedehi بدهی mas'uliyat
مسئولیت

liaison *râbet* رابط

liar *duruq gu* دروغ گو

liberation *âzâdi* آزادی

librarian *ketâb dâr* کتابدار

library *ketâb khâne* کتابخانه

Libya *libi* لیبی

lice *shepesh* شپش

license *tasdiq* تصدیق
(c) *gavâhinâme* گواهینامه

lick (v) *lisidan (lis)* (لیس) لیسیدن

licking *lis* لیس

lid *dar* در

lie (c) *duruq* دروغ *kezb* کذب
(v) *duruq goftan* دروغ گفتن

lieutenant *sotvân* ستوان

life guard *nejât qariq* نجات غریق

life *omr* عمر *hayât* حیات
(c) *zendegi* زندگی *zist* زیست

lifetime *omr* عمر

lift (v) *boland kardan* بلند کردن

light (beams) *nur* نور

light (day light) *roshanâyi* روشنایی

light (lamp) *cherâq* چراغ

light (vs dark) *roshan* روشن

light (vs heavy) *sabok* سبک

light (adj) *foruzân* فروزان

lightening *sâ'eqe* صاعقه

lighter *fandak* فندک

like (v) *dust dâshtan* دوست داشتن
mesl مثل

likelihood *ehtemâl* احتمال

likeness *shebh* شبه

lily *susan* سوسن *zanbaq* زنبق

limb *andâm* اندام *ozv* عضو

lime *âhak* آهک

limit *hadd* حد (v) *mahdud
kardan* محدود کردن

limitation *qeyd* قید *mahdudiyat* محدودیت

limited *ma'dud* معدود *mahdud* محدود

limp *shal* شل *lakht* لخت
(v) *langidan (lang)* (لنگ) لنگیدن

limping *langânlangân* لنگ لنگان

line (of writing) *satr* سطر

line of longitude *nesf onnahâr* نصف النهار

line *khat* خط

lineage *nasab* نسب

linen *malâfe* ملافه

lining *âstar* آستر

link *ettesâl* اتصال *râbete* رابطه

lion *shir* شیر

lip *lab* لب

lipstick *mâtik* ماتیک (c) *rozhe lab* رژلب

liquor store *mashrub forushi* مشروب فروشی

list *fehrest* فهرست *list* لیست

listen (v) *gush dâdan* گوش دادن

listener (c) *shenavande* شنونده
mostame' مستمع

literacy *savâd* سواد

literature *adabiyyât* ادبیات

little boy *pesarak* پسرک

little by little *kamkam* کم کم

little fellow *mardak* مردک

little *kami* کمی (c) *kam* کم
andak اندک

live (adj) *zende* زنده
livelihood *gozarân* گذران
lively *fa'âl* فعال
liver *kabed* کبد (inf) *jegar* جگر
living (c) *omr* عمر *ma'ishat* معیشت
lizard *mârmulak* مارمولک
load *bâr* بار (v) *por kardan* پر کردن
(v) *bâr zadan* بار زدن
loan *qarz* قرض *talab* طلب
lobster *kharchang* خرچنگ
local (anatomical) *moze'i* موضعی
local (internal) *dâkheli* داخلی
local (native) *mahalli* محلی *bumi* بومی
locality *mahal* محل
location *makân* مکان
lock *qofl* قفل
locker *qafase* قفسه
locksmith *qoflsâz* قفل ساز
locust *malakh* ملخ
lodge *mosâferkhâne* مسافر خانه
log *konde* کنده
logic *manteq* منطق
logical *manteqi* منطقی
lollipop *âbnabât* آب نبات
London *landan* لندن
loneliness *tanhâyi* تنهایی
lonely *tanhâ* تنها
long live *zende bâd* زنده باد
long *tavil* طویل *tulâni* طولانی
(c) *derâz* دراز *boland* بلند
longitudinal *tuli* طولی
look for (v) *gashtan (gard)* گشتن
(گرد)

look *negâh* نگاه
loop *halqe* حلقه
loose *laq* لق *shol* شل
looting *chapâvol* چپاول *qârat* غارت
lord *rabb* رب (c) *sarvar* سرور
lorry *bârkesh* بارکش
lose (v) *gom kardan* گم کردن
loser *bâzande* بازنده
loss *latme* لطمه *khesârat* خسارت
zâye'e ضایعه *bâkht* باخت *zarar*
ضرر (v) *bâkhtan (bâz)* باختن (باز)
lot, a *besyâr* بسیار
loud *boland* بلند
loudspeaker *bolandgu* بلند گو
lounge *mobl* مبل
louver *bâdkesh* بادکش
love *eshq* عشق
lovemaking *ashqbâzi* عشقبازی
mo'âsheqe معاشقه
lover *khâter khâh* خاطر خواه
âsheq عاشق *ma'shuqe* معشوقه
low (frequency) *kutâh* کوتاه
low life *past* پست
low *pâyiyn* پایین
lozenge *lozi* لوزی
luck *shâns* شانس
luckily *khoshbakhtâne* خوشبختانه
lucky *khosh shans* خوش شانس
khoshbakht خوشبخت
lullaby *lâlâyi* لالایی
lump *qodde* غده
lunar eclipse *khusuf* خسوف
lunch *nâhâr* ناهار
lung *riye* ریه *shosh* شش

lust *shahvat* شهوت

lustful *shahvat angiz* شهوت انگیز

luxury *luks* لوکس

lymph *lanf* لنف

lyric *qazal* غزل   *sorud* سرود

m

Macedonia maqduniye مقدونیه

mach (game) mosâbeqe مسابقه

machine gun âtash bâr آتشبار mosalsal مسلسل

machinery mashin âlât ماشین آلات

mad majnun مجنون (c) divâne دیوانه

madness jonun جنون

magazine majalle مجله

magic sho'bade شعبده jâdu جادو

magician jâdugar جادوگر sâher ساحر sho'bade bâz شعبده باز

magnet âhan robâ آهن ربا

magnetic meqnâtisi مغناطیسی

magnificent azim عظیم

magnifying glass zarrebin ذره بین

maid kolfat کلفت

mail post پست

mailman nâme rasân نامه رسان

main omde عمده

major (military rank) sargord سرگرد

major general sarleshkar سرلشکر

major asli اصلی

majority aksariyyat اکثریت

make a deal (v) mo'âmele kardan معامله کردن

make a mistake (v) eshtebâh kardan اشتباه کردن

make an appointment (v) garâr gozashtan قرار گذاشتن vaqt gereftan وقت گرفتن

make love (v) ashqbâzi kardan عشقبازی کردن

make up gerim گریم bazak بزک (c) ârâyesh آرایش

make sâkht ساخت (v) sâkhtan (sâz) ساختن (ساز) (v) dorost kardan درست کردن

making face at dahan kaji دهن کجی

maladjusted nâsâzgâr ناسازگار

male nar نر mozakkar مذکر

mammal pestândâr پستاندار

man mard مرد

manage (v) edâre kardan اداره کردن

management modiriyyat مدیریت

manager modir مدیر

mandarin nârengi نارنگی

manger âkhor آخور

mango anbe انبه

mangy ekbiri اکبیری

manhood mardi مردی

manifestation mazhar مظهر

manifesto bayâniye بیانیه

mankind bashar بشر âdam آدم ensân انسان

manner raftâr رفتار kerdâr کردار manesh منش nahve نحوه

mansion kâkh کاخ

mantle shenel شنل

manual (guide) dastur olamal دستورالعمل

manual dasti دستی

manure pehen پهن

manuscript neveshte نوشته

many besyâr بسیار ziyâd زیاد kheyli خیلی

map naqshe نقشه

marble (beads) *mohre* مهره

marble (stone) *marmar* مرمر

March *mârs* مارس

march *sân* سان

marching *mârsh* مارش

mare *mâdiyân* ماديان

margin *hâshiye* حاشيه

marine *daryâyi* دريايى

maritime *daryâyi* دريايى

mark (score) *nomre* نمره

mark *neshâne* نشانه *alâmat* علامت

market *bâzâr* بازار

marriage contract *aqd* عقد

marriage portion *kâbin* كابين

marriage *ta'ahhol* تاهل
zanâshuyi زناشويى *ezdevaj* ازدواج

married man *zandâr* زندار

married woman *shohardâr*
شوهردار

married *mota'ahhel* متاهل

marry (v) *arusi kardan* عروسى كردن
(v) *ezdevâj kardan* ازدواج كردن

Mars *bahrâm* بهرام *merrikh* مريخ

martial *nezâmi* نظامى *jangi* جنگى

martyr *shahid* شهيد

martyrdom *shahâdat* شهادت

Mary *maryam* مريم

masculine *nar* نر *mozakkar* مذكر
mardâne مردانه

masculinity *mardi* مردى

mash *pure* پوره (v) *kubidan (kub)*
كوبيدن (كوب)

mashed *leh* له

masher *gushtkub* گوشت كوب

mask *mâsk* ماسك *neqâb* نقاب

mason *bannâ* بنا

mass *jerm* جرم *hajm* حجم *tude*
توده

massacre *koshtâr* كشتار *qatl* قتل

massage *mâsâzh* ماساژ

masseur *dallâk* دلاك

master *khâje* خواجه *sarvar* سرور
seyyed سيد *ostâd* استاد

masterpiece *shâhkâr* شاهكار

mastery *tabahhor* تبحر

masturbate (v) *estemnâ kardan*
استمناع كردن

masturbation *estemnâ* استمناع
(inf) *jalq* جلق

mat *hasir* حصير

match (sort) (v) *jur kardan*
جور كردن

matches *kebrit* كبريت

mate (friend) *dust* دوست
(inf) *rafiq* رفيق

mate (in chess) *mât* مات

material *jesm* جسم (adj) *mâddi*
مادى (adj) *nafsâni* نفسانى *mâdde*
ماده

maternal aunt *khâle* خاله

maternal uncle *dâyi* دايى

maternity *mâdari* مادرى

math *hesâb* حساب

mathematician *riyâzidân* رياضى دان

mathematics *riyâziyât* رياضيات

mating *joftgiri* جفت گيرى

matrimony *nekâh* نكاح

mattress *toshak* تشك

mature *bâleq* بالغ (v) *bozorg
shodan* بزرگ شدن (v) *bâleq
shodan* بالغ شدن

matured *jâ oftâde* جا افتاده

maturity *boloq* بلوغ

mausoleum *gur* گور

maximum *hadde aksar* حد اکثر

may be (c) *shâyad* شاید *balke* بلکه

May *meh* مه

may *shâyad* شاید

mayor *shahrdâr* شهردار

maze *mâz* ماز

me *man* من *marâ* مرا

meadow *chamanzâr* چمنزار *charâgâh* چراگاه *marta'* مرتع

meal *qazâ* غذا

mean (person) *nâkas* ناکس

mean *motavasset* متوسط *mo'addel* معدل

meaning *mafhum* مفهوم *ma'nâ* معنا *ma'ni* معنی

meaningful *ma'nidâr* معنی دار

means *tariq* طریق *asbâb* اسباب

meantime *zemn* ضمن

meanwhile *zemnan* ضمناً

measles *sorkhak* سرخک

measure *peymâne* پیمانه *andâze* اندازه (v) *sanjidan (sanj)* سنجیدن (سنج)

measurement *sanjesh* سنجش

meat *gusht* گوشت

Mecca *makke* مکه

mechanic *mekânik* مکانیک

mechanical *mekâniki* مکانیکی *mashini* ماشینی

mechanised *mekânize* مکانیزه *motori* موتوری

medal *medâl* مدال

Medes *mâd* ماد

median *miyâne* میانه *namâ* نما

mediation *miyânji gari* میانجی گری

mediator *miyânji* میانجی

medical doctor *pezeshk* پزشک

medical *tebbi* طبی

medicine (drug) *marham* مرحم (c) *dâru* دارو

medicine (profession) (c) *pezeshki* پزشکی *tebb* طب

meeting *neshast* نشست *ejlâs* اجلاس *molâqât* ملاقات *didâr* دیدار

melancholy *mâlikhuliyâ* مالیخولیا

melody *navâ* نوا *naqme* نغمه

melon *kharboze* خربزه

melt (v) *âb shodan* آب شدن

melted *godâkhte* گداخته *mozâb* مذاب

melting *zob* ذوب

member of parliament *vakil* وکیل *namâyande* نماینده

member *ozv* عضو

membership *ozviyyat* عضویت

membrane *qeshâ* غشا

memento *khâtere* خاطره

memories *khâterât* خاطرات

memorising *hefz* حفظ

memory *hâfeze* حافظه *khâter* خاطر

mend *ta'mir* تعمیر

menstruation *heyz* حیض *periyod* پریود (c) *qâ'edegi* قاعدگی

mental hospital *timârestân* تیمارستان *bimârestâne ravâni* بیمارستان روانی

mental *ravâni* روانی

mentioned *mazbur* مذبور *mazkur* مذکور

mentor *ostâd* استاد *morabbi* مربی

meow *miyu* میو

mercenary *ajir* اجیر *mozdur* مزدور

merchandise *kâlâ* کالا

merchant *bâzargân* بازرگان

merciful *bakhshande* بخشنده

mercury *jive* جیوه

mercy *marhamat* مرحمت *rahm* رحم

mere *mahz* محض *serf* صرف

merely *serfan* صرفا

merit *orze* عرضه *salâhiyat* صلاحیت *kârâyi* کارآیی *estehqâq* استحقاق *liyâqat* لیاقت (c) *shâyestegi* شایستگی

message *payâm* پیام *peyqâm* پیغام

messenger (c) *qâsed* قاصد *nabi* نبی

Messiah *masih* مسیح

messy *kasif* کثیف

metal *felezz* فلز

metallic *felezzi* فلزی

metamorphosis *maskh* مسخ

metaphor *este'âre* استعاره

metempsychosis *tanâsokh* تناسخ

meteor *shahâb* شهاب *shahâb sang* شهاب سنگ

meter *metr* متر

method *ravesh* روش *shive* شیوه

metropolitan *shahri* شهری

Mexico *mekzik* مکزیک

mid day (c) *zohr* ظهر *nimruz* نیمروز

middle age *miyân sâl* میان سال

Middle East *khâvare miyâne* خاور میانه

middle *miyâni* میانی

midget *kutule* کوتوله

midnight *nime shab* نیمه شب

midwife (c) *mâmâ* ماما *qâbele* قابله

midwifery *mâmâyi* مامایی

migrant *mohâjer* مهاجر

migrate (v) *mohâjerat kardan* مهاجرت کردن

migrating *kuch* کوچ

migration *mohâjerat* مهاجرت

milch *shirdeh* شیرده

mild *molâyem* ملایم *khafif* خفیف

military expedition *lashkarkeshi* لشکرکشی

military policeman *dezhbân* دژبان

military *nezâmi* نظامی *jangi* جنگی

milk tooth *dandâne shiri* دندان شیری

milk *shir* شیر (v) *dushidan (dush)* دوشیدن (دوش)

Milky Way *kahkashân* کهکشان

millimetre *milimetr* میلی متر

million *milyon* میلیون

millionaire *milyoner* میلیونر

mimicry *taqlid* تقلید

minaret *menâr* منار

mince (v) *charkh kardan* چرخ کردن

minced   charkh karde چرخ کرده
kubide کوبیده   qeyme قیمه
mind   zehn ذهن
mine (pronoun)   man من
mine   ma'dan معدن
mineral water   âbe ma'dani آب
معدنی
mineral   ma'dani معدنی
minor   saqir صغیر
minority   aqalliyat اقلیت
mint   na'nâ نعنا
minus   menhâ منها
minute (time)   daqiqe دقیقه
miracle   mo'jeze معجزه
mirage   sarâb سراب
mirror   âyne آینه
miscarriage   seqt سقط
miscellaneous   motafarreqe متفرقه
mischief   sharr شر
mischievous   bad zât بد ذات
miserable   badbakht بدبخت
mafluk مفلوک
misery   nekbat نکبت   balâ بلا
(c) zellat ذلت   falâkat فلاکت
misfortune   nekbat نکبت   balâ بلا
(c) badbakhti بدبختی
misled   (v) gomrâh kardan
گمراه کردن
miss (feel absence)   (v) del tang
shodan دلتنگ شدن
miss   (c) khânom خانم   dushize
دوشیزه
missile   mushak موشک
missing   qâyeb غایب
(c) gomshode گمشده   mafqud
مفقود

mission   ma'muriyat ماموریت
missionary   moballeq مبلغ
mist   meh مه
mistake   qalat غلط   (c) eshtebâh
اشتباه   sahv سهو   khatâ خطا
mistress   ma'shuqe معشوقه
mistrust   zann ظن
misty   mehâlud مه آلود
mix   (v) makhlut kardan مخلوط کردن
mixed   darham درهم   âmikhte
آمیخته   (c) mokhtalet مختلط
(inf) qâti قاتی
mixture   (c) makhlut مخلوط
ma'jun معجون
moan   (v) nâlidan (nâl) نالیدن (نال)
moaning   shivan شیون
mobile phone   telefone hamrâh
تلفن همراه
mobile   motaharrek متحرک
(c) sayyar سیار
mobilization   basij بسیج
mockery   maskharebâzi مسخره بازی
maskhare مسخره
mode   tarz طرز
model   sarmashq سرمشق   model
مدل
moderate   mo'tadel معتدل   miyâne
ro میانه رو
moderation   miyâne ravi میانه روی
modern   modern مدرن   jadid جدید
modernised   motajadded متجدد
modest   forutan فروتن   motavâze'
متواضع
modesty   tavâzo' تواضع
moist   martub مرطوب   namnâk
نمناک   tar تر   نمناک

moisture rotubat رطوبت nam نم

mole khâl خال

molecule molokol ملکول

moment lahze لحظه moqe' موقع

moment, at the fe'lan فعلا

momentarily lahze be lahze لحظه
به لحظه

monarchist saltanat talab سلطنت
طلب

monastery deyr دیر some'e
صومعه

Monday doshanbe دوشنبه

money lover pulaki پولکی

money pul پول

Mongolia moqolestân مغولستان

monk râheb راهب

monkey meymun میمون

monopoly enhesâr انحصار

month mâh ماه

monthly mâhâne ماهانه

moon mâh ماه

moonlight mahtâb مهتاب

morale ruhiyye روحیه

more (adv) kheyli خیلی
(adj) bishtar بیشتر

morning bâmedâd بامداد (c) sobh
صبح

Morocco marâkesh مراکش

morsel loqme لقمه

mortal margbâr مرگبار fâni فانی

mortality margomir مرگ و میر

mortar shell khompâre خمپاره

mortgage qest قسط

mortification riyâzat ریاضت

mortuary qassâl khâne غسال خانه

Moscow mosko مسکو

Moses musâ موسی

Moslem mosalmân مسلمان
moslem مسلم

mosque masjed مسجد

mosquito net pashe band پشه بند

mosquito pashe پشه

most bishtar بیشتر

motel mosâferkhâne مسافر خانه

mother mâdar مادر

motherland mihan میهن

motherly mâdarâne مادرانه

motion jonbesh جنبش takân تکان

motivate (v) barangikhtan
(barangiz) بر انگیختن (برانگیز)
(v) angikhtan (angiz) انگیختن (انگیز)

motivation angize انگیزه

motive moshavveq مشوق

motor bike motorsiklet موتور سیکلت

motorcycle motor موتور
motorsiklet موتور سیکلت

motorised motori موتوری

motorway (tollway) otubân اتوبان

motto sho'âr شعار

mould (fungi) kapak کپک

mould (shape) qâleb قالب

moulder rikhtegar ریخته گر

mouldy kapak zade کپک زده

mountain climbing kuh navardi
کوه نوردی

mountain range reshte kuh رشته
کوه

mountain ranges kuhestân
کوهستان

mountain side kuhpâye کوه پایه

mountain *kuh* کوه

mountaineering *kuh peymâyi* کوه پیمایی

mountainous *kuhestâni* کوهستانی

mourn (v) *azâdâri kardan* عزاداری کردن

mourner *azâdâr* عزادار

mourning (c) *azâ* عزا *sogovâri* سوگواری *sug* سوگ

mouse *mush* موش

moustache *sebil* سبیل

mouth *dahân* دهان

move (v) *harakat kardan* حرکت کردن (v) *jâbejâ kardan* جابجا کردن

movement *harakat* حرکت

movie script *filmnâme* فیلم نامه

movie *sinemâ* سینما *film* فیلم

Mr *âqâ* آقا

Mrs *khânom* خانم

much *ziyâd* زیاد

mucus *khelt* خلط

mud brick *khesht* خشت

mud *gel* گل

muddy *gelâlud* گل آلود

mudguard *gelgir* گلگیر

muggy *sharji* شرجی

mule *qâter* قاطر

multiple *mazrab* مضرب

multiplication (math) *zarb* ضرب

multiplication *taksir* تکثیر

mum (c) *mâmân* مامان *nane* ننه

mumbling *mennmenn* من من

mummy *mumiyâ* مومیا

murder *khunrizi* خون ریزی *âdam koshi* آدمکشی *qatl* قتل (v) *koshtan (kosh)* کشتن (کش)

murdered *maqtul* مقتول

murderer *jâni* جانی *jenâyat kâr* جنایت کار (c) *qâtel* قاتل

muscle *azole* عضله *mâhiche* ماهیچه

museum *muze* موزه

mushroom *qârch* قارچ

music *musiqi* موسیقی *muzik* موزیک *âhang* آهنگ

musical instrument *sâz* ساز

musical performance *navâzandegi* نوازندگی

musician (c) *navâzande* نوازنده *motreb* مطرب *musiqidân* موسیقی دان

must *bâyad* باید

mustard *khardal* خردل

mutation *jahesh* جهش

mute *gong* گنگ *sâmet* صامت *lâl* لال (c) *bisedâ* بی صدا لال

muttering *mennmenn* من من

mutual agreement *tafâhom* تفاهم

muzzle *puze band* پوزه بند *puze* پوزه

myopia *nazdikbini* نزدیک بینی

myopic *nazdikbin* نزدیک بین

myself *khodam* خودم

mysterious *marmuz* مرموز

mystery *ramz* رمز *râz* راز

mysticism *erfân* عرفان

myth *afsâne* افسانه

n

nail (organ) nâkhon ناخن
nail clippers nâkhon gir ناخن گیر
nail polish lâk لاک
nail mikh میخ
naive nâshi ناشی sâde ساده zudbâvar باور زود
naked berahne برهنه (c) lokht لخت
name (c) esm اسم nâm نام
named mosum موسوم
nanny nane ننه (c) dâye دایه lale لله
nap chort چرت
nappy pushak پوشک
narcotic mokhadder مخدر
narghile qaliyân قلیان
narration naql نقل
narrative sargozasht سرگذشت ravâyat روایت hekâyat حکایت
narrator naqqâl نقال
narrow bârik باریک tang تنگ
nasal tudamâqi تودماغی
nation (c) mellat ملت qom قوم
national melli ملی
nationality tâbe'iyat تابعیت melliyat ملیت
native ahl اهل bumi بومی
natural tabi'i طبیعی
nature (physical) tabi'at طبیعت
nature tinat طینت fetrat فطرت mâhiyat ماهیت
naughtiness sheytâni شیطانی
naughty nâqolâ ناقلا sheytân شیطان

nausea tahavvo' تهوع
naval daryâyi دریایی
navigation nâvbari ناوبری
navigator nâvbar ناوبر
near nazdik نزدیک nazd نزد pahlu پهلو
nearsighted nazdikbin نزدیک بین
nearsightedness nazdikbini نزدیک بینی
neat pâkize پاکیزه
necessarily lozuman لزوما
necessary zaruri ضروری lâzem لازم
necessity hâjat حاجت ehtiyâj احتیاج zarurat ضرورت
neck gardan گردن
necklace gardan band گردنبند
nectarine shalil شلیل
need lozum لزوم ehtiyâj احتیاج niyâz نیاز (v) ehtiyâj dâshtan احتیاج داشتن (v) lâzem dâshtan لازم داشتن (v) niyâz dâshtan نیاز داشتن
needle suzan سوزن
needy niyâz mand نیاز مند mohtâj محتاج faqir فقیر
negation nafy نفی
negative manfi منفی
negativist manfibâf منفی باف
negligence qaflat غفلت
negligent sahl angâr سهل انگار qâfel غافل
negotiation mozâkere مذاکره
neighing shihe شیهه
nephew khâhar zâde خواهر زاده barâdar zâde برادر زاده
nerve asab عصب

nerveless *lash* لش

nervous *asabi* عصبی

nest (c) *lâne* لانه *âshiyâne* آشیانه

net *tur* تور

network *shabake* شبکه

neutral *bitaraf* بی طرف *khonsâ* خنثی

never ever *mabâdâ* مبادا

never *hich vaqt* هیچ وقت *abadan* ابدا

New Zealand *zelânde no* زلاند نو

new *tâze* تازه *no* نو

newborn *nozâd* نوزاد *noraside* نورسیده

news agency *ruzname forushi* روزنامه فروشی

news *akhbâr* اخبار *khabar* خبر

newspaper *ruznâme* روزنامه

next *ba'di* بعدی

nib *nuk* نوک

nice *khub* خوب

nickname *konye* کنیه

niece *khâhar zâde* خواهر زاده *barâdar zâde* برادر زاده

night blindness *shabkuri* شبکوری

night raid *shabikhun* شبیخون

night shift *shab kâri* شب کاری

night *shab* شب

nightingale *bolbol* بلبل

nightly *shabâne* شبانه

nightmare *kâbus* کابوس

nine *noh* نه

nineteen *nuzdah* نوزده

nineteenth *nuzdahom* نوزدهم

ninetieth *navadom* نودم

ninety *navad* نود

ninth *nohom* نهم

nip *gâz* گاز

nippers *anbor* انبر

nipple *pestânak* پستانک

no *na* نه

Noah *nuh* نوح

nobility *nejâbat* نجابت

nobles *ashrâf* اشراف

noise *sarosedâ* سروصدا *sholuqi* شلوغی

noisy *por saro seda* پرسروصدا *sedâdâr* صدادار

nomads *kuchneshin* کوچ نشین *ashâyer* عشایر

nomination *nâmzadi* نامزدی

nominee *kândid* کاندید *nâmzad* نامزد

non-existence *nisti* نیستی

nonsense *jafang* جفنگ *mozakhraf* مزخرف *chert* چرت

noon *zohr* ظهر

normal *tabi'i* طبیعی

north *shomâl* شمال

northern *shomâli* شمالی

Norway *norvezh* نروژ

Norwegian *novezhi* نروژی

nose *bini* بینی

nostalgia *qorbat* غربت

nosy *fozul* فضول

notary public office *mahzar* محضر *daftarkhâne* دفترخانه

notary public *sardaftar* سردفتر

note (money) *eskenâs* اسکناس

notebook daftarche دفترچه daftar
دفتر

notice molâheze ملاحظه ettelâ
اطلاع (v) motavajjeh shodan
متوجه شدن

noun esm اسم

novel (book) român رمان

November novâmr نوامبر

novice tâzekâr تازه کار nâshi ناشی
no âmuz نو آموز

now aknun اکنون hâlâ حالا alân
الان

noxious muzi موذی

nude berahne برهنه (c) lokht لخت

nudity lokhti لختی

nuisance mozâhemat مزاحمت
aziyyat اذیت mozâhem مزاحم

numb kerekh کرخ bihess بی حس

number te'dâd تعداد shomâre
شماره adad عدد nomre نمره

numbering nomre gozâri نمره
گذاری

nun râhebe راهبه

nurse aid behyâr بهیار

nurse parastâr پرستار

nursery rhyme sorud سرود

nursery parvareshgâh پرورشگاه
shirkhârgâh شیرخوارگاه

nursing parastâri پرستاری

nurturing parvaresh پرورش

nutritional moqazzi مغذی

nymph huri حوری

o

oak بلوط *balut*

oath عهد *ahd* قسم *qasam* سوگند *sogand*

obedience تمکین *tamkin* اطاعت *etâ'at*

obedient حرف شنو *harf sheno* مطیع *moti'*

obese چاق *châq*

obey (v) پیروی کردن *peyravi kardan* (v) اطاعت کردن *etâ'at kardan*

object (grammar) مفعول *maf'ul*

object جسم *jesm* شیئی *shey'*

objection اعتراض *e'terâz*

objective مرام *marâm* (adj) عینی *eyni*

obliged مجبور *majbur*

oblique مورب *movarrab* مایل *mâyel*

obscene مبتذل *mobtazal* قبیح *qabih* مستهجن *mostahjan* زننده *zanande*

obscenity قباحت *qabâhat*

observance مراعات *morâ'ât*

observant مراقب *morâqeb*

observation مشاهده *moshâhede*

observatory رصدخانه *rasad khâne*

observer ناظر *nâzer*

obstacle مانع *mân'*

obvious آشکار *âshkâr* بدیهی *badihi* معلوم *ma'lum*

occasion موقع *moqe'*

occasionally گاهگاهی *gâhgâhi*

occupation (job) شغل *shoql*

occupation اشغال *eshqâl* تصرف *tasarrof*

occupy (v) اشغال *eshqâl kardan* کردن

occurrences حوادث *havâdes*

ocean اقیانوس *oqiyânus*

Oceania اقیانوسیه *oqiyânusiye*

October اکتبر *oktobr*

odd فرد *fard*

odor رایحه *râyehe* (c) بو *bu*

oesophagus مری *meri*

of course البته *albatte*

offence توهین *tohin* خلاف *khelâf* جرم *jorm*

offend (v) اهانت *ehânat kardan* کردن

offended دلخور *delkhor* دلگیر *delgir*

offender خلاف کار *khelâf kâr*

offensive متجاوز *motajâvez*

offer تعارف *ta'ârof* (v) تعارف کردن *ta'ârof kardan*

office of justice دادگستری *dâdgostari*

office دفتر *daftar* اداره *edâre*

officer افسر *afsar*

official notice ابلاغ *eblâq*

official (adj) رسمی *rasmi* (n) مامور *ma'mur*

offspring نسل *nasl*

often اغلب *aqlab*

Oh God خدایا *khodâyâ*

oil (cooking) روغن *roqan*

oil (fat) چربی *charbi*

oil (petrol) نفت *naft*

oil tanker نفتکش *naftkesh*

oily چرب *charb* روغنی *roqani*

ointment *pomâd* پماد
okay *khub* خوب bâshe باشه
old (age) *pir* پیر
old man *pirmard* پیرمرد
old woman *pirzan* پیرزن
old *qadimi* قدیمی *kohne* کهنه
old-fashioned *ommol* امل
oleaster *senjed* سنجد
olfaction *buyâyi* بویایی
olfactory *shâmme* شامه
olives *zeytun* زیتون
omelet *khâgine* خاگینه
omen *fâl* فال
ominous *nahs* نحس
on the contrary *baraks* برعکس
on time *bemoqe'* به موقع
on *ru* رو
one fifth *khoms* خمس
one self *khod* خود
one third *sols* ثلث
onion *piyâz* پیاز
only *faqat* فقط
opaque *mât* مات *keder* کدر
open lid *sargoshâde* سر گشاده
open *bâz* باز (v)(c) *bâz kardan* باز
کردن (v) *eftetâh kardan* افتتاح کردن
opening *dahane* دهانه *manfaz*
منفذ
opera *operâ* اپرا
operate *amal kardan* عمل کردن
operation *amal* عمل
operator (telephone) *operâtor*
اپراتور *telefon chi* تلفن چی

ophthalmologist *chesmpezeshk*
چشم پزشک
opinion poll *nazarkhâhi* نظر خواهی
opinion *aqide* عقیده *nazar* نظر
opium poppy *khashkhâsh*
خشخاش
opium *teryâk* تریاک
opponent *mokhâlef* مخالف *taraf*
طرف
opportunist *forsattalab* فرصت طلب
opportunity *forsat* فرصت
opposed *aleyh* علیه
opposite (contrary) *zedd* ضد
mokhâlef مخالف
opposite (front) *ruberu* روبرو
moqâbel مقابل
oppressed *mazlum* مظلوم
setamdide ستمدیده
oppressive *zurgu* زورگو
oppressor *setamgar* ستمگر
optician *cheshm pezeshk* چشم
پزشک
optimistic *khoshbin* خوش بین
option *ekhtiyâr* اختیار *gozine* گزینه
optometrist *binâyi sanj* بینائی سنج
or *yâ* یا
oracle *qeybgu* غیبگو
orange (colour) *nârenji* نارنجی
orange (fruit) *porteqâl* پرتقال
orbit *madâr* مدار
orchestra *orkestr* ارکستر
order (discipline) *tartib* ترتیب
nazm نظم
order (e.g a meal) *sefâresh*
سفارش

order (imperative) farmân فرمان
dastur دستور farmâyesh فرمایش
hokm حکم (v) dastur dâdan دستور
دادن (v) farmân dâdan فرمان دادن

order arms pâfang پافنگ

ordinarily ma'mulan لامعمو

ordinary âddi عادی ma'muli
معمولی

organ andâm اندام ozv عضو

organization tashkilât تشکیلات
sâzemân سازمان

orient mashreq مشرق sharq شرق

origin asl اصل mansha' منشا

original asli اصلی

orphan bipedaro mâdar بی پدر و
مادر yatim یتیم

orthopaedist shekaste band
شکسته بند

other (c) digar دیگر sâyer سایر

others digarân دیگران

ouch âkh آخ

our mân مان mâ ما

ours mâ ما

out of order kharâb خراب

outbreak shoyu' شیوع

outburst favarân فوران toqyân
طغیان

outdoor birun بیرون

outlook cheshmandâz چشم انداز

outpatient sarpâyi سرپایی

output bâzdeh بازده

outset shoru' شروع

outside khârej خارج birun بیرون

outsider ajnabi اجنبی qaribe غریبه

outskirts pirâmun پیرامون

ovary tokhmdân تخمدان

oven ojâq اجاق

over ruye روی

overcast gerefte گرفته

overcharging gerân forushi گران
فروشی

overflowing toqyân طغیان

overindulgence ziyâderavi زیاده
روی

overnight shabâne شبانه

overstatement eqrâq اغراق
qolovv غلو mobâleqe مبالغه

overtaking sebqat سبقت

overthrown monqarez منقرض

oviparous tokhm ozâr تخم گذار

ovum tokhmak تخمک

owl joqd جغد

owner sâheb صاحب mâlek مالک

ownership mâlekiyat مالکیت
melkiyyat ملکیت

ox gâv گاو

oxygen oksizhen اکسیژن

oyster sadaf صدف

P   **102**

p

pace *qadam* قدم

pacific *ârâm* آرام

pacifier *pestânak* پستانک

pack (v) *bastebandi kardan* بسته
بندی کردن

package *baste* بسته

packing *bastebandi* بسته بندی

packsaddle *pâlân* پالان

pact *peymân* پیمان *mo'âhede*
معاهده *qarârdâd* قرارداد *misâq*
میثاق

paddle *pâru* پارو

padlock *qofle zanjir* قفل زنجیر

paedophilia *lavât* لواط

page *safhe* صفحه

pagination *safhebandi* صفحه بندی

pain killer *mosakken* مسکن

pain *dard* درد

painful *dardnâk* دردناک

paint *rang* رنگ

paintbrush *qalam mu* قلم مو

painter *rang zan* رنگ زن
naqqâsh نقاش

painting *tâblo* تابلو *naqqâshi*
نقاشی

pair *zoj* زوج *joft* جفت

pal *dust* دوست *rafiq* رفیق

palace *qasr* قصر *kâkh* کاخ

palate *kâm* کام *mazâq* مذاق

pale *pazhmorde* پژمرده *rang*
paride رنگ پریده

paleontology *dirine shenâsi* دیرینه
شناسی

Palestine *felestin* فلسطین

palm (tree) *nakhl* نخل

palm grove *nakhlestân* نخلستان

palm reading *kafbini* کف بینی

palm *kaf* کف

palpitation *tapesh* تپش

pampered *nâz parvarde* ناز پرورده

pamphlet *jozve* جزوه

pan *tâve* تاوه *lagan* لگن

pancreas *lozolme'de* لوزالمعده

panic *tars* ترس

panting *lahlah* له له

pants *shalvâr* شلوار

paper (article) *maqâle* مقاله

paper (sheet) *kâqaz* کاغذ

parachute *chatr* چتر

parachutist *chatr bâz* چترباز

parade *rezhe* رژه

paradigm *sige* صیغه

paradise *ferdos* فردوس *jannat*
جنت *behesht* بهشت (c)

parallel *motavâzi* متوازی *movâzi*
موازی

paralysed *lang* لنگ *falaj* فلج
chollaq چلاق

paralysis *falaji* فلجی

parasite *angal* انگل

paratrooper *chatr bâz* چترباز

parcel *baste* بسته

parenthetical *mo'tareze* معترضه

parents *pedaro mâdar* پدر و مادر

parish *mahalle* محله

park *pârk* پارک

parking *pârk* پارک

parliament *majles* مجلس

parrot tuti طوطی
parrot-like tutivâr طوطی وار
parsley ja'fari جعفری
partial joz'i جزئی
participant sahim سهیم
participation moshârekat مشارکت
particle zarre ذره
particles zarrât ذرات
particularly makhsusan مخصوصا
partisan cherik چریک
partner sharik شریک
partnership sherâkat شراکت moshârekat مشارکت
partridge kabk کبک
party (political) hezb حزب
party bazm بزم (c) mehmâni مهمانی sur سور ziyâfat ضیافت
pass away (v) fot kardan فوت کردن
pass masir مسیر (v) gozashtan (gozar) گذشتن (گذر)
passage (hole) majrâ مجرا
passage (route) gozargâh گذرگاه
passenger sarneshin سرنشین (c) mosâfer مسافر
passer-by âber عابر rahqozar رهگذر
passion shahvat شهوت
passive (grammar) majhul مجهول
passive monfa'el منفعل
passport gozarnâme گذر نامه
past participle mâziye ba'id ماضی بعید
past gozashte گذشته mâzi ماضی

paste chasb چسب khamir خمیر (v) chasbidan (chasb) چسبیدن (چسب)
pasture charâgâh چراگاه marta' مرتع
pasturing charâ چرا
patch pine پینه
patience hosele حوصله sabr صبر
patient (ill) mariz مریض
patricide pedar koshi پدرکشی
patriot mihan parast میهن پرست
patriotism mihan parasti میهن پرستی
patrol qarâvol قراول keshik کشیک gashti گشتی gasht گشت
pattern qavâre قواره olgu الگو
patting navâzesh نوازش
pause ta'khir تاخیر ta'ammol تامل derang درنگ maks مکث tavaqqof توقف
pavilion qorfe غرفه
paw panje پنجه
pay ojrat اجرت (v) pardâkhtan (pardâz) پرداختن (پرداز) mozd مزد
payment pardâkht پرداخت
peace lover solhtalab صلح طلب
peace âshti آشتی solh صلح ârâmesh آرامش
peaceful solhâmiz صلح آمیز
peach shaftâlu شفتالو
peacock tâvus طاووس
peak oj اوج qolle قله nuk نوک
peanut bâdâm zamini بادام زمینی
pear golâbi گلابی
pearl dorr در (c) morvârid مروارید

pebble rig ریگ
pedal rekâb رکاب
peddler doregard دوره گرد
dastforush دست فروش
pederast luti لوطی
pedestrian piyâde پیاده âber عابر
rahqozar رهگذر
pee shâsh شاش
peg mikh میخ
pelvis lagan لگن
pen name mosta'âr مستعار
pen khodkâr خودکار
penal jazâyi جزایی keyfari کیفری
penalty (c) jarime جریمه jazâ جزا
pencil sharpener medâd tarâsh
مدادتراش
pencil medâd مداد
pendulum pândol پاندول
penetration nofuz نفوذ
penicillin penisilin پنی سیلین
penis (inf) kir کیر âlat آلت
pension mostamerri مستمری
people khâlq خلق (c) mardom
مردم ashkhâs اشخاص
pepper felfel فلفل
per capita sarâne سرانه
per month mâhiyâne ماهیانه
percent dar sad درصد
perception edrâk ادراک dark درک
daryâft دریافت
perfect kâmel کامل
perform (v) eqdâm kardan اقدام
کردن
performance eqdâm اقدام
perfume atr عطر

perhaps balke بلکه shâyad شاید
period (mensturation) nobat
قاعدگی
period (time) dore دوره
permanent mândegâr ماندگار
(c) dâ'em دائم pâydâr پایدار
permissible jâyez جایز ravâ روا
permission (c) ejâze اجازه ezn
اذن
permit javâz جواز (c) ejâze
dâdan اجازه دادن
perpendicular qâ'eme قائمه
Persian speaker fârsi zabân
فارسی زبان
Persian fârsi فارسی
persimmon khormâlu خرمالو
persistence esrâr اصرار semâjat
سماجت
persistent semej سمج
person âdam آدم nafar نفر
shakhs شخص fard فرد kas کس
personal shakhsi شخصی fardi
فردی
personality shakhsiyyat شخصیت
personnel carrier nafar bar نفربر
personnel kârkonân کارکنان kâdr
کادر
perspiration araq عرق
perspire (v) araq kardan عرق کردن
pertinent marbut مربوط
pervert monharef منحرف fâsed
فاسد
pessimistic badbin بدبین
pest âfat آفت
pet ahli اهلی râm رام dast âmuz
دست آموز

petition *dâdkhâst* دادخواست

petrol *benzin* بنزین

petroleum *naft* نفت

phantom *shabah* شبه

Pharaoh *fer'on* فرعون

pharmacist *dârusâz* داروساز

pharmacy *dârukhâne* داروخانه

pharynx *halq* حلق

phase *marhale* مرحله

pheasant *qarqâvol* قرقاول

phenomenon *padide* پدیده

Philippines *filipin* فیلیپین

philosopher *filsuf* فیلسوف

philosophical *falsafi* فلسفی

philosophy *falsafe* فلسفه

phone box *bâje ye telefon* باجه تلفن

phone card *kârte telefon* کارت تلفن

phoney *kalak* کلک *qollâbi* قلابی *alaki* الکی

photo *aks* عکس

photographer *akkâs* عکاس

photography *akkâsi* عکاسی

phrase *ebârat* عبارت

physical training *tarbiyat badani* تربیت بدنی

physician (c) *doktor* دکتر *tabib* طبیب

physicist *fizikdân* فیزیکدان

physics *fizik* فیزیک

pick up (v) *bardâshtan (bar dâr)* برداشتن (بردار)

pick *kolang* کلنگ (v) *chidan (chin)* چیدن (چین)

pickles *torshi* ترشی

pickpocket *jib bor* جیب بر

picture *shakl* شکل *aks* عکس *tasvir* تصویر

piece *tekke* تکه *qat'e* قطعه

pig *khuk* خوک

pigeon fancier *kaftar bâz* کفتر باز

pigeon *kabutar* کبوتر *kaftar* کفتر

pile *tude* توده

pilgrimage (v) *ziyârat kardan* زیارت کردن

pill *hab* حب (c) *qors* قرص

pillar *sotun* ستون

pillow *poshti* پشتی *motakkâ* متکا (c) *bâlesh* بالش

pillowcase *rubaleshi* روبالشی

pilot *khalabân* خلبان

pimp *jâkesh* جاکش *koskesh* کس کش *qoromsâq* قرمساق

pimple *jush* جوش

pin *suzan* سوزن *sanjâq* سنجاق

pine tree *kâj* کاج

pineapple *ânânâs* آناناس

pink *surati* صورتی

pioneer *pishro* پیشرو *pish âhang* پیش آهنگ

pipe (plumbing) *lule* لوله

pipe (smoking) *chopoq* چپق

Pisces *hut* حوت

piss *jish* جیش (v) *jish kardan* جیش کردن (v) *shâshidan (shâsh)* شاشیدن (شاش) *shâsh* شاش

pistachio *peste* پسته

pistol *tapânche* طپانچه

pit *godâl* گودال *châle* چاله

pitcher *kuze* کوزه

pity *heyf* حیف

pivot *mehvar* محور

place *makân* مکان *jâyegâh* جایگاه
mahal محل

placenta *joft* جفت

plague *tâ'un* طاعون

plain (geography) *jolge* جلگه
dasht دشت

plain (simple) *sâde* ساده

plaintiff *modda'i* مدعی *shâki* شاکی

plan *tarh* طرح *naqshe* نقشه

plane tree *chenâr* چنار

planet earth *koreye zamin* کره زمین

planet *sayyâre* سیاره *kore* کره

planning *tarhrizi* طرحریزی

plant *giyâh* گیاه (v) *kâshtan (kâr)*
کاشتن (کار)

plaster *gach* گچ *zamâd* ضماد

plastic *pelâstik* پلاستیک *nâylon*
نایلون

plate (dish) *boshqâb* بشقاب

plate (number) *plâk* پلاک

plateau *falât* فلات

platform *sakku* سکو

platter *sini* سینی

play (in theatre) *namâyesh nâme*
نمایشنامه *namâyesh* نمایش

play an instrument (v) *zadan*
(zan) زدن (زن)

play music (v) *navâkhtan (navâz)*
نواختن (نواز)

play *bâzi* بازی (v) *bâzi kardan*
بازی کردن

player *bâzikon* بازیکن

playful *bâzigush* بازیگوش

playwright *namâyesh nâme*
nevis نمایشنامه نویس

pleasant *matlub* مطلوب *matbu'*
مطبوع

please *lotfan* لطفا

pleased *khoshnud* خوشنود

pleasure *hazz* حظ *eysh* عیش
(c) *lezzat* لذت

pledge (depoit) *gero* گرو

pledge (oath) *qasam* قسم

plenty *farâvân* فراوان

pliers *gâz anbor* گاز انبر

plough *shokhm* شخم

ploughshare *gâvâhan* گاو آهن
khish خیش

plug (electricity) *doshakhe*
دوشاخه

plum *âlu* آلو *goje* گوجه

plumb line *shâqul* شاقول

plunder *târâj* تاراج

pneumonia *zâtorriye* ذات الریه
sine pahlu سینه پهلو

pocket size *jibi* جیبی *baqali* بغلی

pocket *jib* جیب

poem *sh'r* شعر

poet *shâ'er* شاعر

poetic *shâ'erâne* شاعرانه

poetry *she'r* شعر

point (dot) *noqte* نقطه

point (fraction) *momayyez* ممیز

point (mark) *nomre* نمره

point (topic) *nokte* نکته

point out (v) *eshâre kardan* اشاره
کردن (v) *neshân dâdan* نشان دادن

pointing *eshâre* اشاره

poise   *matânat* متانت

poison   *samm* سم   *zahr* زهر

poisoned   *masmum* مسموم

poisoning   *masmumiyat* مسمومیت

poisonous   *sammi* سمی

poker   *poker* پوکر

Poland   *lehestân* لهستان

polar   *qotbi* قطبی

pole   *qotb* قطب

police headquarters   *shahrebâni* شهربانی

police station   *kalântari* کلانتری

police   *polis* پلیس

policy   *mashy* مشی   (c) *siyâsat* سیاست

polish   *seyqal* صیقل

polite   *mo'addab* مودب

politeness   *adab* ادب

political   *siyâsi* سیاسی

politician   *siyâsat madâr* سیاستمدار

politics   *siyâsat* سیاست

pollen   *garde* گرده

pollination   *garde afshâni* گرده افشانی

polling   *nazarkhâhi* نظر خواهی

pollute   (v) *âlude kardan* آلوده کردن

polluted   *âlude* آلوده

pollution   *âludegi* آلودگی

polo-stick   *chogân* چوگان

polygon   *chand zel'i* چند ضلعی

polytheist   *moshrek* مشرک

pomegranate   *anâr* انار

pond   *tâlâb* تالاب

pool (game)   *bilyârd* بیلیارد

pool (swimming)   *estakhr* استخر

poor thing   *teflak* طفلک

poor   *bichiz* بیچیز   *tohidast* تهیدست   *meskin* مسکین   *mofles* مفلس   *mostmand* مستمند   (c) *faqir* فقیر

pop corn   *balâl* بلال

popular   *ma'ruf* معروف

popularity   *mahbubiyat* محبوبیت

population   *jam'yyat* جمعیت   *nofus* نفوس

porcupine   *juje tiqi* جوجه تیغی

pornographic   *mostahjan* مستهجن

pornography   *akshâye seksi* عکس‌های سکسی

port   *bandar* بندر

porter   *hammâl* حمال   (c) *bârbar* باربر

portion   *bakhsh* بخش   *qesmat* قسمت

portrayer   *naqqâsh* نقاش

position   *moze'* موضع   *post* پست

possession   *mâlekiyat* مالکیت   *melkiyyat* ملکیت

possessor   *sâheb* صاحب

possibility   *emkân* امکان

possible   *momken* ممکن

possibly   *shâyad* شاید

post card   *kârt postâl* کارت پستال

post office   *postkhâne* پستخانه

post   *post* پست

postage   *hazineye post* هزینه پست

poster   *puster* پوستر

postman   *postchi* پستچی

posturised   *pâstorize* پاستوریزه

potato   *sib zamini* سیب زمینی

potential *belqovve* بالقوه

potion *davâ* دوا

pottery *sofâlgari* سفال گری

pound (v) *kubidan (kub)* کوبیدن (کوب)

pour (v) *rikhtan (riz)* ریختن (ریز)

poverty *faqr* فقر

powder *gard* گرد *garde* گرده *pudr* پودر *khâke* خاکه

power *qovve* قوه (c) *qodrat* قدرت *niru* نیرو *qovvat* قوت *tavân* توان

powerful *nirumand* نیرومند (c) *qavi* قوی *moqtader* مقتدر

practical *amali* عملی

practically *amalan* عملاً

practice *mashq* مشق

praise *taqdir* تقدیر *sanâ* ثنا *hamd* حمد *niyâyesh* نیایش (v) *ta'rif kardan* تعریف کردن

pram *kâleske* کالسکه *doroshke* درشکه

prawn *meygu* میگو

pray (v) *do'â kardan* دعا کردن

prayer (c) *namâz* نماز *salât* صلات

precedence *taqaddom* تقدم

precious *qeymati* قیمتی *gerân* گران *bahâ* گرانبها

precise *daqiq* دقیق

precision *deqqat* دقت

predatory *darande* درنده

predicate *mosnad* مسند

prediction *pish guyi* پیشگویی

predominant *mosallat* مسلط

preference *tarjih* ترجیح

prefix *pishvand* پیشوند

pregnancy *bârdâri* بارداری *hâmelegi* حاملگی

pregnant *âbestan* آبستن *bârdâr* باردار *hâmele* حامله

prejudice *ta'assob* تعصب *tab'iz* تبعیض

preliminary *moqaddamâti* مقدماتی

prelude *pish darâmad* پیش درآمد

premises *chârdivâri* چاردیواری

preoccupation *mashguliyat* مشغولیت

prepare (v) *âmâde kardan* آماده کردن (v) *farâham kardan* فراهم کردن

prepared *âmâde* آماده *mohayyâ* مهیا

presbyopia *pir chesmi* پیرچشمی

prescription *noskhe* نسخه *tajviz* تجویز

presence *hozur* حضور *pish* پیش

present participle *mâziye naqli* ماضی نقلی

present *hâl* حال *konuni* کنونی *pish kesh* پیشکش *hâzer* حاضر (v) *ehdâ kardan* اهدا کردن

preserved *qoroq* قرق

presidency *riyâsat* ریاست

president *ra'is jomhur* رئیس جمهور

press *matbu'ât* مطبوعات (v) *feshâr dâdan* فشار دادن

pressure *feshâr* فشار

prestige *heysiyat* حیثیت

pretend (v) *jelve dâdan* جلوه دادن

pretentious *motazâher* متظاهر

pretty *zibâ* زیبا

prevalence ravâj رواج shoyu' شیوع

prevalent shâye' شایع

prevention pish giri پیشگیری jelogiri جلوگیری

previous qabl قبل pishin پیشین qabli قبلی

prey (c) to'me طعمه shekâr شکار seyd صید

price qeymat قیمت

priceless gerân bahâ گرانبها

prick nish نیش

pride fakhr فخر mobâhât مباهات qorur غرور

priest keshish کشیش

primary school dabestân دبستان

primary ebtedâyi ابتدایی moqaddamâti مقدماتی avvaliye اولیه

prime Minster nakhost vazir نخست وزیر

prince shâhzâde شاهزاده

princess shâhzâde شاهزاده

principal (c) ra'is رئیس modir مدیر

principle asâsi اساسی asli اصلی

principles usul اصول

print house châpkhâne چاپ خانه

print châp چاپ (v) châp kardan چاپ کردن

printed châpi چاپی

priority taqaddom تقدم

prism manshur منشور

prison bâzdâshtgâh بازداشتگاه habs حبس (c) zendân زندان

prisoner (inmate) zendâni زندانی

prisoner (of war) asir اسیر

privacy khalvat خلوت

private (soldier) sarbâz سرباز

private mahramâne محرمانه khususi خصوصی

privatisation khususi sâzi خصوصی سازی

privilege emtiyâz امتیاز

prize jâyeze جایزه

probability ehtemâl احتمال

problem moshkel مشکل mas'ale مسئله

procedure ravesh روش ravand روند

process farâyand فرآیند ravand روند

producer tolid konande تولید کننده

product farâvorde فرآورده mahsul محصول

production tolid تولید

profanity kofr کفر

profession kâr کار takhassos تخصص

professional herfeyi حرفه ای

profile nimrokh نیمرخ

profit sud سود manfa'at منفعت naf' نفع fâyede فایده

profitability sud dehi سود دهی

profitable sudmand سودمند

profound amiq عمیق

prognosis pish âgahi پیش آگهی

prognostication qeybguyi غیبگویی

program barnâme برنامه

progress pishraft پیشرفت taraqqi ترقی

progressive motaraqqi مترقی

prohibit (v) *man' kardan* منع کردن
prohibition *momâne'at* ممانعت *man'* منع
project *tarh* طرح
projection *barâmadegi* برآمدگی
projector *porozhoktor* پروژکتور
prominent *barjaste* برجسته
promise *mi'âd* میعاد (c) *qol* قول
(v) *qol dâdan* قول دادن
promised *mo'ud* موعود
prone (position) *damar* دمر
prone (adj) *mosta'ed* مستعد
pronoun *zamir* ضمیر
pronunciation *talaffoz* تلفظ
proof *madrak* مدرک
proofreading *qalatgiri* غلط گیری
propaganda *tabliq* تبلیغ *tarvij* ترویج
propeller *parvâne* پروانه
proper *khâs* خاص *monâseb* مناسب
property (asset) *melk* ملک
property (character) *khâsiyat* خاصیت
prophecy *pish guyi* پیشگویی *qeybguyi* غیبگویی *nobovvat* نبوت
prophet *peyqambar* پیغمبر *rasul* رسول *payâmbar* پیامبر
prophetic *nabavi* نبوی
prophets *anbiyâ* انبیا
proportion *tanâsob* تناسب
proportionate *motanâseb* متناسب
proposal *pishnahâd* پیشنهاد
proposing (marriage) *khâstegâri* خواستگاری

proposition *qaziyye* قضیه
proprietor *sâheb* صاحب *mâlek* مالک
prose *nasr* نثر
prosecution *peygard* پیگرد
prostitute *lakkâte* لکاته *jalab* جلب (c) *fâheshe* فاحشه *jende* جنده *qahbe* قحبه *ruspi* روسپی *khodforush* خودفروش
prostitution (c) *fahshâ'* فحشا (inf) *jendegi* جندگی
protect (v) *hefâzat kardan* حفاظت کردن (v) *mohâfezat kardan* محافظت کردن (v) *hemâyat kardan* حمایت کردن
protection *mohâfezat* محافظت *hefâzat* حفاظت *hemâyat* حمایت
protector *mohâfez* محافظ
protégé (c) *tahtolhemâye* تحت الحمایه *dastneshânde* دست نشانده *noche* نوچه
protest *e'terâz* اعتراض (v) *e'terâz kardan* اعتراض کردن
protester *mo'tarez* معترض
proud *moftakhar* مفتخر
prove (v) *esbât kardan* اثبات کردن
proverb *zarbohmasal* ضرب المثل
province (c) *ostân* استان *iyâlat* ایالت
provision *tahiyye* تهیه
prunes *âluche* آلوچه
psychiatrist *ravân pezeshk* روان پزشک
psychiatry *ravân pezeshki* روان پزشکی
psychic *ravâni* روانی

psychologist *ravân shenâs* روانشناس

psychology *ravân shenâsi* روانشناسی

psychotherapy *ravân darmâni* روان درمانی

pub *meykhâne* میخانه

puberty *boloq* بلوغ

pubis *sharmgâh* شرمگاه *zehâr* زهار

public prosecutor *dâdsetân* دادستان *modda'i olumum* مدعی العموم

public *omum* عموم *alani* علنی *omumi* عمومی

publication *nashr* نشر

publications *nashriyyât* نشریات

publicity *shohrat* شهرت

publish (v) *enteshâr dâdan* انتشار دادن

publisher *nâsher* ناشر

puddle *dast andâz* دست انداز *godâl* گودال

puff (c) *fut* فوت *pof* پف

puke *estefrâq* استفراغ

pull (v) *keshidan (kesh)* کشیدن (کش)

pulley *qerqere* قرقره

pulpit *manbar* منبر

pulse *zarabân* ضربان *nabz* نبض

pump *tolombe* تلمبه

pumpkin *kadu* کدو

punch *mosht* مشت

puncher *surâkhkon* سوراخ کن

puncture *panchari* پنچری

punishment *keyfar* کیفر *tanbih* تنبیه

pupil (of eye) *mardomak* مردمک

pupil (student) *shâgerd* شاگرد

puppy *tule* توله *tule sag* توله سگ

purchase *kharid* خرید

pure *motlaq* مطلق *pâk* پاک *nâb* ناب (c) *khâles* خالص

puree *pure* پوره

purely *serfan* صرفا

purity *effat* عفت

purple *arqavâni* ارغوانی

purpose *maqsud* مقصود *hadaf* هدف

purse *kif* کیف

pursuit *ta'qib* تعقیب

pus *cherk* چرک

push *feshâr* فشار (v) *feshâr dâdan* فشار دادن

pussy cat *pishi* پیشی

put (v) *gozâshtan (gozâr)* گذاشتن (گذار)

puzzle *jadval* جدول *mo'ammâ* معما

q

quack shârlâtân شارلاتان

quadrangle chârgush چارگوش

quadruped châhârpâ چهارپا
chârpâ چارپا

quail belderchin بلدرچین

qualified (person) madrakdâr
مدرک دار tahsil karde تحصیلکرده

qualitative keyfi کیفی

quality keyfiyyat کیفیت

quantitative kammi کمی

quantity meqdâr مقدار kamiyyat
کمیت

quarantine qarantine قرنطینه

quarrel (c) da'vâ دعوا nezâ' نزاع
jedâl جدال setize ستیزه
moshâjere مشاجره

quarter yek châhârom یک چهارم
(c) rob' ربع chârak چارک

quatrain dobeyti دوبیتی

quatrains robâ'iyyât رباعیات

queen malake ملکه

question porsesh پرسش (c) so'âl
سئوال

queue saf صف

quick châbok چابک (c) tond تند
zud زود

quiet bisarosedâ بی سروصدا ârâm
ساکت (c) sâket آرام

quill qalam قلم

quilt lahâf لحاف

quince beh به

quiver tarkesh ترکش

quotation naqle qol نقل قول naql
نقل

quotient bahre بهره

r

rabbi *khâkhâm* خاخام
rabbit *khargush* خرگوش
race (ethnicity) *nezhâd* نژاد
race (game) *mosâbeqe* مسابقه *kurs* کورس
racial *nezhâdi* نژادی *qomi* قومی
racism *nezhâd parasti* نژاد پرستی
racist *nezhâd parast* نژاد پرست
rack *tâqche* طاقچه
radiation *tâbesh* تابش
radiator *râdiyator* رادیاتور
radio *râdiyo* رادیو
radish *torob* ترب
radius *sho'â'* شعاع
rail road *râh âhan* راه آهن
railway *râh âhan* راه آهن
rain *bârân* باران
rainbow *qosqazah* قوس قزح (c) *rangin kamân* رنگین کمان
raincoat *bârâni* بارانی
rainfall *bârandegi* بارندگی
raise (v) *boland kardan* بلند کردن
raisins *maviz* مویز
rake *shenkesh* شنکش
rally *gerdehamâyi* گرد هم آیی
ram *quch* قوچ
ramrod *sonbe* سنبه
ranch *mazre'e* مزرعه
random *shânsi* شانسی *tasâdofi* تصادفی
ranger *jangalbân* جنگلبان
rank *raste* رسته *daraje* درجه *maqâm* مقام *rotbe* رتبه
rape *tajâvoz* تجاوز

rapid *sari'* سریع
rare *nâyâb* نایاب *kamyâb* کمیاب *nâder* نادر
rascal *bisaro pâ* بی سروپا *sharur* شرور
rash *jush* جوش
raspberry *tameshk* تمشک
rat *mush* موش
rate *mazanne* مظنه (c) *nerkh* نرخ
rating *darajebandi* درجه بندی
ratio *tanâsob* تناسب *nesbat* نسبت
rational *ma'qul* معقول
rattle box *jeqjeqe* جغجغه
raw *khâm* خام
rays *ashe'e* اشعه
razor *tiq* تیغ
reach (v) *rasidan (ras)* رسیدن (رس)
reaction *aksolamal* عکس العمل *bâztâb* بازتاب
read (v) *khândan (khân)* خواندن (خوان)
readable *khânâ* خوانا
reader *khânande* خواننده
readiness *âmâdegi* آمادگی
ready *âmâde* آماده *hâzer* حاضر
real *haqiqi* حقیقی *vâqe'i* واقعی
realise (v) *dark kardan* درک کردن
reality *haqiqat* حقیقت *vâqe'iyat* واقعیت
rear admiral *daryâdâr* دریادار
rear *aqab* عقب
reason *dalil* دلیل
reasonable *ma'qul* معقول
reasoning *estedlâl* استدلال
rebel *shureshi* شورشی

rebuke mo'âkheze مواخذه
receipt qabz قبض (c) rasid رسید
receive (v) daryâft kardan دریافت
کردن
receiver (phone) gushi گوشی
receiver girande گیرنده
recent navin نوین (c) akhir اخیر
recently akhiran اخیرا
reception (office) paziresh پذیرش
reception (party) pazirâyi پذیرایی
recipient girande گیرنده
recital zekr ذکر telâvat تلاوت
reciting qerâ'at قرائت
recognise (v) shenâkhtan
شناختن (shenâs) (شناس)
recognition shenâsâyi شناسایی
shenâkht شناخت
recommendation tosiye توصیه
reconciliation (c) sâzesh سازش
âshti آشتی solh صلح
record (history) pishine پیشینه
record (song) safhe صفحه
record player gerâmâfon گرامافون
recording zabt ضبط
recovery shafâ شفا (c) behbud
بهبود
recruitment estekhdâm استخدام
rectangle mostatil مستطیل
recurrence tanâvob تناوب
(c) tekrâr تکرار
recurrent mokarrar مکرر
red (c) qermez قرمز sorkh سرخ
redemption kaffâre کفاره
reduce (v) kâstan (kâh) کاستن (کاه)
reduced nâzel نازل

reduction (c) kâhesh کاهش
tanazzol تنزل
reed bed neyzâr نیزار
referee (mach) dâvar داور
referee (reference) mo'arref معرف
reference marja' مرجع mo'arref
معرف
referral morâje'e مراجعه roju'
رجوع
refinery pâlâyeshgâh پالایشگاه
reflection pezhvâk پژواک
en'ekâs انعکاس
reflex aksolamal عکس العمل
bâztâb بازتاب
reform eslâh اصلاح
reformist mosleh مصلح
refraining mozâyeqe مضایقه
refreshing farahbakhsh فرحبخش
refugee âvâre آواره
(c) panâhande پناهنده
refusal emtenâ' امتناع
refuse (v) emtenâ' kardan امتناع
کردن
regard hormat حرمت
regime nezâm نظام
region mantaqe منطقه hozeye
حوضه nâhiye ناحیه
regional mantaqeyi منطقه ای
register daftar دفتر
registered sefâreshi سفارشی
registration nâm nevisi نام نویسی
sabt ثبت
regression qahqarâ قهقرا
regressive mortaje' مرتجع
regret ta'asof تاسف (v) hasrat
khordan حسرت خوردن

regretful *nâdem* نادم

regular *monazzam* منظم

regulator *nâzem* ناظم

reindeer *gavazn* گوزن

reins *lejâm* لجام

rejected *matrud* مطرود *mardud* مردود

rejection *tard* طرد

relation *ertebât* ارتباط *rabt* ربط *râbete* رابطه *nesbat* نسبت

relationship *mo'âsherat* معاشرت *nesbat* نسبت *ertebât* ارتباط

relative (adj) *nesbi* نسبى (n) *khish* خویش

relatively *nesbatan* نسبتا

relatives *bastegân* بستگان *nazdikân* نزدیکان

relativity *nesbiyat* نسبیت

relax (v) *esterâhat kardan* استراحت کردن

relaxation *ârâmesh* آرامش *esterâhat* استراحت

release *morakhkhasi* مرخصی (v) *âzâd kardan* آزاد کردن

relevant *marbute* مربوطه

reliable *hesâbi* حسابى (c) *mo'tabar* معتبر

reliance *takye* تکیه *e'temâd* اعتماد

relieved *âsude* آسوده

religion (c) *din* دین *mazhab* مذهب *shari'at* شریعت

religious duty *farize* فریضه

religious law *feqh* فقه *shar'* شرع

religious leader *emâm* امام

religious *dindâr* دیندار *dini* دینى (c) *mazhabi* مذهبى *motadayyen* متدین

reluctance *ekrâh* اکراه

remaining *bâqimânde* باقیمانده *baqiyye* بقیه

remains *baqâyâ* بقایا

remedy *alâj* علاج *shafâ* شفا *châre* چاره

remind (v) *gushzad kardan* گوشزد کردن

remorse *nedâmat* ندامت

remorseful *pashimân* پشیمان

remote *dur* دور *part* پرت

remove (v) *barchidan (bar chin)* برچیدن (برچین)

renewed *mojaddad* مجدد

rennet *shirdân* شیردان

renovate (v) *bâzsâzi kardan* بازسازی کردن

renovation *nosâzi* نوسازی *bâzsâzi* بازسازی

rent *kerâye* کرایه *ejâre* اجاره (v) *kerâye kardan* کرایه کردن (v) *ejâre kardan* اجاره کردن

repair *ta'mir* تعمیر (v) *ta'mir kardan* تعمیر کردن

repeated *mokarrar* مکرر

repel (v) *daf' kardan* دفع کردن

repelling *daf'* دفع

repetition *tekrâr* تکرار

repetitious *mokarrar* مکرر *tekrâri* تکراری

replace (v) *ta'viz kardan* تعویض کردن

replacement *ta'viz* تعویض

reply *javâb* جواب (v) *javâb dâdan* جواب دادن

report *gozâresh* گزارش (v) *gozâresh dâdan* گزارش دادن

reporter *khabarnegâr* خبرنگار *gozâresh gar* گزارش گر

representation *namâyandegi* نمایندگی

representative *namâyande* نماینده

repression *sarkubi* سرکوبی

reprimand *tobikh* توبیخ

reproduction *taksir* تکثیر (c) *tolide mesl* تولید مثل

reproof *tobikh* توبیخ

reptile *khazande* خزنده

republic *jomhuri* جمهوری

reputation *heysiyat* حیثیت *shohrat* شهرت

request *taqâzâ* تقاضا *darkhâst* درخواست *khâhesh* خواهش (v) *darkhâst kardan* درخواست کردن

require (v) *niyâz dâshtan* نیاز داشتن

requirement *hâjat* حاجت *ehtiyâj* احتیاج *niyâz* نیاز

rescue *nejât* نجات

research *pazhuhesh* پژوهش *tahqiq* تحقیق

researcher *mohaqqeq* محقق

resemblance *moshâbehat* مشابهت *shabâhat* شباهت *tashâboh* تشابه

reserve *zakhire* ذخیره

reservoir *manba'* منبع *makhzan* مخزن

residence *maskan* مسکن *sokunat* سکونت *eqâmat* اقامت

resident *moqim* مقیم *sâken* ساکن

residential *maskuni* مسکونی

residue *bâqi* باقی

resign (v) *este'fa dâdan* استعفا دادن

resignation *este'fa* استعفا *kanâre giri* کناره گیری

resist (v) *esteqâmat kardan* استقامت کردن

resistance *tâb* تاب *istâdegi* ایستادگی *moqâvemat* مقاومت

resistant *moqâvem* مقاوم

resolution *qarâr* قرار *qat'nâme* قطعنامه

resort *tavassol* توسل

respect (attention) *ehterâm* احترام (v) *ehterâm kardan* احترام کردن

respect (relation) *lahâz* لحاظ

respected *mohtaram* محترم *arjomand* ارجمند

respectfully *mohtaramâne* محترمانه

respiration *nafas* نفس *tanaffos* تنفس

respite *forje* فرجه

response *pâsokh* پاسخ

responsibility *mas'uliyat* مسئولیت

responsible *mas'ul* مسئول *mo'azzaf* موظف

rest (relax) *esterâhat* استراحت (v) *esterâhat kardan* استراحت کردن

rest (residue) *bâqimânde* باقیمانده *bâqi* باقی *baqiyye* بقیه

restaurant *resturân* رستوران

restoration *bâzsâzi* بازسازی

restore (v) *bâzsâzi kardan* بازسازی کردن

restrict (v) *mahdud kardan* محدود کردن

restricted *mahdud* محدود
restriction *mahdudiyat* محدودیت
result *asar* اثر *samar* ثمر *natije* نتیجه
resurrection day *qiyâmat* قیامت *ma'âd* معاد *mahshar* محشر
resurrection *rastâkhiz* رستاخیز
retailer *khorde forush* خرده فروش
retaliation *qesâs* قصاص *talâfi* تلافی
retarded *aqab oftâde* عقب افتاده
retina *shabakiyye* شبکیه
retire (v) *bâzneshaste shodan* بازنشسته شدن
retired (c) *bâzneshaste* بازنشسته *khâne neshin* خانه نشین
retirement *bâzneshastegi* بازنشستگی
retreat *aqab neshini* عقب نشینی (v) *aqab neshini kardan* عقب نشینی کردن
retribution *mokâfât* مکافات
return *bâzgasht* بازگشت *bâzgashtan* بازگشتن (v) *marâje'at kardan* مراجعت کردن (v) *bargashtan (bargard)* برگشتن (برگرد)
returning *marâje'at* مراجعت
reveal *efshâ' kardan* افشا کردن *fâsh kardan* فاش کردن
revealing *efshâ'* افشا
revenge *enteqâm* انتقام
revengefulness *kinejuyi* کینه جویی
reversed *ma'kus* معکوس
review *barrasi* بررسی *morur* مرور (v) *barrasi kardan* بررسی کردن

revolt *sarkeshi* سرکشی *fetne* فتنه *qiyâm* قیام *shuresh* شورش (v) *eqteshâsh kardan* اغتشاش کردن (v) *shuridan (shur)* شوریدن (شور)
revolution *enqelâb* انقلاب
revolve (v) *gardidan (gard)* گردیدن (گرد)
revolver *sheshlul* ششلول *tapânche* طپانچه
reward (c) *pâdâsh* پاداش *ajr* اجر
rhinoceros *kargadan* کرگدن
rhyme *qâfiye* قافیه
rhythmical *mozun* موزون
rib *dande* دنده
ribbon *rubân* روبان *navâr* نوار
rice field *shâlizâr* شالیزار
rice *berenj* برنج
rich *dârâ* دارا *qani* غنی (c) *servat mand* ثروتمند
riddle *chistân* چیستان *mo'ammâ* معما
rider *savâr* سوار
ridge *tiqe* تیغه
ridicule (v) *maskhare kardan* مسخره کردن *rishkhand* ریشخند *tamaskhor* تمسخر
ridiculous *khânde dâr* خنده دار *maskhare* مسخره
rifle pit *sangar* سنگر
rifle *tofang* تفنگ
right away *foran* فورا
right now *hamin alân* همین الان
right *sahih* صحیح *dorost* درست *râst* راست
righteous *nikukâr* نیکوکار
rights *hoquq* حقوق

right-wing *jenahe rast* جناح راست

rim *zeh* زه **labe** لبه **kamâne** كمانه

ring *halqe* حلقه **angoshtar** انگشتر

ringdove *qomri* قمرى

ringlet *fer* فر

riot *âshub* آشوب **balvâ** بلوا
eqteshâsh اغتشاش (c) *shuresh*
شورش

riotous *âshubgar* آشوبگر

rip up (v) *shekâftan (shekâf)*
شكافتن (شكاف)

ripe *raside* رسيده

ripped *daride* دريده

risk *khatar* خطر

rivalry *reqâbat* رقابت

river *rud khâne* رودخانه **rud** رود

Riyal *riyâl* ريال

road *jâdde* جاده **râh** راه

roaring *qorresh* غرش

roasted *sorkh karde* سرخ كرده
beryân بريان

rob (v) *dastbord zadan* دستبرد زدن
(v) *dozdidan (dozd)* دزديدن (دزد)

robber *sâreq* سارق

robbery *serqat* سرقت **dozdi** دزدى

rock *sakhre* صخره **sang** سنگ

rocket *mushak* موشك

rod *mile* ميله

rodents *javandegân* جوندگان

roll (v) *qaltidan (qalt)* غلتيدن (غلت)
(v) *charkhidan (charkh)* چرخيدن
(چرخ)

roller *qaltak* غلتك

romantic *asheqâne* عاشقانه

roof *bâm* بام

room *otâq* اتاق

roommate *ham otaqi* هم اتاقى

rooster *khurus* خروس

root *bon* بن (c) *rishe* ريشه

rope (c) *tanâb* طناب *rismân*
ريسمان

rose garden *golestân* گلستان

rose *gole sorkh* گل سرخ

rose-water *golâb* گلاب

rot (v) *pusidan (pus)* پوسيدن (پوس)
(v) *gandidan (gand)* گنديدن (گند)

rotate (v) *dor zadan* دور زدن
(v) *gardidan (gard)* گرديدن (گرد)

rotation *charkhesh* چرخش **dor**
دور

rotten *fâsed* فاسد **gandide** گنديده

rough *nâhanjâr* ناهنجار **khashen**
خشن

round the clock *shabâne ruz* شبانه
روز

round (c) *gerd* گرد **modavvar**
مدور

roundabout *meydân* ميدان **falake**
فلكه

route *masir* مسير **jâdde** جاده **râh**
راه

routine *ruzmarre* روزمره

row *rade* رده **radif** رديف

royal *shâhâne* شاهانه **saltanati**
سلطنتى

royalist *saltanat talab* سلطنت طلب
shâhparast شاه پرست

rub (v) *mâlidan (mâl)* ماليدن (مال)

rubber (eraser) *pâkkon* پاكن

rubber *kâ'uchu* كائوچو **lâstik**
لاستيك

rubbing   *mâlesh* مالش

rubbish   (c) *âshqâl* آشغال   *nokhâle* نخاله

rubella   *sorkhje* سرخجه

ruby   *la'l* لعل

rude   *porru* پررو   *gostâkh* گستاخ

rudiments   *moqaddamât* مقدمات

rue   *hasrat* حسرت

rug   *farsh* فرش

ruin   (v) *az beyn bordan* از بین بردن

ruined   *makhrube* مخروبه

ruins   *kharâbe* خرابه

rule   *qâ'ede* قاعده   (v) *hokumat kardan* حکومت کردن

ruler (governor)   *farmânravâ* فرمانروا

ruler (measuring)   *khatkesh* خط کش

rumor   *cho* چو   (c) *shaye'e* شایعه

run   (v) *davidan (dav)* دویدن (دو)

rural shoe   *châroq* چاروق

rural   *rustâyi* روستایی

rush   *ajale* عجله

Russia   *rusiye* روسیه

rust   *zang* زنگ

rusty   *zang zade* زنگ زده

ruthless   *zâlem* ظالم   *birahm* بیرحم

S 120

s

sable *samur* سمور

sabotage *kârshekani* کارشکنی *ekhlâl* اخلال

sack *kise* کیسه

sacrifice (v) *fadâ kardan* فدا کردن (v) *isâr kardan* ایثار کردن (v) *qorbâni kardan* قربانی کردن

sacrifice *jân nesâri* جان نثاری

sad *qamgin* غمگین *mota'asser* متاثر (c) *nârâhat* ناراحت

saddle *zin* زین

saddlebag *khorjin* خورجین

safe (adj) *amn* امن *iman* ایمن

safe (n) *sanduq* صندوق *gâv sanduq* گاو صندوق

safety *imani* ایمنی

saffron *za'ferân* زعفران

sagacious *farzâne* فرزانه

sail *bâdbân* بادبان

sailor *malavân* ملوان *daryânavard* دریانورد

saint *moqaddas* مقدس *qeddis* قدیس

saints *oliyâ* اولیا

salami *kâlbâs* کالباس

salary *hoquq* حقوق

sale *forush* فروش

salesman *forushande* فروشنده

saliva *bozâq* بزاق

salt *namak* نمک

saltshaker *namak dân* نمک دان *namak pâsh* نمک پاش

salty *shur* شور

salvation *nejât* نجات

sample *nemune* نمونه

sampling *nemune bardâri* نمونه برداری

sanatorium *âsâyeshgâh* آسایشگاه

sanction *tahrim* تحریم

sand *rig* ریگ *mâse* ماسه *shen* شن

sandy *sheni* شنی

sarcasm *matalak* متلک *ta'ne* طعنه *kenâye* کنایه

sarcastic *kenâye âmiz* کنایه آمیز *ta'ne âmiz* طعنه آمیز

Satan *sheytân* شیطان

satanic *sheytâni* شیطانی

satellite *mâhvâre* ماهواره

satire *latife* لطیفه (c) *tanz* طنز

satirist *tanznevis* طنز نویس

satisfaction *erzâ'* ارضا *rezâyat* رضایت

satisfactory *rezâyat bakhsh* رضایت بخش

satisfied *râzi* راضی

satisfy (v) *erzâ' kardan* ارضا کردن

Saturday *shanbe* شنبه

Saturn *keyvân* کیوان

saucer *na'lbaki* نعلبکی

Saudi Arabia *arabestân* عربستان

savagery *tavahhosh* توحش

savant *dânâ* دانا

save (v) *pasandâz kardan* پس انداز کردن *nejât dâdan* نجات دادن

saving *zakhire* ذخیره

savings *pas andâz* پس انداز

saviour *monji* منجی *nâji* ناجی

saw arre ارّه (v) arre kardan ارّه کردن

say (v) goftan (guy) (گوی) گفتن

scabies gâl گال jarb جرب

scaffold chub bast چوب بست

scale tarâzu ترازو meqyâs مقیاس

scandal fazâhat فضاحت eftezâh افتضاح (c) rosvâyi رسوایی

scar dâq داغ

scarce kamyâb کمیاب nâder نادر

scare (v) tarsidan (tars) ترسیدن (ترس)

scarecrow matarsak مترسک

scared moqaddas مقدس

scarf lachak لچک (c) rusari روسری shâl شال maqne'e مقنعه

scarlet fever makhmalak مخملک

scary (c) tarsnâk ترسناک mahib مهیب makhuf مخوف

scattered parâkande پراکنده

scene sahne صحنه

scented mo'attar معطر

sceptical shakkâk شکاک mashkuk مشکوک

scholar mohaqqeq محقق âlem عالم dâneshmand دانشمند fâzel فاضل

school madrase مدرسه

science elm علم

sciences ulum علوم

scientist dâneshmand دانشمند

scissors qeychi قیچی

scoff sarkoft سرکوفت

scolding sarzanesh سرزنش

scoop chomche چمچه

scorpion aqrab عقرب

scout pish âhang پیش آهنگ

scrambled egg nimru نیمرو

scratch panjul پنجول (v) khâridan خاریدن (khâr) (خار) khâresh خارش

scream jiq جیغ dâd داد faryâd فریاد (v) dâd zadan داد زدن (v) jiq zadan جیغ زدن

screen parde پرده

screw driver âchâr آچار

screw (v) gâyiydan (gây) گاییدن(گای)

scriptwriter filmnâme nevis فیلم نامه نویس

scroll tumâr طومار

scrutiny mushekâfi موشکافی

sculptor peykar tarash پیکرتراش

sculpture peykare پیکره mojassame مجسمه

scum tofâle تفاله

sea shell gush mâhi گوش ماهی

sea bahr بحر (c) daryâ دریا

seacoast kanâre daryâ کناردریا sâhel ساحل

seal (ring) negin نگین mohr مهر

seal polomb پلمب mohr مهر (v) mohr zadan مهر زدن

seaman malavân ملوان jâshu جاشو daryânavard دریانورد

seamanship malavâni ملوانی

search taftish تفتیش kandokâv کندوکاو josteju جستجو (v) josteju kardan جستجو کردن (v) gashtan گشتن (gard) (گرد)

searchlight nurafkan نورافکن

seaside *kenâre daryâ* کنار دریا
sâhel ساحل

season *fasl* فصل

seasonal *musemi* موسمی *fasli* فصلی

seasoning *châshni* چاشنی

seat belt *kamar band* کمربند

second (rank) *dovvom* دوم *sâni*
ثانی

second (time) *sâniye* ثانیه

second hand store *semsâri*
سمساری

second hand *mosta'mal* مستعمل

secondary school *dabirestân*
دبیرستان

secondary *far'i* فرعی

secrecy *pardepushi* پرده پوشی

secret (n) *ramz* رمز (adj *serri*
سری (n) *râz* راز

secretarial job *monshigari*
منشیگری

secretariat *dabirkhâne* دبیرخانه

secretary *monshi* منشی *dabir* دبیر

sect *ferqe* فرقه

section *sho'be* شعبه *bakhsh* بخش
qesmat قسمت

sectional *maqta'i* مقطعی

secular *bidin* بیدین *lâmazhab*
لامذهب *kâfar* کافر

secure *mahfuz* محفوظ

security alarm *dozgir* دزدگیر

security *amniyat* امنیت *imani*
ایمنی

sedative *mosakken* مسکن *ârâm
bakhsh* آرام بخش

sediment *tah neshin* ته نشین
rosub رسوب

see (v) *didan (bin)* دیدن (بین)

seed *habbe* حبه (c) *tokhm* تخم
bazr بذر *dâne* دانه

seedless *bidâne* بی دانه

seedling *neshâ* نشا

seeker *juyande* جوینده *tâleb* طالب

see-saw *allâkolang* آلاکلنگ

segment *qat'e* قطعه

seizure *qash* غش

select (v) *bargozidan (bar gozin)*
برگزیدن (v) *entekhâb kardan*
انتخاب کردن

selected *gozide* گزیده

selection *entekhâb* انتخاب
gozinesh گزینش

self burning *khod suzi* خودسوزی

self indulgent *tanparvar* تن پرور

self *nafs* نفس *khishtan* خویشتن
khod خود

self-conceit *khod bini* خودبینی

self-control *khoddâri* خودداری

selfish *khodkhâh* خودخواه

selfishness *khodpasandi*
خودپسندی *khodkhâhi* خودخواهی

self-learner *khod âmuz* خود آموز

self-possessed *matin* متین

self-sacrificer *jânbâz* جانباز

self-service *self servis* سلف
سرویس

sell (v) *forukhtan (forush)* فروختن
(فروش)

seller *forushande* فروشنده

semen *mani* منی

semi-final *nime nahâyi* نیمه نهایی

send (v) *e'zâm kardan* اعزام کردن
(v) *ersâl kardan* ارسال کردن
(v) *ferestâdan (ferest)* (فرستادن
(فرست)
sender *ferestande* فرستنده
senile (c) *mosen* مسن *fartut*
فرتوت
senility *kohulat* کهولت
senior *arshad* ارشد
sensational *shurangiz* شورانگیز
sense *mafhum* مفهوم *hess* حس
senses *havâs* حواس
sensible *mahsus* محسوس
sensitivity *hassâsiyat* حساسیت
sentence *jomle* جمله
sentiment *âtefe* عاطفه
separate (v) *jodâ kardan* جدا کردن
separate *jodâ* جدا
separation *farâq* فراق
September *septâmr* سپتامبر
sergeant *goruhbân* گروهبان
serial *mosalsal* مسلسل
series *majmu'e* مجموعه *seri* سری
serious *mohemm* مهم *jeddi* جدی
seriously *jeddan* جدا
sermon *mo'eze* موعظه *roze* روضه
khotbe خطبه
serpent *mâr* مار
servant *mostakhdem* مستخدم
châkar چاکر (c) *nokar* نوکر
khâdem خادم *khedmatkâr* خدمتکار
bande بنده *pish khedmat* پیشخدمت
server *khâdem* خادم
servile *khâye mâli* خایه مالی
serving *khedmat* خدمت

sesame *konjod* کنجد
session *jalase* جلسه
set up (v) *nasb kardan* نصب کردن
set *majmu'e* مجموعه *dastgâh*
دستگاه
settle (v) *jâ oftâdan* جا افتادن
settlement *mosâlehe* مصالحه
esteqrâr استقرار
seven *haft* هفت
seventeen *hifdah* هفده
seventeenth *hifdahom* هفدهم
seventh *haftam* هفتم
seventy *haftad* هفتاد
several (adj) *mota'added* متعدد
(adv) *chandin* چندین
severe *shadid* شدید
severity *sheddat* شدت
sew (v) *dukhtan (duz)* (دوختن (دوز
sewer *manjalâb* منجلاب
sewerage *fâzelâb* فاضلاب
sewing *khayyâti* خیاطی
sex *jensiyyat* جنسیت
sexism *jense gerayi* جنس گرایی
sexual intercourse *nazdiki* نزدیکی
sexual *jensi* جنسی
sexuality *jensiyyat* جنسیت
shade *sâybân* سایبان *sâye* سایه
shadow *sâye* سایه
shaft *mil* میل *mile* میله
shaggy *pashmâlu* پشمالو
shake *takân* تکان (v) *jonbidan*
(jonb) جنبیدن (جنب) (v) *larzidan*
(larz) لرزیدن (لرز)
shaky *larzân* لرزان
shallow *sathi* سطحی

shame fazâhat فضاحت
sharmandegi شرمندگی (c) khejâlat
sharm شرم خجالت
shameful nang âvar ننگ آور
nangin ننگين (c) khejâlat âvar
خجالت آور
shameless bihayâ بی حيا
shampoo shampo شامپو
shanty house âlunak آلونک
shape shakl شکل
share jire جيره dong دنگ
(c) sahm سهم
shared moshtarak مشترک
shares sahâm سهام
shark kuse کوسه
sharp tiz تيز
sharp-pointed nuktiz نوک تيز
shave (v) tarâshidan (tarâsh)
تراشيدن (تراش)
shaver rish tarash ريش تراش
she u او (c) ân آن
sheath niyâm نيام
sheep dung peshgel پشگل
sheep trotters kalle pâche کله پاچه
sheep gusfand گوسفند
sheepshearing pashm chini پشم
چينی
sheet barg برگ
shelf qafase قفسه komod کمد
shell sadaf صدف lâk لاک pust
پوست
shelling golule bârân گلوله باران
shelter panâhgâh پناهگاه
shepherd chupân چوپان
sheriff kalântar کلانتر

shield separ سپر
shiism tashayyo' تشيع
Shiites shi'e شيعه
shine (v) tâbidan (tâb) تابيدن (تاب)
(v) derakhshidan (derakhsh)
درخشيدن (درخش)
shinny barraq براق
ship keshti کشتی
shipping kashtirâni کشتيرانی
shirt boluz بلوز pirâhan پيراهن
shit goh گه (v) ridan (rin) ريدن
(رين)
shiver (v) larzidan (larz) لرزيدن
(لرز)
shivery larzân لرزان
shoe kafsh کفش
shoe-horn pâshne kesh پاشنه کش
shoemaker kaffâsh کفاش
shooting shellik شليک tirandâzi
تيراندازی
shop keeper maqâzedâr مغازه دار
forushande فروشنده
shop dokân دکان maqâze مغازه
forushgâh فروشگاه
shopping plaza pâsâzh پاساژ
markaze kharid مرکزخريد
shore karâne کرانه sâhel ساحل
short cut miyân bor ميان بر
short (adj) kutâh کوتاه
shortage kambud کمبود noqsân
نقصان
shortcoming kutâhi کوتاهی
shorts (pants) (n) shalvarak
شلواركوتاه shalvar kutah شلوارک
shot (bullet) tir تير golule گلوله
shot (injection) âmpul آمپول

shoulder arms *dush fang* دوش فنگ

shoulder strap *sardushi* سردوشی

shoulder *ketf* کتف *kul* کول (c) *shâne* شانه

shouting *faryâd* فریاد

shovel *bil* بیل

show off *poz* پز *efâde* افاده *khodnamâyi* خودنمایی

show *namâyesh* نمایش (v) *neshân dâdan* نشان دادن

shower *ragbâr* رگبار

shrimp *meygu* میگو

shrine *ziyâratgâh* زیارتگاه *haram* حرم *marqad* مرقد *mazâr* مزار *maqbare* مقبره

shrink (v) *âb raftan* آب رفتن

shroud *kafan* کفن

shrub *bute* بوته

shy *khejâlati* خجالتی *kamru* کمرو

shyness *hojb* حجب

sick *bimâr* بیمار (c) *mariz* مریض

sickle *dâs* داس

sickness *marizi* مریضی *maraz* مرض

side walk *piyâde ro* پیاده رو

side *zel'* ضلع *jahat* جهت *samt* سمت *taraf* طرف

siege *mohâsere* محاصره

sifter *qarbâl* غربال

sigh *âh* آه (v) *âh keshidan* آه کشیدن

sight *namâ* نما *did* دید

sign *neshân* نشان *alâmat* علامت (v) *emzâ' kardan* امضا کردن

signalman *didebân* دیده بان

signature *emzâ'* امضا

significance *ahamiyat* اهمیت

silence *khâmushi* خاموشی (c) *sokut* سکوت

silent *gong* گنگ (c) *sâket* ساکت

silk *abrisham* ابریشم

silly *safih* سفیه *ablah* ابله

silver *noqreyi* نقره ای *noqre* نقره

similar *moshâbeh* مشابه *nazir* نظیر *shabih* شبیه

similarity *moshâbehat* مشابهت *shabâhat* شباهت *tashâboh* تشابه

simile *este'âre* استعاره

simple *sâde* ساده

sin *ma'siyat* معصیت (c) *gonâh* گناه

since *az* از

sincere *biriyâ* بی ریا

sincerely *erâdatmand* ارادتمند

sincerity *samimiyat* صمیمیت

sing (v) *khândan (khân)* خواندن (خوان) (v) *âvâz khândan (âvâz khân)* آواز خواندن (آواز خوان)

singer *khânande* خواننده

single (bachelor) *mojarrad* مجرد

single (one) *tak* تک

singlet *araqgir* عرق گیر

singular *mofrad* مفرد

sinister *nahs* نحس

sink *foru raftan* فرو رفتن *qarq shodan* غرق شدن

sip *jor'e* جرعه

sir (c) *âqâ* آقا *gorbân* قربان

siren *sut* سوت

sister *khâhar* خواهر

sit down (v) neshastan (neshin) نشستن (نشین)

sit for a test (v) emtahân dâdan امتحان دادن

sit (v) neshastan (neshin) نشستن (نشین)

situation ozâ' اوضاع moqe'iyyat موقعیت

six hundred sheshsad ششصد

six shesh شش

sixteen shânzdah شانزده

sixty shast شصت

size andâze اندازه

skate sorsore سرسره

skepticism tardid تردید

sketch tarh طرح

skewer sikh سیخ

skiing eski اسکی

skill mahârat مهارت

skilled mâher ماهر

skimmer kafgir کفگیر

skin pust پوست

skinny lâqar لاغر

skirt dâman دامن

skull jomjome جمجمه

sky scraper âsemân kharâsh آسمان خراش

sky âsemân آسمان

slang âmiyâne عامیانه

slant movarrab مورب mâyel مایل

slap keshide کشیده chak چک sili سیلی (v) chak zadan چک زدن

slaughter koshtâr کشتار zebh ذبح

slaughterhouse koshtârgâh کشتارگاه

slave qolâm غلام barde برده bande بنده

sledge hammer potk پتک

sledge surutme سورتمه

sleep khâb خواب (v) khâbidan خوابیدن (خواب) (khâb)

sleeping bag kise khâb کیسه خواب

sleeping pill qorse khâb قرص خواب

sleepwalking khâb gardi خواب گردی

sleepy khâb âlud خواب آلود

sleeve âstin آستین

slide (v) laqzidan (laqz) لغزیدن (لغز)

slight joz'i جزئی

slip laqzesh لغزش (v) laqzidan (laqz) لغزیدن (لغز)

slippers dampâyi دمپائی

slippery laqzân لغزان laqzande لغزنده liz لیز

slogan sho'âr شعار

slope sarâziri سرازیری nashib نشیب sarpâyiyni سرپایینی shib شیب sarâshib سراشیب شیب

slow kond کند yavâsh یواش âheste آهسته

sludge lajan لجن

slurring over mâst mâli ماست مالی

sluttish shalakhte شلخته

small haqir حقیر mohaqqar محقر (c) kuchek کوچک

smallpox âbele آبله

smart zerang زرنگ bâhush باهوش هوش

smell bu بو (v) bu kardan بو کردن (v) buyidan (buy) بوییدن (بوی)

smile   *tabassom* تبسم   *labkhand* لبخند

لبخند (v) *labkhand zadan* لبخند زدن

smog   *qobâr* غبار   *meh* مه

smoke   *dud* دود

smoking pipe   *pip* پیپ

smooth   *narm* نرم

smuggle   *qâchâq* قاچاق

smuggler   *qâchâqchi* قاچاقچی

smut   *dude* دوده

snail   *halazun* حلزون

snake charmer   *mârgir* مارگیر

snake   *mâr* مار

snatch   (v) *qâpidan (qâp)* قاپیدن (قاپ)

sneer   *puzkhand* پوزخند

sneeze   *atse* عطسه   (v) *atse kardan* عطسه کردن

snitching   *nâkhonak* ناخنک

snoring   *khorkhor* خرخر

snort   *khornâs* خرناس

snot   *fin* فین

snow   *barf* برف

snowy storm   *kulâk* کولاک

snug   *denj* دنج

so and so   *kazâyi* کذایی

soap   *sâbun* صابون

soccer   *futbâl* فوتبال

social worker   *madadkâr* مددکار

social-democratic   *sosyal-domokrat* سوسیال دمکرات

socialist   *sosyalist* سوسیالیست

societies   *javâme'* جوامع

society   *jâme'e* جامعه   *ejtemâ'* اجتماع

sociology   *jâme'e shenâsi* جامعه شناسی

socks   *jorâb* جوراب

soft   *âheste* آهسته   *narm* نرم

soil   *khâk* خاک

soiled   *khâki* خاکی

solar system   *manzume shamsi* منظومه شمسی

solar   *shamsi* شمسی   *khorshidi* خورشیدی

solder   *lahim* لحیم

soldier   *sarbâz* سرباز

sole (of feet)   *kafe pâ* کف پا

sole (only)   *tanhâ* تنها

solid   *jâmed* جامد

solidification   *enjemâd* انجماد

solids   *jâmedât* جامدات

solution (liquid)   *mahlul* محلول

solution   *hall* حل

solve   (v) *hall kardan* حل کردن

some   *barkhi* برخی   *meqdâri* مقداری   *ba'zi* بعضی   *chand* چند

somebody   *kesi* کسی

someone   *kesi* کسی

somersault   *poshtak* پشتک

something   *chizi* چیزی

sometimes   *gahgâh* گهگاه   *gâhi* گاهی

son   *pesar* پسر

song   *âvâz* آواز   *tarâne* ترانه

son-in-law   *dâmâd* داماد

soon   *zud* زود   *bezudi* بزودی

soothe   (v) *ârâm kardan* آرام کردن

soothing   *taskin* تسکین

sophistry   *maqlate* مغلطه

sore throat galu dard گلو درد
sore dardnâk دردناک
sorrow anduh اندوه qosse غصه
qam غم
sorry mota'assef متاسف
sort jur جور (v) jur kardan جور
کردن
sorting dastebandi دسته بندی
soul ravân روان jân جان ruh روح
sound sot صوت sedâ صدا
sour torsh ترش
source sarcheshme سرچشمه
mansha' منشا manba' منبع marja'
مرجع
sourness torshi ترشی
south janub جنوب
souvenir armaqân ارمغان kâdo
کادو
Soviet shuravi شوروی
sow (v) kâshtan (kâr) کاشتن (کار)
space jâ جا fazâ فضا
spaceship safine سفينه
fazâpeymâ فضاپیما
Spain espâniyâ اسپانیا
sparkle jaraqqe جرقه
sparrow hawk qerqi قرقی
sparrow gonjeshk گنجشک
spatial fazâyi فضایی
speak (v) harf zadan حرف زدن
speaker sokhangu سخنگو
spear nize نیزه
spearmint na'nâ نعنا
special makhsus مخصوص
specialist kârshenâs کارشناس
motakhasses متخصص

specialty takhassos تخصص
species gune گونه
specific moshakhkhas مشخص
makhsus مخصوص
specified mo'ayyan معین
specimen nemune نمونه
spectacles eynak عینک
spectator tamâshâchi تماشاچی
spectrum teyf طیف
speech (c) goftâr گفتار sokhan
سخن kalâm کلام
speechless lâl لال
speed sor'at سرعت
spell afsun افسون jâdu جادو
telesm طلسم sehr سحر
spelling emlâ' املا
spend (v) gozarândan (gozaran)
گذراندن (گذران)
spices adviye ادویه
spicy tond تند
spider ankabut عنکبوت
spin (v) ristan (ris) ریستن (ریس)
spinach esfenâj اسفناج
spine nokhâ' نخاع
spinning nakh risi نخ ریسی
spiral mârpich مارپیچ
spirit (drink) araq عرق
spirit (soul) ruh روح
spiritual ruhâni روحانی ma'navi
معنوی
spirituality ma'naviyat معنویت
ruhâniyat روحانیت
spit tof تف
spiteful moqrez مغرض
splashing shorshor شرشر

spleen tahâl طحال
split peas lape لپه
split jodâyi جدایی   tarak ترک
spoiled lus لوس
spokesman sokhangu سخنگو
sponge esfanj اسفنج
sponger moftkhor مفتخور
spook shabah شبح
spool qerqere قرقره
spoon qâshoq قاشق
sport varzesh ورزش
spot noqte نقطه
spotted khâldâr خالدار
spreading nashr نشر
spring (coil) fanar فنر
spring (season) bahâr بهار
spring (water) chesme چشمه
sprinkle (v) pâshidan (pâsh)
پاشیدن (پاش)
sprout javâne جوانه
spur mehmiz مهمیز
spy jâsus جاسوس
squad jukhe جوخه
square (root) majzur مجذور   jazr
جذر
square (roundabout) meydân
میدان
square (shape) morabba' مربع
squat chombâtme چمباتمه
squeeze (v) foshordan (feshâr)
فشردن (فشار)
squint luch لوچ
squirm (v) lulidan (lul) لولیدن (لول)
squirrel sanjâb سنجاب
srew (n) pich پیچ

Sri Lanka serilânkâ سریلانکا
stab (v) châqu zadan چاقو زدن
stability davâm دوام   sobât ثبات
stabilization tasbit تثبیت
stable (adj) mota'âdel متعادل
sâbet ثابت
stable (n) establ اصطبل   tavile
طویله
stadium estâdiyom استادیوم
staff kâdr کادر   kârkonân کارکنان
stage (phase) marhale مرحله
stage (theatre) sahne صحنه
stagnant râked راکد
stagnation rokud رکود
stain lakke لکه
stair pelle پله
stairway râh pelle راه پله
stale bayât بیات
stalk sâqe ساقه
stall tavile طویله
stalled lang لنگ
stamina poshtkâr پشتکار
stammering loknat لکنت
stamp (postal) tambr تمبر
stamp (seal) mohr مهر
stand up (v) boland shodan بلند
شدن   (v) istâdan (ist) ایستادن (ایست)
stand dakke دکه   (v) istâdan (ist)
ایستادن (ایست)
standard me'yâr معیار
star setâre ستاره
starch neshâste نشاسته
starling sâr سار
stars setâregan ستارگان

start shoru' شروع (v) âqâz
آغاز کردن kardan

starvation qahti قحطی gorosnegi
گرسنگی

state (express) hâlat حالت
(v) ezhâr kardan اظهار کردن

state (government) dolat دولت

state (province) iyâlat ایالت

statement ezhâr اظهار

station istgâh ایستگاه

stationery shop nevesht afzâr
forushi نوشت افزار فروشی

stationery lavâzem ottahrir لوازم
التحریر nevesht afzâr نوشت افزار

statistics âmâr آمار

statue (position) sha'n شان
mansab منصب manzelat منزلت

statue (scaplture) tandis تندیس
mojassame مجسمه

stay (v) mândan (mân) ماندن (مان)

steal (v) dozdidan (dozd) دزدیدن
(دزد)

stealing dozdi دزدی

steam bokhâr بخار

steel fulâd فولاد pulâd پولاد

steelyard qapân قپان

steep sarâziri سرازیری sarâshib
سراشیب

steering-wheel farmân فرمان

stem sâqe ساقه

step (phase) marhale مرحله

step (stairs) pelle پله

stepbrother baradar khânde برادر
خوانده

stepdaughter nâdokhtari نادختری

stepfather nâpedari ناپدری

stepmother nâmâdari نامادری
zanbâbâ زن بابا

stepson nâpesari ناپسری

stereotype kelishe کلیشه

sterile aqim عقیم nâzâ نازا

sterility nâzâyi نازایی

stern abus عبوس

stew pan qâblame قابلمه

stew khoresh خورش

stewardess mehmân dâr مهماندار

stick asâ عصا

sticker aksbargardân عکس بر گردان

sticky chasbnâk چسبناک chasbân
چسبان lazej لزج

stiff seft سفت

stimulus moharrek محرک

sting nish نیش (v) gazidan (gaz)
گزیدن (گز)

stingy khasis خسیس

stink gand گند

stipend shahriye شهریه

stipendiary hoquq begir حقوق بگیر

stirrup rekâb رکاب

stitch bakhiye بخیه (v) bakhiye
zadan بخیه زدن

stock mojudi موجودی sahâm سهام

stockings jorâb جوراب

stomach me'de معده shekam
شکم

stone sang سنگ

stonecutter sangtarâsh سنگتراش

stoning sangsâr سنگسار

stood up mo'attal معطل

stool chârpâye چارپایه

stop (in travel) tavaqqof توقف

stop (station)   istgâh   ایستگاه

stop!   ist   ایست

stoppage   gir   گیر

storage   makhzan   مخزن

store (shop)   dokân   دکان   maqâze
مغازه   forushgâh   فروشگاه

store (warehouse)   anbâr   انبار

storey   tabaqe   طبقه

stork   laklak   لکلک

storm   tufân   طوفان

story   dâstân   داستان   qesse   قصه

storyteller   naqqâl   نقال   qessegu
قصه گو

stove   ojâq   اجاق

straight   mostaqim   مستقیم

strainer   âbkesh   آبکش   sâfi   صافی

strait   tange   تنگه

strange   ajib   عجیب

stranger   qaribe   غریبه   bigâne
بیگانه

stratum   lâye   لایه

strawberry   tut ferangi   توت فرنگی

street   khiyâbân   خیابان

strength   qodrat   قدرت   niru   نیرو

strict   sakht   سخت

strictly   akidan   اکیدا

strike   e'tesâb   اعتصاب

string   band   بند   rismân   ریسمان
nakh   نخ

stroke   sekte   سکته   zarbe   ضربه

stroll   (v) qadam zadan   قدم زدن

strong   nirumand   نیرومند   qavi   قوی

structure   sâkhtemân   ساختمان
sâkht   ساخت   sâkhtâr   ساختار

struggle   talâsh   تلاش   kushesh
کوشش   taqallâ   تقلا   (v) kushidan
کوشیدن (کوش)   (kush)

stubborn   kalle shaq   کله شق   lajuj
لجوج   lajbâz   لجباز   khodra'y
خودرای

student (in school)   dânesh âmuz
دانش آموز

student (in university)   dânesh ju
دانشجو

student   mohassel   محصل
shâgerd   شاگرد

study   tahsil   تحصیل   motâle'e   مطالعه
(v) mottale' kardan   مطالعه کردن
(v) dars khândan   درس خواندن

stuff   (v) chapândan (chapân)
چپاندن (چپان)

stuffy   khafe   خفه

stunned   mabhut   مبهوت

stunning   heyrat angiz   حیرت انگیز

stupid   ahmaq   احمق   kodan   کودن
pakhme   پخمه   ablah   ابله

stupidity   hemâqat   حماقت
khariyyat   خریت

stutterer   alkan   الکن

stuttering   loknat   لکنت

style   shive   شیوه   sabk   سبک

stylish   shik   شیک

sub   mâdun   مادون

subcutaneous   zirpusti   زیر پوستی

subdivision   shâkhe   شاخه

subject (in grammar)   fâ'el   فاعل

subject (topic)   mozu'   موضوع
matlab   مطلب

sublime   mota'âl   متعال

submarine   zirdaryâyi   زیردریایی

submission *taslim* تسليم
submissive *râm* رام
submissively *mazlumâne* مظلومانه
submissiveness *mazlumiyat*
مظلوميت
subordinate *zirdast* زيردست
subpoena *jalb* جلب
subscribe (v) *âbnumân shodan*
آبونمان شدن
subscriber *moshtarek* مشترک
subscription *eshterâk* اشتراک
âbnumân آبونمان
subsidiary *far'* فرع
subsiding *forukesh* فروکش
subsistence *ma'âsh* معاش
substance *mâdde* ماده
substitute *jâneshin* جانشين
(v) *avaz kardan* عوض کردن
substitution *ta'viz* تعويض
subtitles *zir nevis* زيرنويس
subtle *daqiq* دقيق
subtraction *menhâ* منها
suburb *home* حومه
subway *metro* مترو
success *movaffaqiyyat* موفقيت
successful (c) *movaffaq* موفق
kâmiyâb کامياب
successive *motavâli* متوالی *pey*
dar pey پی در پی *peyâpey* پياپی
successor *jâneshin* جانشين
such *chenin* چنين
suck (v) *makidan (mak)* مکيدن
(مک)
suckle (v) *makidan (mak)* مکيدن
(مک)

sudden *nâgahâni* ناگهانی
suddenly *nâgâh* ناگاه *nâgahân*
ناگهان
suffering *ranj* رنج
sufficient *kâfi* کافی
suffix *pasvand* پسوند
suffocation *khafeqân* خفقان
Sufi *sufi* صوفی
Sufism *tasavvof* تصوف
sugar bowl *qandân* قندان
sugar cane *neyshakar* نيشکر
sugar cube *qand* قند
sugar *shekar* شکر
suggestion *pishnahâd* پيشنهاد
suicide *entehâr* انتحار (c) *khod*
koshi خودکشی
suitable *monâseb* مناسب
suitcase *chamadân* چمدان
sulphur *gugerd* گوگرد
sultanas *keshmesh* کشمش
sum *jam'* جمع *majmu'* مجموع
sumac *somâq* سماق
summary *chakide* چکيده
(c) *kholâse* خلاصه
summer crop *seyfi* صيفی
summer *tâbestân* تابستان
summit *qolle* قله
summon *farâkhâni* فراخوانی
(v) *ehzâr kardan* احضارکردن
(v) *talabidan (talab)* طلبيدن (طلب)
ehzâr احضار
sun glasses *eynak âftâbi* عينک
آفتابی
sun *âftab* آفتاب *khorshid* خورشيد
sunburnt *âftab zade* آفتاب زده

Sunday yek shanbe یکشنبه
sunflower âftâbgardân آفتاب گردان
Sunnite sonni سنی
sunny âftabi آفتابی
sunrise tolu' طلوع
sunset qorub غروب
sunshade sâybân سایبان
super power abar godrat ابرقدرت
superb âli عالی
superficial sathi سطحی zâheri ظاهری
superior mâfoq مافوق bartar برتر
superstitions mohumât موهومات khorâfât خرافات
supervision nezârat نظارت
supervisor sarparast سرپرست
supplement motammem متمم
supplementary mokammel مکمل
supplier kârpardâz کارپرداز
supplies âzuqe آذوقه
supply (c) rasândan (rasân) (رسان) رساندن
support hemâyat حمایت jânebdâri جانبداری (v) hemâyat kardan حمایت کردن
supporter tarafdâr طرفدار poshtibân پشتیبان hâmi حامی
suppose (v) farz kardan فرض کردن
supposition gomân گمان farz فرض
suppository shiyâf شیاف
supreme commander sar farmândeh سرفرمانده
sure albatte البته hatman حتماً
surf moj موج

surface sath سطح
surgeon jarrâh جراح
surgery (clinic) matab مطب
surgery (operation) jarrâhi جراحی
surname fâmily فامیلی
surplus mâzâd مازاد
surprise ta'ajjob تعجب shegefti شگفتی
surprised motahayyer متحیر mota'ajjeb متعجب
surprising ta'ajjob âvar تعجب آور shegeft angiz شگفت انگیز
surrender taslim تسلیم
surround (v) ehâte kardan احاطه کردن
surrounding mohit محیط dorobar دوروبر
surveying naqshe keshi نقشه کشی
survival baqâ بقا
suspect maznun مظنون
suspended mo'allaq معلق âvizân آویزان
suspicion shak شک zann ظن
suspicious mashkuk مشکوک shakkâk شکاک
sustenance ruzi روزی
suture bakhiye بخیه
swallow (v) bal'idan (bal') بلعیدن
swallow chelchele چلچله parastu پرستو
swallowing bal' بلع
swamp bâtlâq باتلاق
swan qu قو
sway navasân نوسان
swear (oath) qasam قسم sogand سوگند

swear (word) *nasezâ* ناسزا
(v) *fohsh dâdan* فحش دادن   *fohsh*
فحش
sweat (v) *araq kardan* عرق کردن
sweating *araq* عرق
sweep (v) *jâru kardan* جارو کردن
sweet *shirin* شیرین
sweetbrier *nastaran* نسترن
sweetness *shirini* شیرینی
swelling *âmâs* آماس
swim suit *mâyo* مایو
swimmer *shenâgar* شناگر
swimming *âbtani* آبتنی   *shenâ* شنا
switch *kelid* کلید
Switzerland *suvis* سویس
sword lily *gelâyol* گلایل
sword *shamshir* شمشیر
symbol *namâd* نماد
symmetrical *qarine* قرینه
sympathetic *delsuz* دلسوز
synagogue *kanise* کنیسه
synonym *motarâdef* مترادف
syntax *nahv* نحو
synthetic *masno'i* مصنوعی
syringe *sorang* سرنگ
syrup *sharbat* شربت
system *dastgâh* دستگاه

t

table (chart) nemudâr نمودار jadval جدول

table (e.g. office) miz میز

table football futbâl dasti فوتبال دستی

table tennis pinkponk پینک پونک

tablecloth rumizi رومیزی sofre سفره

tablet qors قرص

tact saliqe سلیقه

tactic raviyye رویه

tactile lâmese لامسه basâvâyi بساوایی

tag barchasb برچسب

tail dom دم

tailor duzande دوزنده khayyât خیاط (v) dukhtan (duz) دوختن (دوز)

take (carry) (v) bordan (bar) بردن (بر)

take (get) (v) gereftan (gir) گرفتن (گیر)

take (pick up) (v) bardâshtan (bar dâr) بر داشتن (بردار)

take a nap (v) chort zadan چرت زدن

take a seat (v) neshastan (neshin) نشستن (نشین)

take an exam (v) emtahân dâdan امتحان دادن

take into account (v) gonjândan (gonjân) گنجاندن (گنجان)

take lessons (v) dars khândan درس خواندن

take photo (v) akkâsi kardan عکاسی کردن (v) aks gereftan عکس گرفتن

taking care of (v) negahdâri نگهداری

tale sargozasht سرگذشت dâstân داستان qesse قصه

talent nobuq نبوغ este'dâd استعداد

talented mosta'ed مستعد

talk sohbat صحبت (v) harf zadan حرف زدن

talkative porchâne پرچانه harrâf حراف por harf پر حرف

tall boland بلند qadboland قدبلند

tambourine tonbak تنبک dâyere دایره daf دف

tampons tampân تمپان

tangent momâs مماس

tangible mahsus محسوس

tanner dabbâq دباغ

tannery charm sâzi چرم سازی

tap shir شیر

tape navâr نوار

tar qir قیر

target hadaf هدف neshâne نشانه

tariff ta'refe تعرفه

tassel mangule منگوله

taste maze مزه ta'm طعم (v) chashidan (chash) چشیدن (چش)

tasteless binamak بی نمک

tasty laziz لذیذ bâmaze با مزه khoshmaze خوشمزه

tattooing khâl kubi خال کوبی

taunt sarkuft سرکوفت

tax mâliyât مالیات

taxi stand *istgâhe tâksi* ایستگاه تاکسی

taxi *tâksi* تاکسی

tea cup *estekân* استکان

tea house *qahvekhâne* قهوه خانه

tea *chây* چای

teach (v) *âmuzesh dâdan* آموزش دادن
(v) *dars dâdan* درس دادن

teacher *dabir* دبیر *âmuzgâr* آموزگار
modarres مدرس
(c) *mo'allem* معلم

teaching *tadris* تدریس

team *tim* تیم

teapot *guri* قوری

tear (cry) *ashk* اشک

tearful *geryân* گریان

tease (v) *aziyyat kardan* اذیت کردن

teat *pestân* پستان

technical *fanni* فنی

technique *fann* فن

teenage *nojavâni* نوجوانی

teenager *nojavân* نوجوان

Tehran *tehrân* تهران

telegram *telegerâf* تلگراف

telephone *telefon* تلفن

telescope *teleskop* تلسکوپ

television *televiziyon* تلویزیون

tell (v) *goftan (guy)* گفتن (گوی)

telltale *choqolli* چوقلی

temper *mezâj* مزاج *tabi'at* طبیعت
kholq خلق

temperament *mezâj* مزاج

temperature (fever) *tab* تب

temperature *harârat* حرارت
(weather) *damâ* دما

tempered *âbdide* آبدیده

temple *ma'bad* معبد

temporary *movaqqat* موقت

ten *dah* ده

tenant *mosta'jer* مستاجر *kerâye neshin* کرایه نشین

tend (v) *gerâyidan (gerây)* گراییدن (گرای)

tendency *meyl* میل *tamâyol* تمایل
gerâyesh گرایش

tender (delicate) (adj) *latif* لطیف

tender (n) *mozâyede* مزایده
monâqese مناقصه

tenderness *zarâfat* ظرافت *latâfat* لطافت

tennis *tenis* تنیس

tense *zamân* زمان

tent dwelling *châdorneshini* چادر نشینی

tent *châdor* چادر

term (condition) *shart* شرط

term (period) *dore* دوره

terminal *pâyâne* پایانه

termite *muryâne* موریانه

territory *sarzamin* سرزمین
qalamro قلمرو

test result *kârnâme* کارنامه

test *emtahân* امتحان *test* تست
âzemun آزمون *âzemâyesh* آزمایش
(v) *âzemâyesh kardan* آزمایش کردن

testicle *beyze* بیضه (inf) *khâye* خایه

testimony *shahâdat* شهادت

text (c) *matn* متن *matlab* مطلب

textile factory *pârche bâfi* پارچه بافی

textile *bâftani* بافتنی

texture *bâft* بافت

thankful *mamnun* ممنون
motashakker متشکر

thanking *sepâsgozâri* سپاسگزاری

thanks *mercy* مرسی

thanksgiving *shokrgozâri*
شکرگذاری

that (complementiser) *ke* که

that (demonstrative) *ân* آن

thawed *mozâb* مذاب

theatre *te'âtr* تئاتر

theft *serqat* سرقت *dozdi* دزدی
dastbord دستبرد

theism *khodâ parasti* خداپرستی

theist *khodâ shenâs* خداشناس

then *ba'd* بعد *pas* پس

theology student *talabe* طلبه

theology *elâhiyât* الهیات

theoretical *nazari* نظری

theory *nazarriye* نظریه

therapy *darmân* درمان

thermometer *damâsanj* دماسنج

these *inhâ* اینها

thesis *pâyân nâme* پایان نامه
resâle رساله

they *ishân* ایشان (c) *ânhâ* آنها

thick *koloft* کلفت *zakhim* ضخیم

thickness *zakhâmat* ضخامت

thief *sâreq* سارق (c) *dozd* دزد

thigh *rân* ران

thin (person) *lâqar* لاغر

thin (things) *bârik* باریک *nâzok*
نازک

thing *chiz* چیز

think (v) *fekr kardan* فکر کردن

third *sâles* ثالث (c) *sevvom* سوم

thirst *atash* عطش

thirsty *teshne* تشنه

thirteen *sizdah* سیزده

thirty *si* سی

this year *emsal* امسال

this *in* این

thorn *khâr* خار

thorough *kâmel* کامل

thought *andishe* اندیشه *tafakkor*
تفکر (c) *fekr* فکر

thousand *hezâr* هزار

thread *nakh* نخ

threadbare *nakhnomâ* نخ نما

threat *tahdid* تهدید

three thundered *sisad* سیصد

three *se* سه

three-quarters *se chaharom* سه
چهارم

throat *kherkhere* خرخره (c) *galu*
گلو *holqum* حلقوم

throne *masnad* مسند

throughout *sarâsar* سراسر
sartâsar سرتاسر

thrush *barfak* برفک

thumb *shast* شست

thunder *tondar* تندر *âseman*
آسمان غره *ra'd* رعد *qorre*

Thursday *panj shanbe* پنج شنبه

thus *pas* پس

ticket *belit* بلیت

tickling *qelqelak* قلقلک

tick-skinned *pust koloft* پوست
کلفت

tide *jazro mad* جذر ومد

tidy *morattab* مرتب

tie (c) *kerâvât* كراوات *fokol* فكل
(v) *bastan (band)* بستن (بند)
(c) *gereh zadan* گره زدن

tight (e.g clothes) *chasbân* چسبان
tang تنگ

tight (strong) *mohkam* محكم *seft* سفت

tiler *kâshikâr* كاشى كار

tilt (v) *kaj shodan* كج شدن

tilted *kaj* كج

timber *alvâr* الوار *chub* چوب

time (era) *zamân* زمان

time (frequency) *bâr* بار
martabe مرتبه *daf'e* دفعه *nobat* نوبت

time (hour) *sâ'at* ساعت

timid *kamru* كمرو

timidity *sharm* شرم

tin (a metal) *qal'* قلع

tin (can) *quti* قوطى

tinsel *pulak* پولك

tiny *kuchek* كوچك (c) *riz* ريز
kuchulu كوچولو

tip (peak) *nuk* نوك

tip (reward) *an'âm* انعام

tired *khaste* خسته

tiresome *khaste konande* خسته كننده

tissue (body) *bâft* بافت *nasj* نسج

tissue (paper) *dastmâl kâqazi* دستمال كاغذى

title (e.g. of land) *sanad* سند
qabâle قباله

title (topic) *nâm* نام *onvân* عنوان

to *be* به

toady *motamalleq* متملق

toast (v) *bereshte kardan* برشته كردن

toasted *bereshte* برشته

tobacco *tanbâku* تنباكو *tutun* توتون

today *emruz* امروز

toddler *kudak* كودك

together *bâham* با هم

toilet *tuvâlet* توالت

tolerance (c) *tahammol* تحمل
shakibâyi شكيبايى

tolerant *sabur* صبور

toll *avârez* عوارض

tomato paste *robb* رب

tomato *goje farangi* گوجه فرنگى

tomb *gur* گور *zarih* ضريح *boq'e* بقعه
ârâmqâh آرامگاه

tombstone *loh* لوح

tomorrow *fardâ* فردا

tongs *anbor* انبر

tonic (syrup) *sharbat* شربت

tonight *emshab* امشب

tonsil *loze* لوزه

too *niz* نيز *hamchenin* همچنين
(c) *hamintor* همينطور

tool *abzâr* ابزار *âlat* آلت

tooth *dandân* دندان

toothbrush *mesvâk* مسواك

toothpaste *khamir dandân* خمير دندان

top (c) *bâlâ* بالا *sar* سر *sadr* صدر

topic *mozu'* موضوع *onvân* عنوان
matlab مطلب

topknot *kâkol* کاکل

topography *naqshe bardâri* نقشه برداری

torah *torât* تورات

torch (with battery) *cherâq qovve* چراغ قوه

torch *mash'al* مشعل

torment *azâb* عذاب *zajr* زجر

torn *gosikhte* گسیخته (c) *pâre* پاره

tornado *gerdbâd* گردباد

torture *shekanje* شکنجه

total *kolli* کلی

totally *kollan* کلا

touch (v) *dast zadan* دست زدن

touching *lams* لمس

touchstone *mahak* محک

tour *gardesh* گردش (c) *tur* تور

tourist *jahângard* جهانگرد

towards *be taraf e* بطرف

towel *hole* حوله

tower *borj* برج

towing *boksel* بوکسل

town *shahr* شهر

township *shahrestân* شهرستان

toxic *sammi* سمی

trace *radd* رد

trachea *nây* نای

trachoma *tarâkhom* تراخم

trade *dâdo setad* دادوستد *mo'âmele* معامله *kasb* کسب *pishe* پیشه *herfe* حرفه

trader *tâjer* تاجر

tradesman *kâseb* کاسب

tradition *rasm* رسم *sonnat* سنت *orf* عرف

traffic congestion *râh bandân* راه بندان

traffic *taraddod* تردد *rafto-âmad* رفت و آمد

tragedy *fâje'e* فاجعه

tragic *faji'* فجیع *qamangiz* غم انگیز

train *qatâr* قطار

trainee *kârâmuz* کارآموز

trainer *morabbi* مربی

traitor *khiyânat kâr* خیانت کار *khâ'en* خائن

tram *qatâr barqi* قطار برقی

tranquilliser *ârâm bakhsh* آرام بخش

tranquillity *âsudegi* آسودگی

transfer (v) *enteqâl dâdan* انتقال دادن (v) *jâbejâ kardan* جابجا کردن *enteqâl* انتقال

transformation *degarguni* دگرگونی *tahavvol* تحول

transient *gozarâ* گذرا *nâpâydâr* ناپایدار

transition *enteqâl* انتقال

translation job *motarjemi* مترجمی

translation office *dârottarjome* دارالترجمه

translation *tarjome* ترجمه

translator *motarjem* مترجم

transmission *serâyat* سرایت

transparent (c) *shaffâf* شفاف *zolâl* زلال

transportation *hamlo naql* حمل و نقل

transporters *hâmel* حامل

trap *dâm* دام

trapezoid *zuzanaqe* ذوزنقه

travel *mosâferat* مسافرت *safar* سفر

traveller *mosâfer* مسافر

tray *sini* سینی

treason *khiyânat* خیانت

treasure *ganj* گنج *ganjine* گنجینه

treasurer *khazâne dâr* خزانه دار

treasury *khazâne* خزانه

treat (v) *mo'âleje kardan* معالجه کردن

treatment *mo'âleje* معالجه

treaty *peymân* پیمان *mo'âhede* معاهده *qarârdâd* قرارداد *ahdnâme* عهدنامه

tree *derakht* درخت

tremble (v) *larzidan (larz)* لرزیدن (لرز)

tremor *ra'she* رعشه *larzesh* لرزش

trench *sangar* سنگر

trial (court) *mohâkeme* محاکمه

trial (test) *emtahân* امتحان

triangular *segush* سه گوش

tribal chief *khân* خان

tribe *qabile* قبیله *il* ایل *tâyefe* طایفه *qom* قوم

trick *neyrang* نیرنگ *bâmbul* بامبول *hoqqe* حقه *hile* حیله (c) *kalak* کلک *kalak zadan* (v) کلک زدن

tricycle *secharkhe* سه چرخه

tridimensional *sebo'di* سه بعدی

trigger (of a gun) *mâshe* ماشه

trim (v) *kutâh karadan* کوتاه کردن (v) *morattab kardan* مرتب کردن

trinity *taslis* تثلیث

trip *mosâferat* مسافرت *safar* سفر

triplet *seqolu* سه قلو

tripod *sepâye* سه پایه

triumph *qalabe* غلبه *piruzi* پیروزی

trivial *joz'i* جزئی *nâchiz* ناچیز

troops *qoshun* قشون

tropical *garmsir* گرمسیر

trouble (c) *moshkel* مشکل *gereftâri* گرفتاری

trousers *shalvâr* شلوار

trousseau *jahiziye* جهیزیه

trowel *mâle* ماله

truck *bârkesh* بارکش (c) *kâmiyon* کامیون

true *sahih* صحیح *haqiqi* حقیقی (c) *dorost* درست *râst* راست

trumpet *sheypur* شیپور

truncated *monqate'* منقطع

trunk *badane* بدنه *tane* تنه

trust *bâvar* باور *etminân* اطمینان *e'temâd* اعتماد (v) *e'temâd kardan* اعتماد کردن (v) *etminân kardan* اطمینان کردن

trustworthy *amin* امین

truth *râsti* راستی *haqiqat* حقیقت

truthfulness *râst guyi* راست گویی

try on (v) *emtahân kardan* امتحان کردن

tube *lule* لوله

tuberculosis *sel* سل

Tuesday *seshanbe* سه شنبه

tuition fee *shahriye* شهریه

tulip *lâle* لاله

tumble (v) *qaltidan (qalt)* غلتیدن (غلت)

tummy *shekam* شکم

tumour *qodde* غده

tune *âhang* آهنگ

tunnel (c) *tunel* تونل *naqb* نقب

turban *ammâme* عمامه

turkey (bird) *boqalamun* بوقلمون

Turkey *torkiye* ترکیه

Turkish bath *garmâbe* گرمابه
hammam حمام

turmeric *zardchube* زردچوبه

turmoil *dâdo bidâd* دادوبیداد

turn (v) *gashtan (gard)* (گرد) گشتن
(v) *pichidan (pich)* (پیچ) پیچیدن
nobe نوبه *nobat* نوبت

turnip *shalqam* شلغم

turquoise *firuze* فیروزه

turtle *lâkposht* لاک پشت

twelve *davazdah* دوازده

twentieth *bistom* بیستم

twenty *bist* بیست

twice *dobâr* دوبار

twig *nahâl* نهال

twilight *sahar* سحر

twinge *suzesh* سوزش

twins *doqulu* دوقلو

twist *tâb* تاب *pich khordegi* پیچ
پیچ *pich* خوردگی

twittering *chahchahe* چهچهه

two thundered *divist* دویست

two way *dotarafe* دوسره

two *do* دو

type *tip* تیپ *no'* نوع (v) *tâyp* تایپ
کردن

typhoid fever *hasbe* حصبه

typhoon *tufân* طوفان

typical *âdi* عادی *no'i* نوعی

tyre *lâstik* لاستیک

u

ugliness *zeshti* زشتی

ultimatum *oltimâtom* التیماتوم

ultrasound *ulterâsând* اولتراساند

umbilicus *nâf* ناف

umbrella *chatr* چتر

umpire *dâvar* داور

unable *âjez* عاجز *nâtavân* ناتوان

unaware *bikhabar* بی خبر

uncertain *moraddad* مردد

uncertainty *ebhâm* ابهام

unchaste *nânajib* نانجیب

unclean *nâpâk* ناپاک

uncooked *nâpokhte* ناپخته

under *pâyiyn* پایین *zir* زیر

underage *saqir* صغیر

underground *zirzamini* زیرزمینی

underpants *zirshalvâri* زیرشلواری

undershirt *zirpirâhan* زیر پیراهن

understand (v) *fahmidam (fahm)* فهمیدن (فهم)

understanding *fahm* فهم

underwear *zirpush* زیرپوش

undesirable *nâmatbu'* نامطبوع

unemployed *bikâr* بیکار

unemployment *bikâri* بیکاری

uneven *nâhamvâr* ناهموار

unexpectedly *sarzade* سرزده

unfair *nâhaq* ناحق

unfinished *nime kâre* نیمه کاره

unfit *nabâb* ناباب

unfortunate (c) *badbakht* بدبخت *falakzade* فلک زده

unfortunately *mota'assefâne* متاسفانه

ungrateful *nâshokr* ناشکر

unhappy *nârâhat* ناراحت

uniform *rupush* روپوش

unintelligible *nâmafhum* نامفهوم

unintentional *qeyre amdi* غیر عمدی

union *ettehâd* اتحاد

unions *ettehadiye* اتحادیه

unique *tak* تک

united *mottahed* متحد

universe *gity* گیتی (c) *hasti* هستی *âlam* عالم

university *dâneshgâh* دانشگاه

unjust *zâlemâne* ظالمانه

unkind *nâmehrabân* نامهربان

unknown *gomnâm* گمنام *nâshenâs* ناشناس

unless *magar* مگر

unlikely *ba'id* بعید

unlimited *nâmahdud* نامحدود

unmanly *nâ javân mard* ناجوانمرد

unnatural *qeyre tabiyi* غیر طبیعی

unpleasant *nâgovâr* ناگوار

unripe *nâras* نارس *kâl* کال

unsafe *nâ amn* نا امن

unsaid *nâgofte* ناگفته

unstable *motaqayyer* متغیر

untidy *nâmorattab* نامرتب

until *tâ* تا

untimely *nâbehengâm* نابهنگام

untrue *kâzeb* کاذب

unusual *qyre addi* غیر عادی

unwanted *nâkhâste* ناخواسته
unwell *mariz* مریض
up *bâlâ* بالا
uphill *sarbâlâyi* سربالایی
uprising *qiyâm* قیام
upset stomach *rudel* رودل
upside down *ma'kus* معکوس
urban *shahri* شهری
urgent *ezterâri* اضطراری *fori* فوری
urinal *lagan* لگن
urinate (v)(inf) *jish kardan* جیش
کردن (v)(c) *edrâr kardan* ادرار کردن
(v)(inf) *shâshidan (shâsh)* شاشیدن
(شاش)
urine *jish* جیش (c) *edrâr* ادرار
shâsh شاش
us *mâ* ما
USA *iyâlâte mottahedeye âmrikâ*
ایالات متحده آمریکا
usage *masraf* مصرف *kârbord*
کاربرد
use *estefâde* استفاده *fâyede* فایده
(v) *este'mâl kardan* استعمال کردن
(v) *estefâde kardan* استفاده کردن
used *kohne* کهنه
useful *mofid* مفید
usual *motadâvel* متداول *âdi* عادی
ma'mul معمول *ma'muli* معمولی
usually *ma'mulan* معمولا
usurer *nozul khâr* نزول خوار *rebâ
khâr* ربا خوار
usury *rebâ* ربا
utensil *zarf* ظرف
uterus *rahem* رحم
utmost *nahâyat* نهایت

V

vacant *khâli* خالی
vacation *ta'tilat* تعطیلات
vaccination *vâksinâsyon* واکسیناسیون
vagabond *darbedar* دربدر *lât* لات
vagina *mahbel* مهبل (inf) *kos* کس
vague *mobham* مبهم
vain (c) *puch* پوچ *abas* عبث
valency *zarfiyyat* ظرفیت
valid *mo'tabar* معتبر
valley *darre* دره
value *bahâ* بها *arj* ارج (c) *arzesh* ارزش *qadr* قدر
valve *dariche* دریچه *supâp* سوپاپ
van *vânet* وانت
vanity *takabbor* تکبر
vapour *bokhâr* بخار
variable *motaqayyer* متغیر
varied *motafâvet* متفاوت
various *rangârang* رنگارنگ *mokhtalef* مختلف *gunâgun* گوناگون
vase *goldân* گلدان
vast *pahnâvar* پهناور
vegetables *sabzi* سبزی
vehicles *vasâyele naqliye* وصایل نقلیه
veil *neqâb* نقاب *ruband* روبند
vein *siyâhrag* سیاهرگ *rag* رگ
velocity *shetâb* شتاب
velvet *makhmal* مخمل
venereal *moqârebati* مقاربتی *âmizeshi* آمیزشی
venesection *hejâmat* حجامت
Venetian blinds *kerkere* کرکره

vengeance *enteqâm* انتقام
venom *samm* سم *zahr* زهر
ventilation *tahviye* تهویه
venue *mahal* محل
Venus *nâhid* ناهید *zohre* زهره
verb *fe'l* فعل
verbal *lafzi* لفظی *shafâhi* شفاهی
verbose *harrâf* حراف
verification *ta'yiyd* تایید
verse (of Koran) *âye* آیه
vertebra *mohre* مهره
vertebrate *mohre dârân* مهره داران
vertical *amudi* عمودی
vertigo *sargije* سرگیجه
very *kheyli* خیلی
vessel (ship) *kashti* کشتی *nâv* ناو
vessel (vein) *rag* رگ
vestibule *dehliz* دهلیز
veterinary *dâm pezeshki* دامپزشکی
via *tavassot* توسط
vibration *navasân* نوسان *erte'âsh* ارتعاش
vice president *nâyeb ra'is* نایب رئیس
vice versa *baraks* برعکس
vicinity *havâli* حوالی
victim *to'me* طعمه *âsib dide* آسیب دیده (c) *qorbâni* قربانی
victory *fath* فتح (c) *piruzi* پیروزی
view point *negaresh* نگرش
view *durnamâ* دورنما *manzare* منظره *cheshmandâz* چشم انداز *did* دید
viewer *binande* بیننده
viewpoint *didgâh* دیدگاه

village (c) *deh* ده *qariye* قریه
rustâ روستا

villager *rustâyi* روستایی (c) *dehâti*
دهاتی

villages *dehât* دهات

vine *mo* مو

vinegar *serke* سرکه

vineyard *tâkestân* تاکستان

violation *naqz* نقض *takhallof*
تخلف

violence *dast derâzi* دست درازی

violet (colour) *banafsh* بنفش

violet (flower) *banafshe* بنفشه

viper *af'i* افعی

virgin *bâkereh* باکره

virginity *bakârat* بکارت

virtue *hosn* حسن *fazl* فضل
taqvâ تقوا

virus *virus* ویروس

visa *ravâdid* روادید *vizâ* ویزا

viscosity *qelzat* غلظت

visible *mar'i* مرئی

vision *binâyi* بینایی

visit *molâqât* ملاقات *didâr* دیدار
(v) *didan (bin)* دیدن (بین) (v) *didâr
kardan* دیدار کردن

visitor (guest) *mehmân* مهمان

visitor (in jail) *molâqâti* ملاقاتی

visual *binâyi* بینایی

vital *hayâti* حیاتی

vitamin *vitâmin* ویتامین

vocal *nâteq* ناطق

voice *sot* صوت (c) *sedâ* صدا

voiced *sedâdâr* صدادار *mosavvat*
مصوت

voiceless *bivâk* بی واک

void *khâli* خالی (c) *bâtel* باطل

volatile *farrâr* فرار

volcano *âtash feshân* آتشفشان

volume (copy) *jeld* جلد

volume (measurement) *hajm*
حجم *gonjâyesh* گنجایش

voluntarily *dâvtalabâne* داوطلبانه

volunteer *dâvtalab* داوطلب

voluptuous *shahvat parast* شهوت
پرست

vomit (v) *estefrâq kardan* استفراغ
کردن *qayy* قی (c) *estefrâq* استفراغ

vote *ra'y* رای

vowel *mosavvat* مصوت *vâke* واکه

voyeurism *cheshmcharâni* چشم
چرانی

vulgar *âmiyâne* عامیانه

vulture *karkas* کرکس *lâshkhor*
لاشخور

w

wage dastranj دسترنج dastmozd
دستمزد (c) mozd مزد mavâjeb
مواجب

wailing faqân فغان zuze زوزه

waist kamar کمر

wait (v) istâdan (ist) (ایست) ایستادن
(v) motazer budan منتظر بودن

waiter khedmatkâr خدمتکار
(c) gârson گارسن pish khedmat
پیشخدمت

wake up (v) bidâr shodan بیدار شدن

wall flower shabbu شب بو

wall divâr دیوار

walnut gerdo گردو

wanderer sargardân سرگردان

want (v) khâstan (khâh) خواستن
(خواه)

war game mânovr مانور

war nabard نبرد nezâ' نزاع
(c) jang جنگ

wardrobe ganje گنجه komod کمد

warehouse anbâr انبار

warm garm گرم

warm-blooded khun garm خون
گرم

warn (v) ekhtâr kardan اخطار کردن

warning ebrat عبرت (c) ekhtâr
اخطار tazakkor تذکر

warrant officer ostovâr استوار

warrant mojavvez مجوز

warranty tazmin تضمین zamânat
ضمانت

warship nâv ناو

wart zegil زگیل

wash stand dast shuyi دستشویی

wash (v) shostan (shur) شستن
(شور)

washing machine mashine
lebasshuyi ماشین لباس شویی

washing shosteshu شستشو

wasp zanbur زنبور

waste (v) esrâf kardan اسراف کردن
talaf تلف

watch out (v) ehtiyât kardan احتیاط
کردن (v) pâyiydan (pây) پاییدن
(پای)

watch (n) sâ'at ساعت

watch (v) tamâshâ kardan
تماشاکردن

watchmaker sâ'at sâz ساعت ساز

watchman gârd گارد negahbân
نگهبان

water colour âbrang آب رنگ

water heater âbgarmkon آب
گرمکن

water sprinkler âbpâsh آب پاش

water âb آب

waterfall âbshar آبشار

watermelon hendevâne هندوانه

watery raqiq رقیق

wave moj موج

wavy ferferi فرفری mojdar دار موج

wax mum موم

way râh راه

we mâ ما

weak za'if ضعیف

weakening taz'if تضعیف

weakness za'f ضعف

wealth servat ثروت

wealthy *puldâr* پولدار *qani* غنی
servat mand ثروتمند

weapons *aslahe* اسلحه

wear out (v) *farsudan (farsâ)*
فرسودن (فرسا)

wear (v) *pushidan (push)* پوشیدن
(پوش)

weary *bizâr* بیزار *khaste* خسته

weasel *râsu* راسو

weather cock *bâdnamâ* بادنما

weather *havâ* هوا *âbohavâ* آب و
هوا

weave (v) *bâftan (bâ)* بافتن (باف)

weaving *nassâji* نساجی

wedding *ezdevâj* ازدواج *arusi*
عروسی

wedlock *arusi* عروسی

Wednesday *châhârshanbe*
چهارشنبه

week *hafte* هفته

weep (v) *gerye kardan* گریه کردن

weeping *gerye* گریه

welcome (v) *esteqbâl kardan*
استقبال کردن *khoshâmad* خوشامد
pishvâz پیشواز

welder *jushkâr* جوش کار

welfare *âfiyat* عافیت (c) *refâh* رفاه

well (hole) *châh* چاه

well (ok) *khub* خوب

well being *sehhat* صحت

well digger *châh kan* چاه کن
moqanni مقنی

well done *mâshâllâ* ماشالله
(c) *âfarin* آفرین *bârakallâh* بارک الله

well known *sarshenâs* سرشناس
mashhur مشهور

west *maqreb* مغرب *qarb* غرب

western *qarbi* غربی

westerner *farangi* فرنگی (c) *qarbi*
غربی

westernised *farangi ma'âb* فرنگی
ماب *qarb zade* غربزده (c) ماب

wet *khis* خیس *tar* تر

whale *nahang* نهنگ

what time *key* کی

what (c) *chi* چی *che* چه

wheat *gandom* گندم

wheel *charkh* چرخ

wheelchair *sandaliye charkhdar*
صندلی چرخدار

when *key* کی

where *kojâ* کجا

whether *che* چه

which *kodâm* کدام

whimper *nâle* ناله

whimsical *mohum* موهوم

whip *tâziyâne* تازیانه

whirligig *ferfere* فرفره

whirlpool *gerdâb* گرداب

whiskers *sebil* سبیل

whisper *najvâ* نجوا *pechpech*
پچ پچ *zamzame* زمزمه

whistle *sut* سوت

white skin *sefid pust* سفید پوست

white *sefid* سفید

who *ki* کی

whole *hame* همه *koll* کل *tamâm*
تمام

wholesale *omdeforushi* عمده فروشی

wholesaler *omde forush* عمده
فروش

whom ki کی

whooping cough siyâh sorfe سیاه سرفه

whore lakkâte لکاته fâheshe فاحشه (c) jende جنده qahbe قحبه ruspi روسپی khodforush خودفروش

whorehouse fâheshe khâne فاحشه خانه

whoremonger khânom bâz خانم باز

why cherâ چرا

wick fetile فتیله

wicked palid پلید bad jens بد جنس khabis خبیث razl رذل sharur شرور nâbekâr نابکار

wickedness sharârat شرارت

wide pahn پهن goshâd گشاد

widespread shâye' شایع

widow bive بیوه arz عرض

width pahnâ پهنا

wife ayâl عیال (c) zan زن

wig kolâh gis کلاه گیس

will (death will) vasiyyat وصیت

will (intention) qasd قصد erâde اراده

win (v) bordan (bar) بردن (بر) (v) barande shodan برنده شدن

wind bâd باد

windfall qanimat غنیمت

window panjare پنجره

windy bâdi بادی

wine (c) sharâb شراب mey می

wing (e.g. bird) bâl بال

wing (e.g. party) jenâh جناح

wink (v) cheshmak zadan چشمک زدن

winner barande برنده

winter zemestân زمستان

wiped out (v) mahv kardan محو کردن

wipers barf pakkon برف پاکن

wire sim سیم

wireless bisim بی سیم

wireman simkesh سیمکش

wisdom aql عقل

wise kherad mand خردمند fahmide فهمیده âqel عاقل

wisely âqelâne عاقلانه

wish (v) ârezu kardan آرزو کردن (c) ârezu آرزو morâd مراد

wishbone janâq جناق

with bâ با

withdraw (v) aqab neshini kardan عقب نشینی کردن (v) kenâr raftan کنار رفتن

withdrawal aqab neshini عقب نشینی

withdrawn gushe gir گوشه گیر

without bedune بدون bi بی

witness shâhed شاهد govâh گواه

wolf gorg گرگ

woman zan زن

womaniser zanbâz زن باز

womb rahem رحم

wonder (v) ta'ajjob kardan تعجب کردن

wood chub چوب takhte تخته

woodpecker dârkub دارکوب

woof pud پود

wool spinning pashm risi پشم ریسی

wool pashm پشم

woollen pashmi پشمی

word (c) kalame کلمه lafz لفظ loqat لغت

work out narmesh نرمش

work (v) kâr kardan کار کردن kâr کار

worker kârgar کارگر

workshop kârgâh کارگاه

world cup jâme jahâni جام جهانی

world ruzgâr روزگار donyâ دنیا jahân جهان

worm kerm کرم

worn out (c) kohne کهنه mondares مندرس mostahlak مستهلک

worried moztareb مضطرب negarân نگران

worry ezterâb اضطراب daqdaqe دغدغه (c) negarâni نگرانی

worship setâyesh ستایش (v) ebâdat kardan عبادت کردن (v) parastidan (parast) پرستیدن (پرست) ebâdat عبادت parastesh پرستش

worshiper setâyesh gar ستایشگر

worth arzesh ارزش

worthy sezâvâr سزاوار qâbel قابل shâyeste شایسته

wound jarâhat جراحت (c) zakhm زخم

wounded zakhmi زخمی majruh مجروح

wrap (v) bastebandi kardan بسته بندی کردن (v) pichidan (pich) پیچیدن (پیچ)

wrapping bastebandi بسته بندی

wrath asabâniyat عصبانیت khashm خشم

wrathful qazabnâk غضبناک

wrench (v) chelândan (chelân) چلاندن (چلان)

wrestling koshti کشتی

wriggle (v) lulidan (lul) لولیدن (لول)

wrinkle chin چین (v) chin khordan چین خوردن choruk چروک

wrinkled chin khorde چین خورده

wrist moch مچ

write (v) nagâshtan (negâr) نگاشتن (نگار) (v)(c) neveshtan (nevis) نوشتن (نویس)

writer mo'allef مولف negârande نگارنده (c) nevisande نویسنده

writing nevisandegi نویسندگی ta'lif تالیف

written katbi کتبی

wrong (c) qalat غلط avazi عوضی

y

yard *hayât* حیاط

yawn *khamyâze* خمیازه
dahandarre دهن دره

year *sâl* سال

yearly *sâliyâne* سالیانه

yeast *mâye* مایه *mokhammer* مخمر

yell *faryâd* فریاد (v) *na're zadan* نعره زدن *na're* نعره

yellow *zard* زرد

yelping *zuze* زوزه

yes *bale* بله (inf) *âre* آره

yesterday *diruz* دیروز

yield *sud* سود

yoghurt *mâst* ماست

yogi *mortâz* مرتاض

yolk *zarde* زرده

you (plural/polite) *shomâ* شما

you (singular/familiar) *to* تو

young *javân* جوان

youngster *nojavân* نوجوان

youth *javâni* جوانی

z

zeal *qeyrat* غیرت
zealous *mota'asseb* متعصب
zebra *gurkhar* گورخر
zero *sefr* صفر
zinc *roy* روی
Zionism *sahyonism* صهیونیسم
zipper *zip* زیپ
zone *mantaqe* منطقه
zoo *bâq vahsh* باغ وحش
zoology *jânavar shenâsi* جانورشناسی
Zoroastrian *zartosht* زرتشت
Zoroastrians *zartoshti* زرتشتی
zygote *notfe* نطفه

a

âb darmâni آب درمانی hydrotherapy

âb kardan آب کردن to melt something

âb raftan آب رفتن to shrink

âb shodan آب شدن to melt

âb آب water

abâ عبا clergy's cloak

âbâd آباد habitable, inhabited

abad ابد forever, eternity

ab'âd ابعاد dimensions

abadan ابدا never, not at all

âbâdi آبادی habituation, village

âbân آبان eighth month of Iranian calendar

abar godrat ابرقدرت super power

abas عبث vain, useless

âbdâr آبدار juicy

âbdide آبدیده tempered

âbe garm آب گرم hot water

âbe ma'dani آب معدنی mineral water

âbe mive آب میوه juice

âbele آبله smallpox

âber bank عابر بانک automatic teller

âber عابر pedestrian, passer-by

âberu rizi آبروریزی disgrace, discredit

âberu آبرو respect, honour, credit

âbestan shodan آبستن شدن to get pregnant

âbestan آبستن pregnant

âbgarmkon آب گرمکن water heater

âbgusht آبگوشت broth, soup

âbi آبی blue

âbjo آبجو beer

âbkesh آبکش strainer

ablah ابله stupid, silly

âbnabât آب نبات lollipop, candy

âbnumân shodan آبونمان شدن to subscribe

âbnumân آبونمان subscription

âbohavâ آب و هوا weather, climate

âbpâsh آب پاش water sprinkler

âbpaz آب پز boiled in water

abr ابر cloud

âbrang آب رنگ water colour

abri ابری cloudy

abrisham ابریشم silk

abru ابرو eyebrow

âbshar آبشار waterfall

âbtani kardan آبتنی کردن to bath, to swim

âbtani آبتنی bathing, swimming

abus عبوس frowning, cross, stern

âbyâr آبیار irrigator

âbyâri kardan آبیاری کردن to irrigate

âbyâri آبیاری irrigation

abzâr ابزار tool, device

âbzi آبزی aqueous, marine

âchâr آچار screw driver

adab kardan ادب کردن to discipline

âdâb آداب ceremonies, formalities

adab ادب politeness, discipline, civility

153 ADABIYYÂT

adabiyyât ادبیات literature

a'dâd اعداد numbers, digits

adad عدد number, figure, digit

adâlat عدالت justice, fairness

âdam kosh آدمکش assassin, killer

âdam koshi آدمکشی homicide, murder

âdam آدم human, mankind, person

adam عدم absence, lack

âdâms آدامس chewing gum

adas عدس lentil

adasi عدسی lens, lentiform

âdat kardan عادت کردن to be addicted, to habituate

âdat عادت habit, practice, custom, menstruation

âddi عادی typical, ordinary

âdel عادل fair, just

adelâne عادلانه justly

âdi عادی ordinary, usual, typical

adl عدل justice, fairness

âdres آدرس address

adviye ادویه spices, condiments

âfaridan (âfarin) آفریدن (آفرین) to create

âfarin آفرین well done!

âfat آفت pest, plague

af'i افعی viper

âfiyat bashe! عافیت باشه bless you!

âfiyat عافیت health, welfare, happiness

afrâd افراد individuals

afrâshtan (afrâz) افراشتن (افراز) to raise, to elevate

afrukhtan (afruz) افروختن (افروز) to light, to provoke

afsâne افسانه fiction, myth

afsâr افسار bridle, head-stall

afsar افسر officer

afsorde افسرده depressed

afsordegi افسردگی depression

afsun افسون charm, spell

afsus افسوس regret, alas

âftab zade آفتاب زده sunburnt, sunstruck

âftab آفتاب sun

âftâbe آفتابه ewer

âftâbgardân آفتاب گردان sunflower

âftabi آفتابی sunny

afv kardan عفو کردن to forgive

afv عفو forgiveness, pardon

afzâyesh dâshtan افزایش داشتن to increase

afzâyesh افزایش increase, growth

âgâh kardan آگاه کردن to warn, to inform

âgâh آگاه aware, conscious

âgahi kardan آگهی کردن to advertise, to announce

âgahi آگهی advertisement, announcement

agar اگر if, in case

âh keshidan آه کشیدن to sigh

âh آه sigh, alas

âhak آهک lime

ahâli اهالی inhabitants, citizens

ahamiyat اهمیت importance, significance

âhan robâ آهن ربا magnet

âhan آهن iron
âhang آهنگ tune, music
âhangar آهنگر blacksmith
âhangsâz آهنگ ساز composer
ahd kardan عهد کردن to promise
ahd عهد agreement, era, oath
ahdâf اهداف goals, aims
ahdnâme عهدنامه treaty, pact
âheste آهسته slow, soft
ahkâm احکام commands, orders, sentences
ahl اهل native, inhabitant, citizen
ahli اهلی domestic, pet
ahmaq احمق fool, stupid
ahriman اهریمن devil, Satan
ahrom اهرم lever
âhu آهو deer
ahvâl احوال conditions, states
âj عاج ivory
ajab عجب surprising, wonderful
ajal اجل death, the hour of death
ajale kardan عجله کردن to hurry
ajale عجله hurry, rush
ajdâd اجداد ancestors
âjez عاجز unable, disabled, unfit
ajib عجیب strange, bizarre
âjil آجیل dried nuts and fruits
ajir kardan اجیر کردن to hire
ajir اجیر hired worker, mercenary
ajnabi اجنبی foreigner, alien, outsider
ajnâs اجناس goods, commodities
âjor آجر brick
ajr اجر reward, compensation

ajsâm اجسام bodies, substances, materials
ajul عجول hasty, impatient
ajzâ' اجزا parts, components
âkh آخ ouch! oh!
âkhar آخر last, end, finish
akhbâr اخبار news information
âkherat آخرت futurity, afterlife
âkherin آخرین final, latest, the last one
âkherozzamân آخر الزمان end of the world
akhir اخیر recent, late, last
akhiran اخیرا recently
akhlâq اخلاق morals, ethics, habits
akhm اخم frown, disapproving look
âkhor آخور manger
âkhund آخوند clergy, theologian
akidan اکیدا strictly, emphatically
akkâs عکاس photographer
akkâsi kardan عکاسی کردن to take photo
akkâsi عکاسی photography
aknun اکنون now, at present
aks gereftan عکس گرفتن to take photo
aks عکس photo, picture, image
aksaran اکثرا mostly, generally
aksariyyat اکثریت majority
aksbardâri عکسبرداری taking an X ray
aksbargardân عکس بر گردان sticker
aksolamal عکس العمل reaction, reflex
alaf علف grass, herb

alâj علاج cure, remedy

alaki الكی groundless, phoney

âlam عالم world, universe

alam علم banner, flag

alâmat علامت sign, mark, proof

alâmate ekhtesâri علامت اختصاری abbreviation

alamshange الم شنگه commotion, nuisance

alân الان now, just now

alangu النگو bracelet

alani علنی open, public, overt

alâqe علاقه interest, concern, affection

alâqemand علاقمند interested, concerned

âlât آلات instruments, tools

âlat آلت tool, penis

alâve bar علاوه بر in addition to

âlbâlu آلبالو black cherry

albatte البته of course, sure

âlbom آلبوم collection, album

aldang الدنگ clown, lout

alefbâ الفبا alphabet

âlem عالم scientist, scholar

aleyh علیه against, opposed

âli عالی sublime, grand, superb

alil علیل invalid, disabled

alkan الکن stutterer

alkol الکل alcohol

allâh الله God

allâkolang آلاکلنگ see-saw

âlmân آلمان Germany

almâs الماس diamond

almosannâ المثنی duplicate copy

alo الو hello! (answering)

âlu آلو plum

âluche آلوچه prunes

âlude kardan آلوده کردن to contaminate, to pollute

âlude آلوده contaminated, polluted

âludegi آلودگی pollution

âlunak آلونک hut, shanty house

alvâr الوار timber

alvât الواط rascal, wanton

âlyâzh آلیاژ alloy

âmadan (ây) آمدن (آی) to come

âmâde kardan آماده کردن to prepare

âmâde آماده ready, prepared

âmâdegi آمادگی readiness, fitness

amâken اماکن places, locations

amal kardan عمل کردن to act, to operate

âmâl آمال desires, hopes

amal عمل act, action, operation

amalan عملا practically

amale عمله labourer

amali عملی practical, addict

amaliyyât عملیات operations, procedures

amalkard عملکرد function, revenue

amân امان safety, security, amnesty

amânat امانت honesty, deposit

âmâr آمار statistics, census

âmâs آماس swelling, edema

âmbulâns آمبولانس ambulance

amdi عمدی deliberate, intentional, on purpose

âmel عامل agent, factor

âmikhtan (âmiz) (آمیختن)آمیز to mix, to blend

âmikhte آمیخته mixed

âmin آمین amen!

amin امین trustworthy, honest

amiq عمیق deep, profound

amir امیر prince, chief

âmiyâne عامیانه slang, vulgar, folk

âmizesh kardan آمیزش کردن to make an intercourse

âmizesh آمیزش intercourse

âmizeshi آمیزشی venereal

amlâk املاک estates, properties

ammâ اما but

ammâme عمامه turban

âmme عامه common people, the public

amme عمه paternal aunt

amn امن peaceful, safe

amniyat امنیت security, peace

âmorzesh آمرزش forgiveness

âmpul zandan آمپول زدن to give a shot, to give an injection

âmpul آمپول shot, injection

amrâz امراض diseases

amri امری imperative

amu عمو paternal uncle

amudi عمودی vertical

âmukhtan (âmuz) (آموختن)آموز to learn

âmuzande آموزنده instructive

âmuzesh dâdan آموزش دادن to instruct, to teach

âmuzesh didan آموزش دیدن to learn, to take lessons

âmuzesh آموزش instruction, education

âmuzeshgâh آموزشگاه education center

âmuzgâr آموزگار teacher

amvâj امواج waves, tides

amvât اموات the dead

ân آن that, he, she, it

an'âm انعام tip (gratuity)

ânânâs آناناس pineapple

anâr انار pomegranate

anbâr انبار warehouse, store

anbe انبه mango

anbiyâ انبیا prophets

anbor انبر tongs, nippers

anbuh انبوه thick, crowded

andak اندک little, few

andâm اندام body, limb, organ

andâze اندازه size, measure

andishe اندیشه thought, contemplation

anduh اندوه grief, sorrow

ânfulânzâ آنفولانزا flue, influenza

angal انگل parasite

angikhtan انگیختن to motivate, to stimulate

angize انگیزه motivation, stimulant

angosht kardan انگشت کردن to put finger in, to tamper, to molest

angosht انگشت finger

angoshtar انگشتر ring (on finger)

angur انگور grapes
âni آنی instantly, immediately
anjâm dâdan انجام دادن to do, to fulfil
anjâm انجام fulfilment, ending
anjir انجیر fig
anjoman انجمن association, assembly
ankabut عنکبوت spider
ânten آنتن antenna, aerial
ântibiyutik آنتی بیوتیک antibiotics
anvâ' انواع kinds, sorts
âpândis آپاندیس appendix (body part)
âqâ آقا Mr., sir, gentleman
aqab neshini kardan عقب نشینی کردن to retreat, to withdraw
aqab neshini عقب نشینی retreat, withdrawal
aqab oftâde عقب افتاده retarded, remaining behind
aqab عقب back, behind, rear
aqallan اقلا at least
aqalliyat اقلیت minority
âqâz kardan آغاز کردن to start, to begin
âqâz آغاز start, beginning
aqd عقد marriage contract
âqebat عاقبت at last, end, conclusion
âqed عاقد a notary marrying a couple
âqel عاقل wise, sane
âqelâne عاقلانه wisely, wise
aqide dâshtan عقیده داشتن to believe

aqide عقیده belief, faith, opinion
aqim عقیم barren, sterile
aqiq عقیق agate
aql عقل wisdom, intellect, common sense
aqlab اغلب often
aqlâni عقلانی intellectual, rational
aqrab عقرب scorpion
aqrabe عقربه hand (of watch)
aqsâm اقسام kinds, varieties
aqsât اقساط instalment, portions
âqush آغوش hug
aqvâm اقوام tribes, ethnic groups
âr عار shame, disgrace
arab عرب Arab
arabestân عربستان Saudi Arabia
ârâm bakhsh آرام بخش sedative, tranquilliser
ârâm kardan آرام کردن to soothe, to calm down
ârâm آرام quiet, pacific
ârâmesh آرامش rest, peace, relaxation
ârâmqâh آرامگاه tomb, grave
araq kardan عرق کردن to sweat, to perspire
araq khor عرق خور habitual drinker
arâq عراق Iraq
araq عرق sweating, perspiration, spirit, distillate
araqgir عرق گیر singlet, underwear
ârâye umumi آرای عمومی polls
ârâyesh آرایش make-up
ârâyeshgâh آرایشگاه barber shop, hair dressing

ârâyeshgar آرایشگر hairdresser, barber

arâzel اراذل hoodlums, rascals

arâzi اراضی lands, territories

arbâb ruju ارباب رجوع client

arbâb ارباب boss, masters

arbade عربده drunken brawl

ârd آرد flour

âre آره yes (info)

ârenj آرنج elbow

âreze عارضه complication, happening

ârezu kardan آرزو کردن to wish

ârezu آرزو wish, desire

ârezumand آرزومند hopeful, eager

âriyâ آریا Aryan race

arj ارج value, esteem

arjomand ارجمند valuable, respected

ârmân آرمان ideal, aim

armani ارمنی Armenian

armaqân ارمغان present, souvenir

âroq zadan آروغ زدن to burp

âroq آروغ burp

arqâm ارقام figures, numbers

arqavâni ارغوانی purple

arre kardan اره کردن to saw

arre اره saw

arse عرصه field, arena

arshad ارشد elder, senior

arshe عرشه deck

ârshiv آرشیو archives

artesh ارتش army, military

arus عروس bride, daughter-in-law

arusak عروسک doll

arusi kardan عروسی کردن to marry

arusi عروسی wedding, marriage, wedlock

arvâh ارواح spirits, ghosts

ârvâre آرواره jaw

arz ارز foreign currency, exchange

arz عرض width, breadth, remark

arzân ارزان cheap, inexpensive

arzesh ارزش value, worth

ârzhântin آرژانتین Argentina

âs آس ace

asâ عصا cane, stick

asab عصب nerve

asabâni عصبانی angry, furious, nervous

asabâniyat عصبانیت anger, wrath

asabi عصبی nervous, touchy

asal عسل honey

âsân آسان easy

âsânsor آسانسور elevator

asar gozâshtan اثر گذاشتن to affect, to impress

asar اثر effect, result, impression

asâs اثاث furniture

asâs اساس basis, foundation

asâsi اساسی principle, basic

asâsnâme اساسنامه constitution, fundamental

âsâyesh آسایش relaxation, convenience

âsâyeshgâh آسایشگاه sanatorium

asb savari اسب سواری horse riding

asb اسب horse

asbâb اسباب means, tools, instruments

âsemân kharâsh آسمان خراش sky scraper

âsemân qorre آسمان غره thunder

âsemân آسمان sky

âsh آش soap, porridge

âshâmidani آشامیدنی beverage

ash'âr اشعار poems

a'shâr اعشار decimal

ashâyer عشایر tribes, nomads

ashe'e اشعه rays

âshenâ shodan آشنا acquaintance, friend, familiar

âshenâ آشنا شدن to be familiar

âshenâyi آشنایی friendship, familiarity

âsheq shodan عاشق شدن to fall in love

âsheq عاشق lover, in love

asheqâne عاشقانه loving, romantic

âshiyâne آشیانه nest, den

ashk rikhtan اشک ریختن to cry

ashk اشک tear (cry)

ashkâl اشکال pictures, forms

âshkâr آشکار evident, obvious

ashkhâs اشخاص persons, people

âshofte kardan آشفته کردن to disturb

âshofte آشفته disturbed, agitated

âshpaz آشپز cook

âshpazi kardan آشپزی کردن to cook

âshpazi آشپزی cooking

âshpazkhâne آشپزخانه kitchen

âshqâl آشغال rubbish, garbage

ashrâf اشراف aristocrats, nobles

ashrâr اشرار rebels

âshti آشتی peace, reconciliation

âshub آشوب riot, disturbance

âshubgar آشوبگر riotous, agitator

âsib dide آسیب دیده damaged, victim, injured

âsib آسیب harm, damage

asir kardan اسیر کردن to capture

asir اسیر captive, prisoner

âsiyâ آسیا Asia

asl اصل basis, genuine, origine

aslahe اسلحه arms, weapons, armaments

asli اصلی original

âsm آسم asthma

âsperin آسپرین aspirin

asr عصر afternoon, age, era

asrâne عصرانه afternoon tea

asrâr اسرار secrets, mysteries

ast است is

âstar آستر lining, first coat

âstin آستین sleeve

âsude آسوده relieved, comfortable

âsudegi آسودگی tranquillity, comfort

âsuri آسوری Assyrian

âtash bâr آتشبار machine gun

âtash bas آتش بس cease-fire

âtash bâzi آتشبازی fireworks

âtash feshân آتشفشان volcano

âtash kade آتشکده (Zoroastrian) fire temple

âtash neshân آتش نشان fire fighter

âtash neshâni آتش نشانی fire station

âtash parast آتش پرست fire worshiper

âtash suzi آتش سوزی a fire

âtash آتش fire

atash عطش thirst, craving

atbâ' اتباع citizens, nationals

âtefe عاطفه emotion, sentiment, affection

atiqe عتیقه antique, relic

atr عطر perfume, fragrance, aroma

atrâf اطراف sides, surroundings

atse kardan عطسه کردن to sneeze

atse عطسه sneeze

avâkher اواخر near the end, latter parts

avâmer اوامر commands

âvâr آوار debris

âvardan (âvar) آوردن (آور) to bring

âvâre آواره homeless, refugee

avârez عوارض taxes, charges, toll

avâset اواسط middle parts

avâyel اوایل beginnings, early parts

avaz kardan عوض کردن to substitute, to exchange, to change, to return

âvâz khândan (âvâz khân) آواز خواندن (آواز خوان) to sing

âvâz آواز song

avaz عوض substitute, exchange, change, return

avazi عوضی wrong, mistaken

âvikhtan (âviz) آویختن (آویز) to hang

âvizân آویزان suspended, pending

âvril آوریل April

avval اول first, initial, first-rate

avvalan اولا firstly

avvalin اولین the first

avvaliye اولیه primary

âyâ آیا whether (a question word)

ayâl عیال wife

a'yân اعیان nobles

âyande آینده future

ayâr عیار standard (of gold), carat

âyât آیات verses (of Koran)

âye آیه verse (of Koran)

âyele عایله family, wife and children

âyeq عایق non-conductor, insulator

âyin آیین custom, ceremony

âyne آینه mirror

ayyâm ایام days, times

ayyâsh عیاش pleasure seeking, epicure

az beyn bordan از بین بردن to destroy, to ruin

az beyn raftan از بین رفتن to be destroyed, to be ruined

az از since, from

a'zâ اعضا members, organs

azâ عزا mourning

azâb عذاب torment, pain, agony

azab عذب bachelor, single

âzâd kardan آزاد کردن to free, to release

âzâd آزاد free (not bound)

âzâdâne آزادانه freely

azâdâr عزادار mourner

azâdâri kardan عزاداری کردن
to mourn

âzâdi khâh آزادی خواه freedom
seeker

âzâdi آزادی freedom, liberation

azamat عظمت grandeur, eminence

azân اذان call to prayer

âzâr dâdan آزار دادن to harass

âzar آذر ninth month of Iranian
calendar

âzâr آزار harassment

azbar ازبر by memory, by heart

âzemâyesh kardan آزمایش کردن
to test, to examine

âzemâyesh آزمایش test,
examination

âzemâyeshgâh آزمایشگاه
laboratory

âzemâyeshi آزمایشی experimental

âzemude آزموده experienced

âzemun آزمون test, exam

âzhâns آژانس agency

azim عظیم grand, huge,
magnificent

azimat kardan عزیمت کردن
departure, leaving

azimat عزیمت departure, leaving

aziyyat kardan اذیت کردن
nuisance, teasing

aziyyat اذیت nuisance, teasing

aziz عزیز dear, esteemed, darling

azl kardan عزل کردن to dismiss,
to sack

azl عزل dismissal, sacking

azm عزم intention, will,
determination

azole عضله muscle

âzuqe آذوقه supplies, provisions

B 162

b

bâ با with

bâbâ بابا father, dad

ba'ba' بع بع bleating

bachche بچه child

bachchegâne بچگانه childish

bad dahan بد دهن foul mouth

bad jens بد جنس malicious, wicked

bâd kardan باد کردن to blow

bad zât بد ذات mischievous, mean

bâd باد wind, swelling

bad بد bad, evil, ill

ba'd بعد next, later, then

bâdâm zamini بادام زمینی peanut

bâdâm بادام almond

badan بدن body

ba'dan بعدا afterwards, later on

badane بدنه frame, trunk

bâdbâdak بادبادک kite

badbakht بدبخت miserable, unfortunate

badbakhti بدبختی misfortune, bad luck

bâdbân بادبان jib, sail

badbin بدبین pessimistic

badbiyâri بد بیاری bad luck

bâdemjân بادمجان eggplant

bâdi بادی windy, pneumatic

badi بدی badness, fault

ba'di بعدی next

badihi بدیهی obvious

bâdkesh بادکش cupping, louver

bâdkonak بادکنک balloon

bâdnamâ بادنما weather cock

badr بدر full moon

bâdsanj باد سنج anemometer

bâdzan باد زن fan, blower

bâ'es shodan باعث شدن to cause

bâ'es باعث cause, motive

bâft بافت tissue, texture

bâftan (bâf) (باف) بافتن to weave

bâftani بافتنی textile

bahâ بها price, value, cost

bâham با هم together

bahâne juyi بهانه جویی seeking excuses

bahâne بهانه excuse, pretext

bahâr بهار spring

bahâyi بهایی Baha'i

bahâyiyat بهائیت Baha'ism

bahbah به به excellent, well done

bahman بهمن eleventh month of Iranian calendar

bahr بحر sea

bahrâm بهرام mars

bahre بهره quotient, interest

bahrebardâri kardan بهره برداری کردن to exploit

bahrebardâri بهره برداری exploitation, operation

bahrekeshi بهره کشی exploitation

bahs kardan بحث کردن to discuss, to argue

bahs بحث discussion, argument

bâhush با هوش intelligent, smart

ba'id بعید far, distant, unlikely

bâje ye telefon باجه تلفن phone box

bakereh باکره virgin

163

BAKHIL

bakhil بخیل jealous, miserly

bakhiye zadan بخیه زدن to stitch

bakhiye بخیه suture, stitch

bakhsh بخش part, portion, section

bakhshande بخشنده generous, merciful

bakhshidan (bakhsh) بخشیدن (بخش) to forgive

bakhshnâme بخشنامه circular, directive

bâkht باخت loss

bakht بخت chance, luck

bâkhtan باختن to loss

bâl بال wing

bal' بلع swallowing

bâlâ raftan بالا رفتن to climb

bâlâ بالا up, top, upper part

balâ بلا disaster, misfortune, misery

balad budan بلد بودن to know

balad بلد familiar, guide

balâl بلال corn, pop corn

balam بلم small boat

bâlâye بالای above

bale بله yes

bâleq shodan بالغ شدن to mature

bâleq بالغ mature, adult

bâlesh بالش pillow, cushion

bal'idan (bal') بلعیدن to swallow

bâlini بالینی clinical

balke بلکه maybe, perhaps

balqur بلغور groats

balut بلوط oak

balvâ بلوا riot, disturbance

bâm بام roof

bam بم bass, low voice

bâmaze با مزه tasty

bâmbul بامبول trick

bâmedâd بامداد morning

banâ بنا building, construction

banâder بنادر ports, harbours

banafsh بنفش violet

banafshe بنفشه violet, pansy

banâgush بناگوش cavity behind the ear

band bâzi بند بازی acrobatics, rope-walking

band e kafsh بند کفش lace

band بند band, rope, joint, string

bandar بندر port, harbour

bande بنده slave, servant

bândpichi باند پیچی bandage

bang بنگ hashish

bâni بانی founder, builder

bânk بانک bank

bannâ بنا builder, mason

bânovân بانوان ladies, women

bânu بانو lady

bâq vahsh باغ وحش zoo

bâq باغ garden

baqâ بقا survival, permanence

baqal kardan بغل کردن to cuddle, to hug

baqal بغل a cuddle, hug

baqali بغلی pocket-size

baqâyâ بقایا remains, remnants

bâqbâni باغبانی gardening

bâqelâ باقلا broad bean

BÂQI
164

bâqi باقی rest, residue, left

bâqimânde باقیمانده remaining, rest

baqiyye بقیه rest, remaining

bâqlavâ باقلوا a kind of pastry

baqqâl بقال grocer

baqqâli بقالی grocery

bar aleyh بر علیه against

bar angikhtan (bar angiz) بر (برانگیز) انگیختن to motivate, to encourage

bar hasb e بر حسب in terms of, for

bâr zadan بار زدن to load

bâr بار load, time

barâbar برابر equal, same

barâbari برابری equality

baradar khânde برادر خوانده step brother

barâdar shohar برادر شوهر husband's brother

barâdar zâde برادر زاده niece or nephew

barâdar zan برادرزن wife's brother

barâdar برادر brother

barâdari برادری brotherhood

barâdarkhânde برادر خوانده half brother

bârakallâh بارک الله well down

barakat برکت blessing

baraks برعکس vice versa, on the contrary

barâmadan برآمدن to appear, to rise

barâmadegi برآمدگی projection, outgrowth

bârân باران rain

barande shodan برنده شدن to win

barande برنده winner

bârandegi بارندگی rainfall

bârâni بارانی raincoat

barâvard برآورد estimate, evaluation

barâye برای for, in order to

bârbar باربر porter

barchasb برچسب label, tag

barchidan (bar chin) برچیدن (برچین) to remove, to put an end

bârdâr باردار pregnant

bârdâri بارداری pregnancy

bardâshtan (bar dâr) بر داشتن (بردار) to pick up, to take

barde برده slave

barf pakkon برف پاکن wipers

barf برف snow

barfak برفک thrush, TV flakes

barg برگ leaf, sheet, page

bargashtan (bargard) برگشتن (برگرد) to return, to go back

bargozâr kardan برگذار کردن to celebrate, to held

bargozâri برگذاری celebration

bargozidan (bar gozin) برگزیدن to choose, to select

bârik باریک narrow, thin

barjaste برجسته projecting, prominent

barkanâr kardan برکنار کردن to discharge, to dismiss

barkanâr برکنار discharged, dismissed

bârkesh بارکش lorry, truck

barkhâstan (bar khiz) برخاستن (برخیز) to rise, to get up

barkhelâf برخلاف against, contrary

barkhi برخی some

barkhordan (bar khor) برخوردن (برخور) to clash, to bump into

barmalâ برملا revealed, public

barnâme برنامه program

barq gereftan برق گرفتن to electrocute

barq برق electricity

barqarâr kardan برقرار کردن to establish

barqarâr برقرار established, continuing

barraq براق shinny, bright

barrasi kardan بررسی کردن to inspect, to review

barrasi بررسی inspection, review

barre بره lamb

bartar برتر higher, superior

bârut باروت gunpowder

bârvar kardan بارورکردن to fertilise

bârvar بارور fertile

barzakh برزخ limbo, uncertainty

barzegar برزگر farmer

bas بس enough

basâmad بسامد frequency

basâvâyi بساوایی sense of touch, tactile

bâsh! باش be

bashar بشر human, mankind

bashardust بشردوست humanitarian

bâshe باشه ok

bâshgâh باشگاه club

bashshâsh بشاش cheerful, smiling

basij بسیج mobilization, preparation

basirat بصیرت insight

basketbâl بسکتبال basketball

bastan (band) بستن (بند) to close, to tie, to fasten

bastani بستنی ice cream

bâstânishenâsi باستان شناسی archaeology

bâstânshenass باستان شناس archaeologist

bastari kardan بستری کردن to hospitalise

bastari بستری hospitalised

baste بسته package, parcel, closed

bastebandi kardan بسته بندی کردن to pack, to wrap

bastebandi بسته بندی packaging, packing, wrapping

bastegân بستگان relatives

batâlat بطالت idleness, laziness

bâtel kardan باطل کردن to cancel

bâtel باطل void, useless

bâten باطن conscious, inner part

bâtlâq باتلاق swamp

bâtri باطری battery

bâvar kardan باور کردن to believe

bâvar باور belief, trust

bavâsir بواسیر haemorrhoids

bayân kardan بیان کردن to express, to explain

bayân بیان expression, explanation

bayâniye بيانيه declaration, manifesto

bayât بيات stale

bâyegâni بايگانى archives

bâyer باير idle land, barren

bâyesti بايستى must

bâz kardan باز کردن to open

bâz باز open, wide, hawk

bazak بزک make up, grooming

bâzande بازنده loser

bâzâr بازار market

bazarak بزرک linseed, flax

bâzargân بازرگان merchant, trader

bâzargâni بازرگانى commerce, business

bâzâri بازارى businessman, commercial

bazâz بزاز cloth-dealer

bâzdâsht kardan بازداشت کردن to arrest

bâzdâsht بازداشت detention, arrest

bâzdâshtgâh بازداشتگاه detention center, prison

bâzdeh بازده output, efficiency

bâzdid kardan بازديد کردن to inspect, to audit

bâzdid بازديد inspection, audit

bâzgasht بازگشت return, homecoming

bâzgashtan بازگشتن to return

bâzi kardan بازى کردن to play

bâzi بازى game, sport, play

ba'zi بعضى some, a few

bâzigar بازيگر actor

bâzigush بازيگوش playful, careless

bâzikon بازيکن player

bâzju بازجو investigator, interrogator

bâzjuyi kardan بازجويى کردن to investigate, to interrogate

bâzjuyi بازجويى investigation, interrogation

bâzkhâst بازخواست interrogation

bazm بزم party, feast

bâzmânde بازمانده survivor

bâzneshaste shodan بازنشسته شدن to retire

bâzneshaste بازنشسته retired

bâzneshastegi بازنشستگى retirement, superannuating

bâzpors بازپرس inspector

bâzporsi بازپرسى interrogation, investigation

bazr بذر seed, grain

bâzras بازرس inspector

bâzsâzi kardan بازسازى کردن to restore, to renovate

bâzsâzi بازسازى restoration, renovation

bâztâb بازتاب reflex, reaction

bâzu بازو arm

bâzuband بازوبند bracelet, armlet

be dar bordan (be dar bar) بدر بردن (بدر بر) to save, to escape

be salamati بسلامتى cheers!

be taraf e بطرف towards

be به to, at, by, in

bedehi بدهى debt, liability

bedehkâr بدهکار in debt, indebted

bedune بدون without

beh به quince

behbud بهبود recovery, improvement

behdâsht بهداشت health care, health

behdâshti بهداشتی hygienic

behesht بهشت paradise, heaven

behtar بهتر better

behtarin بهترین the best

behyâr بهیار nurse aid

bejoz بجز except

bekr بکر virgin, intact

belderchin بلدرچین quail

belit بلیت ticket

belqovve بالقوه potential

bemoqe' به موقع on time, timely

benzin بنزین petrol, gasoline

berahne برهنه naked, nude

berenj برنج rice, brass

bereshte kardan برشته کردن to toast

bereshte برشته toasted, browned

berjis برجیس Jupiter

beryân بریان roasted, grilled, barbequed

be'sat بعثت becoming a prophet

beshkan بشکن finger snap

besmellâah بسم الله in the name of God

bestânkâr بستانکار creditor

besyâr بسیار many, a lot

bey'âne بیعانه deposit

bey'at بیعت loyalty, homage

beyn بین middle, between, among

beynolmelali بین المللی international

beyraq بیرق flag

beytolmâl بیت المال public budget

beyze بیضه testicle

bezâ'at بضاعت financial ability, means

bezehkâr بزهکار delinquent, criminal

bezudi بزودی soon

bi بی without

bi'âr بی عار shameless, lazy

bibi بی بی mistress of the house

bichâre بیچاره helpless, poor

bichiz بیچیز poor

bidâne بی دانه seedless

bidâr shodan بیدار شدن to wake up

bidâr بیدار awake, alert

bidasto pâ بی دست و پا clumsy, resource less

biderang بیدرنگ immediately, quickly

bidin بیدین atheist, secular

bigâne بیگانه foreign, alien, stranger

bigonâh بیگناه innocent, sinless

bihâl بی حال ill, weak, exhausted

bihayâ بی حیا immodest, shameless, rude

bihejâb بی حجاب unveiled, uncovered

bihess بی حس numb, anaesthetised

bihosele بی حوصله impatient, irritable

bijâ بی جا inappropriate

bikâr بیکار unemployed

bikâri بیکاری unemployment

bikh بیخ root, bottom

bikhabar بی خبر unaware, ignorant

bikhâbi بی خوابی insomnia

bikhânemân بی خانمان homeless

bikhâsiyat بی خاصیت ineffective, useless

bikhiyâl بی خیال absent minded, thoughtless

bil بیل shovel

bim بیم fear, panic

bimâr بیمار ill, sick

bimârestân بیمارستان hospital

bimâri بیماری illness, disease

bime kardan بیمه کردن to insure

bime بیمه insurance, guarantee

bimnâk بیمناک fearful, afraid

bimohregân بی مهرگان invertebrates

binamak بی نمک tasteless

binande بیننده viewer, watcher

binâyi sanj بینائی سنج optometrist

binâyi بینایی visual, vision

bini بینی nose

bi'orze بی عرضه incapable, incompetent

bipanâh بی پناه homeless, shelterless

biparde بی پرده frank, open

bipedaro mâdar بی پدر و مادر orphan

birabt بی ربط irrelevant

birâhe بیراهه by-way

birahm بیرحم cruel, ruthless

biriyâ بی ریا sincere, frank

birun kardan بیرون کردن to expel

birun بیرون outside, outdoor

bisaro pâ بی سروپا rascal

bisaro tah بی سروته incoherent, empty

bisarosedâ بی سروصدا quiet, hush-hush

bisavâd بی سواد illiterate

bisavâdi بی سوادی illiteracy

bisedâ بی صدا quiet, mute

bishtar بیشتر more, most

bisim بی سیم wireless

bist بیست twenty

bistom بیستم twentieth

bitafâvot بی تفاوت indifferent

bitaraf بی طرف neutral

bivâk بی واک voiceless

bivâsete بی واسطه direct

bive بیوه widow

biyâbân بیابان desert, wilderness

bizâr بیزار weary, disgusted

bo'd بعد dimension, distance

bohrân بحران crisis

bohrâni بحرانی critical

boht بهت stunning, amazement

bohtân بهتان false accusation

bokhâr بخار steam, vapour

bokhâri بخاری heater, fireplace

boks بوکس boxing

boksel بوکسل towing

boland kardan بلند کردن to lift, to raise

boland parvâz بلند پرواز ambitious

boland shodan بلند شدن to get up, to stand up

boland بلند loud, tall, long

bolandgu بلند گو loudspeaker

bolbol بلبل nightingale

boloq بلوغ maturity, puberty

bolqârestân بلغارستان Bulgaria

boluz بلوز shirt, blouse

bomb بمب bomb

bombafkan بمب افکن bomber

bombârân kardan بمباران کردن to bombard

bombârân بمباران bombardment

bon بن base, root

bonbast بن بست dead end, no through road

bongâh بنگاه agency, institution

bonyâd بنیاد base, foundation

bonyân بنیان foundation, structure

bonye بنیه health, physical condition

boqche بقچه bundle, cloth wrapper

boq'e بقعه tomb

boqranj بغرنج complicated, intricate

boqz بغض spite, hatred

borâde براده filings, shavings

bordan (bar) (بر) بردن to take, to win

bores zadan برس زدن to brush

bores برس brush

boridan (bor) (بر) بریدن to cut

borj برج tower, month

boshke بشکه barrel

boshqâb بشقاب plate, dish

bostân بستان garden

bot بت idol

botri بطری bottle

boz بز goat

bozâq بزاق saliva

bozorg kardan بزرگ کردن to foster, to grow

bozorg shodan بزرگ شدن to grow up, to mature

bozorg بزرگ large, big, grown up

bozorgrâh بزرگراه freeway, highway

bozorgsâl بزرگسال adult, grown up

bu kardan بو کردن to smell

bu بو smell, odour

budan (bast) (هست) بودن to be

budâyi بودائی Buddhist

budje بودجه budget

bufe بوفه buffet

buluk بلوک block, civil parish

bulur بلور crystal

bumi بومی native, local, indigenous

buq بوق horn

buqalamun بوقلمون turkey

bur بور blond, light-coloured

burân بوران snow-storm blizzard

buse بوسه kiss

busidan (bus) (بوس) بوسیدن to kiss

bute بوته bush, shrub

buyâyi بویایی olfaction

buyidan (buy) (بوی) بوییدن to smell

ch

châbok چابک agile, quick

châdor zadan چادر زدن to camp

châdor چادر veil, tent

châdorneshini چادر نشینی nomadic, tent dwelling

châgukesh چاقو کش hoodlum, knife stabber

châh kan چاه کن well digger

châh چاه well, hole

châhâr râh چهار راه intersection

châhâr چهار four

châhârdah ma'sum چهارده معصوم 14 innocents

châhârdah چهارده fourteen

châhârpâ چهارپا quadruped

châhârshanbe چهارشنبه Wednesday

chahchahe چهچهه twittering

chak zadan چک زدن to slap

châk چاک cleft, crack

chak چک slap

châkar چاکر servant

chakâvak چکاوک lark

châkhân چاخان exaggeration, charlatan

chakhmâq چخماق flint

chakidan (chak) چکیدن (چک) to drip, to trickle

chakide چکیده summary

chakkosh چکش hammer

chakme چکمه boot, high boot

châknây چاکنای glottis

châle چاله pit, trench, hole

chamadân چمدان suitcase

chaman zan چمن زن lawn mower

chaman چمن grass, lawn

chamanzâr چمنزار meadow

chanbare چنبره hoop, circle, curl

chand zel'i چند ضلعی polygon

chand چند some, few, how, how many

chandân چندان so, as much as

chandin چندین several, many

châne zadan چانه زدن to bargain

châne چانه chin

chang zadan چنگ زدن to grasp

chang چنگ harp, claw

changak چنگک hook

changâl چنگال fork, claws

chap dast چپ دست left handed

châp kardan چاپ کردن to print

châp چاپ print, edition, press

chap چپ left

chapândan (chapân) چپاندن (چپان) to stuff, to push into

chapar چپر wattle, fence

chapâvol چپاول looting, fleecing

chape چپه capsized

chapgerâ چپگرا leftist

châpi چاپی printed, typographical

chapidan (chap) چپیدن (چپ) to packed into a place

châpkhâne چاپ خانه press, print house

châplus چاپلوس flatterer, toady sit

châq چاق fat, obese

châqu zadan چاقو زدن to stab

châqu چاقو knife

charâ چرا grazing, pasturing

charâgâh چراگاه pasture, meadow

chârak چارک quarter

charande چرنده grazer

charb jabân چرب زبان glib tongued

charb چرب fatty, oily, greasy

charbi چربی fat, oil

charbidan (charb) (چرب) چربیدن to exceed

chârchub چارچوب frame, skeleton

chârdivâri چاردیواری house, premises

châre چاره remedy, cure

chârgush چارگوش quadrangle, square

charidan (char) چریدن to graze

charkh dande چرخ دنده gear

charkh kardan چرخ کردن to mince

charkh karde چرخ کرده minced

charkh savâri چرخ سواری cycling

charkh چرخ wheel, bicycle

charkhesh چرخش spinning, rotation

charkhidan (charkh) چرخیدن (چرخ) to turn, to roll

charm sâzi چرم سازی tannery

charm چرم leather

châroq چاروق rural shoe

chârpâ چارپا quadruped

chârpâye چارپایه stool

chârshâne چارشانه broad-shouldered

chasb چسب glue, paste

chasbân چسبان sticky, tight

chasbidan (chasb) چسبیدن (چسب) to glue, to paste

chasbnâk چسبناک sticky, adhesive

chashâyi چشایی gustatory

chashidan (chash) چشیدن (چش) to taste

châshni چاشنی seasoning, dressing

chatr bâz چترباز parachutist, paratrooper

chatr چتر umbrella, parachute

châvosh چاوش herald

chây چای tea

châyiydan (chây) چاییدن (چای) to chill, to catch cold

che چه what, whether

cheft چفت latch, hasp

chegune چگونه how

chegunegi چگونگی condition, circumstance

chehel چهل forty

chehre چهره face

chek chek چک چک dropping, dripping

chek kardan چک کردن to check

chek چک checking, bank check

chekke kardan چکه کردن to leak

chekke چکه drop, leaking

chelândan (chelân) چلاندن to squeeze, to wrench

chelchele چلچله swallow

chelcherâq چلچراغ chandelier

chelle چله a period of forty days

chenânche چنانچه if, in case

chenânke چنانکه as

chenâr چنار plane tree

chenin چنین such, such as

cheqadr چقدر how much, how many

cherâ چرا why

cherâq qovve چراغ قوه torch (flashlight)

cherâq چراغ light, lamp, lantern

cherik چریک guerilla, partisan

cherk چرک pus, filth

cherknevis چرکنویس draft, rough copy

chert چرت irrelevant, nonsense

cheshm bandi چشم بندی juggling

cheshm baste چشم بسته blindfold

cheshm pezeshk چشم پزشک optician

cheshm pushi چشم پوشی forbearance, tolerance

cheshm zakhm چشم زخم harm by evil's eye

cheshm چشم eye

cheshmak zadan چشمک زدن to wink, to blink

cheshmak چشمک wink, blink, twinkle

cheshmandâz چشم انداز view, outlook

cheshmcharâni چشم چرانی voyeurism, ogling

chesm dâsht چشمداشت expectation hope

chesm roshani چشم روشنی gift, present

chesme چشمه spring, source

chesmpezeshk چشم پزشک ophthalmologist

chetor چطور how

chi چی what

chidan (chin) چیدن (چین) to pick, to pluck, to clip

chin khordan چین خوردن to wrinkle

chin khorde چین خورده wrinkled, crumpled

chin چین China, wrinkle, crease, wave

chini چینی Chinese, chinaware

chiregi چیرگی victory, dominance

chistân چیستان riddle, puzzle

chit چیت printed cotton

chiz چیز thing, object

chizi چیزی something

cho andâkhtan چو انداختن to spread a rumor

cho چو rumor

chodan چدن cast iron

chogân چوگان polo-stick, bat

chollaq چلاق crippled, paralyzed

chomâq چماق club

chombâtme چمباتمه squat

chomche چمچه ladle, scoop

chon چون because, for

chopoq keshidan چپق کشیدن to smoke a pipe

chopoq چپق calumet, pipe

choqolli چوقلی telltale, complaining

choqondar چغندر beet

chort zadan چرت زدن to take a nap

chort چرت nap

chortke چرتکه abacus

choruk چروک wrinkle, crease

chos چس silent wind, fizzle

chub bast چوب بست scaffold

chub panbe چوب پنبه cork

chub چوب wood, timber, log

chubdasti چوبدستی walking stick, cane

chupân چوپان shepherd

D

d

dabbâq دباغ tanner

dabbe دبه flask

dabestân دبستان primary school

dabir دبیر secretary, teacher

dabirestân دبیرستان high school, secondary school

dabirkhâne دبیرخانه secretariat, registering office

dâd zadan داد زدن to scream

dâd داد scream, justice

dad دد wild, beast

dâdan (dah) دادن (ده) to give

dâdâsh داداش brother

dâdgâh دادگاه court (legal)

dâdgostari دادگستری office of justice

dâdkhâst دادخواست petition, complaint

dâdo bidâd دادوبیداد brawl, turmoil

dâdo setad دادوستد deal, business, trade

dâdras دادرس judge

dâdsetân دادستان public prosecutor

dâ'em دائم permanent, constant

daf' kardan دفع کردن to repel, to discharge

daf دف tambourine

daf' دفع repelling, discharge

daf'e دفعه time, instance

dafn kardan دفن کردن to bury

dafn دفن burial

daftar دفتر notebook, office, register

daftarche دفترچه notebook

daftardâr دفتردار bookkeeper

daftarkhâne دفترخانه notary public

dah ده ten

dahan kaji دهن کجی making face at

dahân دهان mouth

dahanbin دهن بین whimsical

dahandarre دهن دره yawning

dahâne دهانه bridle, opening, entrance

dahe دهه decade

dâkhel داخل inside, in, interior

dâkheli داخلی internal, local

dakhl دخل income, profit, cash register

dakhme دخمه tomb, crypt

dakke دکه stand, booth, stall, kiosk

dâlân دالان hall, corridor

dalil â دلیل آوردن to give a reason, to argue

dalil دلیل reason, cause

dallâk دلاک masseur, barber

dallâl دلال broker, dealer

dalqak دلقک clown

dâm pezeshki دامپزشکی veterinary

dâm دام trap, domestic animal

damâ دما temperature

dâmâd داماد groom, son-in-law

dâman دامن lap, skirt

dâmane دامنه foothill, extent, amplitude

damâqe دماغه cape, prow

damar دمر prone, lying face downwards

damâsanj دماسنج thermometer

damidam (dam) دمیدن (دم) to blow, to puff

dampâyi دمپائی slippers

dânâ دانا wise, savant

dandân quruche دندان قروچه grating the teeth

dandân دندان tooth

dandâne shiri دندان شیری milk tooth

dandânpezeshk دندانپزشک dentist

dandânsâz دندانساز dentist

dande دنده rib, gear (of a vehicle)

dâne دانه seed, grain, piece

dânesh âmuz دانش آموز student (in primary or secondary school)

dânesh ju دانشجو student (university)

dânesh دانش knowledge

dâneshgâh دانشگاه university

dâneshkade دانشکده faculty, college

dâneshmand دانشمند scientist, scholar

dânestan (dân) دانستن (دان) to know (some thing)

dâng دانگ share, sixth part

dâq داغ hot, scar, bereavement

daqal دغل fraud, deceitful

daqdaqe دغدغه apprehension, worry

dâqdâr داغدار bereaved

daqiq دقیق subtle, careful, precise

daqiqe دقیقه minute (60 seconds)

dar âmadan (dar ây) در آمدن (در آیی) to come out

dar âvardan (dar âvar) در آوردن (در آور) to bring out, to earn

dar bâz kon در باز کن bottle opener, can opener

dar kardan (dar kon) در کردن (در کن) to let off, to fire off

dar raftan (dar rav) در رفتن (در رو) to escape, to dislocate, to flee

dar raftegi در رفتگی dislocation

dar sad درصد percent

dâr دار gallows

dar در door, lid, cap, in, at, by

dârâ دارا rich, possessor

dârâbi دارابی grapefruit

darajât درجات degrees, ranks

daraje درجه degree, rank, thermometer

darajebandi درجه بندی graduation, rating

darak درک hell

darâmad درآمد income

darande درنده beast, predatory, fierce animal

dârâyi دارایی assets, belongings

darbân دربان door keeper, porter

darband دربند narrow pass or alley

darbâr دربار court (royal)

darbast دربست exclusive, whole

darbedar دربدر homeless, vagabond

dârchin دارچین cinnamon

dard kardan درد کردن to ache

dard درد pain, ache, agony

dardnâk دردناک painful, sore

dargir shodan درگیر شدن to get involved, to fight

dargozasht درگذشت passing away, demise

darham درهم chaotic, mixed

dari دری Dari, a dialect of Persian in Afghanistan

dariche دریچه hatch, shatter, valve

daride دریده torn, ripped, impudent

dariq دریغ alas, denial, refusal

darj درج insertion, publishing

dark kardan درک کردن to understand, to realise

dark درک perception, comprehension

darkhâst kardan درخواست کردن to request

darkhâst درخواست request, petition

dârkub دارکوب woodpecker

darmân درمان cure, healing, therapy

darmânde درمانده hopeless, desperate

darmângâh درمانگاه clinic

dârottarjome دارالترجمه translation office

darre دره valley, gorge

dars dâdan درس دادن to teach, to give lessons

dars khândan درس خواندن to study, to learn, to take lessons

dars درس lesson, lecture

darsad درصد percent

dâru دارو medicine, drug

dârukhâne داروخانه pharmacy, chemist

darun درون in, inside, interior

daruni درونی internal, inner

dârusâz داروساز pharmacist, chemist

darvâze دروازه gate, goal

darvâzebân دروازه بان gateman, goalkeeper

darvish درویش Dervish, mystic, poor

daryâ kanâr دریاکنار seacoast, beach

daryâ دریا sea

daryâche دریاچه lake

daryâdâr دریادار rear admiral

daryâft kardan دریافت کردن to receive

daryâft دریافت receipt, perception

daryânavard دریانورد seaman, sailor

daryâsâlâr دریاسالار admiral

daryâyi دریایی marine, naval, maritime

darz درز suture, crack

dâs داس flax, sickle

dasht دشت plain, field

dâshtan (dâr) داشتن (دار) to have

dasise دسیسه plot, conspiracy

dast âmuz دست آموز pet

dast andâz دست انداز bump, puddle

dast andâzi دست اندازی aggression, invasion

dast âviz دست آویز excuse, pretext

dast dâshtan دست داشتن to be involved

dast derâzi دست درازی aggression, violence

dast duz دست دوز hand sewn

dast khat دست خط hand writing

dast khorde دست خورده touched, used

dast pâche دستپاچه hasty, excited

dast pokht دست پخت hand-cooked

dast sâz دست ساز handmade

dast shuyi دستشویی washstand, toilet

dast zadan دست زدن to touch

dast دست hand, side, deck, set

dâstân داستان story, tale

dastband zadan دستبند زدن to handcuff

dastband دستبند bracelet, handcuff

dastbord zadan دستبرد زدن to rob, to steal

dastbord دستبرد theft, robbing

dastbus دستبوس kissing superior's hand

daste gol دسته گل bouquet, flower bunch

daste دسته handle, bunch, group

dastebandi دسته بندی sorting, grouping, classification

dastforush دست فروش peddler, hawker

dastgâh دستگاه system, set, apparatus

dastgire دستگیره handle, knob

dasti دستی hand made, manual

dastkesh دستکش gloves

dastmâl دستمال handkerchief

dastmâli دستمالی touching, fingering

dastmozd دستمزد wage, earning

dastnamâz دستنماز ablution before praying

dastneshânde دست نشانده protégé, stooge

dastranj دسترنج wage

dastrasi دسترسی access, availability

dastshuyi دستشویی bathroom

dastur dâdan دستور دادن to order

dastur olamal دستورالعمل manual, guide

dastur دستور order, direction, grammar

dastyâr دستیار assistant, aid

da'vâ kardan دعوا کردن to argue, to fight

da'vâ دعوا fight, quarrel, argument

davâ دوا medicine, potion

davâm دوام durability, stability

dâvar داور judge, referee, umpire

da'vat kardan دعوت کردن to invite

da'vat دعوت invitation

davazdah دوازده twelve

davidan (dav) دویدن (دو) to run

dâvtalab داوطلب volunteer, candidate

dâvtalabâne داوطلبانه voluntarily

dâye دایه nanny

dâyer دایر established, opened

dâyere دایره circle, round, tambourine

dâyi دایی maternal uncle

dayyus دیوث cuckold

debsh دبش acrid, cool

defâ' kardan دفاع کردن to defend

defâ' دفاع defense, resistance

degarguni دگرگونی change, transformation

deh ده village

dehât دهات villages

dehkade دهکده small village

dehliz دهلیز hallway, vestibule

dehqân دهقان farmer

dekhâlat kardan دخالت کردن to interfere, to intervene

dekhâlat دخالت interference, intrusion

del bastan دل بستن to be attached emotionally

del tang shodan دلتنگ شدن to miss (feel absence)

del دل heart, guts, belly

delâvar دلاور brave, courageous

delbar دلبر charming, sweetheart

delbastegi دلبستگی attachment, affection

delchasb دلچسب pleasing, enjoyable

deldâri دلداری condolence

delgarm دلگرم confident, assured

delgir دلگیر offended

delir دلیر brave, bold

deljuyi دلجویی appeasement, affability

delkhâh دلخواه desirable, ideal

delkharâsh دلخراش heart-breaking, harrowing

delkhor دلخور annoyed, offended

delkhoshi دلخوشی delight, happiness

delsard دلسرد disappointed, discouraged

delsuz دلسوز compassionate, sympathetic

deltang دلتنگ gloomy, nostalgic

demokrasi دمکراسی democracy

denj دنج cozy, snug

deq دق fatal grief

deqqat دقت attention, precision

derakhshân درخشان shinny, bright

derakhshidan (derakhsh) درخشیدن (درخش) to shine, to glow

derakht درخت tree

derang درنگ pause, delay

derâz دراز long, prolonged, tall

derâzâ درازا length

dero kardan درو کردن to harvest

dero درو harvest

desâmr دسامبر December

deser دسر dessert

deshne دشنه dagger

dey دی tenth month of Iranian calendar

deym دیم dry farming

deyn دین debt

deyr دیر monastery, convent

dezh دژ castle, fort

dezhbân دژبان military policeman

dezhkhim دژخیم executioner

did دید view, vision, sight

didan (bin) (بین) دیدن to see, to visit

didani دیدنی worthy of seeing

didâr kardan دیدار کردن to visit, to meet

didâr دیدار visit, meeting

didebân دیده بان watchman, signalman

didgâh دیدگاه viewpoint

dido bâzdid دید و باز دید visiting each other

dig دیگ boiler, pot

digar دیگر other, another, next, more

digarân دیگران others, other people

digari دیگری another, the other one

diksheneri دیکشنری dictionary

diktâtor دیکتاتور dictator

dikte دیکته spelling, dictation

din دین religion, faith

dindâr دیندار religious

dini دینی religious

diplom دیپلم diploma holder

dir kardan دیر کردن to be late, to delay

dir دیر late, delayed

dirine shenâsi دیرینه شناسی paleontology

diruz دیروز yesterday

dirvaqt دیر وقت late

dis دیس big plate

dishab دیشب last night

div دیو demon, devil

divâne دیوانه mad, crazy, insane

divâr دیوار wall, partition

divist دویست two thundered

diyabeti دیابتی diabetic

diyâr دیار region, country

diye دیه fine, blood money

dizi دیزی small cooking pot, a Persian dish.

do دو two

do'â kardan دعا کردن to pray, to give blessing

do'â دعا prayer, blessing

dobâr دوبار twice

dobâre دوباره again

dobb دب bear

dobeyti دوبیتی quatrain

dobini دوبینی diplopia

dochâr دچار afflicted with, involved in

docharkhe دوچرخه bicycle

docharkhesavar دوچرخه سوار cyclist

dockarkhe savâri دوچرخه سواری cycling

dodel دودل double minded, hesitant

dogâne دوگانه double

dogme دگمه button

dohol دهل kettledrum

dojânebe دوجانبه bilateral

dojin دوجین a dozen

dokân دکان shop, store

dokhâniyât دخانیات tobacco products

dokhtar khânde دخترخوانده
adopted daughter

dokhtar دختر girl, daughter, virgin

dokhtarâne دخترانه girlish, for girls

doktor دکتر doctor, physician

dolat دولت government, state, wealth

dolul دولول double barreled

dom دم tail

domal دمل abscess

donbâl kardan دنبال کردن to follow

donbâl دنبال rear, behind, following

donbalân دنبلان sheep's testicle

donbâledâr دنباله دار continuous

dong دنگ share

donyâ دنیا world, universe

doqulu دوقلو twins

dor zadan دور زدن to turn, to rotate

dor دور turn, rotation

dorage دورگه hybrid, half blooded

dorâhi دوراهی junction

dorân دوران era, period, age

dore didan دوره دیدن to be trained, to take a course

dore دوره period, term, course

doregard دوره گرد hawker, peddler

dornâ درنا crane

dorobar دوروبر around, surrounding

doroshke درشکه carriage, pram

dorosht درشت large, coarse, big

dorost kardan درست کردن to make, to build, to correct

dorost درست right, true, exact

dorr در pearl

doru دورو double faced

dorud دورود greeting, praise

dosare دوسره return trip

doshâkhe دوشاخه plug (electricity)

doshanbe دوشنبه Monday

doshman دشمن enemy

doshmani دشمنی hostility, animosity

doshnâm دشنام curse, swearing

doshvâr دشوار difficult, hard

dost dokhtar دوست دختر girlfriend

dost pesar دوست پسر boyfriend

dotarafe دوسره two way, return, bilateral

dovvom دوم second

dozabâne دوزبانه bilingual

dozd دزد thief, robber, snitcher

dozdaki دزدکی secret, covert

dozdgir دزدگیر security alarm, thief-catcher

dozdi دزدی theft, robbery, stealing

dozdidan (dozd) (دزد) دزدیدن to steal, to rob, to kidnap

dozist دوزیست amphibious

duble دوبله dubbing

dud دود smoke, smog

dude دوده smut, lampblack

dudi دودی smoked, dark

dudkesh دودکش chimney

dudmân دودمان dynasty, lineage

dukhtan (duz) (دوز) دوختن to sew, to tailor

duq دوغ a drink made of yogurt, salt and water

dur دور far, remote

durandish دوراندیش farsighted

durbin furushi دوربین فروشی
camera shop

durbin دوربین binoculars, camera

durbini دوربینی farsightedness

durnamâ دورنما landscape, view

duruq goftan دروغ گفتن to lie

duruq qu دروغ گو liar

duruq دروغ lie, false

dush fang دوش فنگ shoulder arms

dushidan (dush) دوشیدن (دوش)
to milk

dushize دوشیزه girl, miss

dust dâshtan دوست داشتن to like

dust دوست friend, mate, pal

dustâne دوستانه friendly, hospitable

dusti دوستی friendship

duzakh دوزخ hell

duzande دوزنده tailor

e

ebâdat kardan عبادت کردن
to worship

ebâdat عبادت worship

ebâdgâh عبادت گاه a place for worship

ebârat عبارت phrase, expression

ebhâm ابهام ambiguity, uncertainty

eblâq ابلاغ giving an official notice

eblis ابلیس devil, Satan

ebrat عبرت lesson, warning

ebri عبری Hebrew

ebtedâ ابتدا beginning, first

ebtedâyi ابتدایی elementary, primary

ebtekâr ابتکار innovation, initiative

edâlat عدالت justice

e'dâm kardan اعدام کردن to execute

e'dâm اعدام execution

edâme dâshtan ادامه داشتن to continue

edâme ادامه continuation, prolongation

edâre kardan اداره کردن to manage, to administer

edâre اداره office, administration

edqâm kardan ادغام کردن to combine, to integrate

edqâm ادغام combination, integration

edrâk ادراک perception

edrâr kardan ادرار کردن to urinate

edrâr ادرار urine

efâde افاده show off, boasting

effat عفت purity, modesty

efrât افراط immoderation, exaggeration

efrite عفریته female demon, astringent

efshâ' kardan افشا کردن to reveal, to disclose

efshâ' افشا revealing, disclosing

eftâr افطار breaking a fast

eftekhâr kardan افتخار کردن to be proud of

eftekhâr افتخار honour, dignity

eftetâh kardan افتتاح کردن to open, to commence

eftetâh افتتاح opening, commencement

eftezâh افتضاح scandal, disgrace

ehânat kardan اهانت کردن to insult, to offend

ehânat اهانت insult, offence

ehâte kardan احاطه کردن to surround

ehâte احاطه surrounding, siege

ehdâ kardan اهدا کردن to dedicate, to present

ehdâ اهدا dedication, present

ehsân احسان charity, favour

ehsâs kardan احساس کردن to feel

ehsâs احساس feeling, sentiment

ehtekâr احتکار hoarding, forestalling

ehtemâl احتمال probability, likelihood

ehterâm kardan احترام کردن to respect

ehterâm احترام respect, regard

ehtiyâj dâshtan احتياج داشتن to need

ehtiyâj احتياج necessity, requirement, need

ehtiyât kardan احتياط کردن to be careful, to watch out

ehtiyât احتياط caution

ehzâr kardan احضارکردن to call, to summon

ehzâr احضار calling, summoning

ejâre kardan اجاره کردن to rent, to hire

ejâre اجاره rent, hire, lease

ejâze dâdan اجازه دادن to permit

ejâze اجازه permission

ejbâri اجباری compulsory, forceful

ejlâs اجلاس meeting, session

ejrâ' kardan اجرا کردن to execute, to enforce

ejrâ' اجرا execution, enforcement

ejtemâ' اجتماع meeting, society, gathering

ejtenâb kardan اجتناب کردن to avoid

ejtenâb اجتناب avoidance, abstinence

ekbiri اکبیری nasty, mangy

ekhlâl اخلال trouble, sabotage

ekhrâj kardan اخراج کردن to dismiss, to fire

ekhrâj اخراج dismissal

ekhtâr kardan اخطار کردن to warn, to notify

ekhtâr اخطار notification, warning

ekhtelâl اختلال disorder, disturbance

ekhtelâs اختلاس embezzlement

ekhterâ' kardan اختراع کردن to invent

ekhterâ' اختراع invention, innovation

ekhtiyâr اختیار authority, power, option

ekrâh اکراه reluctance, dislike

elâhe الهه goddess

elâhi الهی divine, o god

elâhiyât الهیات theology

elhâm kardan الهام کردن to inspire

elhâm الهام inspiration

ellat علت reason, cause

elm علم science, knowledge

elqâ' kardan الغاء کردن to abolish

elqâ' الغاء abolition, elimination

eltehâb التهاب inflammation, excitement

eltemâs kardan التماس کردن to beg

eltemâs التماس begging, requesting

emâm امام religious leader

emâmat امامت leadership

emâmzâde امامزاده religious shrine

emârat عمارت building, construction

emddad امداد help, assistance

emkân امکان possibility, feasibility

emlâ' املا spelling, dictation

emperâtor امپراتور emperor

emperâtori امپراتوری empire

emruz امروز today

emsal امسال this year

emshab امشب tonight

emtahân dâdan امتحان دادن to sit for a test, to take an exam

emtahân kardan امتحان کردن to try on

emtahân امتحان exam, trial, test

emtedâd امتداد extension, length

emtenâ' kardan امتناع کردن to refuse

emtenâ' امتناع refusal, abstention

emtiyâz امتياز privilege, advantage, point

emzâ' kardan امضا کردن to sign

emzâ' امضا signature

enabiye عنبيه iris

enâyat عنايت favour, kindness

enbessat انبساط expansion

en'ekâs انعكاس reflection, reaction

enerezhi انرژی energy

enfejâr انفجار explosion, eruption

engâr انگار think thou, as if

engelis انگليس England

enhelâl انحلال termination, dissolution

enherâf انحراف deviation, diversion

enhesâr انحصار monopoly

enhesâri انحصاری monopolistic, exclusive

enjemâd انجماد freezing, solidification

enjil انجيل Bible

enkâr kardan انكار کردن to deny

enkâr انكار denial

enqebâz انقباض contraction

enqelâb انقلاب revolution, upheaval

enqerâz انقراض downfall, decline

ensâf انصاف equity, justice

ensân انسان mankind, human

ensâniyat انسانيت humanity, courtesy

enserâf dâdan انصراف دادن to give up

enserâf انصراف giving up, changing mind

enshâ' انشا composition, writing

enshâ'allâh انشا الله god willing

enshe'âb انشعاب branching, separation

entefâyi انتفاعی profit producing

entehâ انتها end, limit

entehâr انتحار suicide

entekhâb kardan انتخاب کردن to select, to elect

entekhâb انتخاب election, selection

enteqâd kardan انتقاد کردن to criticize

enteqâd انتقاد criticism

enteqâl dâdan انتقال دادن to transfer

enteqâl انتقال transition, transfer

enteqâm انتقام revenge, vengeance

entesâb kardan انتصاب کردن to appoint

entesâb انتصاب appointment

enteshâr dâdan انتشار دادن to publish

enteshâr انتشار publishing, broadcasting

entezâmi انتظامی disciplinary

entezâr dâshtan انتظار داشتن
to expect

entezâr انتظار waiting, expectation

enzebât انضباط discipline, order

eqâmat اقامت residence, staying

eqdâm kardan اقدام کردن action, performance

eqdâm اقدام action, performance

eqmâ' اغما faint, coma

eqrâq kardan اغراق کردن to exaggerate

eqrâq اغراق exaggeration, overstatement

eqrâr kardan اقرار کردن to confess

eqrâr اقرار confession

eqtebâs kardan اقتباس کردن to adapt

eqtebâs اقتباس adaptation, citation

eqtesâd اقتصاد economy

eqteshâsh kardan اغتشاش کردن to revolt

eqteshâsh اغتشاش riot, revolt

erâdat ارادت inclination, devotion

erâdatmand ارادتمند sincere, sincerely

erâde اراده will, intention

erfân عرفان mysticism

ers bordan ارث بردن to inherit

ers ارث inheritance, legacy

ersâl kardan ارسال کردن to dispatch, to send

ersâl ارسال remittance, dispatch

ershâd kardan ارشاد کردن to guide

ershâd ارشاد guiding, leading

ersi ارثی congenital

erte'âsh ارتعاش vibration, trembling

ertebât ارتباط connection, relation

ertefâ' ارتفاع height, altitude

erzâ' kardan ارضا کردن to satisfy

erzâ' ارضا satisfaction

esârat اسارت captivity, capture

esbât kardan اثبات کردن to prove

esbât اثبات proof, verification

esfanj اسفنج sponge

esfenâj اسفناج spinach

eshâl اسهال dysentery, diarrhoea

eshâre kardan اشاره کردن to point out

eshâre اشاره pointing, hint, gesture

eshkâl اشکال difficulty, hardness

eshq عشق love, passion

eshqâl kardan اشغال کردن to occupy

eshqâl اشغال occupation, invasion

eshqbâzi kardan عشقبازی کردن to make love

eshqbâzi عشقبازی lovemaking, love affair

eshtebâh kardan اشتباه کردن to make a mistake

eshtebâh اشتباه mistake, error

eshtehâ اشتها appetite

eshterâk اشتراک partnership, subscription

eshtiyâq اشتیاق eagerness, enthusiasm

eshve عشوه coyness, playfulness

eskele اسکله dock

eskenâs اسکناس note (money)

eski اسکی skiing

eslâh kardan اصلاح کردن
to correct, to cut one's hair

eslâh اصلاح correction, reform,
haircut

eslâm اسلام Islam

esm اسم name, noun

esme kuchik اسم کوچک Christian
name

espâniyâ اسپانیا Spain

esrâf kardan اصراف کردن to waste

esrâf اصراف extravagance,
wasting

esrâr kardan اصرار کردن to insist

esrâr اصرار insistence, persistence

establ اصطبل stable, mews

estâdiyom استادیوم stadium

estakhr استخر pool (swimming)

este'âre استعاره metaphor, simile

estebdâd استبداد dictatorship

este'dâd استعداد talent, gift

estedlâl kardan استدلال کردن
to argue

estedlâl استدلال argument,
reasoning

este'fa kardan استعفا کردن to resign

este'fa استعفا resignation

estefâde kardan استفاده کردن to use

estefâde استفاده use, benefit

estefrâq kardan استفراغ کردن
to vomit

estefrâq استفراغ vomiting, puke

estehlâk استهلاک spending away,
consuming

estehqâq استحقاق merit, right

estehzâr استحضار notice,
information

estekâk اصطکاک friction, contact

estekân استکان tumbler-shaped,
tea cup

estekhdâm kardan استخدام کردن
to employ

estekhdâm استخدام employment,
recruitment

estekhrâj kardan استخراج کردن
to extract

estekhrâj استخراج extraction,
drawing out

estelâh اصطلاح term, idiom

este'mâl kardan استعمال کردن
to use

este'mâl استعمال usage, application

este'mâr kardan استعمار کردن
to colonize

este'mâr استعمار colonization

estemnâ kardan استمناع کردن
to masturbate

estemnâ استمناع masturbation

esteqâmat kardan استقامت کردن
to resist

esteqâmat استقامت resistance,
endurance

esteqbâl kardan استقبال کردن
to welcome

esteqbâl استقبال welcome,
reception

esteqlâl استقلال independence,
liberty

esteqrâ استقرا induction

esteqrâr استقرار settlement

esterâhat kardan استراحت کردن
to rest, to relax

esterâhat استراحت resting, relaxation

estesmâr استثمار exploitation

estesnâ استثنا exception, exclusivity

estetâr استتار camouflage, under cover

estevâ استوا equator

estizâh kardan استیضاح کردن to impeach

estizâh استیضاح impeachment

etâ'at kardan اطاعت کردن to obey

e'tebâr اعتبار credit, importance

e'telâf ائتلاف coalition, alliance

e'temâd kardan اعتماد کردن to trust

e'temâd اعتماد trust, reliance

e'tenâ kardan اعتنا کردن to care, to pay attention

e'tenâ اعتنا care, attention

e'teqâd اعتقاد belief, faith

e'terâf kardan اعتراف کردن to confess

e'terâf اعتراف confession

e'terâz kardan اعتراض کردن to protest

e'terâz اعتراض protest, objection

e'tesâb kardan اعتصاب کردن to go on a strike

e'tesâb اعتصاب strike

e'tiyâd اعتیاد addiction

etlâf اتلاف wasting, losing

etminân kardan اطمینان کردن to trust

etminân اطمینان confidence, trust

ettefâq اتفاق event, incident

ettehâd اتحاد alliance, union

ettehadiye اتحادیه unions

ettehâm اتهام accusation, charge

ettelâ اطلاع information, notice

ettelâ'ât اطلاعات information, news

ettelâ'iyye اطلاعیه announcement

ettesâl اتصال link, junction

eyâdat عیادت visiting the sick

eyb عیب fault, shortcoming

eybjuyi عیبجویی criticism

eyd عید festival, feast, celebration

eydi عیدی new year's gift

eynak âftâbi عینک آفتابی sun glasses

eynak عینک glasses, spectacles

eyne عین identical, similar

eyni عینی objective

eysh عیش pleasure, fun

eyvân ایوان balcony

ezâfe kardan اضافه کردن to add, to increase

ezâfe اضافه excess, extra

e'zâm kardan اعزام کردن to dispatch, to send

e'zâm اعزام dispatch, sending off

ezdehâm ازدحام crowd, gathering

ezdevâj kardan ازدواج کردن to marry

ezdevâj ازدواج marriage, wedding

ezdiyâd ازدیاد increasing, increase

ezhâr kardan اظهار کردن to express, to state

ezhâr اظهار expression, statement

ezhâriyye اظهاریه declaration

ezn اذن permission

ezterâb اضطراب anxiety, worry

ezterâri اضطرارى urgent

f

fa'âl فعال active, lively, energetic

fa'âliyat فعالیت action, activity, effort

fadâ فدا sacrifice, devotion

fadâkâr فداکار devoted, self-sacrificing

fâ'el فاعل subject, actor, factor, agent

fâheshe khâne فاحشه خانه brothel, whorehouse

fâheshe فاحشه prostitute, whore

fahm فهم understanding, comprehension

fahmidam (fahm) (فهم) فهمیدن to understand

fahmide فهمیده wise, intelligent

fahshâ' فحشا prostitution

fâje'e فاجعه disaster, tragedy, catastrophe

faji' فجیع tragic, horrible, brutal

fajr فجر dawn

fakhr kardan فخر کردن to boast

fakhr فخر pride, boasting

fakk فک jaw

fâktor فاکتور invoice, list, bill

fâl فال omen, fortune

falaj فلج paralysed, paralysis

falak فلک destiny, fortune, bastinado

falâkat فلاکت poverty, misery

falake فلکه round about, belt pulley

falakzade فلک زده unfortunate, miserable

falât فلات plateau

fâlbin فال بین fortune teller

fa'le فعله labourer

fâlgiri فال گیری fortune telling

falsafe فلسفه philosophy, reason

falsafi فلسفی philosophical

fâmil فامیل family

fâmily فامیلی familial, surname

fan فن technique, skill

fanâ فنا destruction, mortality, annihilation

fanar فنر spring, coil

fandak فندک lighter

fandoq فندق hazelnut

fâni فانی mortal, transitory, finite

fanlând فنلاند Finland

fann فن technique

fanni فنی technical

fântezi فانتزی fancy goods

fânus فانوس lantern, bellows

faqân فغان wailing, groaning

faqat فقط only, just

fâqed فاقد missing, lacking

faqid فقید the late, deceased

faqih فقیه clergy

faqir فقیر poor, needy, beggar

faqr فقر poverty, impoverishment

far' فرع secondary, subsidiary, subdivision

farâgereftan (farâgir) (فرا) فراگرفتن گیر to learn, to embrace

farâham kardan فراهم کردن to prepare

farâham فراهم available, ready

farahbakhsh فرحبخش pleasant, refreshing

farâkhâni فراخوانی recall, summon

farâmush kardan فراموش کردن to forget

farâmush فراموش forgetting, disregarding

farâmushi فراموشی amnesia, forgetfulness, laps of memory

farânesavi فرانسوی French

farânese فرانسه France

farang فرنگ overseas, abroad, west

farangi ma'âb فرنگی ماب westernised

farangi فرنگی westerner

farâq فراق separation, departure

farâqat فراغت leisure, rest

farâr فرار escape, running away

farârasidan (farâras) فرا رسیدن (فرارس) to arrive, to come

farâri فراری escapee, fugitive

farâvân فراوان many, a lot, plenty, numerous

farâvâni فراوانی abundance, plentifulness

farâvorde فرآورده product

farâyand فرآیند process

fard فرد person, individual, single, odd

fardâ فردا tomorrow

fardi فردی personal, individual

fâreq فارغ free, disengaged, released

fâreqottahsil shodan فارغ التحصیل شدن to graduate

fâreqottahsil فارغ التحصیل graduate

fâreqottahsili فارغ التحصیلی graduation

farhang فرهنگ culture, dictionary

farhangestân فرهنگستان academy

farhangi فرهنگی cultural

far'i فرعی secondary, minor, subordinate

farib فریب deceit, deception, cheating

faribande فریبنده deceitful, charming, enticing

farize فریضه religious duty

farjâm فرجام end, termination, appeal

farmân dâdan فرمان دادن to order

farmân فرمان order, command, steering-wheel

farmândâr فرماندار governor general

farmândâri فرمانداری governor's office

farmândeh فرمانده commander

farmândehi فرماندهی command office, headquarter

farmânravâ فرمانروا ruler

farmâyesh فرمایش order, remarks, words

farmudan (farmâ) فرمودن (فرما) to order, to say, to do (Pol)

farq فرق difference, discrimination, parting of hair, head

farrâr فرار vaporizable, volatile

farrâsh فراش servant, waiter, janitor, office boy

farsang فرسنگ length unit, 6 kilometre

farsâyesh فرسایش erosion, wearing out

farsh فرش rug, carpet

fârsi zabân فارسی زبان Persian speaker

fârsi فارسی Persian, Farsi, Native language of Iran

farsudan (farsâ) (فرسودن (فرسا to wear out, to erode, to exhaust

farsude فرسوده worn out, eroded

fart فرط excess

fartut فرتوت old, senile

farvardin فروردین, the first month of Iranian calendar

faryâd فریاد scream, shouting, yell

farz kardan فرض کردن to suppose, to assume

farz فرض supposition, assumption

farzand e rezâ'i فرزند رضائی foster-child

farzand khânde فرزند خوانده adopted child

farzand فرزند child, offspring

farzâne فرزانه wise, sagacious

farziyye فرضیه hypothesis

fasâd فساد corruption, decay, deterioration

fâsed فاسد corrupt, rotten, perverted

fâsele فاصله distance, interval, extent

fâsh kardan فاش کردن to reveal, to expose

fâsh فاش revealed, obvious, overt

faskh فسخ dissolution, cancellation, termination

fasl فصل season, chapter, section

fâteh فاتح victor, conqueror, champion

fâtehe فاتحه praying for the dead

fath فتح victory, triumph

fatq فتق hernia, rupture

fatvâ فتوا religious opinion

favarân فوران eruption, outbreak, outburst

favvâre فواره fountain

fâyede فایده use, profit, utility

fazâ فضا space, area

fazâhat فضاحت disgrace, scandal, shame

fazânavard فضانورد astronaut

fazâpeymâ فضاپیما spaceship

fazâyi فضایی spatial

fâzel فاضل spiritual, scholar

fâzelâb فاضلاب drainage, sewerage

fazl فضل excellence, merit, virtue

fazle فضله bird dropping, dung

fehrest فهرست index, list, glossary

fekr kardan فکر کردن to think

fekr فکر thought, thinking, mind

fe'l فعل verb, action

fe'lan فعلا currently, at the moment

felân فلان such and such, a certain person

felestin فلسطین Palestine

felezz فلز metal

felezzi فلزی metallic

felfel فلفل pepper

fenjân فنجان cup

feqdân فقدان lack, absence, shortage

feqh فقه religious law

fer فر curl, ringlet, oven

ferâmâsoneri فراماسونرى freemasonry

ferdos فردوس paradise

ferekâns فرکانس frequency

fereshte فرشته angel

ferestâdan (ferest) (فرست) فرستادن to send, to despatch, to export, to mail

ferestâde فرستاده messenger, envoy

ferestande فرستنده sender, broadcaster, radio station

ferfere فرفره peg-top, whirligig

ferferi فرفرى curly, wavy

ferni فرنى a type of pudding

fer'on فرعون Pharaoh

ferqe فرقه sect, faction, denomination

ferz فرز quick, agile, fast

fesenjân فسنجان a type of stew

feshang فشنگ cartridge

feshâr dâdan فشار دادن to press, to push

feshâr فشار force, pressure, strain, push

feshare khun فشار خون blood pressure

feshârsanj فشارسنج barometer

feshfeshe فشفشه torpedo, rocket

feshorde فشرده pressed, condensed, compressed

fetile فتیله wick

fetne فتنه revolt, conspiracy, trouble

fetr فطر End of Ramadan

fetrat فطرت nature, disposition, instinct

fetri فطرى innate, inborn

fevriye فوریه February

feys فیس boasting

feyz فیض blessing, profit

fil فیل elephant

filipin فیلیپین Philippines

film فیلم film, movie

filmbardâr فیلم بردار cinematographer

filmbardâri فیلم بردارى shooting a film

filmnâme nevis فیلم نامه نویس scriptwriter

filmnâme فیلم نامه movie script

filsuf فیلسوف philosopher

fin kardan فین کردن to blow nose

fin فین snot

firuze فیروزه azure, turquoise

fizik فیزیک physics

fizikdân فیزیکدان physicist

fohsh dâdan فحش دادن to swear

fohsh فحش swear word, curse, abusive language

fokâhi فکاهى humorous, funny

fokol فکل tie, collar

foqolâde فوق العاده brilliant, great

foran فورا immediately, right away

fori فورى urgent, express

forje فرجه respite, delay

form فرم form, figure

formul فرمول formula

forsat talab فرصت طلب opportunist

forsat فرصت opportunity, chance, occasion

foru raftan فرو رفتن to sink, to go in

foru فرو down, deep

forud âmadan فرود آمدن to land, to descend

forud فرود descending, going down, landing

forudgâh فرودگاه airport

forugozâri فروگذاری neglect, refrain

forukesh فروکش subsiding, allaying

forukhtan (forush) فروختن (فروش) to sell

foruraftegi فرورفتگی dent, depression, cavity

forush فروش sale, selling, auction

forushande فروشنده shopkeeper, seller, salesman

forushgâh فروشگاه store, shop, market

forushi فروشی for sale

forutan فروتن humble, modest

foruzân فروزان bright, light

foshordan (feshâr) فشردن (فشار) to squeeze, to press

foshorde فشرده intensive, pressed

fot kardan فوت کردن to pass away, to die

fot فوت death, passing away

fozul فضول intruder, nosy, meddler

fozulât فضولات waste matters, excrement

fulâd فولاد steel

furushqahe zanjireyi فروشگاه زنجیره ای department store

fut kardan فوت کردن to blow

fut فوت blow, puff

futbâl dasti فوتبال دستی table football

futbâl فوتبال football, soccer

futbâlist فوتبالیست football player

g

gach گچ chalk, plaster

gahgâh گهگاه sometimes

gâhgâhi گاهگاهی occasionally, once in a while

gâhi گاهی sometimes

gahvâre گهواره cradle, crib, hammock

gâl گال scabies

galangedan گلنگدن breechblock

galle گله cattle, herd, flock

galu dard گلو درد sore throat

galu گلو throat

gâm گام step, pace, gait

gand گند stink, foul smell

gandidan (gand) گندیدن (گند) to rot, to decompose, to spoil

gandide گندیده rotten, spoiled

gandom گندم wheat

ganj گنج treasure

ganje گنجه cupboard, cabinet, wardrobe

ganjine گنجینه treasure, store

gap zadan گپ زدن to chat up

gap zani گپ زنی chatting

gap گپ chat, chattering

gar گر bald, mangy, scabbed

garâr gozashtan قرار گذاشتن to make a an appointment

garâr قرار date (appointment)

gârâzh گاراژ garage

garche گرچه although

gârd گارد guard, watchman

gard گرد dust, powder

gardan band گردنبند necklace

gardan koloft گردن کلفت bully, ruffian

gardan گردن neck

gardândan (dardân) گرداندن (گردان) to turn, to spin, to rotate

garde afshâni گرده افشانی pollination

garde گرده pollen, powder

gardesh گردش walk, touring, circulation, excursion

gardgiri kardan گردگیری کردن to dust

gardidan (gard) گردیدن (گرد) to turn, to rotate, to revolve

gâri گاری cart

garm گرم warm, hot, passionate

garmâ گرما heat, warmth

garmâbe گرمابه Turkish bath

garmâzadegi گرمازدگی heat stroke, exhaustion

garmi گرمی heat, warmth, affection

garmkhâne گرمخانه greenhouse

garmsir گرمسیر tropical, warm climate

gârson گارسن waiter

gasht گشت tour, walk, patrol

gashtan (gard) گشتن (گرد) to search, to look for, to turn

gashti گشتی patrol

gâv sanduq گاو صندوق safe (box)

gâv گاو cow, ox, bull

gâvâhan گاو آهن ploughshare

gavâhinâme گواهینامه certificate, license

gavazn گوزن deer, reindeer

gâvcharân گاو چران cowboy

gâyiydan (gây) گاییدن (گای) to fuck, to screw

gâz anbor گاز انبر pliers

gâz gereftan گازگرفتن to bite

gâz گاز bite, nip, gas, gauze

gazand گزند damage, injury

gâzdâr گازدار gassy

gazidan (gaz) گزیدن (گز) to bite, to sting

gâzo'il گازوئیل gasoline

gedâ گدا beggar

gedâyi kardan گدایی کردن to beg

gedâyi گدایی begging

gel گل mud, clay

gelâlud گل آلود muddy

gelâviz گل آویز grappling, scuffling

gelâyol گلایل sword lily

gele kardan گله کردن to complain

gele گله complaint, grievance

gelgir گلگیر mudguard, fender

gelim گلیم coarse carpet

geram گرم gram

gerâmâfon گرامافون record player

gerâmi گرامی dear, honourable, respectful

gerân bahâ گرانبها precious, valuable, priceless

gerân forushi گران فروشی overcharging, fleecing

gerân گران expensive, costly

gerâni گرانی expensiveness, high cost

gerâyesh گرایش tendency, inclination

gerâyidan (gerây) گراییدن (گرای) to intend, to believe, to tend

gerd گرد round, circular

gerdâb گرداب whirlpool, swirl

gerdâvari گردآوری gathering, compiling

gerdbâd گردباد cyclone, hurricane, tornado

gerdehamâyi گرد هم آیی rally

gerdo گردو walnut

gereftan (gir) گرفتن (گیر) to get, to take, to hold, to catch

gereftâr گرفتار involved, captured, very busy

gereftâri گرفتاری trouble, preoccupation, entanglement

gerefte گرفته dull, taken, closed, overcast

gereh zadan گره زدن to knot, to tie

gerim گریم make up

geris گریس grease

gero گرو bond, pledge, pawn

gerogân گروگان hostage, pledge

geryân گریان weeping, tearful

gerye kardan گریه کردن to cry, to weep

gerye گریه crying, weeping, tears

geshniz گشنیز coriander

gij shodan گیج شدن to be confused, to get dizzy

gij گیج dizzy, giddy, confused

giji گیجی dizziness, giddiness

gilâs گیلاس cherry, glass

gir گیر difficulty, stoppage, clog

girâ گیرا attractive, grasping

girande گیرنده receiver, recipient

girboks گیربکس gearbox

gire گیره clip, hairpin, clamp

girodâr گیرودار in the heat of, conflict

gis گیس women's hair

gishe گیشه ticket office, counter

gitâr گیتار guitar

gity گیتی cosmos, universe

give گیوه cotton shoes

giyâh گیاه plant, herb

god گود deep, profound

godâkhte گداخته melted, smelted

godâl گودال pit, ditch, puddle

godâze گدازه lava

godi گودی depth, groove

goftan (guy) گفتن (گوی) to say, to tell

goftâr گفتار speech, discourse, statement

goftegu kardan گفتگو کردن to converse, to discuss, to have a dialogue

goftegu گفتگو conversation, dialogue, dispute

gofto shenud گفت وشنود conversation, dialogue

goh گه shit, faeces

goje farangi گوجه فرنگی tomato

goje گوجه plum

gol forush گل فروش florist

gol گل flower, goal

golâb گلاب rose-water

golâbi گلابی pear

golchin گلچین selection, digest

goldân گلدان vase, flowerpot

golduzi گلدوزی embroidery

gole sorkh گل سرخ rose

golestân گلستان rose garden

golf گلف golf

golule bârân گلوله باران shelling, cannonade

golule گلوله bullet, shot, ball

gom kardan گم کردن to lose

gom گم lost, missing

gomân گمان guess, supposition, supposition

gomâshtan (gomâr) گماشتن (گمار) to appoint, to assign, to employ

gomnâm گمنام anonymous, unknown, incognito

gomrâh kardan گمراه کردن to misled, to deceive

gomrok گمرک customs

gomshode گمشده lost, missing, misplaced

gonâh kardan گناه کردن to sin

gonâh گناه sin, guilt, fault

gonâhkâr گناه کار sinner, guilty, offender

gonbad گنبد dome, arch

gonde گنده large, huge

gong گنگ dumb, mute, silent

gonjândan (gonjân) گنجاندن (گنجان) to include, to contain, to take into account

gonjâyesh گنجایش capacity, volume, size

gonjeshk گنجشک sparrow

gor گر flame, blaze

gorâz گراز boar

gorbân قربان sir (polite address)

gorbe گربه cat

gorg گرگ wolf

gorikhtan (goriz) گریختن (گریز) to escape, to flee, to run away

goriz گریز escape, runaway

gorosne گرسنه hungry, starved

gorosnegi گرسنگی hunger, starvation

goruh گروه group, band

goruhân گروهان company

goruhbân گروهبان sergeant

goruhe khuni گروه خونی blood type

goshâd گشاد wide, broad, loose

goshâyesh گشایش opening, improvement

goshne گشنه hungry

gosikhte گسیخته broken, torn, disconnected

gosil گسیل despatching, sending

gostâkh گستاخ rude, bold

gostaresh گسترش expansion, extension

govâh گواه witness, testimony

govâhi گواهی certificate, evidence, diploma

govâresh گوارش digestion

govâreshi گوارشی digestive

gozarâ گذرا transient, temporary

gozarân گذران livelihood, means of subsistence

gozarândan (gozaran) گذراندن (گذران) to spend, to pass, to transmit

gozâresh dâdan گزارش دادن to report

gozâresh gar گزارش گر reporter, journalist, newscaster

gozâresh گزارش report, news

gozargâh گذرگاه passage, crossing

gozarnâme گذر نامه passport

gozasht گذشت passing, concession, forgiveness

gozâshtan (gozâr) گذاشتن (گذار) to put, to place, to set, to deposit, to let, to leave

gozashtan (gozar) گذشتن (گذر) to pass, to cross, to forgive, to give up

gozashte گذشته past, bygone, last

gozashtegân گذشتگان the deceased

gozide گزیده chosen, selected

gozine گزینه option, selection

gozinesh گزینش selection, choice

gugerd گوگرد sulphur

gul khordan گول خوردن to be cheated

gul zadan گول زدن to deceit, to cheat

gul گول deceit, deception

gunâgun گوناگون various, diverse

gune گونه kind, species, type, cheek

guni گونی big sack to carry fabrics

gur گور grave, tomb, mausoleum

gurestân گورستان cemetery, graveyard

guri قوری teapot

guril گوریل gorilla

gurkan گورکن badger

gurkhar گورخر zebra

gusâle گوساله calf

gusfand گوسفند sheep

gush dâdan گوش دادن to listen

gush mâhi گوش ماهی sea shell

gush گوش ear

gushe gir گوشه گیر isolated, withdrawn

gushe گوشه corner, angle

gushi گوشی receiver, earphone, headphone

gushmâli گوشمالی small punishment

gusht گوشت meat

gushtâlu گوشتالو plump, chubby, fat

gushte khuk گوشت خوک ham

gushtkhâr گوشت خوار carnivore

gushtkub گوشت کوب masher

gushvâre گوشواره earring

gushzad kardan گوشزد کردن to remind, to hint

guvatr گواتر goitre

guyâ گویا expressive, clear, self-evident

guyande گوینده broadcaster, announcer

guyesh گویش dialect

guz گوز fart

guzidan (guz) گوزیدن (گوز) to fart

h

hab حب pill

habbe حبه grain, seed

habs kardan حبس کردن to block, to jail

habs حبس prison, jail

hâd حاد acute

hadaf هدف aim, target, goal

hadafgiri هدف گیری aiming

hadar هدر waste, futile

hadd حد limit, extent

hadde aksar حد اکثر maximum

hâdese حادثه accident, event

hadis حدیث religious narrations

hads zadan حدس زدن to guess

hads حدس guess, assumption

hâfeze حافظه memory, recollection

haffâri حفاری digging, excavation

hafr kardan حفر کردن to dig

hafr حفر digging, excavation

haft هفت seven

haftâd هفتاد seventy

haftâdom هفتادم seventieth

hafte هفته week

haftegi هفتگی weekly

haftom هفتم seventh

haftsad هفتصد seven hundred

hâg هاگ spore

hâjat حاجت necessity, requirement

hâji حاجی one who pilgrims Mecca

hajj حج pilgrimage to Mecca

hajm حجم capacity, mass, volume

hajmi حجمی cubic

hajv هجو lampoon, satire

hâkem حاکم governor, ruling

hâki حاکی indicating, designating

hakk حک engraving, carving

hakkâki حکاکی engraving

hâl حال present, condition

hâlâ حالا now, at the moment

halab حلب tin

halâk هلاک death, perished, downfall

halâkat هلاکت death, ruin

halâl zâde حلال زاده legitimate child

halâl حلال legitimate, permissible

hâlât حالات conditions, circumstances

hâlat حالت state, mood, case

halazun حلزون snail, cochlea

hâle هاله halo, aura

halim حلیم porridge made of wheat

hall kardan حل کردن to dissolve, to solve

hall حل dissolving, solution

hallâji kardan حلاجی کردن to analyze

halq حلق pharynx

halqe حلقه ring, loop, link

halvâ حلوا sweet paste

ham hame همهمه noise, commotion, turmoil

ham ma'ni هم معنی synonymous

ham otaqi هم اتاقی roommate

ham qadd همقد of the same hight or size

ham sen همسن of the same age

ham vatan هم وطن compatriot, fellow citizen

ham zisti همزیستی coexistence

ham هم also, too, both, either, likewise

hamâhang هماهنگ coordinated, harmonious

hamâhangi هماهنگی harmony, coordination

hamân همان the same, that very same

hamânâ همانا indeed, certainly

hamânand همانند alike, identical, like, same

hamâse حماسه epic poem

hamâvâzi هم آوازی chorus, concord

hambastari هم بستری sleeping together

hamchenân همچنان accordingly, in that way

hamchenin همچنین too, as well

hamcheshmi همچشمی rivalry, competition

hamd حمد praise

hamdam همدم companion, confident, intimate

hamdardi همدردی sympathy

hamdast همدست collaborator, accomplice

hamdasti همدستی collaboration, conspiracy, complot

hamdeli همدلی agreement, consensus

hamdigar همدیگر one another, each other

hame porsi همه پرسی referendum

hame همه all, every, whole, everyone

hamegi همگی all, whole, entire

hamegir همه گیر epidemic

hâmel حامل carrier, transporters

hâmele حامله pregnant

hâmelegi حاملگی pregnancy

hamgen همگن congenial, cohort

hamgerâ همگرا convergent

hâmi حامی supporter, protector

hamin alân همین الان right now

hamin ke همینکه as soon as, when, just as

hamin همین only this, this same

hamishe همیشه always, forever

hamishegi همیشگی permanent, everlasting

hamjavâr همجوار neighbour, adjacent

hamjens همجنس homogeneous

hamjes bâz همجنس باز homosexual

hamkâr همکار colleague, co-worker, fellow member

hamkâri kardan همکاری کردن to cooperate, to collaborate

hamkâri همکاری cooperation, collaboration

hamkelâs همکلاس classmate

haml kardan حمل کردن to carry

haml حمل carrying, transport

hamle kardan حمله کردن to attack, to rush

hamle حمله attack, rush, assault

hamlo naql حمل و نقل
transportation, conveyance

hammâl حمال carrier, porter

hammâm حمام bath, Turkish bath

hamnishini هم نشینی
companionship, friendship

hamno' هم نوع homogenous,
same race or species

hamotâqi هم اطاقی roommate

hamqatâr همقطار colleague, co-
worker

hamrâh همراه companion, fellow,
company

hamrâhi همراهی accompanying,
escorting

hamsafar همسفر travel companion,
fellow traveller

hamsâl همسال of the same age

hamsân همسان alike, same

hamsar همسر spouse, husband,
wife

hamsâye همسایه neighbour

hamsâyegi همسایگی
neighbourhood, vicinity

hamshahri همشهری fellow citizen,
fellow townsman

hamshekam هم شکم twin

hamshire همشیره sister

hamsohbat هم صحبت interlocutor

hamtâ همتا match, peer, equal

hamvâr هموار plane, flat, level

hamvâre همواره always, ever, all
the time

hamyâri همیاری cooperation

hamzabân همزبان speaking the
same language

hamzâd همزاد twin, born together

hamzamân همزمان concurrent,
contemporary, simultaneous

hanâ حنا henna

hang هنگ regiment

hangoft هنگفت enormous, large,
huge

hanjare حنجره larynx

hanuz هنوز yet, still

haq koshi حق کشی injustice

haq shenâs حق شناس grateful

haq حق right, duty, privilege

haqâyeq حقایق facts

haqiqat حقیقت truth, reality, fact

haqiqi حقیقی real, true

haqir حقیر humble, small, modest

haqqâniyat حقانیت truth,
legitimacy

har chand هر چند although,
though

har che هر چه whatever, what

har cheqadr هر چه قدر as much
as, whatever

har do هر دو both

har kodâm هر کدام each

har ruz هر روز every day

hâr هار rabid, mad

har هر each, any, every

harakat kardan حرکت کردن
to move, to depart

harakat حرکت movement, motion,
departure

harâm kardan حرام کردن to prohibit
by religious law

harâm حرام prohibited, illegitimate

haram حرم shrine, holy tomb

haramsarâ حرمسرا harem

harâmzâde حرامزاده bustard, illegitimate

harârat حرارت heat, temperature

harâs هراس fear, fright, dread

harâsân هراسان scared, fearful, frightened

harâsidan (harâs) هراسیدن (هراس) to scare, to be afraid

harâsnâk هراسناک dreadful, frightful

harbe حربه weapon, excuse

harf sheno حرف شنو obedient, heedful

harf zadan حرف زدن to speak, to talk

harf حرف talking, letter, speech

hargâh هرگاه whenever, in case

hargez هرگز never, not at all, ever

hâri هاری rabidness

harif حریف rival, opponent

harim حریم boundary, limit

hariq حریق fire

harir حریر silk

haris حریص greedy

harjo marj talab هرج و مرج طلب anarchist

harjo marj هرج و مرج chaos, anarchy, confusion

harkas هرکس anybody, everybody, anyone

harrâf حراف talkative, verbose

harrâj kardan حراج کردن to auction

harrâj حراج on sale, auction

harz هرز vain, worn out, waste

harze هرزه libertine, lewd, profligate

harzegi هرزگی libertinism, profligacy

hasad حسد jealousy

hasbe حصبه typhoid fever

hâsel khiz حاصل خیز fertile, productive

hâsel حاصل produce, crop, harvest

hâshâ حاشا denial

hashare kosh حشره کش insecticide

hashare shenâs حشره شناس entomologist

hashare حشره bug, insect

hashari حشری lustful, horny

hashish حشیش hashish

hâshiye حاشیه margin, edge, border

hasht هشت eight

hashtâd هشتاد eighty

hashtâdom هشتادم eightieth

hashtom هشتم eighth

hashtpâ هشت پا octopus

hashtsad هشتصد eight hundred

hasir حصیر mat

hasrat khordan حسرت خوردن to regret

hasrat حسرت regret, rue

hassâs حساس sensitive, critical

hassâsiyat حساسیت sensitivity, allergy

hast هست is, there is

hastand هستند they are, are

haste هسته nucleus, stone of fruit

hasteyi هسته ای nuclear

hasti هستی existence, life, being

hasud حسود jealous, envious

hatk هتک dishonouring, violating, rape

hatman حتماً sure, certainly

hatmi حتمی certain, indispensable

hattâ حتی even

hattâki هتاکی swearing, defamation

hattal emkân حتی الامکان as far as possible

havâ هوا air, weather, atmosphere

havâdâr هوادار admirer, fan, supporter

havâdes حوادث accidents, occurrences

havâkesh هواکش air vent, chimney

havâkhori هواخوری walking for pleasure, strolling

havâle حواله draft, transfer, assignment

havâli حوالی vicinity, environs

havânavard هوانورد navigator, airman, pilot

havâpeymâ هواپیما aeroplane

havâpeymâyi هواپیمایی aviation, airline

havâr هوار loud cry, scream

havas bâz هوسباز whimsical, playful, capricious

havas rân هوسران whimsical, playful, capricious

havâs حواس senses, memory

havas هوس violent desire, passion, whim, longing

havas هوس کردن to long for

havâshenâsi هواشناسی meteorology

havâyi هوایی aerial, related to air

havâzi هوازی aerobe

hâvi حاوی containing, comprising

havij هویج carrot

havu هوو a rival wife

havvâ حوا Eve

havvâri حواری disciple, apostle

hayâ حیا decency, modesty

hayâhu هیاهو commotion, brawl, noise

hayât حیات life, living

hayât حیاط yard, courtyard

hayâti حیاتی vital

hayejân âvar هیجان آور exciting, moving, stimulating

hayejân هیجان excitement, agitation

hâyhây های های noisy crying

hayulâ هیولا monster

hâzeme هاضمه digestive

hâzer حاضر ready, prepared, present

hazf kardan حذف کردن to delete, to eliminate

hazf حذف deletion, elimination

hazine هزینه expense, cost, charge

hazineye post هزینه پست postage

hazm kardan هضم کردن to digest

hazrat حضرت highness, excellency

hazyân goftan هذیان گفتن
to hallucinate

hazyân هذیان delirium,
hallucination

hazz kardan حظ کردن to enjoy

hazz حظ enjoyment, pleasure

hebbe هبه gift, donation,
endowment

hedâyat kardan هدایت کردن
to guide, to lead

hedâyat هدایت guidance, leading,
conduction

hedye هدیه gift, present

hefâzat kardan حفاظت کردن
to protect

hefâzat حفاظت protection,
shielding

hefdah هفده seventeen

hefdahom هفدهم seventeenth

hefz حفظ memorising, protecting,
guarding

hejâ هجا syllable

hejâb حجاب covering, wearing veil

hejâmat حجامت venesection

hejâyi هجایی syllabic

hejdah هجده eighteen

hejdahom هجدهم eighteenth

hejji هجی spelling

hejle حجله bridal chamber

hejrân هجران separation, isolation

hejrat هجرت departure, migration,
prophet's migration from Mecca
to Medina

hejri هجری related to Hejrat

hejriye qamari هجری قمری Islamic
lunar calendar

hejriye shamsi هجری شمسی
Iranian solar calendar

hekâyat حکایت story, anecdote,
narrative

hekhâmaneshi هخامنشی
Achaemenid

hekmat حکمت wisdom,
philosophy

hektâr هکتار hectare

hel هل cardamoms

helâl هلال crescent, new moon

helhele هلهله cheers, exultation,
applauding

hemâqat حماقت stupidity,
foolishness

hemâyat kardan حمایت کردن
to protect, to support

hemâyat حمایت protection,
support

hemmat همت ambition, aspiration,
effort

hend هند India

hendese هندسه geometry

hendesi هندسی geometrical

hendevâne هندوانه watermelon

hendi هندی Indian

hendochin هندوچین Indochina

hendu هندو Hindu

hengâm هنگام time, occasion

heqârat حقارت inferiority, scorn

heram هرم pyramid

herâst حراست guarding, guard

herfe حرفه job, profession, trade

herfeyi حرفه ای professional

heroin هروئین heroin

hers حرص greed

hesâb dâr حساب دار accountant, bookkeeper

hesâb kardan حساب کردن to calculate, to pay bills

hesâb حساب account, calculation, math

hesâbi حسابی reasonable, reliable

hesâdat حسادت jealousy, envy

hesâr حصار fence, wall

hess kardan حس کردن to feel

hess حس feeling, sense

hey'at هیئت board, council

heybat هیبت awe, dignity, appalling presence

heyf حیف pity

heyhât هیهات alas

heykal هیکل figure, shape, body

heyn حین during, at the moment of

heyrân حیران amazed, astound

heyrat angiz حیرت انگیز puzzling, stunning

heys حیث regard, respect

heysiyat حیثیت prestige, reputation

heyvân حیوان animal, beast

heyvâni حیوانی brutal, beastly

heyz حیض menstruation

hezânat حضانت fostering, custody

hezâr هزار thousand

hezâre هزاره millennium

hezârom هزارم thousandth

hezârpâ هزارپا myriapod

hezb حزب party

hich chiz هیچ چیز nothing, anything

hich gâh هیچ گاه never, ever

hich gune هیچگونه under no condition

hich jâ هیچ جا nowhere

hich kâre هیچ کاره good for nothing, worthless

hich kas هیچ کس no one, nobody

hich kodâm هیچ کدام neither, none of them

hich vaqt هیچ وقت never, ever

hich yek هیچیک no one, none

hich هیچ nothing, not, no, any, none

hicho puch هیچ و پوچ nothing, vain, futile

hijdah هجده eighteen

hile حیله trick, deceit

hipâtit هپاتیت hepatitis

hipnotism هیپنوتیزم hypnosis

hite حیطه domain, enclosure

hiz هیز catamite, lascivious

hizom هیزم firewood

ho kardadan هو کردن to defame

hobâb حباب bubble, globe

hobubât حبوبات grains, cereals

hochi هوچی rumour monger, totter

hodhod هدهد hoopoe

hodud حدود limits, boundaries

hohuq begir حقوق بگیر stipendiary

hojâj حجاج Hajjis

hojb حجب modesty, shyness

hojre حجره old type of business office

hojum هجوم attack, rush, invasion

hokm حکم sentence (prison), conviction, order

hokrân حکمران ruler, governor

hokumat kardan حکومت کردن to govern, to rule

hol dâdan هل دادن to push

hol kardan هول کردن to startle

holand هلند Holland, Netherlands

hole حوله towel

holnâk هولناک terrifying, frightening, horrendous, scary

holqum حلقوم throat, pharynx

home حومه suburbs, outskirts

honar هنر art, craft, skill, talent

honarestân هنرستان technical school

honari هنری artistic

honarmand هنرمند artist, artistic, industrious

honarpishe هنرپیشه actor, artist, movie star

hoqqe bâz حقه باز impostor, cheat

hoqqe حقه trick, cheating

hoquq dân حقوقدان lawyer

hoquq حقوق rights, salary

hoquqe bashar حقوق بشر human rights

hoquqe madani حقوق مدنی civil rights

hoquqi حقوقی civil, legal

hormat حرمت respect, regard

horuf حروف letters

hosele حوصله patience, tolerance

hoshdâr dâdan هشدار دادن to warn

hoshdâr هشدار warning, alert, beware

hosn حسن beauty, virtue

hotel هتل hotel

hoveydâ هویدا obvious, apparent, appearing

hoviyyat هویت identity, identification

hoz حوض pond, pool, basin

hozeye حوضه region, area, district

hozur حضور presence, attendance

hozzâr حضار audience

hulu هلو peach

huri حوری Nymph

hush هوش intelligence, memory, sense

hushyâr هوشیار aware, alert, cautious

hut حوت Pisces

i

ijâd kardan ایجاد کردن to create

ijâd ایجاد creation, production

il ایل tribe, clan

imân ایمان faith, belief

iman ایمن safe, secure

imani ایمنی security, safety

in این this

ingilis انگلیس England

ingilisi انگلیسی English

inhâ اینها these

injâ اینجا here

injâneb اینجانب I (polite)

irâd gereftan ایراد گرفتن to criticize,
to blame

irân ایران Iran

irâni ایرانی Iranian

irland ایرلند Ireland

isâ عیسی Jesus

isâr ایثار sacrifice, generosity

ishân ایشان they (Pol)

ist ایست stop!

istâdan (ist) ایستادن (ایست)
to stand, to stand up, to wait

istâdegi ایستادگی resistance,
insistence

istgâh ایستگاه station, stop

istgâhe metro ایستگاه مترو subway
station

istgâhe tâksi ایستگاه تاکسی taxi
stand

iyâlat ایالت province, state

iyâlâte mottahedeye âmrikâ
ایالات متحده آمریکا USA

izad ایزد God

j

jâ oftâdan جا افتادن to settle

jâ oftâde جا افتاده matured

jâ جا place, seat, space

ja'be جعبه box, case, carton

jâbejâ kardan جابجا کردن to transfer, to move

jâbejâ جابجا displaced, dislocated

ja'beye komaâhaye avvaliyye جعبه کمکهای اولیه first-aid kit

jabin جبین forehead

jad جد grandfather

jâdde جاده path, road, route

jâdu جادو magic, spell, charm

jâdugar جادوگر magician

jadval جدول table, kerb, puzzle

jafang جفنگ nonsense, silly

ja'fari جعفری parsley

jahâd جهاد holy war

jahâlat جهالت ignorance

jahân جهان world, universe

jahângard جهانگرد tourist

jahâni جهانی universal, global

jahannam جهنم hell

jahât جهات directions, reasons

jahat جهت direction, side, cause

jâhel جاهل ignorant, unlearned

jahesh جهش jump, mutation

jahiziye جهیزیه trousseau

jahl جهل ignorance

jâhtalabi جاه طلبی ambition

jâjim جاجیم coarse woollen blanket

jak جک jack (for car)

jâkesh جاکش pimp

jâkhâli جاخالی blank space, missing

ja'l kardan جعل کردن to forge

ja'l جعل forgery, fabrication

jalab جلب deceitful, prostitute

jalâl جلال glory, grandeur

jalase جلسه session, meeting

jalb جلب arrest, subpoena

jâleb جالب attractive, interesting

jâlebâsi جالباسی clothes hanger

jallâd جلاد executioner

jalq جلق masturbation

jam' âvari جمع آوری collection, gathering

jam' kardan جمع کردن to add, to collect, to gather

jâm جام cup, pane

jam' جمع sum, addition, group

jamâ' جماع intercourse, coitus

jamâ'at جماعت congregation, community

jam'an جمعا totally, altogether

jâme jahâni جام جهانی world cup

jâme varzeshi جام ورزشی league

jâme' جامع comprehensive, universal

jâmed جامد solid, firm

jâmedât جامدات solids

jâme'e shenâsi جامعه شناسی sociology

jâme'e جامعه community, society

jân dâdan جان دادن to die

jân feshâni جانفشانی devotion, self sacrifice

jân nesâri جان نثاری devotion, sacrifice

jân جان soul, power, essence, life

janâb 'âli جنابعالی your excellency

janâb جناب excellency, highness

jânamâz جانماز a cloth for praying

janâq جناق wishbone, sternum

jânavar shenâsi جانورشناسی zoology

jânavar جانور animal, beast

janâze جنازه corpse, carcass

jânbâz جانباز self-sacrificer

janbe جنبه side, beside to, adjacent

jândar جاندار animate

jândârân جانداران fauna

jâneb جانب side, direction

jânebdâri جانبداری support

jâneshin جانشین successor, substitute

jang afzâr جنگ افزار weapon, arms

jang kardan جنگ کردن to fight

jang جنگ war, battle

jangal zodayi جنگل زدایی deforestation

jangal جنگل forest, wood, bush

jangalbân جنگلبان forester, ranger

jangande جنگنده fighter

jangi جنگی martial, military

jangju جنگجو fighter, belligerent

jâni جانی criminal, murderer

janin جنین fetu's, embryo

janjâl جنجال commotion, brawl

jannat جنت paradise

janub جنوب south

jarâ'ed جراید newspapers

jarâ'em جرائم crimes, fines

jarâhat جراحت injury, wound

jârakhti جارختی clothes hanger

jaraqqe جرقه spark, sparkle

jarasaqil جرثقیل crane

jarayân جریان flowing, circulation

jarb جرب scabies

jârchi جارچی pubic crier, herald

jâri جاری flowing, running, current

jarime جریمه fine, penalty

jarrâh جراح surgeon

jarrâhi جراحی surgery

jâru kardan جارو کردن to sweep

jâru جارو broom

jasad جسد corpse, carcass

jasârat جسارت courage, boldness

jashn gereftan جشن گرفتن to celebrate

jashn جشن festival, celebration

jashnvare جشنواره festival

jâshu جاشو seaman

jasur جسور bold, daring

jâsus جاسوس spy, agent

jâsusi جاسوسی espionage, spying

javâb dâdan جواب دادن to answer, to reply

javâb جواب answer, reply

javâher furush جواهر فروش jeweller

javâher جواهر jewellery, gems

javâherât جواهرات jewellery

javâme' جوامع societies

javân mard جوانمرد generous, brave

javân marg جوانمرگ dying in youth

javân جوان young

javandegân جوندگان rodents

javâne جوانه bud, sprout

javâni جوانی youth

javâz جواز permit, licence

jâvedân جاودان eternal, perpetual

jâvid جاوید eternal, immortal

javidan (jav) (جو) جویدن to chew

javv جو atmosphere, space

jâyegâh جایگاه place, quarter

jâyez جایز permissible

jâyeze جایزه prize, award

jazâ جزا penalty, punishment

jazâyer جزایر islands

jazâyi جزایی penal

jazb kardan جذب کردن to absorb

jazb جذب absorption

jâzebe جاذبه gravity, attraction

jazire جزیره island

jazr جذر square root

jazro mad جذر ومد tide, flux and reflux

jazzâb جذاب attractive, charming

jebhe جبهه frontline

jedâl جدال quarrel, brawl

jeddan جدا seriously

jeddi جدی serious, energetic

jegar جگر liver, guts

jegarsuz جگرسوز painful, heart-rending

jeld جلد cover, copy, volume

jelf جلف indecent, immodest

jelo جلو front, ahead, advanced

jelogiri جلوگیری prevention, hindrance

jelve dâdan جلوه دادن to pretend

jenâh جناح wing, side

jenahe chap جناح چپ left-wing

jenahe rast جناح راست right-wing

jenâyat kâr جنایت کار criminal, murderer

jenâyat جنایت crime, murder, offence

jenâyi جنایی criminal

jende khâne جنده خانه brothel

jende جنده prostitute, whore

jendegi جندگی prostitution

jengir جن گیر exorcist

jenn جن jinni, jinn

jens جنس kind, gender, goods, made (of)

jense gerayi جنس گرایی sexism

jensi جنسی sexual

jensiyyat جنسیت sexuality, sex

jeqjeqe جغجغه rattle box

jerm جرم body, mass

jesm جسم body, object, material

jeyrân جیران gazelle, deer

jib bor جیب بر pickpocket

jib جیب pocket

jibi جیبی pocket size

jin جین jeans

jip جیپ jeep

jiq zadan جیغ زدن to scream, to cry

jiq جیغ scream, cry

jire جيره allocation, share

jirjirak جيرجيرک cricket (insect)

jish kardan جيش کردن to piss, to urinate

jish جيش piss, urine

jive جيوه mercury

jo جو barley

jobrân kardan جبران کردن to compensate

jobrân جبران compensation, indemnity

jodâ kardan جدا کردن to separate

jodâ جدا separate, loose

joft جفت pair, even, couple, placenta

joftak جفتک kicking

joftgiri جفت گيری mating, coitus

jogandomi جوگندمی grey

johar جوهر essence, ink

jok جوک joke

jolân جولان show off, flaunting

jolbak جلبک seaweed, algae

jolge جلگه plain

jom'e جمعه Friday

jomhuri جمهوری republic

jomjome جمجمه skull, cranium

jomle جمله sentence (words), all

jonbesh جنبش movement, motion

jonbidan (jonb) (جنب) جنبيدن to move, to shake

jong جنگ anthology, collection

jonob جنب having a wet dream

jonub جنوب south

jonun جنون madness, insanity

joqd جغد owl

jor جور cruelty, tyranny

jorâb جوراب socks, stockings

jor'at جرات courage, daring

jor'e جرعه sip, draught

jorm جرم crime, offence

josse جثه built, bulk

josteju kardan جستجو کردن to search

josteju جستجو search, quest

joz جز except

joz' جزء part, section, ingredient

jozâm جذام leprosy

joz'i جزئی slight, trivial, partial

joz'iyât جزئيات details

jozve جزوه pamphlet, lecture notes

juhud جهود Jew, Jewish

juje kabâb جوجه کباب chicken kebab

juje tiqi جوجه تيغی porcupine

juje جوجه chicken, chick

jukhe جوخه squad, section

jur kardan جور کردن to sort, to match, to solve

jur جور sort, type, assorted

jush جوش acne, pimple, rash

jushidan (jush) (جوش) جوشيدن to boil

jushide جوشيده boiled, stewed

jushkâr جوش کار welder

juyande جوينده seeker, finder

juybâr جويبار brook, small river

k

kabâb کباب kebab, roasted meat

kabâbi کبابی kebab seller

kabed کبد liver

kâbin کابین marriage portion

kâbine کابینه cabinet (government)

kabir کبیر mature, great

kabise کبیسه leap year

kabk کبک partridge

kâbl کابل cable

kabud کبود dark blue

kâbus کابوس nightmare

kabutar کبوتر pigeon

kachal کچل bald, having scalp disease

kadbânu کدبانو housewife

kadkhodâ کدخدا headman, elder man

kâdo کادو souvenir

kâdr کادر personnel, staff, frame

kadu کدو pumpkin

kaf کف foam, bubble, palm, floor, clapping

kafan کفن shroud, grave clothes

kâfar کافر unbeliever, secular, pagan

kafbini کف بینی chiromancy, palm reading

kâfe کافه cafeteria

kaffâre کفاره ransom, redemption, alms

kaffâsh کفاش shoemaker

kafgir کفگیر skimmer

kâfi کافی enough, sufficient

kafsh duzak کفشدوزک ladybird

kafsh کفش shoe

kaftar bâz کفتر باز pigeon fancier

kaftâr کفتار hyena

kaftar کفتر pigeon

kâfur کافور camphor

kâh کاه hay, straw

kâhen کاهن Jewish priest

kâhesh کاهش decrease, deduction, reduction

kahkashân کهکشان The Milky Way, galaxy

kâhu کاهو lettuce

kaj shodan کج شدن to tilt

kâj کاج pine tree

kaj کج tilted, slanting, crooked

kak کک flea

kâkh کاخ palace, mansion

kâkol کاکل topknot, forelock

kakomak کک و مک freckles

kâl کال unripe, premature

kal کل bald

kâlâ کالا goods, merchandise, product

kalâfe کلافه hank, network, distressed

kalak zadan کلک زدن to trick, to fool

kalak کلک trick, phoney

kalâm کلام word, speech

kalam کلم cabbage

kalame کلمه word

kalân کلان big, large, massive

kalântar کلانتر sheriff

kalântari کلانتری police station

kalâq کلاغ crow

kâlbâs كالباس salami

kâlbod shekâfi كالبد شكافى autopsy

kâlej كالج college

kâleske كالسكه carriage, coach, pram

kalimi كليمى Jew

kallâsh كلاش sponger, charlatan

kalle pâche كله پاچه sheep trotters

kalle shaq كله شق stubborn

kalle كله head, top, mind

kalukh كلوخ clod

kam khuni كمخونى anaemia

kam shodan كم شدن to decrease

kâm كام palate, mouth

kam كم few, little, less

kamân كمان bow, arc

kamânche كمانچه a musical instrument

kamâne كمانه hoop, rim

kamar band كمربند belt, waistband, seat belt

kamar كمر waist

kambud كمبود shortage, deficit, lack

kâmel كامل complete, perfect, thorough

kami كمى a little

kamin كمين ambush, lying in wait

kâmiyâb كامياب successful, prosperous

kâmiyon كاميون lorry, truck

kamiyyat كميت quantity

kamkam كم كم little by little

kammi كمى quantitative

kamrang كم رنگ light, faint, pale

kamru كمرو shy, timid

kamtar كمتر lesser, fewer, less often

kamtarin كمترين least

kamyâb كمياب rare, scarce

kanaf كنف cannabis, hemp

kânâl كانال canal

kanâr كنار side, edge, away, beside

kanâre giri كناره گيرى resignation, quitting

kandan (kan) كندن (كن) to dig, to take off, to engrave, to pick, to pull off

kandekâri كنده كارى engraving, carving

kândid كانديد candidate, nominee, applicant

kandokâv كندوكاو search, investigation

kandu كندو hive

kane كنه leech

kangar كنگر acanthus

kanise كنيسه synagogue

kaniz كنيز female servant

kankâsh كنكاش deliberation, research

kânun كانون centre, focus

kapak zade كپك زده mouldy

kapak كپك mould, must

kapar كپر hut

kâput كاپوت bonnet, condom

kâqaz كاغذ paper, letter

kâr gardân كارگردان director, stage manager

kâr kardan كار كردن to work

kâr کار work, job, profession

kar کر deaf

karafs کرفس celery

kârâgâh کارآگاه detective

karam کرم generosity, courtesy

kârâmuz کارآموز trainee, apprentice, beginner

karâne کرانه coast, shore

kârâyi کارآیی efficiency, merit

kârbord کاربرد application, use

kârd کارد knife

kardan (kon) (کن) کردن to do, to make, to fuck (slang)

kârdân کاردان experienced, efficient

kare کره butter

kârfarmâ کارفرما employer

kargadan کرگدن rhinoceros

kârgâh کارگاه workshop, studio

kârgar کارگر worker, labourer

kârgari کارگری labour work, construction work

kârgozâr کارگزار agent, correspondent

kârgozini کارگزینی recruitment, human resources

kari کری deafness

kârikâtor کاریکاتور cartoon, caricature

kârkard کارکرد output, yield

karkas کرکس vulture

kârkhâne کارخانه factory

kârkonân کارکنان personnel, employees, crew

kârkoshte کارکشته experienced

kârmand کارمند employee, office worker

kârnâme کارنامه test result

kârpardâz کارپرداز supplier, in charge of supplies

kârshekani کارشکنی sabotage, obstruction

kârshenâs کارشناس expert, specialist

kârshenâsi کارشناسی expertise, bachelor degree

kârt postâl کارت پستال post card

kârt کارت card

kârte e'tebâri کارت اعتباری credit card

kârte shenâsâyi کارت شناسایی identification card

kârte telefon کارت تلفن phone card

kârton کارتن carton, board box

kârvân کاروان caravan, convoy

kârvarzi کارورزی internship, training

kas کس person, kin, someone

kasabe کسبه traders, merchants

kasâd کساد stagnant, stale, dull market

kasâlat âvar کسالت آور boring

kasâlat کسالت illness, being unwell

kasb کسب earning, job, trade

kâse کاسه bowl, socket

kâseb کاسب tradesman, merchant

kasel کسل tired, bored, sluggish

kâsh کاش I wish

kâshef کاشف discoverer

kashf kardan کشف کردن to discover

kashf كشف discovery, deciphering
kashfiyât كشفيات discoveries
kâshi كاشى glazed tile
kâshikâr كاشى كار tiler
kashk كشك dried whey
kashki كشكى groundless, without bases
kâshtan (kâr) كاشتن (كار) to plant, to sow
kashti كشتى ship, vessel
kashtirâni كشتيرانى sailing, shipping
kasif كثيف dirty, messy, untidy, filthy
kâsni كاسنى chicory
kasr كسر decimal, deduction, fraction
kâstan (kâh) كاستن (كاه) to reduce, to decline, to decrease
katâni كتانى cotton, linen
katbi كتبى written
kate كته boiled rice
katibe كتيبه inscription
kâtolik كاتوليك catholic
kâ'uchu كائوچو rubber
kavir كوير salt desert
kâvosh كاوش digging, excavation, search
kazâyi كذايى so and so
kâzeb كاذب fake, false, untrue
ke كه when, that
kebrit كبريت matches
keder كدر blurred, dim, dull, opaque
kefâlat كفالت guardianship

kefâyat كفايت adequacy, sufficiency
kelâj كلاج clutch (car)
kelâs كلاس class, grade, classroom
kelid كليد key, switch
kelisâ كليسا cathedral, church
kelishe كليشه cliché, stereotype
kenâr raftan كنار رفتن to withdraw, to go away
kenâr كنار beside
kenâre daryâ كنار دريا seaside
kenâye âmiz كنايه آميز sarcastic
kenâye zadan كنايه زدن to be sarcastic
kenâye كنايه irony, sarcasm
keneft كنفت insulted, disgraced
kenise كنيسه synagogue
kerâvât كراوات tie
kerâye kardan كرايه كردن to lease, to rent, to hire
kerâye neshin كرايه نشين tenant, renter
kerâye كرايه lease, rent, hire, fare
kerdâr كردار behaviour, deed, manner
kerekh كرخ numb
kerem كرم cream
kerkere كركره Venetian blinds
kerm khordegi كرم خوردگى tooth decay, decay
kerm كرم worm
kesâfat kâri كثافت كارى dirty work, making mess
kesâfat كثافت dirt, filth, mess

kesh کش elastic band, rubber band

keshâle کشاله groin

keshâvarz کشاورز farmer

keshâvarzi کشاورزی agriculture, farming

keshesh کشش attraction, draught

keshidan (kesh) کشیدن (کش) to pull, to draw, to drag

keshide کشیده extended, pulled, long, slap

keshik کشیک guard, patrol, post

keshish کشیش priest

keshmakesh کشمکش struggle, conflict

keshmesh کشمش raisins, sultanas

kesho کشو drawer

kesht کشت cultivation, plantation

keshti کشتی ship

keshtzâr کشتزار field, farm

keshvar کشور country, homeland

kesi کسی somebody, someone

ketâb dâr کتابدار librarian

ketâb forush کتاب فروش book seller

ketâb forushi کتاب فروشی bookshop

ketâb khâne کتابخانه library

ketâb کتاب book

ketâbche کتابچه booklet

ketf کتف shoulder

ketmân کتمان denial, concealment

key کی when, what time

keyf کیف euphoria, joy, pleasure

keyfar کیفر penalty, punishment

keyfari کیفری penal

keyfi کیفی qualitative

keyfiyyat کیفیت quality

keyhân کیهان cosmos, universe

keyk کیک cake

keyvân کیوان Saturn

kezb کذب lie, untrue

ki کی who, whom

kif کیف purse, bag, briefcase

kilo کیلو kilo

kilometre کیلومتر kilometre

kine کینه animosity, hatred

kinejuyi کینه جویی revengefulness

kir کیر penis

kise khâb کیسه خواب sleeping bag

kise کیسه bag, sack, flannel

kish کیش religion, check mat, shoo (for birds)

kishmât کیش مات checkmate

kist کیست cystitis

kodâm کدام which, which one

kodan کودن stupid, dumb

kodurat کدورت opacity, annoyance

kofr کفر profanity, blasphemy

kohan کهن ancient, archaic

kohne کهنه old, worn out, used, outdated, cloth

kohulat کهولت senility, old age

kojâ کجا where

kolâh bardâr کلاهبردار cheat, fraudulent

kolâh gis کلاه گیس wig

kolâh کلاه hat, helmet, cap

kolang كلنگ pick
kolbe كلبه cottage, hut
kolfat كلفت maid, housemaid
koli كولى gypsy
koliye كليه kidney
koll كل all, whole, entire
kollan كلا entirely, totally
kolli كلى general, total
koloft كلفت thick, coarse
koluche كلوچه cookie
kolye كليه kidney
komak kardan كمك كردن to help
komak كمك help, aid, assistance
komaki كمكى aid, auxiliary, hand, helping
komedi كمدى comedy
komisiyon كميسيون commission
komod كمد wardrobe, shelf
komonist كمونيست communist
kond كند slow, blunt, sluggish
konde كنده log
kongere كنگره congress
konj كنج corner, angle
konjkâvi كنجكاوى curiosity
konjod كنجد sesame
konsert كنسرت a concert
konserv كنسرو canned food
konsul كنسول consul
konsulgari كنسول گرى consulate
konterât كنترات contract, agreement
kontor كنتور counter, meter, gauge
kontorol كنترل control, inspection
konuni كنونى present, current

konyâk كنياك brandy
konye كنيه nickname
kopon كوپن coupon
kord كرد Kurdish
kore كره planet, globe, sphere, Korea
koreye zamin كره زمين planet earth
kork كرك soft hair, fluff
korre كره colt
korset كرست bra, corset
korsi كرسى seat, traditional heater
kos كس vagina, vulva
koshande كشنده fatal, lethal, deadly
koshtan (kosh) كشتن (كش) to kill, to murder
koshtâr كشتار killing, slaughter, massacre
koshtârgâh كشتارگاه slaughterhouse
koshte كشته murdered, killed
koshti كشتى wrestling
koskesh كس كش pimp
kosuf كسوف eclipse of the sun
kot كت jacket
kotak كتك beating
ku كو where is it?
kubidan (kub) كوبيدن (كوب) to pound, to mash, to grind, to bash
kubide كوبيده minced, mashed, pounded
kuch كوچ moving, migrating
kuche كوچه alley, lane
kuchek كوچك small, little, tiny

kuchneshin كوچ نشين nomadic tribes

kuchulu كوچولو tiny, little kid

kud كود fertilizer, compost

kudak كودک child, baby, toddler

kudakestân كودکستان kindergarten

kudaki كودکى childhood

kudetâ كودتا coup

kufte كوفته bruised, a type of meal

kuftegi كوفتگى bruise

kuh navardi كوه نوردى mountain climbing

kuh peymâyi كوه پيمايى mountaineering

kuh كوه mountain

kuhân كوهان hump of camel

kuhestân كوهستان mountain ranges

kuhestâni كوهستانى mountainous, hilly, highlander

kuhpâye كوه پايه mountain side

kuk zadan كوک زدن to stitch

kuk كوک stitch, tune, winding

kuku كوكو vegetable omelette

kul كول shoulder

kulâk كولاک snowy storm

kule poshti كوله پشتى backpack

kuli كولى anchovy

kun كون ass, anus, arse, butt

kunde كون ده passive homo-sexual

kuni كونى passive homo-sexual

kur كور blind

kurân كوران draught, air current

kure كوره crematory, kiln, furnace

kuri كورى blindness

kurkurâne كوركورانه blindly

kurs كورس race

kurtâzh كورتاژ abortion

kuse كوسه shark, thin-bearded

kushesh كوشش effort, struggle, attempt

kushidan (kush) كوشيدن (كوش) to try, to struggle

kutâh كوتاه short, low, brief

kutâhi كوتاهى shortcoming, negligence

kutule كوتوله dwarf, midget

kuy كوى alley, narrow street, quarter

kuze كوزه jug, pitcher

kh

khâb âlud خواب آلود sleepy

khâb gardi خواب گردی sleepwalking

khâb خواب sleep

khabar gozâri خبر گذاری news agency

khabar خبر news, notice

khabarchin خبرچین informer

khabardâr خبردار alert, attention, aware

khabarnegâr خبرنگار correspondent, reporter

khâbgâh خوابگاه dormitory, mess

khâbidan (khâb) خوابیدن (خواب) to sleep

khabis خبیث malicious, wicked

khadamât خدمات services (assistance)

khadame خدمه crew, servants, attendants

khâdem خادم servant, server

khâ'en خائن traitor, betrayer

khafe خفه stuffy, choked

khafeqân خفقان suffocation, oppression

khafif خفیف mild, light

khâgine خاگینه omelet

khâhar khânde خواهر خوانده adopted sister

khâhar shohar خواهر شوهر husband's sister

khâhar zâde خواهر زاده nephew or niece

khâhar zan خواهر زن wife's sister

khâhar خواهر sister

khâhesh خواهش request, wish, desire

khâje خواجه eunuch, master

khâk âlud خاک آلود soiled, dusty

khâk andâz خاک انداز dustpan

khâk sepâri خاک سپاری funeral

khâk خاک soil, earth, land

khâke خاکه powder, dust

khâkestar خاکستر ash

khâkestari خاکستری gray

khâkhâm خاخام rabbi

khâki خاکی soiled, earthly

khâkriz خاکریز embankment, bund

khâl kubi خال کوبی tattooing

khâl خال mole

khal' خلع deposition

khalabân خلبان pilot

khâldâr خالدار spotted

khâle خاله maternal aunt

khâleq خالق creator, maker

khâles خالص pure, unalloyed

khâli خالی empty, void, vacant

khalife خلیفه Caliph

khalij خلیج gulf, bay

khâlq خلق people, creation

khalse خلسه ecstasy

khalvat خلوت privacy, seclusion

khâm خام raw, crude, naïve

kham خم curve, bend

khâme خامه cream

khamide خمیده curved, bent

khamir dandân خمیر دندان toothpaste

khamir خمیر paste, dough

khâmush خاموش quiet, silent, extinct

khâmushi خاموشى black out, silence

khamyâze خميازه yawn

khân خان tribal chief

khânâ خوانا readable, legible

khânande خواننده singer, reader

khânavâde خانواده family, household

khânavâdegi خانوادگى familial

khândan (khân) (خواندن (خوان to read, to sing, to study

khandaq خندق moat, ditch

khande dâr خنده دار funny, ridiculous

khande خنده laughter

khandidan (khand) خنديدن to laugh

khâne dâr خانه دار housewife

khâne neshin خانه نشين retired, staying at home

khâne خانه house, home

khânedân خاندان dynasty, family

khânegi خانگى domestic, house-made

khânemân خانمان household

khâneqâh خانقاه monastery

khânevâr خانوار family

khanjar خنجر dagger

khânom bâz خانم باز whoremonger

khânom خانم lady, Mrs. Mistress

khâr خار thorn, bristle

khârâ خارا granite

kharâb خراب broken, out of order, faulty

kharâbe خرابه ruins

kharboze خربزه melon

kharchang خرچنگ crab, lobster

khardal خردل mustard

khârej خارج outside, abroad, away

khâreje خارجه abroad, foreign country

khâreji خارجى external, foreigner

khâreq olâde خارق العاده extraordinary

khâresh خارش itching, scratching

khargush خرگوش hare, rabbit, bunny

khâri خوارى despise, degradation

kharid خريد purchase, buying

khâridan (khâr) (خاريدن (خار to scratch

kharidan (khar) (خريدن (خر to buy

kharidâr خريدار buyer, customer

khariyyat خريت stupidity, silliness

kharj خرج cost, expense

kharji خرجى allowance, budget

kharmagas خرمگس horsefly, gadfly

kharman خرمن stack, harvest, yield

kharmast خرمست dead drunk

khârobâr forushi خوار و بار فروشى grocery

khârobâr خوار و بار grocer

khâs خاص special, proper

khashâb خشاب loader of rifle magazine

khâshâk خاشاک motes, stalks

khashen خشن rough, coarse

khashkhâsh خشخاش opium poppy

khashm خشم anger, wrath

khashmgin خشمگین angry, furious

khasis خسیس stingy

khâsiyat خاصیت property, use, virtue

khasmâne خصمانه hostile

khâst خواست will, desire

khâstan (khâh) خواستن (خواه) to want, to ask

khaste konande خسته کننده boring, tiresome

khaste خسته tired, worn out, bored

khâste خواسته wish, desire

khâstegâri خواستگاری proposing (marriage)

khat خط line, lane, hand writing

khatâ خطا mistake, offence

khâtam kâri خاتم کاری inlaid work

khatar خطر danger, risk, jeopardy

khatarnâk خطرناک dangerous

khâteme خاتمه conclusion, end

khâter jam' خاطر جمع sure, tranquil

khâter khâh خاطر خواه fond, lover

khâter خاطر mind, sake, memory

khâterât خاطرات memories

khâtere خاطره memory, memento

khatkesh خط کش ruler

khatkeshi خط کشی delineation, drawing lines

khatm ختم termination, funeral service

khatne ختنه circumcision

khattât خطاط calligraphist

khâtun خاتون lady

khâvare dur خاور دور far east

khâvare miyâne خاور میانه middle east

khâviyâr خاویار caviar

khâye mâli خایه مالی flattery, servile

khâye خایه testicle, balls

khayyât خیاط tailor

khayyâti خیاطی sewing, tailoring

khayyer خیر benevolent

khaz خز fur

khazân خزان fall, autumn

khazande خزنده reptile

khazâne dâr خزانه دار treasurer

khazâne خزانه treasury, reservoir

khazar خزر Caspian

khaze خزه algae

khâzen خازن condenser, capacitor

khazidan (khaz) خزیدن (خز) to crawl

khebre خبره expert

khedmat خدمت serving

khedmatkâr خدمتکار servant, waiter

kheffat خفت disgrace, humiliation

khejâlat âvar خجالت آور shameful, embracing

khejâlat zade خجالت زده embarrassed

khejâlat خجالت shame, shyness, embarrassment

khejâlati خجالتی shy, coy

khejel خجل ashamed, embarrassed

khelâf kâr خلاف کار offender

khelâf خلاف offence, violation

khelâfat خلافت caliphate

khelâl خلال interval

khelâs خلاص released, saved

khelqat خلقت creation

khelt خلط mucus

khepel خپل chubby

kherad mand خردمند wise

kherkhere خرخره larynx, throat

khers خرس bear

kherto pert خرت وپرت junk

khesârat خسارت damage, loss

khesht خشت mud brick

kheslat خصلت character, feature

kheyli خیلی many, very, more

kheyr خیر benefit, good

kheyrât خیرات charity

kheyriyye خیریه charity, relief

khiki خیکی fat, flabby

khire خیره dazzled, gazed

khis خیس wet, drenched

khish خویش relative, oneself

khish خیش ploughshare

khishâvand خویشاوند kin, relative

khishtan خویشتن self

khit خیط loss of face

khiyâbân خیابان street, avenue

khiyâl bâfi خیالبافی daydreaming

khiyâl خیال fancy, imagination

khiyâli خیالی imaginary, visionary, fiction

khiyânat kâr خیانت کار traitor

khiyânat خیانت treason

khiyâr خیار cucumber

khod âmuz خود آموز self-learner

khod bini خودبینی self-conceit

khod koshi خودکشی suicide

khod nevis خودنویس fountain pen

khod suzi خودسوزی self burning

khod خود self, oneself

khodâ biyâmorz خدابیامرز God bless his soul

khodâ hâfez خداحافظ good bye, farewell

khodâ hâfezi خداحافظی farewell, good bye

khodâ parasti خداپرستی theism, godliness

khodâ shenâs خداشناس theist

khodâ خدا God, the Lord

khodam خودم myself

khodâvand خداوند God, the Lord

khodâyâ خدایا Oh God!

khodbekhod خودبخود automatically

khoddâri خودداری self-control, continence

khodemâni خودمانی intimate

khodforush خودفروش prostitute, whore

khodkâr خودکار pen (ballpoint), automatic

khodkhâh خودخواه selfish

khodkhâhi خودخواهی selfishness

khodmokhtâri خودمختاری autonomy

khodnamâyi خودنمایی showing off

khodpasandi خودپسندی selfishness

khodra'y خودرای stubborn, wilful

khodro خودرو car, automobile

khof خوف fear, phobia

khoffâsh خفاش bat

khofnâk خوفناک fearful, dreadful

khol خل crazy

kholâse خلاصه summary, brief

kholq خلق temper, temperament

khompâre خمپاره mortar shell

khoms خمس one fifth

khonak خنک cool, chilly

khonsâ خنثی neutral, sexless

khorâfât خرافات superstitions

khord خرد small, tiny, minced

khordâd خرداد third month of Iranian calendar

khordan (khor) خوردن (خور) to eat, to drink

khorde forush خرده فروش retailer

khorde خرده bit, fragment

khordsâl خردسال child, infant

khore خوره leprosy

khoresh خورش stew

khorjin خورجین saddlebag

khorkhor خرخر snoring

khormâ خرما date (edible)

khormâlu خرمالو persimmon

khornâs خرناس snort

khorsand خرسند satisfied, content

khorshid خورشید sun

khorshidi خورشیدی solar

khortum خرطوم elephant's trunks

khoruj خروج exit

khosh akhlâq خوش اخلاق good-tempered, cheerful

khosh gozarâni خوشگذرانی living in pleasure

khosh qiyâfe خوش قیافه handsome

khosh shans خوش شانس lucky

khosh خوش happy, pleasant

khoshâmad خوشامد welcome

khoshbakht خوشبخت lucky, fortunate

khoshbakhtâne خوشبختانه luckily, fortunately

khoshbin خوش بین optimistic

khoshbu خوشبو fragrance, aroma

khoshgel خوشگل beautiful, handsome

khoshhâl خوشحال glad, happy

khoshi خوشی joy, happiness

khoshk خشک dry, dried

khoshkbâr خشکبار dried fruits

khoshki خشکی land, ground, dryness

khoshksâli خشکسالی draught

khoshmaze خوشمزه tasty, delicious

khoshnud خوشنود happy, pleased

khotbe خطبه sermon, exhortation

khub خوب good, OK, well, nice

khubi خوبی goodness, kindness

khud خود helmet, headgear

khuk خوک pig, boar

khukcheye hendi خوکچه هندی guinea pig

khun âlud خون آلود bloody, blood stained

khun âshâm خون آشام blood sucker

khun bahâ خون بها blood money

khun damâq خون دماغ nose bleeding

khun garm خون گرم warm-blooded, kind

khun khâr خون خوار blood thirsty, cruel

khun mordegi خون مردگی ecchymosis

khun خون blood, kinship

khunâbe خونابه serum, bitter tears

khunin خونین bloody

khunrizi خون ریزی haemorrhage, murder

khunsard خونسرد cold-blooded

khurâk خوراک food, meal

khurâki خوراکی edible, food

khurd خرد change (coins)

khurus خروس rooster, cock

khurushân خروشان roaring

khushe خوشه bunch, cluster

khushunat خشونت coarseness, hostility

khusuf خسوف lunar eclipse

khusumat خصومت hostility

khususan خصوصا especially, in particular

khususi sâzi خصوصی سازی privatisation

khususi خصوصی private, personal, special

khususiyyât خصوصیت characteristics, particulars

l

lâ aqal لا اقل at least

lâ ebâli لا ابالی careless, reckless

lâ لا fold, ply, inside, among

lab shekari لب شکری harelip, cleft lip

lab لب lip, edge

labâlab لبالب brimful

labaniyât لبنیات diary products

labe لبه edge, rim

labkhand zadan لبخند زدن to smile

labkhand لبخند smile, sneer

lâbod لابد perhaps, certainly

labu لبو boiled beetroot

lachak لچک scarf

lâf zadan لاف زدن to boast

lâf لاف puff, boast, vaunt

laffâfe لفافه cover, guise

lafz لفظ word

lafzi لفظی verbal

lagad zadan لگد زدن to kick

lagad لگد kick

lagadmâl لگدمال trampled

lagan لگن pelvis, pan, urinal

lahâf لحاف quilt

lahâz لحاظ respect, view, connection

lâhe لاهه the Hague

lahim لحیم solder

lahje لهجه dialect, accent

lahlah له له panting

lahn لحن tune, tone, manner

lahze be lahze لحظه به لحظه gradually, momentarily

lahze لحظه moment, instant

la'in لعین cursed, damned

laj لج spite, grudge

lajâjat لجاجت grudge, stubbornness

lajan لجن sludge, loose mud, morass

lâjavardi لاجوردی azure

lajbâz لجباز stubborn, spiteful

lajuj لجوج stubborn, pig-head

lâk لاک shell, nail polish

lak لک freckle, spot

lâken لاکن but, however

lakht لخت flaccid, limp, lax

lakhte لخته clot, clog

lakkâte لکته prostitute, whore

lakke لکه spot, stain, stigma

laklak لکلک stork

lâkposht لاک پشت turtle, tortoise

lâl لال mute, dumb, speechless

la'l لعل ruby

lâlâyi لالایی lullaby

lâle لاله tulip

lale لله nanny

lam لم leaning

lâmazhab لامذهب secular, atheist

lâmese لامسه sense of touch

lamidan (lam) لمیدن (لم) to loll, to relax, to lean

lâmp لامپ lamp, globe

lams لمس touching, contact

la'n لعن cursing, damning, swearing

la'nat لعنت curse, damning

la'nati لعنتی damned, cursed

landan لندن London

lâne لانه nest, den

lanf لنف lymph

lang لنگ paralysed, crippled, stalled

langânlangân لنگان لنگان limping

langar لنگر anchor, gravity

langargâh لنگرگاه harbour, anchorage

langidan (lang) لنگیدن (لنگ) to limp

lape لپه split peas

laq لق loose, shaky

laqab لقب title, cognomen, epithet

lâqar لاغر thin, skinny

laqv kardan لغو کردن to cancel

laqv لغو cancellation, void

laqzân لغزان slippery, sliding

laqzande لغزنده slippery, sliding

laqzesh لغزش slip, error, mistake

laqzidan (laqz) لغزیدن (لغز) to slip, to slide

lârubi لاروبی dredging

larz لرز shivering, shaking

larzân لرزان shaky, vibrant, shivery

larzesh لرزش tremor, vibration, quake

larzidan (larz) لرزیدن (لرز) to shake, to shiver, to tremble

lâs لاس flirting

lase لثه gum (of teeth)

lash لش lumpish, nerveless

lâshe لاشه corpse, carcass

lashkar لشکر army, force

lashkargâh لشکرگاه camp (army)

lashkarkeshi لشکرکشی military expedition, campaign

lâshkhor لاشخور vulture

lâstik لاستیک rubber, tyre

lât لات vagabond, destitute

latâfat لطافت purity, fineness, tenderness

latif لطیف tender, pure, delicate, fine

latife لطیفه joke, satire, humour

latme zadan لطمه زدن to harm

latme لطمه damage, harm, loss

lavâ لوا banner, flag

lavand لوند coy

lavâsh لواش a type of bread

lavât لواط paedophilia

lavâzem ottahrir لوازم التحریر stationery

lavâzem لوازم necessities, equipments

lâye لایه layer, stratum

lâyehe لایحه bill (legislation)

lâyeq لایق deserved, competent, fit

lazej لزج viscous, slippery, sticky

lâzem dâshtan لازم داشتن to need

lâzem لازم necessary, intransitive, essential

laziz لذیذ delicious, tasty

lebâs لباس clothes, dress, costume

leh له crushed, mashed, squashy

lehestân لهستان Poland

lejâm لجام bridle, reins

lemm لم trick, know how

leng لنگ leg

lenge لنگه pair, half a load, mate

lent لنت (brake) shoe

leqâh لقاح fertilization

lezzat bakhsh لذت بخش delightful, enjoyable

lezzat bordan لذت بردن to enjoy

lezzat لذت pleasure, joy, satisfaction

libi لیبی Libya

lif لیف bathing sponge

limu لیمو lime, lemon

lis لیس licking

lisâns لیسانس bachelor degree

lisidan (lis) (لیس) لیسیدن to lick

list لیست menu, table, list

livân لیوان glass

liyâqat لیاقت merit, virtue, efficiency

liz لیز slippery, viscous

lo لو betrayal, divulging

lo'âb لعاب glaze, coating, polish

lobb لب essence, gist

lobnân لبنان Lebanon

lobnâni لبنانی Lebanese

loh لوح board, tombstone

lokhm لخم lean (meat), boneless

lokht لخت naked, nude, bare

lokhti لختی nakedness, nudity

loknat لکنت stuttering, stammering

lolâ لولا hinge, joint

long لنگ apron, bathing cloth

lop لپ cheek

loqat nâme لغتنامه dictionary

loqat لغت word

loqme لقمه morsel, mouthful

los لوث contaminated, soiled

lotf لطف kindness, favour, courtesy

lotfan لطفا please

loze لوزه tonsil

lozi لوزی lozenge

lozolme'de لوزالمعده pancreas

lozum لزوم necessity, need, essentiality

lozuman لزوما necessarily

lubiyâ لوبیا bean

luch لوچ squint, cross-eyed

luks لوکس luxury, elegant

lul لول intoxicated

lule لوله pipe, tube

lulidan (lul) (لول) لولیدن to squirm, to wriggle

lulu لولو bogyman

lus لوس spoiled

luster لوستر chandelier

luti لوطی pederast, buffoon

m

mâ oshsha'ir ما الشعير barely water

mâ ما we, us, our, ours

ma'âd معاد resurrection day

ma'âref معارف education, culture

ma'âsh معاش living, sustenance

ma'bad معبد temple

mabâdâ مبادا never ever, let it not be

mabâdâ مبادا never, beware

mabâni مبانی bases, essentials

ma'bar معبر passage, road, path

mab'as مبعث the date Mohammed was appointed as prophet

mabda' مبدا foundation, beginning

mabhas مبحث subject, topic, part

mabhut مبهوت stunned, amazed, astonished

mablaq مبلغ amount, fee

mabnâ مبنا bases, foundation

mâch kardan ماچ کردن to kiss

mâch ماچ kiss

mâd ماد Medes

madad مدد help, aid, assistance

madadkâr مددکار social worker

ma'dan معدن mine

madani مدنی civil, civic, urban

ma'dani معدنی mineral

mâdar bozorg مادر بزرگ grandmother

mâdar khânde مادر خوانده stepmother

mâdar shohar مادر شوهر mother in law, husband's mother

mâdar zâdi مادر زاد congenital

mâdar zan مادر زن mother in law, wife's mother

mâdar مادر mother, mum

madâr مدار orbit, circuit, axis

mâdarâne مادرانه motherly

mâdari مادری maternity

madd مد flow (tide)

maddâhi مداحی eulogy, praise

mâdde ماده substance, material, article

mâddi مادی material, corporal

mâde ماده female, feminie

madfan مدفن grave, resting place

madfu' مدفوع excrement, faeces

madfun مدفون buried, entombed

madh مدح praise, eulogy

mâdiyân مادیان mare

madrak مدرک document, papers, proof

madrase مدرسه school, academy, institute

ma'dud معدود few, limited

ma'dum معدوم destroyed, executed, extinct

mâdun مادون inferior, sub-

madyun مدیون in debt, owing

mafâsed مفاسد corruptions, mischief

mafhum مفهوم concept, sense, meaning

mafluk مفلوک miserable, unfortunate

mâfoq مافوق beyond, superior

mafqud مفقود missing, lost

mafsal مفصل joint, articulation

maftul مفتول twisted wire

maf'ul مفعول object, passive homosexual

maf'uli مفعولی objective, accusative

magar مگر unless

magas kosh مگس کش fly swat

magas مگس fly

mâh ماه month, moon, beautiful

mahâfel محافل meetings, sources

mahak محک touchstone, criterion

mahâl محال impossible

mahal محل place, venue, locality

mahalle محله parish, district

mahalli محلی local, native

mâhâne ماهانه monthly

mahâr مهار bridle, harness, leading rope

mahârat مهارت skill, dexterity, mastery

mahâsen محاسن virtues, beauties, beard

mahavvate محوطه surroundings, area, yard

mahbel مهبل vagina

mahbub محبوب beloved, favourite, darling

mahbubiyat محبوبیت popularity

mahdud kardan محدود کردن to limit, to restrict

mahdud محدود limited, confined, restricted

mahdude محدوده confined, area, limit

mahdudiyat محدودیت limitation, restriction

mâher ماهر skilled, expert

mahfaze محفظه case, container

mahfel محفل meeting, circle, gathering

mahfuz محفوظ safe, secure, guarded, learned

mâhi tâbe ماهی تابه frying pan

mâhi ماهی fish, monthly

mahib مهیب scary, terrible, frightening

mâhiche ماهیچه muscle, fillet

mâhigir ماهیگیر fisherman

mâhigiri ماهیگیری fishery

mâhiyâne ماهیانه per month

mâhiyat ماهیت nature, essence, entity

mahkum kardan محکوم کردن to condemn, to charge

mahkum محکوم convicted, condemned

mahkumiyat محکومیت conviction, condemnation

mahlake مهلکه dangerous situation

mahlul محلول solution, liquid

mahr مهر marriage portion, dowry

mahram محرم close kin, confidant

mahramâne محرمانه confidential, private, classified

mahriye مهریه marriage portion, dowry

mahrum kardan محروم کردن to deprive

mahrum محروم deprived, denied

mahrumiyat محرومیت deprivation

mahshar محشر resurrection day

mahshur محشور associated with

mahsub محسوب counted, taken into account

mahsul محصول product, crop, output

mahsus محسوس sensible, tangible

mahtâb مهتاب moonlight

mahtâbi مهتابی florescent, terrace

mâhut ماهوت felt

mahv kardan محو کردن to wipe out, to erase

mahv محو faded, wiped out

mâhvâre ماهواره satellite

mahz محض mere

mahzar محضر notary public office, presence

ma'ishat معیشت living, earning

majalle مجله magazine

mâjarâ ماجرا adventure, event, circumstance

mâjarâju ماجراجو adventurous

majbur مجبور obliged, forced

majhul مجهول passive, unknown

majjani مجانی free (of charge)

majles مجلس parliament, gathering

majma' مجمع assembly, association

majmu' مجموع total, sum

majmu'e مجموعه collection, set, series

majnun مجنون mad, crazy

majrâ مجرا canal, passage, duct

majruh مجروح wounded, injured

ma'jun معجون mixture, electuary

majzub kardan مجذوب کردن to attract

majzub مجذوب attracted, fascinated, absorbed

majzur مجذور square (root)

makân مکان place, location

makâni مکانی local

makhfi kardan مخفی کردن to hide, to cover

makhfi مخفی hidden, secret, covered

makhfiyâne مخفیانه in secret

makhluq مخلوق creature, created, people

makhlut kardan مخلوط کردن to mix

makhlut مخلوط mixed, blended, mixture

makhmal مخمل velvet

makhmalak مخملک scarlet fever

makhmase مخمصه trouble, difficulty

makhraj مخرج outlet, anus, denominator

makhrube مخروبه ruined

makhrut مخروط cone

makhsus مخصوص special, specific

makhsusan مخصوصا especially, particularly

makhuf مخوف scary, terrifying

makhzan مخزن reservoir, storage, warehouse

makidan (mak) (مک) مکیدن to suck, to suckle

makkar مکار deceitful, crafty

makke مکه Mecca

makr مکر trick, deceit

makruh مکروه disapproved by religious law

maks مکث pause, halt

maktab مکتب old-fashioned school

ma'kus معکوس reversed, inverted, upside down

mâl مال property, asset, possession, animal

malâfe ملافه bed sheet, linen

malâj ملاج fontanel

malak ملک angel

malake ملکه queen

malakh ملخ locust

malâl angiz ملال انگیز boring, annoying

malâmat ملامت blame, taunt

malâqe ملاقه ladle

malavân ملوان sailor, seaman

malavâni ملوانی seamanship

mâle ماله trowel

mâlek مالک owner, proprietor, lord

malek ملک king

mâlekiyat مالکیت ownership, possession

mâlesh مالش rubbing, scrubbing

mâlidan (mâl) مالیدن (مال) to rub, to massage

mâlikhuliyâ مالیخولیا melancholy

mâliyât مالیات tax, duty, toll

ma'lul معلول handicapped, invalid, effect

malul ملول weary, sad, bored

ma'luliyat معلولیت invalidity, handicap

ma'lum معلوم obvious, evident

ma'lumât معلومات knowledge, qualifications

mal'un ملعون damned, cursed

malus ملوس cuddly, catamite

mâmâ ماما midwife

mâmân مامان mum, mother

mâmâyi مامایی midwifery

mame مه breast, dummy

mamnu' kardan ممنوع کردن to forbid

mamnu' ممنوع forbidden, restricted

mamnun ممنون thankful, grateful

ma'mul معمول usual, customary

ma'mulan معمولا usually, ordinarily

ma'muli معمولی usual, ordinary

ma'mur مامور official, appointed, agent

ma'muriyat ماموریت mission, duty, assignment

man' kardan منع کردن to prohibit, to forbid

mân مان our, ours, us

man من I, me, mine

man' منع prohibition, forbidding

ma'nâ معنا meaning

manâl منال property, asset

ma'navi معنوی spiritual

ma'naviyat معنویت spirituality

manba' منبع source, reservoir, origin

manbar منبر pulpit, preacher's seat

mândan (mân) ماندن (مان) to stay, to remain, to last

mândegâr ماندگار lasing, permanent

mâne' مانع obstacle, barrier

manesh منش manner, nature, disposition

manfa'at منفعت gain, benefit, profit

manfaz منفذ opening, passage, hole

manfi منفى negative, negation

manfibâf منفى باف negativist

mang منگ dizzy, giddy

mangane منگنه punch, press

mangule منگوله tassel, knot

ma'ni معنى meaning, sense

mani منى semen, sperm

ma'nidâr معنى دار meaningful

manjalâb منجلاب sewer, sewage water

mânovr مانور war game

manqal منقل brazier

mansab منصب position, rank, status

mansha' منشا source, origin

manshur منشور prism, charter

mansub منصوب appointed

mansukh منسوخ obsolete, abolished

mantaqe منطقه area, zone, region

mantaqeyi منطقه اى regional

manteq منطق logic, rationality

manteqi منطقى logical

manut منوط depending, pending

manzare منظره sight, view, landscape

manzel منزل home, house

manzelat منزلت respect, status

manzume منظومه poem, constellation, solar system

manzur منظور purpose, aim, intention

mâqabl ماقبل preceding, before

maq'ad مقعد anus, butt, arse

maqâle مقاله paper, article, essay

maqâm مقام position, rank, status

maqâmât مقامات authorities

maqâze مغازه shop, store

maqâzedâr مغازه دار shop keeper

maqbare مقبره shrine, tomb

maqbul مقبول accepted

maqbun مغبون hoaxed, cheated

maqdam مقدم arrival

maqduniye مقدونيه Macedonia

maqdur مقدور possible, feasible

maqferat مغفرت forgiveness

maqlate مغلطه sophistry

maqlub مغلوب defeated, beaten

maqne'e مقنعه veil, scarf

maqreb مغرب west

maqrur مغرور arrogant, haughty, snobbish

maqruz مقروض indebted

maqsad مقصد destination, aim, intention

maqshush مغشوش disturbed, chaotic

maqsud مقصود aim, purpose, intension

maqta' مقطع section, cut

maqta'i مقطعی temporary, sectional

maqtul مقتول killed, murdered, assassinated

ma'qul معقول reasonable, rational

maqule مقوله category, class

maqz مغز brain

mâr مار snake, serpent

marâ مرا me

marâje'at kardan مراجعه کردن to return

marâje'at مراجعت returning, coming back

ma'rake معرکه battle field, jugglers' display

marâkesh مراکش Morocco

marâm nâme مرامنامه doctrine, articles

marâm مرام aim, objective

marâsem مراسم ceremonies, customs, formalities

maraz مرض illness, disease, sickness

ma'raz معرض exposure, exposed to

marbut مربوط relative, connected, pertinent

marbute مربوطه relevant, related

mârchube مارچوبه asparagus

mard مرد man, male, mankind

mardak مردک little man, little fellow

mardâne مردانه masculine, brave, courageous

mardânegi مردانگی courage, generosity

mardi مردی manhood, masculinity, courage

mardom shenâsi مردم شناسی anthropology

mardom مردم people, folks

mardomak مردمک pupil (of eye)

mardomi مردمی humanity, humanism

mardud مردود failed, rejected, discarded

ma'refat معرفت knowledge, insight, wisdom

marg مرگ death, demise, end

margbâr مرگبار deadly, mortal

mârgir مارگیر snake charmer

margomir مرگ و میر mortality, fatality

marhabâ مرحبا well done, bravo

marhale مرحله stage, step, phase

marham مرحم cure, medicine

marhamat مرحمت favour, mercy, kindness

marhum مرحوم deceased, the late

mar'i مرئی visible, evident

mariz مریض ill, sick, unwell, patient

marizi مریضی illness, sickness, disease

marizkhâne مریضخانه hospital

marja' مرجع source, resort, reference

marjân مرجان coral

markaz مرکز centre, head office, middle

markazi مرکزی central

mârmâhi مارماهی eel

marmar مرمر marble

mârmulak مارمولک lizard

marmuz مرموز mysterious, secretive, mystical

mârpich مارپیچ spiral, helix, coil

marqad مرقد shrine, tomb, grave

marqub مرغوب high quality, desirable

mârs مارس March

mârsh مارش marching

marsiye مرثیه elegy, mourning

marsum مرسوم customary, habitual

marta' مرتع pasture, meadow

martabe مرتبه rank, degree, grade, floor, time, stage

martub مرطوب damp, moist, humid

ma'ruf معروف popular, famous

maryam مریم Mary

marz مرز border, frontier, boundary

marzbân مرزبان frontier guard, border guard

marzneshin مرزنشین borderer, frontiersman

marzobum مرزوبوم country, homeland

masâfat مسافت distance

masâhat مساحت measurement, area, survey

mas'ale مسئله problem, affair

masâleh مصالح interests, materials

mâsâzh ماساژ massage

masdar مصدر infinitive, source

masdud مسدود closed, blocked

mâse ماسه sand

mâsh ماش chikling vetch

mash'al مشعل torch

mâshâllâ ماشالله well done

mashâm مشام smelling

mashâqel مشاغل jobs, occupations

mashaqqat مشقت hardship, difficulty

mâshe ماشه trigger, tongs

mashgul مشغول busy, occupied, engaged

mashguliyat مشغولیت preoccupation, hobby

mashhud مشهود obvious, evident

mashhur مشهور famous, well-known

mashin âlât ماشین آلات machinery

mâshin ماشین car, machine

mashine lebasshuyi ماشین لباس شویی launderette, washing machine

mashini ماشینی mechanical, urban

mashkuk مشکوک doubtful, suspicious, sceptical

mashmul مشمول including, subject to

mashq مشق homework, drill, practice

mashqul مشغول busy, engaged

mashreq مشرق east, orient

mashrub forushi مشروب فروشی liquor store

mashrub khâr مشروب خوار drinker

mashrub مشروب alcoholic drink

mashruh مشروح detailed, comprehensive

mashrut مشروط conditional

mashrute مشروطه constitutional

mashrutiyat مشروطیت constitutionalism

ma'shuqe معشوقه mistress, lover

mashvarat kardan کردن مشورت to consult

mashvarat مشورت consultation

mashy مشی policy, pace

masih مسیح Messiah, Christ

masihi مسیحی Christian

masihiyat مسیحیت Christianity

masir مسیر pass, route, direction

ma'siyat معصیت sin, guilt

masjed مسجد mosque

mâsk ماسک mask

maskan مسکن residence, home

maskh مسخ metamorphosis

maskhare kardan مسخره کردن to ridicule

maskhare مسخره mockery, ridicules

maskharebâzi مسخره بازی horseplay, mockery

maskuni مسکونی residential, inhabited

maskut مسکوت hushed, kept quiet

maslahat مصلحت advisable, good intention

maslak مسلک religion, belief, ideology

maslub مصلوب crucified

masmum مسموم poisoned

masmumiyat مسمومیت poisoning

masnad مسند seat, position, throne

masno'i مصنوعی artificial, forged, synthetic

masraf مصرف consumption, usage

masru' مشروع legitimate, legal

mâst mâli ماست مالی slurring over

mâst ماست yoghurt

mast مست drunk, intoxicated

masti مستی drunkenness, intoxication

mas'ul مسئول in charge, responsible, accountable

mas'uliyat مسئولیت responsibility, liability, duty

ma'sum معصوم innocent, chaste

masun مصون secure, immune

masuniyat مصونیت immunity, security

mât مات astound, amazed, mate, opaque

matab مطب surgery, clinic

mâtaht ماتحت button, ass, anus

matalak متلک sarcasm, taunting

mâtam ماتم mourning, grieving

matânat متانت dignity, poise

matarsak مترسک scarecrow

matbu' مطبوع pleasant, desirable

matbu'ât مطبوعات press, printed materials, newspapers

mate مته drill, auger

mâtik ماتیک lipstick

matin متین self-possessed, dignified

matlab مطلب topic, subject, text

matlub مطلوب desired, demanded, pleasant

matn متن text, context

matrah مطرح under consideration, under attention

matrud مطرود expelled, sate away, rejected

matruk متروک abandoned, deserted

ma'tuf معطوف inclined, focused on, oriented

mavâdde mokhadder مواد مخدر drugs

mavâjeb مواجب wage, salary

mavâlid موالید births

mavât موات uncultivated land

mavâzin موازین standards, scales

maviz مویز raisins

mâye' مایع liquid, fluid

mâye مایه ferment, capital, yeast

mâyel مایل slant, oblique, inclined

mâyo مایو bathing suit, swim suit

ma'yub معیوب defective, faulty

ma'yus مایوس disappointed, hopeless, desperate

mâz ماز maze, twist

mâzâd مازاد excess, surplus

mazanne مظنه price, rate

mazâq مذاق taste

mazâr مزار tomb, shrine

mazbur مزبور mentioned, aforementioned, said

maze مزه taste, flavour

ma'zerat معذرت apology, excuse

mazhab مذهب religion, faith

mazhabi مذهبی religious

mazhar مظهر manifestation, appearance

mâzi ماضی past tense

maziqe مضیقه difficulty, hardship, distress

mâziye ba'id ماضی بعید past participle

mâziye estemrâri ماضی استمراری continuous past

mâziye naqli ماضی نقلی present participle

mazkur مذکور mentioned, said

mazlum مظلوم oppressed

mazlumâne مظلومانه submissively

mazlumiyat مظلومیت submissiveness, innocence

maznun مظنون suspect, mistrustful

mazrab مضرب multiple

mazre'e مزرعه farm, field, ranch

ma'zur معذور excused, exempted

medâd pâkkon مداد پاکن rubber, eraser

medâd tarâsh مدادتراش pencil sharpener

medâd مداد pencil

medâl مدال medal, badge

me'de معده stomach

meh مه fog, mist, smog, May

mehâlud مه آلود foggy, misty, hazy

mehmân dâr مهماندار host(ess), stewardess

mehmân dust مهمان دوست hospitable

mehmân khâne مهمان خانه guest house, inn, hostel

mehmân navâzi مهمان نوازی hospitality

mehmân مهمان guest, visitor

mehmâni مهمانی party, feast

mehmiz مهمیز spur, prick

mehr مهر affection, seventh month of Iranian calendar

mehrâb محراب adytum

mehrebân مهربان kind, affectionate, gracious

mehrebâni مهربانی kindness, affection, compassion

mehvar محور pivot, axis

mekânik مکانیک mechanic

mekâniki مکانیکی mechanical, garage

mekânize مکانیزه mechanised

mekzik مکزیک Mexico

melâk ملاک proof, criterion, basis

melk ملک property, real estate

melkiyyat ملکیت possession, ownership

mellat ملت nation, people

melli ملی national

melliyat ملیت nationality

me'mâr معمار architect

me'mâri معماری architecture

menâr منار minaret, lighthouse

menhâ منها minus, subtraction

mennat منت favour, indebtedness

mennmenn من من mumbling, muttering

menqâr منقار beak, bill, nob

meqdâr مقدار amount, quantity, sum

meqdâri مقداری some

meqnâtisi مغناطیسی magnetic

meqyâs مقیاس scale, measure

mercy مرسی thanks, thank you

meri مری oesophagus

merrikh مریخ Mars

mes مس copper

mesâl مثال example, instance

meshki مشکی black

meskin مسکین poor, needy

mesr مصر Egypt

mesrâ' مصرع half verse

mesvâk zadan زدن مساک to brush one's teeth

mesvâk مساک toothbrush

metr متر meter

metro مترو subway

mey می wine, liquor

me'yâr معیار criterion, standard

meydân میدان square, roundabout, field, opportunity

meygu میگو shrimp, prawn

meykhâne میخانه pub, bar

meykhâre میخواره drinker, alcohol addict

meyl میل desire, will, tendency

meymun میمون monkey, prosperous

meyyet میت dead, corpse

mezâh مزاح joke, jest, kidding

mezâj مزاج condition, temperament, temper

mi'âd میعاد promise, covenant

mihan parast میهن پرست patriot

mihan parasti میهن پرستی patriotism

mihan میهن homeland, motherland

mikh میخ nail, peg

mikhak میخک carnation

mikhi میخی cuneiform

mikrob میکروب germ, microbe

mil میل bar, knitting needle, shaft, axle

milâd میلاد birth, birth of Christ

milâdi میلادی Christian calendar

mile میله rod, shaft, axle

milimetr میلی متر millimetre

milyârd میلیارد billion

milyon میلیون million

milyoner میلیونر millionaire

minâ kâri مینا کاری enamelwork

minâ مینا enamel

mirâs میراث heritage, legacy

misâq میثاق promise, pact, treaty

mish میش ewe

mive میوه fruit

miyân bor میان بر short cut

miyân sâl میان سال middle age

miyân میان middle, between, mid, centre, among

miyâne ravi میانه روی moderation

miyâne ro میانه رو moderate

miyâne میانه middle, median

miyângin میانگین average, median, mean

miyâni میانی middle, central

miyânji gari میانجی گری mediation, arbitration

miyânji میانجی mediator, arbitrator

miyu میو meow

miz میز table, desk

mizân میزان balance, amount, quantity, degree

mizbân میزبان host

mo مو vine

mo'addab مودب polite, courteous

mo'addel معدل mean, median, average

mo'âdel معادل equivalent, equal

mo'âdele معادله equation, parity

mo'âf kardan معاف کردن to excuse, to exempt

mo'âf معاف exempt, excused, forgiven

mo'âfiyat معافیت exemption

mo'âhede معاهده pact, treaty, agreement

mo'âkheze مواخذه reprimanding, rebuke, reproving

mo'âleje kardan معالجه کردن to treat

mo'âleje معالجه treatment, cure, healing

mo'allaq معلق suspended, hanging

mo'allef مولف author, writer

mo'allem معلم teacher, trainer, master

mo'allemi معلمی teaching, instruction

mo'âmele kardan معامله کردن to make a deal

mo'âmele معامله deal, trade, bargain

mo'ammâ معما riddle, puzzle, enigma

mo'ammam معمم clergy

mo'annas مونث female

mo'arref معرف sponsor, referee, introducer

mo'arrefi kardan معرفی کردن to introduce

mo'arrefi معرفی introducing, presenting

mo'âser معاصر contemporary

mo'âsheqe معاشقه love-making, fondling

mo'âsherat معاشرت relationship, company

mo'asser موثر influential, effective, efficient

mo'asses موسس founder

mo'assese موسسه institute, foundation

mo'attal معطل waiting, detained, stood up

mo'attali معطلی delay, suspension

mo'attar معطر scented, aromatic, fragrant

mo'âven معاون assistant, deputy

mo'âveze معاوضه exchange, swap

mo'âyene kardan معاینه کردن to examine (medical)

mo'âyene معاینه examination, check up

mo'ayyan معین specified, fixed, known

mo'azzab معذب uneasy, bothered, uncomfortable

mo'azzaf موظف responsible, ordered

mobâdele مبادله exchange, trade

mobâhât مباهات pride, boasting

mobâhese مباحثه dispute, discussion

mobâleqe âmiz مبالغه آمیز exaggerated

mobâleqe مبالغه exaggeration, overstatement

moballeq مبلغ missionary, publicist

mobârak مبارک blessed, happy

mobârez مبارز fighter, challenger, combatant

mobâreze مبارزه fighting, combat, battle

mobarrâ مبرا exempt, acquitted, cleared

mobâsher مباشر foreman, conductor

mobed موبد Zoroastrian priest

mobham مبهم ambiguous, vague, equivocal

mobl مبل furniture, lounge

mobser مبصر students' representative

mobtadi مبتدی novice, beginner

mobtaker مبتکر resourceful, innovator

mobtalâ مبتلا affected, suffering from, afflicted by

mobtazal مبتذل commonplace, obscene

moch مچ wrist

mochâle مچاله crumpled

mod مد fashion, style

modâfe' مدافع defender, defendant, guard

modâfe'e مدافعه defence

modâkhele مداخله interference, intervention, intrusion

modâm مدام continually, all the time

modarraj مدرج graduated, scaled

modarres مدرس teacher, lecturer

modâvâ مداوا treatment, cure

modâvem مداوم continuous, lasting, enduring

modavvan مدون compiled

modavvar مدور round, spheric

modda'i olumum مدعی العموم public prosecutor

modda'i مدعی claimant, plaintiff

moddat مدت period, duration

model مدل model, design, guide

modir مدیر director, manager, principal, headmaster, editor

modiriyyat مدیریت management, direction, editorship

mo'ed موعد due date, time, deadline

mo'eze موعظه preaching, sermon

mofâd مفاد contents, context

mofassal مفصل detailed, full, elaborate

mofasser مفسر commentator

mofid مفید useful, helpful

mofles مفلس poor, needy

mofrad مفرد singular, single

moft مفت free of charge, complimentary

moftakhar مفتخر proud

mofti مفتی free of charge

moftkhor مفتخور parasite, sponger

mohabbat amiz محبت آمیز affectionate, kind

mohabbat محبت kindness, affection

mohaddab محدب convex

mohâfez محافظ guard, protector

mohâfezat kardan محافظت کردن to protect

mohâfezat محافظت protection, conservation

mohâfezekâr محافظه کار conservative

mohâjer مهاجر immigrant, migrant

mohâjerat kardan کردن مهاجرت to immigrate, to migrate

mohâjerat مهاجرت immigration, migration

mohâjerneshin مهاجر نشین settlement, colony

mohâkeme محاکمه trial, hearing

mohâkemeye sahrâyi محاکمه صحرایی court marshal

mohandes مهندس engineer

mohandesi مهندسی engineering

mohaqqar محقر small, humble

mohaqqeq محقق researcher, scholar

moharrek محرک motive, stimulus

mohâsebe محاسبه calculation, computation

mohâsere محاصره siege, surrounding

mohassel محصل student, learner

mohâvere محاوره conversation, dialogue

mohayyâ مهيا ready, prepared

mohayyej مهيج exciting, provocative, moving

mohebat موهبت gift, blessing

mohemm مهم important, serious

mohemmât مهمات ammunitions

mohen موهن insulting, offensive

mohit محيط environment, surrounding, circumference

mohite zist محيط زيست ecology

mohiti محيطى environmental

mohkam محكم firm, strong, tight

mohlat مهلت deadline, respite, time

mohlek مهلك fatal, lethal, dangerous

mohmal مهمل nonsense, absurd, silly

mohr zadan مهر زدن to seal

mohr مهر seal, stamp, seal ring

mohre dârân مهره داران vertebrate

mohre مهره bead, marble, vertebra

mohtâj محتاج needy, poor

mohtaker محتكر hoarders

mohtaram محترم respected, honourable

mohtaramâne محترمانه respectfully

mohtât محتاط cautious, careful

mohtavi محتوى containing, consisting

mohum موهوم imaginary, fanciful, whimsical

mohumât موهومات superstitions, imaginations

moj موج wave, surge, surf

mojaddad مجدد again, renewed

mojâhed مجاهد fighter of holy war

mojahhaz مجهز equipped, prepared

mojallal مجلل glorious, grand

mojarrad مجرد single, bachelor

mojassame مجسمه statue, sculpture

mojavvez مجوز warrant, licence

mojazzâ مجزا isolated, analysed

mojeb موجب cause, causing

mojer موجر landlord, owner, lender

mo'jeze معجزه miracle

mojrem مجرم guilty, criminal

mojri مجرى director, executive

mojtahed مجتهد high ranking clergyman

mojtame' مجتمع complex, gathering

mojud موجود existing, creature, present

mojudât موجودات creatures, species

mojudi موجودى asset, stock

moka'ab مكعب cube, cubic

mokâfât مكافات retribution, retaliation

mokallaf مكلف bound, mature to practice religion

mokammel مكمل complementary, supplementary

mokarrar مكرر repeated, recurrent, repetitious

mokassar مكسر irregular

mokâtebe مكاتبه correspondence

mokh مخ brain, cerebrum

mokhadder مخدر narcotic

mokhaffaf مخفف abbreviated, short form

mokhâlef مخالف opposed, opponent, opposite

mokhâlefat مخالفت opposition, objection, disagreement

mokhallafât مخلفات accessories, garnishing

mokhammer مخمر fermented, yeast

mokharreb مخرب destructive, vandal

mokhâteb مخاطب addressee

mokhche مخچه cerebellum

mokhles مخلص devoted, sincerely

mokhtalef مختلف various, different, diverse

mokhtalet مختلط mixed, bisexual

mokhtall مختل disturbed, disorganised, disordered

mokhtare' مخترع inventor

mokhtasar مختصر brief, short, abstract

mokul موکول dependent, pending

molâheze ملاحظه consideration, notice, heeding

molâqât ملاقات meeting, visit

molâqâti ملاقاتی visitor

molavvan ملون coloured

molâyem ملایم mild, gentle, quiet

molayyen ملین laxative

molhaq ملحق joined, attached

molhed ملحد atheist, apostate

mollâ ملا clergy, theologian

molokol ملکول molecule

moltafet ملتفت aware, attentive

moltaheb ملتهب inflamed, burning

molud مولود born, generated, birthday

momâne'at ممانعت prevention, prohibition

momâs مماس touching, tangent

momayyez ممیز decimal, point, auditor

momen مومن believer, faithful

momken ممکن possible, feasible

momtad ممتد continuous, extended

momtane' ممتنع abstention, blank vote

monabbat kâri منبت کاری inlaid work, embossment

monabbat منبت inlaid, embossed

monâfât منافات incompatibility, contradiction

monâfeq منافق hypocrite, double-crosser

monâjât مناجات prayer, chanting

monajjem منجم astronomer, astrologer

mon'akes منعکس reflected, echoed

mon'aqed منعقد held, tied, coagulated

monâqese مناقصه tender

monâqeshe مناقشه dispute, controversy

monâseb مناسب proper, suitable, fit

monâsebat مناسبت connection, pertinence, appropriateness

monavvar منور bright, lighted

monâzere مناظره debate, dispute

monazzam منظم disciplined, regular, orderly

mondares مندرس worn out

monfa'el منفعل passive, inactive

monfajer منفجر blown up, exploded

monfajere منفجره explosive

monfared منفرد single, isolated

monhadem منهدم destroyed, demolished

monhal منحل dissolved, closed

monhani منحنی curve, bend

monharef منحرف deviated, pervert

monhaser منحصر confined, exclusive

monjamed منجمد frozen

monjar منجر resulting in, leading to

monji منجی saviour

monker منکر denying, disclaiming

monqabez منقبض contracted

monqaleb منقلب changed, upset, touched

monqarez منقرض overturned, extinct, overthrown

monqate' منقطع cut off, interrupted, truncated

monqazi منقضی expired, ended

monsaref منصرف changing mind, giving up

monsef منصف just, fair

monsefâne منصفانه fair, impartially

monsha'eb منشعب branching, subdivided

monshi منشی secretary

monshigari منشیگری secretarial job

montabeq منطبق conforming, coinciding

montahâ منتها end, extreme, by and large

montakhab منتخب selected, chosen, elected

montaqed منتقد critic

montaqel منتقل moved, posted, transferred

montasher منتشر published, printed, distributed

montazer منتظر waiting, expectant

moqa'arr مقعر concave

moqâbel مقابل front, opposite, against

moqâbele مقابله confrontation, encounter

moqaddam مقدم preferred, foremost

moqaddamât مقدمات rudiments, first steps

moqaddamâti مقدماتی preliminary, primary

moqaddame مقدمه preface, introduction

moqaddarât مقدرات destiny, decrees

moqaddas مقدس holy, scared, saint

moqalled مقلد follower in faith

moqanni مقنی well digger

moqârebat مقاربت intercourse, coition, mating

moqârebati مقاربتی venereal, sexual

moqâren مقارن coinciding with, synchronic

moqarrar مقرر decided, arranged

moqarrarât مقررات rules, regulations, procedures

moqasser مقصر guilty, offender, responsible

moqâte'e kâr مقاطعه کار contractor

moqâte'e مقاطعه contract

moqatta' مقطع interrupted, cut into pieces

moqattar مقطر distilled

moqâvem مقاوم resistant, preserving, enduring

moqâvemat مقاومت resistance, perseverance

moqavvâ مقوا cardboard

moqavvi مقوی tonic, nourishing, strengthening

moqâyer مغایر contradictory, incompatible

moqâyerat مغایرت contradiction, disagreement

moqâyese مقایسه comparison

moqayyad مقید bound, conservative

moqazzi مغذی nutritional, rich

moqe' موقع time, occasion, moment

moqe'iyyat موقعیت position, situation, circumstance

moqim مقیم resident

moqolestân مغولستان Mongolia

moqrez مغرض biased, spiteful

moqtader مقتدر powerful, strong, potent

moqtanam مغتنم valued, useful

moqtazi مقتضی appropriate, advisable

moqtaziyât مقتضیات circumstances, exigencies

moquf موقوف suspended, abolished, stopped

moqufât موقوفات endowment, charity

morâ'ât مراعات observance, consideration

morabbâ مربا jam, preserve

morabba' مربع square, quadrangle

morabbi مربی trainer, coach, mentor, instructor

morâd مراد wish, desire, intension

moraddad مردد uncertain, hesitant

morâje'e مراجعه reference, referral

morakhkhas مرخص released, dismissed, excused

morakhkhasi مرخصی leave of absence, release

morakkab مرکب ink, compound, consist of

morakkabât مرکبات citrus fruits

morâqeb مراقب observant, alert, vigilant

morâqebat مراقبت attention, supervision, watch, guarding

morattab مرتب tidy, orderly, punctual, arranged

mordâb مرداب lagoon, marsh

mordâd مرداد fifth month of Persian calendar

mordan (mir) مردن (میر) to die, to pass away, to abolish

mordani مردنی dying, doomed to death

mordâr مردار corpse

morde مرده dead, deceased, obsolete

mordeshur مرده شور washer of the dead

mored مورد case, instance, application

morid مرید disciple, follower

morovvat مروت compassion, generosity

morq مرغ hen, chicken

morqâbi مرغابی duck

morshed مرشد spiritual guide, instructor

mortad مرتد apostate, a Moslem who denies Islam

morta'esh مرتعش trembling, vibrating, shaking

mortafe' مرتفع high, elevated, raised

mortaje' مرتجع conservative, fanatic, regressive

mortakeb مرتکب committed, doer, guilty

mortâz مرتاض yogi

morur مرور review, passing

morvârid مروارید pearl

mosâbeqe مسابقه competition, race, mach, game

mosâdef مصادف coincident, concurrent

mosâ'ed مساعد in accord, favourable

mosâ'edat مساعدت assistance, aid

mosâ'ede مساعده advance payment

mosâfer مسافر passenger, traveller

mosâferat مسافرت travel, journey, trip

mosâferkhâne مسافر خانه inn, motel, lodge

mosâhebe مصاحبه interview

mosakken مسکن sedative, pain killer

mosâlehe مصالحه compromise, settlement

mosallâ مصلا place for public prayer

mosallah مسلح armed, equipped

mosallahâne مسلحانه armed

mosallam مسلم certain, definite, proved

mosallaman مسلما certainly, undoubtedly, definitely

mosallat مسلط dominant, predominant

mosalmân مسلمان Moslem

mosalmâni مسلمانی being Moslem

mosalsal مسلسل machine gun, chained, serial

mosammam مصمم determined

mosattah مسطح flat, plane

mosâvât مساوات equality

mosâvi مساوی equal, alike, even, the same

mosavvabe مصوبه approved, passed

mosavvat مصوت vowel, voiced

mosen مسن old, aged, senile

moshâbeh مشابه identical, similar, alike

moshâbehat مشابهت similarity, resemblance

moshâhede مشاهده observation, noticing

moshâjere مشاجره quarrel, dispute, debate

moshakhkhas مشخص distinct, specific, distinguished

moshakhkhasât مشخصات features, particulars

moshârekat مشارکت partnership, participation

moshâver مشاور counsellor, advisor

moshâvere مشاوره consultation, advice

moshavveq مشوق motive, patron

moshâye'at مشایعت seeing off, escorting

moshel مسهل laxative

moshkel pasand مشکل پسند fussy, fastidious

moshkel مشکل difficult, hard, problem

moshref مشرف close to, adjacent, near

moshrek مشرک dualist, polytheist

mosht مشت fist, punch, handful

moshtâq مشتاق eager, keen

moshtarak مشترک shared, joint, common

moshtarek olmanâfe' مشترک المنافع commonwealth

moshtarek مشترک subscriber, partner

moshtari مشتری customer, client, Jupiter

moshtbâzi مشت بازی boxing

moshtzan مشت زن boxer

mosibat مصیبت disaster, suffering, catastrophe

mosko مسکو Moscow

mosleh مصلح reformist, peace maker

moslem مسلم Moslem

moslemin مسلمین Moslems

mosnad مسند predicate

mosta'âr مستعار pen name

mostabed مستبد autocrat, dictator

mosta'ed مستعد talented, fit, ready

mostahab مستحب religious precepts

mostahjan مستهجن obscene, pornographic

mostahlak مستهلک worn out, absorbed

mosta'jer مستاجر tenant

mostakber مستکبر arrogant

mostakhdem مستخدم employee, servant, janitor

mostalzem مستلزم requiring

mosta'mal مستعمل second hand, used

mostamar مستمر continuous, constant

mostame' مستمع listener, audience

mosta'mere مستعمره colony

mostamerri مستمری pension

mostanad مستند documentary, supported

mostaqarr مستقر settled, established

mostaqell مستقل independent, autonomous

mostaqim مستقیم straight, direct

mostaqiman مستقیما directly

mostarâh مستراح toilet, lavatory

mostatil مستطیل rectangle

mostmand مستمند poor, needy

mosuf موصوف qualified by, characterised by

mosum موسوم called, named, labelled

mot موت death, demise

mota'added متعدد numerous, several

mota'âdel متعادل balanced, stable

mota'ahhed متعهد committed, bound, obliged

mota'ahhel متاهل married

mota'ajjeb متعجب surprised, amazed

mota'âl متعال exalted, sublime

mota'alleq متعلق belonging, pertaining

mota'asseb متعصب fanatical, zealous

mota'assef متاسف sorry, sad

mota'assefâne متاسفانه unfortunately

mota'asser متاثر sorry, sad, touched

mo'tabar معتبر reliable, valid

motâbeq مطابق according to, equal to, corresponding to

motâbeqat مطابقت conformity, contrast

mo'tâd معتاد addict, hooked on

motadâvel متداول common, usual

motadayyen متدین religious

mo'tadel معتدل mild, moderate, gentle

motafakker متفکر thoughtful, contemplating

motafarreqe متفرقه miscellaneous, different

motafâvet متفاوت different, varied

motahammel متحمل sufferer, patient, sustaining

motaharrek متحرک mobile, moving

motahavvel متحول changing, evolving

motahayyer متحیر astonished, surprised

motahhar مطهر pure, holy, scared

motajadded متجدد modernised, modern

motajâvez متجاوز aggressive, offensive

motakabber متکبر arrogant, snob

motakhasses متخصص expert, specialist

motakkâ متکا pillow

motâlebe مطالبه claiming, demanding

motâle'e مطالعه study, survey, consideration

motallaqe مطلقه divorced

MOTAMADDEN

MOTAMADDEN 248

motamadden متمدن civilised, cultured
motamalleq متملق flattering, toady
motamarkez متمرکز concentrated, centralised
mo'tamed معتمد confidant, trusty
motammem متمم supplement
motanaffer متنفر hating, disgusted
motanâseb متناسب proportionate, symmetrical
motanavve' متنوع various, diverse
motaqalleb متقلب cheater, dishonest
motaqayyer متغیر changing, variable, unstable
motaqâzi متقاضی applicant
mo'taqed معتقد believer, faithful
mo'taqedât معتقدات beliefs, credos
motarâdef مترادف synonym
motaraqqi مترقی advanced, progressive
mo'tarez معترض protester, objecting
mo'tareze معترضه parenthetical
motarjem مترجم translator, interpreter
motarjemi مترجمی translation job
motasaddi متصدی in charge
motashakker متشکر thankful, grateful
motashannej متشنج confused, disturbed
motavajjeh متوجه attentive, directed toward
motavâli متوالی continuous, successive

motavalled متولد born
motavaqqe' متوقع expecting
motavaqqef متوقف stopped, static, still
motavâri متواری run away, escapee
motavasset متوسط mean, average, ordinary
motavâze' متواضع humble, modest
motavâzi متوازی parallel
motazâher متظاهر pretentious
motezâd متضاد opposed, antonym, adverse
moti' مطیع obedient, submissive
motlaq مطلق absolute, pure, definite
motlaqan مطلقا absolutely
motma'enn مطمئن confident, certain, secure
motma'ennan مطمئنا certainly
motor موتور engine, motorcycle
motori موتوری motorised, mechanised
motorsiklet موتور سیکلت motorcycle, motor bike
motreb مطرب musician
mottafeqin متفقین The Allies
mottaham kardan متهم کردن to accuse
mottaham متهم accused, charged, indicted
mottahed متحد united, ally
mottaki متکی relying, depending on
mottale' kardan مطالعه کردن to study

249 MOTTALE'

mottale' مطالعه informed, aware, conscious

mottasel متصل connected, joined, attached

mo'ud موعود promised

movâfeq موافق agree, consenting, congruent

movâfeqat nâme موافقت نامه contract

movâfeqat موافقت agreement, consent

movaffaq موفق successful, prosperous

movaffaqiyyat موفقيت success, prosperity

movâjeh مواجه facing, confronting

movâjehe مواجهه confrontation, encounter

movajjah موجه permitted, justified

movakkel موكل client

movalled مولد generator, producer

movaqqat موقت temporary, casual

movarrab مورب oblique, slant

movarrakh مورخ dated

movarrekh مورخ historian

movâzeb مواظب careful, heedful

movâzebat مواظبت care, heed, watching

movâzene موازنه balance, equilibrium

movâzi موازى parallel

moyassar ميسر possible, feasible

moz موز banana

mozâ'af مضاعف double, extra

mozâb مذاب melted, thawed

mozâf مضاف added

mozâhem مزاحم troublesome, nuisance

mozâhemat مزاحمت nuisance, interruption, inconvenience

mozâkere مذاكره discussion, negotiation

mozakhraf مزخرف absurd, nonsense

mozakkar مذكر male, masculine

mo'zalât معضلات problems, complexities

mozâre' مضارع tense for present and past

mozâyede مزايده auction, bid, tender

mozâyeqe مضايقه refraining, refusal

mozd مزد wage, pay

mozdur مزدور hired worker, mercenary

moze' موضع position, location, situation

moze'i موضعى local

mozerr مضر harmful, damaging

mozhak مژك cilia

mozhde مژده good news

mozhdegâni مژدگانى reward for good news

mozhe مژه eyelash

mozmen مزمن chronic

moztareb مضطرب anxious, restless, worried

mozu' موضوع subject, topic, issue

mozun موزون rhythmical, elegant

mu مو hair

mum موم wax

mumiyâ مومیا mummy

munes مونس companion, confident

murche مورچه ant

murmur مورمور creep (slang)

muryâne موریانه termite

musâ موسی Moses

musemi موسمی seasonal

mush موش mouse, rat

mushak موشک missile, rocket

mushekâfi موشکافی scrutiny, minuteness

musiqi موسیقی music

musiqidân موسیقی دان musician

muyrag مویرگ capillary

muze موزه museum

muzi موذی harmful, noxious

muzik موزیک music

n

nâ amn نا امن unsafe, insecure, dangerous

nâ javân mard ناجوانمرد unmanly, ungenerous

nâ omid نا امید hopeless, desperate

na نه no, neither, nor, not

nâb ناب pure, clean

nabâb ناباب unfit

nâbâleq نابالغ immature, minor

nabarâbari نابرابری inequality

nabard نبرد fight, war, battle

nabât نبات plant, rock sugar

nabâti نباتی related to plants and vegetables

nabavi نبوی prophetic

nâbehengâm نابهنگام untimely, premature

nâbejâ نابجا inappropriate, unwise

nâbekâr نابکار wicked, useless

nâbeqe نابغه genius, gifted

nâbesâmân نابسامان disorganised, chaotic

nabi نبی prophet, messenger

nâbinâ نابینا blind

nâbinâyi نابینایی blindness

nabsh نبش exhumation, corner

nâbud نابود extinct, vanished, devastated

nâbudi نابودی destruction, extinction, devastation

nabz نبض pulse, beating

nâchâr ناچار helpless, inevitably

nâchâri ناچاری helplessness, distress

nâchiz ناچیز trivial, petty

nâdân نادان ignorant, fool

nâdâni نادانی ignorance, illiteracy

nâdem نادم regretful, sorry

nâder نادر rare, scarce

nâdokhtari نادختری step daughter

nâdorost نادرست incorrect, false, wrong

nâf ناف umbilicus, centre

naf' نفع profit, benefit, interest

nafaqe نفقه alimony, subsistence

nafar bar نفربر personnel carrier

nafar نفر individual, person

nafarât نفرات soldiers

nâfarmâni نافرمانی disobedience

nafas نفس breath, respiration, instance

nafis نفیس exquisite, precious, costly

nafkh نفخ swelling, bloating, inflation

nafs نفس essence, self, soul

nafsâni نفسانی material, physical, bodily

naft نفت kerosene, petroleum, oil

nafte khâm نفت خام crude oil

naftkesh نفتکش oil tanker

nafty نفتی oily, related to petroleum

nafy نفی rejection, denial, negation

nâgâh ناگاه suddenly, all at once

nâgahân ناگهان suddenly, out of the blue

nâgahâni ناگهانی unexpected, sudden

nagâshtan (negâr) (نگار) نگاشتن to write, to draw

nâgofte ناگفته unsaid, unmentioned

nâgovâr ناگوار unpleasant, unpalatable

nâgozir ناگزیر inevitable, indispensable

nahâd نهاد subject, nature, disposition

nahâl نهال twig, young tree or shrub

nâhamvâr ناهموار uneven, rough

nahân نهان hidden, concealed

nahang نهنگ whale

nâhanjâr ناهنجار abnormal, rough, coarse

nâhaq ناحق unjustified, unfair

nâhâr khori ناهار خوری dinning room

nâhâr ناهار lunch

nahâyat نهایت extreme, utmost, maximum

nâhid ناهید Venus

nahif نحیف weak, thin, frail

nâhiye ناحیه region, area, district

nahofte نهفته hidden, covert, latent

nahr نهر creek, river, stream

nahs نحس ominous, unlucky, sinister

nahv نحو syntax

nahve نحوه method, way, manner

nahy نهی ban, restrain, forbidding

najes نجس unclean, filthy, polluted

nâji ناجی savoir, saver

najib نجیب noble, decent, chaste

najjar نجار carpenter

najjari نجاری carpentry

nâjur ناجور ill-matched, incongruous

najvâ نجوا whisper

nâkâm ناکام unsuccessful, disappointed, defeated

nakare نکره indefinite

nâkas ناکس detestable, mean, coward

nakh risi نخ ریسی spinning

nakh نخ string, thread

nâkhâste ناخواسته unwanted, uninvited

nakhi نخی cotton

nakhl نخل palm

nakhlestân نخلستان palm grove

nakhnomâ نخ نما threadbare

nâkhodâ ناخدا captain (of ship)

nâkhon gir ناخن گیر nail clippers

nâkhon ناخن nail, claw

nâkhonak ناخنک snitching, pilfering

nâkhosh ناخوش sick, ill

nâkhoshi ناخوشی sickness, illness

nakhost vazir نخست وزیر prime minister

nakhost نخست first, foremost

nakhostin نخستین the first

na'l نعل horseshoe

nâlân نالان groaning, moaning

na'lbaki نعلبکی saucer

na'lband نعلبند farrier

nâle ناله groan, whimper

na'leyn نعلین clergy slippers

nâlidan (nâl) (نال) نالیدن to moan, to groan

nâm nevisi نام نویسی enrolment, registration

nâm نام name, title

nam نم moisture, humidity, dampness

namâ نما sight, index, median

namâd نماد symbol

namad نمد felt

nâmâdari نامادری step mother

nâmafhum نامفهوم unintelligible, vague

nâmahdud نامحدود infinite, unlimited

nâmahram نامحرم stranger, not a close kin

namak dân نمک دان saltshaker

namak pâsh نمک پاش saltshaker

namak zâr نمکزار salt marsh

namak نمک salt, charm

nâma'lum نامعلوم unknown, undecided, vague

nâma'qul نامعقول irrational, illogical

nâmarbut نامربوط irrelevant, unrelated, abusive

nâmard نامرد unmanly, coward

nâmardi نامردی cowardliness, foul play

nâmar'i نامرئی invisible

nâmashru' نامشروع illegitimate, bastard, illegal, illicit

nâmatbu' نامطبوع undesirable

namâya degi نمایندگی representation, delegacy, agency

namâyân نمایان revealed, apparent

namâyande gân نمایندگان representatives, agents, delegates

namâyande نماینده representative, member of parliament, agent

namâyesh gâh نمایشگاه exhibit, fair

namâyesh nâme nevis نمایشنامه نویس playwright

namâyesh nâme نمایشنامه play

namâyesh نمایش show, exhibition, play

namâz نماز prayer

namâzkhân نماز خوان prayer person

namâzkhâne نماز خانه place for praying

nâmborde نامبرده above-mentioned, above-named

nâmdâr نامدار popular, famous

nâme fâmil نام فامیل family name

nâme negâri نامه نگاری correspondence

nâme rasân نامه رسان mailman, postman

nâme نامه letter

nâmehrabân نامهربان unkind, cold

namnâk نمناک damp, moist, muggy

namnam نم نم fine drops, drizzle

nâmonâseb نامناسب improper, unfit, inappropriate

nâmonazzam نامنظم irregular, unorganised, unsystematic

nâmorattab نامرتب clumsy, untidy, disorganised

nâmus ناموس chastity, principle, reputation

nâmzad نامزد fiancée, nominee, candidate, engaged

nâmzadi نامزدی candidature, engagement, nomination

nân âvar نان آور bread winner, supporter

nân نان bread

na'nâ نعنا spearmint, mint

nânajib نانجیب unchaste, not noble

nânavâ نانوا baker

nânavâyi نانوایی bakery

nane ننه mum, nanny

nang âvar ننگ آور disgraceful, shameful

nang ننگ shame, disgrace, scorn

nangin ننگین shameful, disgraceful

nanu ننو hammock

nâpadid ناپدید disappeared, concealed

nâpâk ناپاک dirty, unclean

nâpasand ناپسند indecent

nâpâydâr ناپایدار transient, inconsistent

nâpedari ناپدری stepfather

nâpesari ناپسری stepson

nâpokhte ناپخته raw, crude, uncooked, inexperienced

nâqâbel ناقابل worthless, insignificant

naqb نقب burrow, tunnel, shaft

naqd نقد cash, ready money

naqdi نقدی in cash

nâqel ناقل conductor, carrier, dispatcher

nâqes ناقص incomplete, defective, imperfect

naqiz نقیض contradictory, contrary

naql نقل narration, quotation, transmission

naqle qol نقل قول citation, quotation

naqliye نقلیه transport means, vehicles

naqme نغمه song, melody

nâqolâ ناقلا naughty, cunning, clever

naqqâd نقاد critic, reviewer

naqqâl نقال narrator, storyteller

naqqâre نقاره kettledrum

naqqâsh نقاش painter, portrayer

naqqâshi نقاشی painting, drawing, portraying

naqs نقص fault, deficiency, defect

naqsh نقش picture, design, painting

naqshe bardâri نقشه برداری topography, mapping

naqshe kesh نقشه کش draftsman, planner, drawer

naqshe keshi نقشه کشی drawing, surveying, mapping

naqshe نقشه map, plan, model

nâqus ناقوس bell, chime

naqz نقض violation, breach

nar نر male, man, masculine

nârâhat ناراحت uncomfortable, sad, unhappy, bothered

nârâhati ناراحتی discomfort, annoyance

nâras نارس immature, unripe, green

nârâzi ناراضی dissatisfied, discontented

nard نرد backgammon

narde نرده fence, hedge

nardebân نردبان ladder

na're zadan نعره زدن to yell

na're نعره yell, loud cry, roar

nârej نارنج sour orange

nârengi نارنگی mandarin

nârenjak نارنجک grenade, shell

nârenji نارنجی orange colour

narges نرگس daffodil

nârgil نارگیل coconut

narm نرم soft, smooth, gentle

narmesh نرمش work out, warm up, softness

nâru نارو double cross, foul play

nârvan نارون elm tree

nasab نسب genealogy, lineage

nasabi نسبی consanguineous, ancestral

nâsâzgâr ناسازگار maladjusted, unsuitable

nasb kardan نصب کردن to plant, to install, to set up

nasb نصب planting, installing, setting up

nasezâ ناسزا swear, curse, coarse

na'sh نعش dead body, remains

nâshâyeste ناشایسته indecent, improper

nâshenâs ناشناس unknown, disguised, stranger

nâshenavâ ناشنوا deaf

nâsher ناشر publisher

nâshi ناشی naive, novice, resulting

nashib نشیب slope, descent

nâshigari ناشیگری inexperience, clumsiness

nâshokr ناشکر ungrateful, unthankful

nashr نشر publication, diffusion, spreading

nashriyyât نشریات publications

nasht نشت leak, seeping

nâshtâ ناشتا empty-stomach, breakfast

nashv نشو growth

nasib نصیب share, portion, destiny

nasihat kardan نصیحت کردن to advise

nasihat نصیحت advice, counsel

nasim نسیم breeze

nasj نسج tissue, texture

nasl نسل race, generation, offspring

nasr نثر prose

nassâji نساجی weaving

nastaran نسترن sweetbrier

nasuz نسوز fireproof

nâtamâm ناتمام incomplete, unfinished

natars نترس bold, fearless, brave

nâtavân ناتوان weak, powerless, impotent

nâtavâni ناتوانی weakness, impotence

nâteq ناطق speaking, vocal

natije نتیجه result, consequence

nâto ناتو charlatan

na'uz bellâh نعوذ بالله we seek refuge in God

nâv dân ناو دان drain pipe

nâv ostovâr ناو استوار naval warrant officer

nâv shekan ناو شکن destroyer

nâv ناو warship, vessel, frigate

navâ نوا melody, tune, sustenance

navad نود ninety

navâde نواده grand child

navadom نودم ninetieth

navâkhtan (navâz) نواختن (نواز) to play music, to fondle, to hit

navâr chasb نوارچسب adhesive tape

navâr نوار ribbon, cassette, tape, band

navasân نوسان fluctuation, vibration, sway

navâzande نوازنده musical performer, musician

navâzandegi نوازندگی playing music, musical performance

navâzesh نوازش patting, caress, fondling

navâzidan (navâz) نوازیدن (نواز) to play music, to pat

nâvbân ناوبان lieutenant (navy)

nâvbar ناوبر navigator

nâvbari ناوبری navigation

nâvche ناوچه small boat

nâve havâpeymâbar ناو هواپیما بر aircraft carrier

nave نوه grandchild

navid نوید good news

navin نوین new, recent

nây نای trachea

nâyâb نایاب rare, extinct

nâyeb ra'is نایب رئیس vice president

nâyeb نایب deputy, vice

nâyel نایل achieving, attaining

nâylon نایلون plastic, nylon

nâyzhe نایژه bronchus

nâz parvarde ناز پرورده pampered, spoiled

nâz ناز coyness, demurring

nâzâ نازا sterile, infertile, barren

nazâkat نزاکت elegance, courtesy, etiquette

nazar نظر view, look, glance, opinion

nazari نظری theoretical, speculative

nazarkhâhi نظر خواهی polling, opinion poll

nazarriye نظریه opinion, view, theory

nâzâyi نازایی sterility, infertility

nazd نزد near, by, among, by the side

nazdik نزدیک close, near, about

nazdikân نزدیکان relatives, kin

nazdikbin نزدیک بین nearsighted, myopic

nazdikbini نزدیک بینی nearsightedness, myopia

nazdiki نزدیکی closeness, vicinity, sexual intercourse

nâzel نازل low, reduced, falling

nâzem ناظم regulator, assistant

nâzer ناظر observer, supervisor, watching

nâzidan (nâz) (ناز) نازیدن to boast of, to vaunt

nazir نظیر match, equal, similar

nazm نظم order, regularity, discipline

nâzok nârenji نازک نارنجی fastidious

nâzok نازک thin, tender, slim

nazri نذری vowed, oblatory

nedâ ندا call, evocation

nedâmat ندامت regret, remorse

nefâq نفاق disunion, disharmony, difference

nefekâre نصفه کاره half-finished

nefrat angiz نفرت انگیز disgusting, repugnant

nefrat نفرت hating, disgust, aversion

nefrin نفرین curse, evil words, damnation

negâh نگاه look, glance

negahbân نگهبان guard, watchman, keeper

negahbâni نگهبانی guarding, keeping, watching

negahdâri نگهداری keeping, holding, preserving, taking care of

negâr khâne نگار خانه gallery, painter's studio

negarân نگران worried, anxious, restless

negârande نگارنده author, writer

negarâni نگرانی worry, anxiety

negâresh نگارش writing, composing

negaresh نگرش view point, perception, opinion

negârestân نگارستان picture's gallery, painter's studio

negin نگین gem, of a ring, seal ring

nehzat نهضت movement, resurgence

nejâbat نجابت nobleness, nobility, chastity

nejât qariq نجات غریق life guard

nejât نجات salvation, rescue, relive

nekâh نکاح marriage, matrimony, nuptial

nekbat نکبت adversity, misery, misfortune

ne'mat نعمت comfort of life, grace, blessing

nemudan (nemâ) (نما) نمودن to do, to make, to perform

nemudâr نمودار chart, table, diagram, appearing

nemune bardâri نمونه برداری sampling, biopsy

nemune نمونه sample, specimen, example

neqâb نقاب mask, veil

neqâbdâr نقاب دار veiled, masked

neqâhat نقاهت ailment, indisposition

neqres نقرس gout

nerkh نرخ price, rate

nesâr نثار bestowing, offering

nesbat نسبت relation, ratio, kinship

nesbatan نسبتا relatively

nesbi نسبى relative, comparative

nesbiyat نسبيت relativity

nesf onnahâr نصف النهار line of longitude

nesf نصف half

nesfe نصفه half-done

neshâ نشا seedling

neshâdor نشادر sal ammoniac

neshân dâdan نشان دادن to show, to point out

neshân نشان mark, sign, brand, insignia

neshâne ravi نشانه روى aiming

neshâne نشانه goal, target, mark, reminder

neshâni نشانى address, sign, code word

neshast نشست meeting, sagging, session, subsiding

neshastan (neshin) نشستن (نشين) to sit, to sit down, to take a seat

neshâste نشاسته starch

neshât âvar نشاط آور joyful, cheerful, lively

neshât نشاط joy, freshness

neshiman نشيمن dwelling, lodging

nesye نسيه credit transaction

nevesht afzâr forushi نوشت افزار فروشى stationary shop

nevesht afzâr نوشت افزار stationary

neveshtan (nevis) نوشتن (نويس) to write, to put down

neveshte نوشته written, manuscript

nevisande نويسنده writer, author

nevisandegi نويسندگى writing, authorship

ney نى flute, bamboo

neyrang نيرنگ deceit, trick, fraud

neyshakar نيشكر sugar cane

neyzâr نيزار reed bed

nezâ' نزاع fight, war, quarrel

nezâfat نظافت cleanliness, neatness

nezâm نظام order, regime, military service

nezâmi نظامى limitary, martial

nezârat نظارت supervision, control, inspection

nezâre نظاره watching, looking

nezhâd parast نژاد پرست racist

nezhâd parasti نژاد پرستى racism

nezhâd نژاد race, tribe, ethnicity, breed

nezhâdi نژادى racial, ethnic

niku نيكو good, excellent

nikukâr نيكوكار righteous, charity helper

nili نيلى azure

nim نيم half

nime afrâshte نيمه افراشته half mast

nime jân نيمه جان half dead

nime kâre نيمه كاره incomplete, unfinished

nime nahâyi نيمه نهايى semi-final

nime shab نيمه شب midnight

nime نيمه half, half size

nimkat نيمكت bench, sofa

nimkore نيمكره hemisphere

nimrokh نیمرخ profile, vertical, silhouette

nimru نیمرو scrambled egg

nimruz نیمروز midday

nini نی baby

niru نیرو power, strength, force

nirumand نیرومند powerful, strong

nish نیش a sting, prick

nishtar نیشتر lancet, stylet

nist نیست is not

nisti نیستی non-existence

niyâbat نیابت deputation, delegation

niyâkân نیاکان ancestors

niyâm نیام sheath

niyâyesh نیایش praise, praying

niyâz dâshtan نیاز داشتن to need, to require

niyâz mand نیازمند needy, in need

niyâz نیاز need, requirement, exigency

niyyat نیت intention, will, intent

niz نیز also, too

nize نیزه spear, dart

no âmuz نو آموز novice, apprentice, beginner

no arus نوعروس new bride

no âvari نوآوری invention, innovation

no' dust نوعدوست humanitarian

no نو new, recent, modern

no' نوع type, kind

nobar نوبر first fruit, novel, rare

nobat نوبت turn, time, period

nobati نوبتی in turn, periodic

nobâve نوباوه child, youngster

nobe نوبه turn, intermittent

nobovvat نبوت prophecy, prophetic mission

nobuq نبوغ talent, genius

noche نوچه novice, protégé

nofus نفوس population, lives

nofuz نفوذ influence, penetration

noh نه nine

nohe نوحه elegy, lament

nohekhân نوحه خوان elegist, a hired mourner

nohom نهم ninth

no'i نوعی typical, specific

nojavân نوجوان adolescent, teenager

nojavâni نوجوانی adolescence, teenage

nojum نجوم astrology, astronomy

nokar نوکر servant, butler

nokhâ' نخاع spine

nokhâle نخاله sifting, rubbish

nokhbe نخبه best part, chosen, the best

nokhod نخود chickpea

nokhodchi نخودچی roasted pea

nokte نکته point, pointer

nomovv نمو growth

nomre gozâri نمره گذاری numbering, grading, marking

nomre نمره number, grade, mark, point

noql نقل a type of sweet

noqre نقره silver

noqreyi نقره ای of silver

noqsân نقصان shortage, lack, reduction

noqte نقطه point, dot, spot

noras نورس fresh, young

noraside نورسیده newborn, newcomer, fresh

noruz نوروز the first day of Persian year

norvezh نروژ Norway

nosâkht نوساخت newly built

nosâzi نوسازی renovation

noshdâru نوشدارو antidote

noskhe نسخه prescription, copy

notfe نطفه embryo, zygote

notq نطق speech, lecture

novâmr نوامبر November

novezhi نروژی Norwegian

nozâd نوزاد baby, newborn

nozul khâr نزول خوار usurer

nozul نزول descent, fall, usury

nozzâr نظار spectators, watchers

nuh نوح Noah

nuk نوک tip, nib, peak, top

nuktiz نوک تیز sharp-pointed

nur نور light, flash, beam, brightness

nurafkan نورافکن searchlight, limelight

nurâni نورانی sparkling, glittering, shinning

nurecheshm نورچشم the apple of one's eye, dear

nushâbe نوشابه beverage, drink

nushidan (nush) نوشیدن (نوش) to drink

nushidani نوشیدنی drink, beverage, drinkable

nuzdah نوزده nineteen

nuzdahom نوزدهم nineteenth

o

obâsh اوباش lewd, rascals

obohhat ابهت dignity, glory

obur عبور passing, passage, transit

ofoq افق horizon

ofoqi افقی horizontal

oft افت fall, shortage

ofunat عفونت infection, stink

ofuni عفونی infectious, infected

ohde عهده responsibility, undertaking

oj اوج culmination, highest point, peak

ojâq اجاق oven, fireplace, stove

ojrat اجرت pay, earning

oksizhen اکسیژن oxygen

oktobr اکتبر October

olâd اولاد children

olâq الاغ donkey

olgu الگو pattern, mould

oliyâ اولیا saints

oltimâtom التیماتوم ultimatum

olufe علوفه forage, fodder

olyâhazrat علیاحضرت her majesty

omde forush عمده فروش wholesaler

omde عمده chief, main

omdeforushi عمده فروشی wholesale

omid امید hope, expectation

omidvâr امیدوار hopeful

ommat امت believers, followers

ommol امل old-fashioned

omq عمق depth, intensity

omr عمر life, lifetime, living

omrân عمران development, establishing

omum عموم all, the public, everyone

omumi عمومی universal, public, common

ons انس fellowship, acquaintance

onsor عنصر element, agent

onvân عنوان title, heading, topic

operâ اپرا opera

operâtor اپراتور operator

oqâb عقاب eagle, falcon

oqâf اوقاف charity, pious legacies

oqât اوقات times, hours

oqde عقده complex

oqiyânus اقیانوس ocean

oqiyânusiye اقیانوسیه Oceania

ordak اردک duck

ordangi اردنگی a kick on the back

ordibehesht اردیبهشت second month of Iranian calendar

ordu اردو camp

orf عرف tradition, custom

orib اریب diagonal

orkestr ارکستر orchestra

oryân عریان naked, nude, bare

orze عرضه capability, merit

osâre عصاره extract, essence, juice

osqof اسقف bishop

ostâd استاد professor, master, mentor

ostân استان province

ostândâr استاندار governor

ostekhân استخوان bone

ostovâne استوانه cylinder

ostovâr استوار warrant officer

otâq khâb اتاق خواب bedroom

otâq اتاق room, chamber

otrish اتریش Austria

otubân اتوبان motorway (tollway)

otumobil اتومبیل car, motorcar

ozâ' اوضاع conditions, situation

ozr khâhi عذر خواهی apology, apologising

ozr khâstan عذر خواستن to apologise

ozr عذر excuse, apology

ozv عضو organ, limb, member

ozviyyat عضویت membership

p

pâ dar havâ پا در هوا groundless, uncertain

pâ پا foot

pâche پاچه trotters

pâdâsh پاداش reward, bonus

pâdegân پادگان barracks

pâdeshâh پادشاه king, shah, monarch

pâdeshâhi پادشاهی royalty, kingdom

padide پدیده phenomenon

pâdo پادو footboy, assistant

pâdtan پادتن antibody

pâdzahr پادزهر antidote

pâfang پافنگ order arms

pâfeshâri پافشاری insistence, emphasis

pahlavân panbe پهلوان پنبه cardboard cavalier

pahlavân پهلوان hero, champion

pahlu پهلو side, near

pahn پهن wide, broad, extensive

pahnâ پهنا width, extent

pahnâvar پهناور extensive, vast

pâk پاک clean, pure, innocent

pakar پکر gloomy

pâkat پاکت envelope, paper bag

pakhme پخمه stupid, dumb

pakhsh پخش distribution, broadcast

pâkize پاکیزه neat, clean

pâkkon پاکن eraser, wiper, rubber

pâknevis پاکنویس final draft, revised

palakidan (palak) پلکیدن (پلک) to hang out

pâlân پالان packsaddle

palang پلنگ leopard

pâlâsidan (palâs) پلاسیدن (پلاس) to fade, to wither

pâlâyeshgâh پالایشگاه refinery

palid پلید filthy, wicked

pâlto پالتو coat

panâh پناه shelter, refuge, asylum

panâhande پناهنده refugee, asylum seeker

panâhgâh پناهگاه shelter

panbe risi پنبه ریسی cotton spinning

panbe پنبه cotton

panchari پنچری puncture

pand پند advice, guidance

pândol پاندول pendulum

panir پنیر cheese

panj shanbe پنج شنبه Thursday

panj پنج five

panjâh پنجاه fifty

panjare پنجره window

panje پنجه claw, paw

panjul پنجول scratch, scrape

panke پنکه fan (hand-held)

pans پنس forceps, pin

pânsad پانصد five hundred

pânsemân پانسمان dressing, bandage

pânsiyon پانسیون boarding house, hostel

pânzdah پانزده fifteen

par kande پرکنده plucked (chicken)

par پر feather

pârâf پاراف initialling

parâkande پراکنده scattered, dispersed

parande پرنده bird

parandegân پرندگان birds

parastâr پرستار nurse

parastâri پرستاری nursing

parastesh پرستش worship, adoration

parastidan (parast) پرستیدن (پرست) to worship

parastu پرستو swallow

parcham پرچم flag, banner

pârche bâfi پارچه بافی textile factory

pârche پارچه cloth, fabric

parchin پرچین fence, hedge

pardâkht پرداخت payment, polish

pardâkhtan (pardâz) پرداختن (پرداز) to pay

parde پرده curtain, screen, layer

pardepushi پرده پوشی secrecy

pâre پاره torn, ragged

paresh پرش jump

pargâr پرگار calliper

parhiz پرهیز abstinence, avoidance

parhizkâr پرهیزکار vitreous, godly

pari ruz پریروز day before yesterday

pari پری fairy

paridan (par) پریدن (پر) to fly, to jump, to fade

parishab پریشب the night before

parishân پریشان distressed, disturbed

pârk پارک a park, parking

parkhâsh پرخاش protest, aggression

parkhashgar پرخاشگر aggressive

pârs پارس barking

pârsâl پارسال last year

part پرت remote, deviated

partâb پرتاب throwing, shooting

partgâh پرتگاه crag; wall of rock

parto پرتو ray, beam, light

pârty پارتی connections, party

pâru پارو snow-shovel, paddle

parvande پرونده file, dossier, record

parvâne پروانه butterfly, permit, propeller

parvâr پروار fattened (animal)

parvardegâr پروردگار god, nourisher

parvaresh پرورش nurturing, breeding

parvareshgâh پرورشگاه nursery, orphanage

parvâz پرواز flight

pas andâz پس انداز savings

pas fardâ پس فردا day after tomorrow

pas mânde پس مانده leftover, residue

pas پس then, after, thus

pasand پسند admiration, approval

pasandidan (pasand) پسندیدن (پسند) to choose, to like, to approve

pâsâzh پاساژ shopping plaza

pâsdâr پاسدار Islamic guard

pâsebân پاسبان policeman, guard

pâsebâni پاسبانی guarding, patrolling

pâsgâh پاسگاه rural police station

pashe band پشه بند mosquito net

pashe پشه mosquito, fly

pâshidan (pâsh) (پاش) پاشیدن to sprinkle

pashimân پشیمان regretful, remorseful

pashm chini پشم چینی sheepshearing

pashm risi پشم ریسی wool spinning

pashm پشم wool

pashmak پشمک cotton candy

pashmâlu پشمالو hairy, shaggy

pashmi پشمی woollen

pâshne kesh پاشنه کش shoe-horn

pâshne پاشنه heel

paso pish پس وپیش back and forth

pâsokh پاسخ answer, response

past پست mean, inferior, low life

pâstorize پاستوریزه posturised

pastu پستو closet

pasvand پسوند suffix

pâtil پاتیل dead drunk

patu پتو blanket

pâtuq پاتوق hang out, meeting place

pâvaraqi پاورقی foot-article

payâm پیام message

payâmbar پیامبر prophet, messenger

pâyân nâme پایان نامه thesis, dissertation

pâyân پایان end, finish

pâyâne پایانه terminal

pâydâr پایدار permanent, constant

pâye پایه grade, pillar, basis

pâygâh پایگاه base

pâyiydan (pây) (پای) پاییدن to look out, to watch out

pâyiyn پایین down, low, under

pâyiyz پاییز fall, autumn

pâytakht پایتخت capital city

pazhmorde پژمرده faded, pale, sad

pazhuhesh پژوهش research, appeal

pazirâyi پذیرایی reception, hospitality

paziresh پذیرش admission, acceptance, reception

paziroftan (pazir) (پذیر) پذیرفتن to accept, to admit

pechpech پچ پچ whisper

pedar bozorg پدربزرگ grand father

pedar koshi پدرکشی patricide

pedar shohar پدر شوهر father-in-law (husband)

pedar sukhte پدرسوخته knavish, damn

pedar zan پدرزن father in law (wife's father)

pedar پدر father

pedarâne پدرانه fatherly

pedaro mâdar پدر و مادر parents

pehen پهن dung, manure

pelâstik پلاستیک plastic

pelk پلک eyelid

pelle پله stair, step

pellekân پلکان stairs, steps

penhân پنهان hidden, secret

penisilin پنی سیلین penicillin

periyod پریود menstruation

pesar amme پسر عمه son of paternal aunt

pesar amu پسرعمو son of paternal uncle

pesar bachche پسر بچه young boy

pesar dâyi پسر دایی son of maternal uncle

pesar khâle پسرخاله son of maternal aunt

pesar khânde پسرخوانده adopted son

pesar پسر boy, son

pesarak پسرک little boy

peshgel پشگل sheep dung

pestân پستان beast, teat

pestânak پستانک nipple, pacifier

pestândâr پستاندار mammal

peste پسته pistachio

pey dar pey پی در پی successive, continuous

pey پی foundation, trace

peyâpey پیاپی successive, continuous

peydâ پیدا visible, evident

peydâyesh پیدایش genesis, existence

peygard پیگرد prosecution

peykar tarash پیکرتراش sculptor

peykare پیکره sculpture

peymân پیمان contract, pact, treaty

peymâne پیمانه measure

peymânkâr پیمانکار contactor

peyqâm پیغام message

peyqambar پیغمبر prophet

peyravi kardan پیروی کردن to follow, to obey

peyravi پیروی following, obeying

peyrizi kardan پی ریزی کردن to found

peyrizi پی ریزی founding

peyro پیرو follower, disciple

peyvand پیوند graft, union, relationship

peyvast پیوست attachment, enclosed

peyvastan (peyvand) پیوستن (پیوند) to connect, to join

peyvaste پیوسته connected, continuous

pezeshk پزشک medical doctor

pezeshki پزشکی medicine, medical practice

pezhvâk پژواک echo, reflection

pich khordegi پیچ خوردگی twist, bend

pich پیچ twist, bend, screw

pichak پیچک ivy

pichidan (pich) پیچیدن (پیچ) to turn, to wrap

pichide پیچیده intricate, complicated

pichidegi پیچیدگی intricacy, twist

pile پیله cocoon, abscess, gumboil

pine پینه patch, callous

pinkponk پینک پونک table tennis

pip پیپ smoking pipe

pir chesmi پیرچشمی presbyopia

pirâhan پیراهن shirt, dress

pirâmun پیرامون outskirts, around

pirâste پیراسته trimmed, decorated

pirâyesh پیرایش trimming, ornament

piri پیری old age

pirmard پیرمرد old man

piruzi پیروزی victory, triumph

pirzan پیرزن old woman

pish âgahi پیش آگهی prognosis, warning

pish âhang پیش آهنگ scout, pioneer

pish âmad پیشامد event, accident

pish âpish پیشاپیش beforehand

pish bahâ پیش بها advance payment

pish band پیش بند apron, bib

pish bini پیش بینی forecast, anticipation

pish darâmad پیش درآمد prelude

pish dasti پیش دستی forestalling

pish forush پیش فروش sold in advance

pish giri پیشگیری prevention

pish guyi پیشگویی prediction, prophecy

pish kesh پیشکش present, gift

pish khân پیشخوان counter

pish kharid پیش خرید advance purchase

pish khedmat پیشخدمت waiter, servant

pish namâz پیش نماز prayer leader, chaplain

pish qadam پیش قدم leader, initiator

pish qest پیش قسط first instalment

pish پیش front, before, presence

pishâni پیشانی forehead

pishe پیشه jib, trade, profession

pishfang پیش فنگ present arms

pishi پیشی precedence, pussy cat

pishin پیشین former, previous

pishine پیشینه background, file

pishnahâd پیشنهاد proposal, offer, suggestion

pishraft پیشرفت progress, improvement

pishrafte پیشرفته progressed, advanced

pishravi پیشروی advancement, moving ahead

pishro پیشرو forerunner, pioneer

pishvâ پیشوا leader

pishvand پیشوند prefix

pishvâz پیشواز welcoming

pit پیت tin, container

piyâde ravi پیاده روی walking, hiking

piyâde ro پیاده رو side walk, footpath

piyâde پیاده on foot, pedestrian, infantry

piyâle پیاله cup, bowl, mug

piyâz پیاز onion, bulb

piyâzche پیازچه spring onion, bulbils

plâk پلاک plate, tag

pof پف puff, blowing out

pofyuz پفيوز crabbed, sullen

poker پوکر poker

pokhtan (paz) (پز) پختن to cook

pokhte پخته cooked, experienced

pol پل bridge

polis پليس police

poliver پوليور jumper (sweater)

polo پلو cooked rice

polomb پلمب seal

pomâd پماد ointment

por harf پر حرف talkative, yapping

por kardan پر کردن to fill, to load

por saro seda پرسروصدا noisy

por پر full, loaded, charged

porchâne پرچانه talkative

porov پرو fitting, trying on

porozhoktor پروژکتور projector

porposht پرپشت thick, dense

porru پررو rude

porsesh پرسش question, inquiry

porsidan (pors) (پرس) پرسيدن
to ask a question

porteqâl پرتقال orange

posht پشت back, behind, wrong
side

poshtak پشتک somersault

poshtevâne پشتوانه backing

poshti پشتى cushion, pillow

poshtibân پشتيبان supporter,
patron

poshtkâr پشتکار consistency,
stamina

poshto ru پشت و رو inside out

post پست post, mail, position

postchi پستچى postman

postkhâne پستخانه post office

potk پتک hammer, sledge

poz پز show off

puch پوچ empty, blank, vain

pud پود woof

pudr پودر powder

puk پوک empty, hollow

puke پوکه cartridge-shell

pul پول money, currency

pulâd پولاد steel

pulak پولک tinsel, fish-scale

pulaki پولکى money lover

puldâr پولدار rich, wealthy

pure پوره puree, mash

pushâk پوشاک clothing, dress

pushak پوشک nappy

pushâl پوشال stuffing or packing
material

pushe پوشه file, folder

pushesh پوشش covering, wrap

pushidan (push) (پوش) پوشيدن
to wear, to cover, to hide

pusidan (pus) (پوس) پوسيدن
to decay, to rot

pusidegi پوسيدگى decay,
rottenness

pust kande پوست کنده frank, open

pust koloft پوست کلفت tick-
skinned

pust پوست skin, peel, shell

puste پوسته crust, scale

puster پوستر poster

putin پوتين boot

puyâ پویا searcher

puze band پوزه بند a muzzle

puze پوزه muzzle, chin

puzesh پوزش apology, pardon

puzkhand پوزخند sneer

q

qâb bâzi بازی قاب knucklebone game

qâb قاب frame, case, knucklebone

qabâ قبا cloak

qabâhat قباحت hideousness, obscenity

qabâle قباله title deed, contract

qâbel قابل worthy, deserved, competent

qâbele قابله midwife

qabih قبيح obscene, immoral, indecent

qabil قبيل kind, type

qabile قبيله clan, tribe

qabl قبل before, ago, previous

qâblame قابلمه stew pan, metal bowl

qablan قبلا beforehand, first of all

qabli قبلى previous, last, former

qabqab غبغب double chin, dewlap

qabr قبر grave, tomb

qabrestân قبرستان graveyard, cemetery

qabrkan قبركن gravedigger

qabul قبول acceptance, consent, admitting

qabuli قبولى acceptance, approval, passing (test)

qabz قبض bill, receipt

qabze قبضه handle, clutch

qâchâq قاچاق smuggle, illicit

qâchâqchi قاچاقچى smuggler

qad قد height, size, tallness

qadam zadan قدم زدن to walk, to stroll

qadam قدم pace, footstep

qadaqan غدغن forbidden

qadar قدر destiny

qadboland قدبلند tall

qâder قادر able, competent, capable

qadimi قديمى old, ancient

qadr قدر value, worth, merit

qadrdâni قدردانى appreciation, gratitude

qâ'ede قاعده rule, base

qâ'edegi قاعدگى menstruation, period

qâ'eme قائمه perpendicular

qafas قفس cage

qafase قفسه shelf, locker, bookcase

qâfel غافل negligent, ignorant

qâfele قافله caravan, convoy

qâfelgir غافلگير blitzing, surprisal

qâfiye قافيه rhyme

qaflat غفلت negligence, carelessness

qafqâz قفقاز Caucasia

qahbe قحبه prostitute, whore

qahqahe قهقهه loud laugh

qahqarâ قهقرا regression, retrogression

qahr قهر not speaking with, angry at

qahramân قهرمان hero, champion

qahramâni قهرمانى championship

qahti zade قحطی زده famine-stricken

qahti قحطی famine, starvation

qahve قهوه coffee

qahvechi قهوه چی tea house keeper

qahvekhâne قهوه خانه tea house, bar, café

qahveyi قهوه ای brown

qâjâr قاجار the Qajar dynasty

qal' قلع tin

qalabe غلبه dominance, victory, triumph

qalâf غلاف sheath, case cover

qalam mu قلم مو paintbrush

qalam قلم pen, quill

qalamro قلمرو territory, domain

qalamzani قلمزنی engraving

qalat غلط error, mistake, incorrect, wrong

qalatgiri غلط گیری proofreading

qalb قلب heart, spirit, forged, fake

qalbi قلبی sincere, genuine, cordial

qal'e قلعه fort, castle

qâleb غالب victorious, most, dominant

qâleb قالب mould, model, cast, matrix

qâleban غالبا frequently, often

qaliyân قلیان Hubble bubble, narghile

qallâde قلاده collar (dog's), leash

qalle غله corn, grain, cereals

qaltak غلتک roller, coaster

qaltidan (qalt) غلتیدن (غلت) to roll, to tumble

qam غم sorrow, worry, sadness

qamangiz غم انگیز tragic, saddening

qambâd غمباد goitre

qame قمه dagger

qamgin غمگین sad, gloomy, saddened

qanâri قناری canary

qand قند sugar cube

qandân قندان sugar bowl

qani غنی rich, wealthy

qanimat غنیمت booty, windfall

qannâdi قنادی confectionary, pastry shop

qânun gozâri قانون گذاری legislation

qânun قانون law

qâp قاپ snatching

qapân قپان steelyard, scale

qâpidan (qâp) قاپیدن (قاپ) to snatch, to grab

qâr غار cave

qarâmat غرامت indemnity, damage

qarantine قرنطینه quarantine

qarâr قرار agreement, resolution, appointment, date

qarârdâd قرارداد pact, treaty, contract

qarârdâdi قراردادی conventional

qarârgâh قرارگاه headquarter

qârat غارت plunder, looting

qarâvol قراول guard, patrol

qaraz غرض purpose, grudge, ill-will

qarb غرب west

qarbâl غربال sifter, riddle

qarbi غربی western

qârch قارچ mushroom, fungus

qâri قاری Koran reader

qaribe غریبه alien, stranger, lonely

qarine قرینه symmetrical, match

qariye قریه village

qarize غریزه instinct, nature

qarn قرن centaury

qarniye قرنیه cornea

qarq غرق drowning, sinking, flooded

qârqâr قارقار cawing

qarqare غرغره gargling

qarqâvol قرقاول pheasant

qârre قاره continent

qarz قرض debt, loan, borrowing, lending

qasam قسم oath, pledge, swear

qasâvat قساوت cruelty

qasb غصب usurpation, snatching, seizing

qasd قصد will, intension, purpose

qasdi قصدی intentional

qâsed قاصد messenger, courier

qâsedak قاصدک dandelion

qash غش fit, coma, seizure

qashang قشنگ beautiful

qâshoq قاشق spoon

qasr قصر palace

qassâb قصاب butcher

qassâl khâne غسال خانه a place for washing corpses, mortuary

qassâl غسال one who washes dead bodies, mortician

qat' قطع cutting, amputation, interruption

qat'an قطعا positively, definitely

qatâr barqi قطار برقی tram

qatâr قطار train, sequence

qâte' قاطع decisive, clear-cut

qat'e قطعه piece, section, segment

qâtel قاتل murderer, assassin

qâter قاطر mule

qâti قاتی mixed, mingled

qat'i قطعی definite, final, certain

qatl قتل murder, massacre, assassination

qat'nâme قطعنامه resolution, declaration

qatre chakân قطره چکان dropper

qatre قطره drop, drip

qatur قطور thick, bulky

qavâre قواره pattern, figure, cut

qavi قوی powerful, strong

qavvâs غواص diver

qavvâsi غواصی diving

qâyeb غایب absent, hidden, missing

qâyem mushak قایم موشک hide-and-seek

qâyem قایم firm, secure, strong, hidden

qâyeq قایق boat

qayy قی vomit

qayyem قیم guardian

qâz غاز goose

qazâ غذا food, meal

qazabnâk غضبناک angry, wrathful, infuriated

qazal غزل lyric, love poem

qazâvat قضاوت judgement

qazâyi قضایی judicial

qâzi قاضی judge, justice of peace

qaziyye قضیه case, proposition, clause

qeble قبله praying direction

qebres قبرس Cyprus

qeddis قدیس saint

qedmat قدمت antiquity, oldness

qelqelak قلقلک tickling

qelzat غلظت viscosity, density

qenâ'at قناعت continence, contentment

qerâ'at قرائت reading, reciting

qermez قرمز red

qerqere قرقره spool, pulley

qerqi قرقی sparrow hawk

qesâs قصاص retaliation, punishment

qeshâ غشا membrane, coat

qeshlâq قشلاق winter quarters

qeshr قشر crust, layer, coating

qesm قسم kind, type, class

qesmat قسمت section, portion, fate

qesse قصه story, tale

qessegu قصه گو storyteller

qest قسط instalment, mortgage

qeyb غیب invisible, mysterious

qeybat غیبت backbiting, absence, being away

qeybgu غیبگو clairvoyant, oracle

qeybguyi غیبگویی prophecy, prognostication

qeychi قیچی scissors

qeyd قید adverb, bond, limitation

qeymat قیمت price, fee, cost

qeymati قیمتی precious, costly

qeyme قیمه minced meat

qeymumat قیمومت guardianship

qeyr غیر another, except, other than, without

qeyrat غیرت zeal, jealousy

qeyre addi غیر عادی abnormal, unusual

qeyre addi غیر عادی unusual, strange

qeyre amdi غیر عمدی unintentional

qeyre herfeyi غیر حرفه ای amateur, unprofessional

qeyre momken غیر ممکن impossible

qeyre mostaqim غیر مستقیم indirect

qeyre qâbele fahm غیر قابل فهم incomprehensible

qeyre rasmi غیر رسمی informal, unofficial

qeyre shar'i غیر شرعی illegal, unlawful

qeyre tabiyi غیر طبیعی unnatural

qeysi قیسی a type of apricot

qif قیف funnel

qir قیر tar

qirât قیراط carat

qiyâb غیاب absence, absenteeism

qiyâfe قیافه appearance, pose

qiyâm قیام revolt, rebellion, uprising

qiyâmat قیامت resurrection day

qiyâs قیاس analogy, comparison

qobâr غبار dust, smog

qobârâlud غبار آلود dusty, soiled

qodde غده gland, tumour, lump

qodrat قدرت power, strength

qofl قفل lock

qofle zanjir قفل زنجیر padlock

qoflsâz قفل ساز locksmith

qol قول promise, vow

qolâm غلام servant, slave

qoldor قلدر bully, thug

qolenj قولنج colic

qollâb قلاب hook, drag

qollâbduzi قلابدوزی crocheting

qollâbi قلابی fake, phoney

qolle قله summit, peak, apex

qolovv غلو exaggeration, overstatement

qolve قلوه kidney

qom قوم tribe, nation, sect

qomâr قمار gamble

qomârkhâne قمار خانه casino

qomi قومی racial, ethnical

qomqome قمقمه flask, thermos bottle

qomri قمری ringdove

qonche غنچه bud, sprout, blossom

qondâq قنداق diapers, swaddling bands, gunstock

qoqâ غوغا disturbance, tumult

qor غر grumble, murmur

qor'ân قرآن Koran

qorbâni قربانی sacrifice, victim

qorbat غربت away from home, nostalgia

qorbati غربتی gypsy

qor'e قرعه lottery, draw

qorfe غرفه pavilion, booth, chamber

qormesabzi قرمه سبزی rice with vegetable stew

qoromsâq قرمساق pimp, cuckold

qoroq قرق preserved, restricted

qorresh غرش roaring, thundering

qors قرص pill, tablet, loaf, firm

qorse khâb قرص خواب sleeping pill

qorse zedde hamelegi قرص ضد حاملگی contraceptive pill

qorub غروب sunset, dusk

qorur غرور pride, dignity, vanity

qos قوس bow, arch

qoshun قشون troops, army

qosl غسل ceremonial washing, bathing

qosqazah قوس قزح rainbow

qosse غصه sorrow, gloom, grief

qotb قطب pole

qotbi قطبی polar

qotbnamâ قطب نما compass

qotr قطر diameter

qovvat قوت power, strength, potency

qovve قوه power, energy

qozruf غضروف cartilage

qu قو swan

quch قوچ ram

qul غول giant

qurbâqe غورباغه frog, toad

qure غوره sour grape

qush قوش falcon, hawk

quti قوطی tin, can

quz قوز hunch, hump

r

rabb رب God, lord

râbet رابط connector, liaison

râbete رابطه relation, connection, link

rabt ربط connection, relation

ra'd رعد thunder

radd رد refusal, disproval, trace

radde pâ رد پا footpath, track (footprints)

rade bandi رده بندی classification

rade رده category, row, line

radif ردیف row, line, order

râdiyator رادیاتور radiator

râdiyo رادیو radio

rafiq رفیق friend, pale, mate, buddy

raftan (rav) رفتن (رو) to go

raftâr رفتار behaviour, conduct, manner

rafto âmad رفت و آمد traffic, coming and going

rag رگ vein, artery, vessel

ragbâr رگبار shower

râh âhan راه آهن railway, rail road

râh bandân راه بندان traffic congestion, road obstruction

râh namâ راهنما guide, directory, manual

râh pelle راه پله stairway

râh peymâyi راهپیمایی walking, demonstration

râh راه road, route, way

rahâ رها freed, liberated

râhat راحت comfortable, easy

rahâyi رهایی freedom, salvation

rahbar رهبر leader

rahbari رهبری leadership

râheb راهب monk

râhebe راهبه nun

rahem رحم uterus, womb

rahm رحم mercy, compassion

rahmat رحمت blessing

rahn رهن mortgage, lien

rahqozar رهگذر pedestrian, passer-by

râhro راه رو hall, corridor

râhzan راهزن bandit, highwayman

ra'is jomhur رئیس جمهور president

ra'is رئیس chief, head, director, principal, boss

râked راکد stagnant, standstill

rakht âviz رخت آویز clothes hanger

rakht kan رختکن cloakroom, dressing room

rakht khâb رخت خواب bed, bedding

rakht shuyi رخت شویی clothes washing, laundry

rakht رخت clothes, garment

rakik رکیک obscene, indecent

râm رام domestic, submissive, pet

ram رم scared, shying

ramaq رمق energy

ramazân رمضان fasting month

rammâl رمال fortune teller

ramz رمز code, secret, mystery

rân ران thigh

rânande راننده driver

rânandegi رانندگی driving

rândan (rân) (راندن (ران to drive

rande رنده grater, shredder

rang âmizi رنگ آمیزی coloration

rang paride رنگ پریده pale, faded

rang zan رنگ زن painter

rang رنگ color, paint, hue

rangârang رنگارنگ multicolored, various

rangi رنگی colored, colour (film)

rangin kamân رنگین کمان rainbow

ranj رنج pain, suffering, agony

ranjesh رنجش annoyance, irritation

ranjidan (ranj) (رنجیدن (رنج to be annoyed, to be offended

raqam رقم figure, digit, number

raqbat رغبت desire, relish

râqeb راغب willing, keen

raqiq رقیق diluted, warty

raqqâs رقاص dancer

raqs رقص dancing

raqsidan (raqs) (رقصیدن (رقص to dance

ra's راس head, head of (cattle)

rasad khâne رصدخانه observatory

rasânâ رسانا conductor

rasândan (rasân) (رساندن (رسان to supply, to deliver

rasâne رسانه medium

ra'she رعشه tremor, trembling

rashid رشید brave

rasid رسید receipt

rasidan (ras) (رسیدن (رس to reach, to arrive

raside رسیده ripe, mature

rasidegi رسیدگی investigation, checking

rasm رسم custom, tradition

rasmi رسمی formal, official

rasmiyyat رسمیت formality

râst guyi راست گویی truthfulness

râst راست straight, true, right, upright

râstâ راستا direction

rastâkhiz رستاخیز resurrection

râste راسته fillet, row

raste رسته class, rank

rastegâr رستگار saved, delivered

râsti راستی truth, honesty

râsu راسو weasel

rasul رسول prophet

ravâ روا permissible, fair

ravâdid روادید visa

ravâj رواج currency, prevalence

ravân darmâni روان درمانی psychotherapy

ravân pezeshk روان پزشک psychiatrist

ravân pezeshki روان پزشکی psychiatry

ravân shenâs روانشناس psychologist

ravân shenâsi روانشناسی psychology

ravân روان running, flowing, fluent, soul, spirit

ravand روند process, procedure

ravâne روانه dispatched, sent

ravâni روانى fluency, mental, psychic

ravâyat روايت narrative

ravesh روش method, procedure

raviyye رويه policy, tactic

ra'y راى poll, ballot, vote, opinion

râyegân رايگان free of charge

râyehe رايحه smell, odor, fragrance

râyej رايج current, customary

ra'yyat رعيت inferior, farmer

râz راز secret, mystery

râzdâr رازدار confidant

râzi راضى satisfied, content

razl رذل mean, wicked

razm nâv رزمناو battleship, cruiser

razm رزم fight, battle

razmande رزمنده fighter, combatant

re'âyat رعايت regard, consideration

rebâ khâr ربا خوار usurer

rebâ ربا usury

refâh رفاه welfare, convenience

rehlat رحلت death

rejâl رجال distinguished people

rekâb ركاب pedal, stirrup

reqâbat رقابت competition, rivalry

resâle رساله thesis, dissertation

reshte kuh رشته كوه mountain range

reshte رشته field, line, string

resturân رستوران restaurant

rezâyat bakhsh رضايت بخش satisfactory

rezâyat رضايت satisfaction

rezerv رزرو booking

rezhe رژه parade

ridan (rin) ريدن (رين) to shit, to defecate

rig ريگ pebble, sand, gravel

rikhtan (riz) ريختن (ريز) to pour, to litter, to cast

rikhtegar ريخته گر moulder

rish tarash ريش تراش razor, shaver

rish ريش beard

rishe kani ريشه كنى eradication

rishe ريشه root, origin

rishkhand ريشخند mocking, ridicule

rishu ريشو bearded

rismân ريسمان string, rope

ristan (ris) ريستن (ريس) to spin

riyâkâr رياكار hypocritical

riyâl ريال Rial, Persian currency

riyâsat رياست chairmanship, presidency

riyâzat رياضت mortification, self discipline

riyâzidân رياضى دان mathematician

riyâziyât رياضيات mathematical

riye ريه lung

riz ريز tiny, little, detail

rizesh ريزش pouring, flowing down, collapse

rob' ربع one fourth, quarter

robâ'iyyât رباعيات quatrains

robâyande ربابنده hijacker

robb رب tomato paste

robudan (robây) (ربای) ربودن
to kidnap, to hijack

roftgar رفتگر street sweeper

rofu رفو darning

rofuze رفوزه failed

roju' رجوع reference, referral, returning

rok رک frank, open, blunt

rokh رخ face, rook (in chess)

rokud رکود stagnation, standstill

român رمان novel (book)

ronaq رونق success, prosperity

roqan روغن oil (cooking)

roqani روغنی oily, greasy

roshan روشن light, lit, bright

roshanâyi روشنایی light, brightness

roshandel روشندل blind

roshanfekr روشنفکر intellectual

roshd رشد growth, development

roshve dâdan رشوه دادن to bribe

roshve رشوه bribe, bribery

roshvekhâr رشوه خوار bribe taker

rosub رسوب sediment, dregs

rosvâyi رسوایی scandal, stigma

rotbe رتبه rank, grade, level

rotubat رطوبت moisture

roy روی zinc

royâ رویا dream

royat رویت sight, vision

rozan روزن hole, crack

roze روضه sermon

ru رو face, top, on

rubâh روباه fox

rubaleshi روبالشی pillowcase

rubân روبان ribbon, band

ruband روبند veil, mask

ruberu shodan روبرو شدن to confront

ruberu روبرو face to face, opposite

rubusi روبوسی kissing each other

rud khâne رودخانه river

rud رود river, stream

rudarbâyesti رودربایستی bashfulness, embarrassment

rudarru رو در رو face to face

rude روده intestine, gut, bowel

rudel رودل upset stomach

ruh olqodos روح القدس Holy Spirit

ruh روح spirit, soul, ghost

ruhâni روحانی spiritual, holy, clergy

ruhâniyat روحانیت the clergy, spirituality

ruhiyye روحیه morale

rumizi رومیزی tablecloth

runevesht رونوشت copy

runevisi رونویسی copying

rupush روپوش cover, gown, uniform

rusari روسری scarf

rusiye روسیه Russia

ruspi روسپی prostitute, whore

rustâ روستا village

rustâyi روستایی villager, rural

ruydâd رویداد event, incident

ruye ham rafte روی هم رفته altogether

ruye روی over

ruyiydan (ruy) (روی) روییدن to grow

ruz روز day

ruzâne روزانه daily

ruze khâr روزه خوار fast breaker

ruze روزه fasting, fast

ruzedâr روزه دار one who fasts

ruzgâr روزگار world, circumstance, time

ruzhe lab روژ لب lipstick

ruzi روزی sustenance

ruzmarre روزمره daily, routine

ruzmozd روزمزد daily pay

ruzname forushi روزنامه فروشی newsagency

ruznâme negâr روزنامه نگار journalist

ruznâme negâri روزنامه نگاری journalism

ruznâme روزنامه newspaper

s

sa'âdat سعادت luck, happiness

sâ'at sâz ساعت ساز watchmaker

sâ'at ساعت hour, time, watch

sabab سبب cause, reason

sabad سبد basket, hamper

sabbâbe سبابه index finger

sâbeq سابق former, old

sâbeqe dâr سابقه دار experienced, with a past record

sâbeqe سابقه previous record, antecedent

sâbet ثابت fixed, stable, proved

sabk سبک style

sabok سبک light, soft, undignified

sabr صبر patience, tolerance

sabt ثبت registration, record

sâbun صابون soap

sabur صبور patient, tolerant

sabus سبوس bran

sabz سبز green, greenery, growing

sabze سبزه dark complexion, brunet

sabzi forush سبزی فروش greengrocer

sabzi سبزی vegetables, greenery

sad صد hundred

sadaf صدف oyster, shell

sadame صدمه harm, injury, damage

sadaqe صدقه charity

sadd سد dam, barrier, blockage

sâde ساده simple, easy, naive

sade سده century

sâdeq صادق sincere, honest

sâder konande صادر کننده exporter

sâder صادر exporting

sâderât صادرات exports

sadr صدر top, uppermost

sâ'ed ساعد forearm

sâ'eqe صاعقه lightening

sâf صاف clear, transparent, pure, flat

saf صف queue

safâ صفا purity, serenity, clarity

safar bekheyr سفر بخیر bon voyage!

safar سفر travel, trip, cruise

safarnâme سفرنامه itinerary

safhe kelid صفحه کلید keyboard

safhe صفحه page, sheet, layer, record

safhebandi صفحه بندی pagination

sâfi صافی strainer, sift, purity

safih سفیه silly, lunatic

safine سفینه space ship

safir سفیر ambassador, envoy

safsate سفسطه fallacy

safte سفته draft, exchange bill

sag سگ dog

sahâbe صحابه companions (of prophet)

sahâm سهام shares, stocks

sahâmi سهامی joint-stock

sahar سحر dawn, twilight

sâheb صاحب owner, possessor, proprietor

sâhebkhâne صاحب خانه landlord

sâhel ساحل shore, beach, coast, seaside

sâheli ساحلی coastal

sâher ساحر magician

sahhâfi صحافی bookbinding

sahih صحیح correct, right, true

sahim سهیم participant, partner

sahl angâr سهل انگار careless, negligent

sahl سهل easy

sahm سهم share, stock

sahn صحن courtyard

sahne صحنه scene, theatre, stage

sahrâ صحرا desert, wilderness

sahrâneshin صحرانشین nomad, desert dweller

sahv سهو mistake, error

sahyonism صهیونیسم Zionism

sajde سجده bowing, prostration

sakane سکنه inhabitants, residents

sâken ساکن resident, inhabitant

sâket ساکت quiet, silent

sakhâvat mand سخاوتمند generous

sakhâvat سخاوت generosity

sakhre صخره rock, cliff

sâkht ساخت made, make, structure

sakht سخت difficult, hard, strict, rigid

sâkhtan (sâz) ساختن (ساز) to build, to make

sâkhtâr ساختار structure

sâkhtegi ساختگی artificial, forged

sâkhtemân ساختمان building, structure

sakhtgir سختگیر uncompromising, diligent

sakku سکو platform

sâl سال year, annum

salâh صلاح goodness, advisable

salâhiyat صلاحیت competency, merit, authority

salâm aleykom سلام علیکم hello, greetings

salâm سلام hello, greeting

salâmati سلامتی health

salât صلات prayer

salavât صلوات praise for God and the prophet

sâleh صالح competent, decent

sâlem سالم intact, healthy, safe

sâles ثالث third

sâlgard سالگرد anniversary

salib صلیب cross (religious)

salibi صلیبی crusade, cross shaped

saliqe سلیقه taste, tact

salis سلیس fluent

sâliyâne سالیانه yearly, annual

sâlkhorde سالخورده old, aged

sâlmand سالمند aged, old

salmâni سلمانی barber, hairdresser

sâlnâme سالنامه calendar

sâlon سالن hall, lounge

sâlruz سالگرد anniversary

saltanat talab سلطنت طلب monarchist, royalist

saltanat سلطنت kingdom, monarchy

saltanati سلطنتی royal

sam'ak سمعک hearing aid

samar bakhsh ثمربخش useful, fruitful

samar ثمر fruit, product, result

sâmet صامت mute

sam'i basari سمعی بصری audio-visual

samimi صمیمی sincere, intimate, genuine

samimiyat صمیمیت sincerity

samm سم poison, venom

sammi سمی poisonous, toxic

samt سمت side, direction

samur سمور sable

sân سان parade, march

sanâ ثنا eulogy, praise

sanad سند document, title

san'at صنعت industry, craft

san'ati صنعتی industrial, industrialised

sanâye'e dasti صنایع دستی crafts, hand crafts

sandali صندلی chair, seat

sandaliye charkhdar صندلی چرخدار wheelchair

sanduq صندوق chest, case, safe, cash register

sanduqdâr صندوق دار cashier

sânehe سانحه accident, casualty

sang سنگ stone, rock

sangak سنگگ a type of bread

sangar سنگر trench, rifle pit

sangarbandi سنگربندی entrenchment, fortification

sangdel سنگدل cruel, stone-hearted

sangin سنگین heavy, massive

sangrize سنگریزه gravel

sangsâr سنگسار stoning

sangtarâsh سنگتراش mason, stonecutter

sâni ثانی secondary, second

sâniye ثانیه a second

sanjâb سنجاب squirrel

sanjâq سنجاق pin, hairpin

sanjâqak سنجاقک dragonfly

sanjesh سنجش measurement, testing

sanjidan (sanj) سنجیدن (سنج) to measure, to test

sânsor سانسور censorship

sânt سانت centimetre

sântimetr سانتیمتر centimetre

sâq ساق leg

sâqdush ساقدوش groomsman

sâqe ساقه stem, stalk

saqf سقف roof, ceiling

saqir صغیر minor, underage

saqqez سقز chewing gum

sar farmândeh سرفرمانده supreme commander

sâr سار starling

sar سر head, top, end

sar' صرع epilepsy, fits

sarâb سراب mirage

sarafkande سرافکنده ashamed, disgraced

sarafrâz سرافراز honoured

sarakhs سرخس fern

sarâne سرانه per capita, per head

saranjâm سرانجام end, finally

sarâsar سراسر throughout, all over

sarâshib سراشیب slope, steep

sarâsime سراسیمه confused, in a hurry

saratân سرطان cancer

sarâydâr سرایدار janitor, doorman

sarâziri سرازیری slop, downhill, steep

sarbâlâyi سربالایی uphill

sarbâz سرباز soldier, private

sarcheshme سرچشمه source

sard سرد cold, frigid, discouraged

sardabir سردبیر editor, chief secretory

sardaftar سردفتر notary public

sardâr سردار commander

sardard سردرد headache

sardaste سردسته group leader

sardi سردی coldness, frigidity

sardsir سردسیر cold region

sardushi سردوشی shoulder strap

sâreq سارق robber, thief

sarf صرف spending, consuming, profit

sarfe صرفه benefit, economy, interest

sarfejuyi صرفه جویی economy, providence

sargardân سرگردان wanderer, vagabond

sargarm konande سرگرم کننده entertaining

sargarm سرگرم busy, amused, preoccupied

sargarmi سرگرمی hobby, amusement, entertainment

sargije سرگیجه vertigo, dizziness

sargord سرگرد major

sargoshâde سر گشاده open, open lid

sargozasht سرگذشت adventure, tale, narrative

sarhadd سرحد border, boundary

sarhang سرهنگ colonel

sari' سریع fast, rapid, speedy

sarih صریح frank, explicit, precise

sarjukhe سرجوخه corporal

sarkâr سرکار honorific title in army

sarkarde سرکرده commander, leader

sarkârgar سرکارگر foreman

sarkeshi سرکشی inspection, revolt

sarkoft سرکوفت taunt, scoff

sarkonsul سرکنسول consulate general

sarkubi سرکوبی suppression, repression

sarleshkar سرلشکر major general

sarmâ khordegi سرما خوردگی a cold

sarmâ سرما cold, coldness

sarmâkhordegi سرما خوردگی catching cold

sarmaqâle سرمقاله editorial

sarmashq سرمشق copy, model

sarmâye سرمایه capital

sarmâyedâr سرمایه دار capitalist

285 SARMÂYEDÂRI

sarmâyedâri سرمایه داری capitalism

sarnegun سرنگون capsized, destroyed, upside down

sarneshin سرنشین passenger, crew member

sarnevesht سرنوشت fate, destiny

sarnize سرنیزه bayonet

sarosedâ سروصدا noise, commotion

sarparast سرپرست guardian, supervisor

sarpâyi سرپایی outpatient

sarpâyiyni سرپایینی slope, downhill

sarpichi سرپیچی disobedience, revolt

sarrâfi صرافی currency exchange

sarsari سرسری carelessly

sarshenâs سرشناس well known, famous

sarshir سرشیر cream

sarshomâri سرشماری census

sartâsar سرتاسر throughout, entire

sartip سرتیپ brigadier general

sarv سرو cypress tree

sarvân سروان captain

sarvar سرور leader, master, lord

sarzade سرزده suddenly, unexpectedly

sarzamin سرزمین country, territory

sarzanesh سرزنش blame, scolding

sath سطح surface, level

sathi سطحی shallow, superficial

satl سطل bucket

satr سطر line

sâtur ساطور large knife

savâb ثواب spiritual reward

savâd سواد literacy

savâr سوار rider, mounted, installed

savâre nezâm سواره نظام cavalry

savârkâr سوارکار jockey

sa'y سعی attempt, trying, effort

sâybân سایبان shade, sunshade

sâye سایه shadow, shade

sâyer سایر rest, other

sâyesh سایش friction, abrasion

sâyiydan (sây) ساییدن (سای) to grind, to wear away, to erode

sayyâd صیاد hunter

sayyal سیال fluid, flowing

sayyar سیار mobile, wanderer

sayyâre سیاره planet

sâz ساز musical instrument

sâzande سازنده creative, builder

sâzemân سازمان organization, institution

sâzesh سازش compromise, reconciliation

se chaharom سه چهارم three-quarters

se سه three

sebil سبیل moustache, whiskers

sebo'di سه بعدی tridimensional

sebqat سبقت overtaking, precedence

secharkhe سه چرخه tricycle

sedâ صدا voice, sound, noise, call

sedâdâr صدادار voiced, noisy

sedâqat صداقت honesty, truthfulness

sefârat سفارت embassy

sefâresh سفارش order, advice

sefâreshi سفارشی registered, recommended

sefat صفت attribute, character, adjective

sefid pust سفید پوست white skin, white

sefid سفید white, blank

sefr صفر zero

seft سفت tight, stiff, hard

segush سه گوش triangular

sehhat صحت health, well being, intactness

sehr سحر spell, magic

sekke سکه coin

sekseke سکسکه hiccup

sekte سکته stroke, hear attack

sel سل tuberculosis

selâh سلاح arms, armour

self servis سلف سرویس self-service

sellul سلول cell

selsele سلسله kingdom, dynasty

semâjat سماجت insistence, persistence

semat سمت position, designation

semej سمج persistent, cheeky

semsâri سمساری second hand store

senavâyi شنوایی hearing

senf صنف trade union, class, trade

senjed سنجد oleaster, wild olive

senn سن age

sepâh سپاه army

separ سپر shield, armour, bumper

sepas سپس then, afterwards

sepâsgozâri سپاسگزاری thanking, expressing gratitude

sepâye سه پایه tripod

sepordan (sepâr) (سپر) سپردن to recommend, to give, to deposit

seporde سپرده deposit

septâmr سپتامبر September

seqolu سه قلو triplet

seqt سقط abortion, miscarriage

serâhat صراحت frankness, bluntness, explicitness

serâmik سرامیک ceramic

serâyat سرایت contagion, transmission

serf صرف pure, mere

serfan صرفا merely, purely

seri سری set, series

serial سریال episodic

serish سریش glue

serke سرکه vinegar

serqat سرقت theft, robbery

serri سری secret, classified, confidential

servat mand ثروتمند rich, wealthy

servat ثروت wealth, property

seshanbe سه شنبه Tuesday

setâd ستاد headquarter

setam ستم cruelty, injustice, abuse

setamdide ستمدیده oppressed

setamgar ستمگر cruel, oppressor

setâre shenâs ستاره شناس astronomer

setâre ستاره star, asterisk, fortune

setâregan ستارگان stars

setâyesh gar ستایشگر worshiper

setâyesh ستایش praise, worship

setize ستیزه quarrel, dispute

sevvom سوم third

seyd صید hunt, prey, fishing

seyfi صیفی summer crop

seyl zade سیلزده flood victim

seyl سیل flooding

seyqal صیقل polish, shine

seyr سیر travel, tour, excursion

seyyed سید master, a decent of the prophet

sezâvâr سزاوار deserving, worthy

si سی thirty

sib zamini سیب زمینی potato

sib سیب apple

sidi سی دی CD

sigâr سیگار cigarettes

sigâri سیگاری cigarette smoker

sikh سیخ skewer, stiff

sili سیلی slap

sim pich سیم پیچ armature winder

sim سیم wire, cable

simâ سیما face, vision, appearance

simân سیمان cement, concrete

simkesh سیمکش wireman

sine pahlu سینه پهلو pneumonia

sine سینه breast, chest, bosom

sineband سینه بند bra, bib

sinemâ سینما cinema, movie

sini سینی tray, platter

siqe صیغه temporary marriage, paradigm

sir سیر full, satisfied, fed up, garlic

sirâb سیراب satisfied of drinking

sirâbi سیرابی tripe

sirk سیرک circus

sisad سیصد three thundered

siyâh pust سیاه پوست black coloured

siyâh sorfe سیاه سرفه whooping cough

siyâh zakhm سیاه زخم anthrax

siyâh سیاه black

siyâhat nâme سیاحت نامه tourist's itinerary

siyâhat سیاحت tour, travel, excursion

siyâhrag سیاهرگ vein

siyânor سیانور cyanide

siyâsat madâr سیاستمدار politician

siyâsat سیاست politics, policy

siyâsi سیاسی political

sizdah سیزده thirteen

sizdahbedar سیزده بدر thirteen's of new year's festivity

so'âl سئوال question, inquiry

sobât ثبات stability, firmness

sobh bekheyr صبح بخیر good morning

sobh صبح morning. am

sobhâne صبحانه breakfast

sodur صدور issuing, emission

sofâl سفال crockery, ceramic

sofâlgari سفال گری pottery, crockery

sofre سفره tablecloth

sogand سوگند swear, oath

sogovâri سوگواری mourning, funeral

sohân سوهان file, a type of sweet

sohbat صحبت speech, talk, chat

sohulat سهولت easiness

sokhan parâkani سخن پراکنی broadcasting

sokhan سخن speech, talk

sokhanchini سخن چینی gossip

sokhangu سخنگو spokesman, speaker

sokhanrân سخنران lecturer, speaker

sokhanrâni سخنرانی lecture, oration, speech

sokkân سکان helm

sokkândâr سکاندار helmsman

sokuh شکوه magnificence, glory

sokunat سکونت residence, settlement

sokut سکوت silence, quiet

solh صلح peace, reconciliation, compromise

solhâmiz صلح آمیز conciliatory, peaceful

solhtalab صلح طلب peace lover

sols ثلث third, one third

soltân سلطان king, sultan

solte سلطه dominance, control

som سم hoof

somâkh صماخ tympan, eardrum

somâq سماق sumac

some'e صومعه monastery, convent

sonbâde سنباده grindstone

sonbe سنبه ramrod

sonbol سنبل hyacinth

sonnat سنت tradition

sonni سنی Sunnite

soqât سوغات travel gift

soqut سقوط fall, crash, decline

sorang سرنگ syringe

sorâq سراغ clue, trace

sor'at سرعت speed, rapidity

sorb dar سرب دار leaded (petrol; gas)

sorb سرب lead

sorfe سرفه cough

sorkh karde سرخ کرده roasted, browned, fried

sorkh سرخ red

sorkhak سرخک measles

sorkhje سرخجه rubella

sorkhrag سرخرگ artery

sorme سرمه collyrium

sormeyi سرمه ای dark blue

sorsore سرسره skate

sorud سرود song, lyric, nursery rhyme

sorur سرور happiness, joy

sorush سروش inspiration

sos سوس ketchup

sost سست weak, flabby, slow

sosyal-domokrat سوسیال دمکرات social-democratic

sosyalist سوسیالیست socialist

sot صوت voice, sound

sotun ستون column, pillar

sotvân ستوان lieutenant

so'ud صعود climbing, mounting, ascending

su سو direction, side

sud dehi سود دهی profitability

sud سود benefit, profit, interest

sudmand سودمند profitable, useful, helpful

su'e hâzeme سوء هاضمه indigestion

sufi صوفی Sufi

sug سوگ sorrow, mourning

sukht سوخت fuel, combustion

sukhtan (suz) (سوز) سوختن to burn, to flame, to grieve

sukhtani سوختنی combustible, flammable

sukhtegi سوختگی burn

sukhtgiri سوختگیری fuelling

supâp سوپاپ valve

supur سپور garbage man, street cleaner

sur سور party, feast

surâkh سوراخ hole, puncture, cavity

surâkhkon سوراخ کن puncher

surat hesab صورت حساب bill (shopping)

surat صورت face, form, list, manu

surati صورتی pink

sure سوره a chapter of Koran

surutme سورتمه sledge

susan سوسن lily

susk سوسک cockroach

susmâr سوسمار lizard

sut سوت whistle, siren

suvis سویس Switzerland

suzâk سوزاک gonorrheae

suzân سوزان burning, flaming, smarting

suzan سوزن needle, pin, injection

suzanbân سوزن بان switch man

suzesh سوزش burn, pain, twinge

sh

shab bekheyr شب بخیر good evening, good night

shab kâri شب کاری night shift

shab neshini شب نشینی evening party

shab شب night, eve, evening

shabah شبح phantom, ghost, spook

shabâhat شباهت similarity, resemblance

shabake شبکه net, network

shabakiyye شبکیه retina

shabâne ruz شبانه روز day and night, round the clock

shabâne شبانه nightly, every night, overnight

shabâneruzi شبانه روزی all the time, boarding-house

shabbu شب بو wall flower

shabih شبیه similar, alike

shabikhun شبیخون night raid, ambush

shabkuri شبکوری night blindness

shabnam شبنم dew

shâd شاد happy, glad

shâdi شادی happiness

shadid شدید severe, intense

shâdravân شادروان the late, the deceased

shâ'er شاعر poet

shâ'erâne شاعرانه poetic, poetical

shafâ شفا cure, remedy, recovery

shafâhi شفاهی verbal, oral

shaffâf شفاف transparent

shaftâlu شفتالو peach

shâgerd شاگرد student, pupil, apprentice

shâgerdi شاگردی apprenticeship, training

shâh شاه king, Shah

shahâb sang شهاب سنگ meteor

shahâb شهاب meteor

shahâdat شهادت martyrdom, testimony

shahâmat شهامت bravery, greatness

shâhâne شاهانه kingly, royal

shâhanshâh شاهنشاه king, emperor

shâhdâne شاهدانه hempseed

shâhed شاهد witness, testifier

shâhi شاهی kingship, cress

shahid شهید martyr

shâhkâr شاهکار masterpiece

shâhnâme شاهنامه the Shah name book, epic of kings

shâhparast شاه پرست royalist

shahr شهر city, town

shâhrag شاهرگ carotid artery

shâhrâh شاهراه highway

shahrdâr شهردار mayor

shahrebâni شهربانی police headquarters

shahrestân شهرستان township

shahri شهری urban, metropolitan

shahrivar شهریور sixth month of Iranian calendar

shahriye شهریه tuition fee, stipend

shahrneshin شهرنشین city dweller, citizen

shâhtut شاه توت black mulberry

shahvat angiz شهوت انگیز lustful, sexy, arousing

shahvat parast شهوت پرست voluptuous, lustful

shahvat شهوت lust, passion

shâhzâde شاهزاده prince, princess

shajarenâme شجره نامه genealogy

shajarshenas شجره شناس genealogist

shak شک doubt, suspicion, indecision

shakar شکار sugar

shâkh شاخ horn

shâkhe شاخه branch, subdivision

shakhs شخص individual, person

shakhsi شخصی personal, civilian, private

shakhsiyyat شخصیت personality, entity

shâki شاکی suer, plaintiff

shakibâyi شکیبایی patience, tolerance

shakkâk شکاک sceptical, suspicious

shakl شکل figure, shape, form, picture

shâl شال scarf

shal شل crippled, limp

shalakhte شلخته clumsy, sluttish

shalil شلیل nectarine

shâlizâr شالیزار rice field

shallâq شلاق lash, whip

shalqam شلغم turnip

shalvâr شلوار pants, trousers

shalvarak شلوارک short

shâm شام dinner, supper

sham' شمع candle

sham'dân شمعدان chandelier

sham'dâni شمعدانی geranium

shâmel شامل including, containing

shâmme شامه sense of smell, olfactory

shâmpâni شامپانی champagne

shâmpâyn شامپاین champagne

shampo شامپو shampoo

shamshir bâzi شمشیربازی fencing

shamshir شمشیر sword

shamsi شمسی solar

sha'n شان dignity, status

shanbe شنبه Saturday

shâne شانه shoulder, comb

shanidan (shenav) شنیدن (شنو) to hear, to listen

shâns شانس luck, chance

shânsi شانسی random, accidentally

shânzdah شانزده sixteen

shappare شب پره bat

shaqâyeq شقایق corn poppy

shâqel شاغل employed, incumbent

shaqiqe شقیقه forehead

shâqul شاقول plumb line

shar' شرع religious law

sharâb شراب wine

sharaf شرف honour, dignity

sharâfat شرافت dignity, honour

sharârat شرارت wickedness, vice, vandalism

sharayân شریان artery

sharâyet شرایط conditions, terms

sharbat شربت syrup, tonic

shardâri شهرداری city council

shar'e شرعی lawful, legal

sharh شرح description, explanation

sharhe hâl شرح حال biography

shari'at شریعت religious law, religion

sharif شریف noble, honourable

sharik شریک partner, associate

sharji شرجی sultry, muggy

shârlâtân شارلاتان charlatan, quack

sharm شرم shame, timidity, pudency

sharmande شرمنده ashamed, embarrassed

sharmandegi شرمندگی embarrassment, shame

sharmâvar شرم آور disgraceful, indecent

sharmgâh شرمگاه pubis

sharmsâr شرمسار ashamed, disgraced

sharq شرق east, orient

sharqi شرقی eastern

sharr شر evil, mischief

shart شرط condition, bet, term

shartbandi شرط بندی betting, bid

sharti شرطی conditional

sharur شرور wicked, mischievous

shâsh شاش urine, piss, pee

shâshidan (shâsh) شاشیدن (شاش) to urinate, to piss

shast شست thumb

shast شصت sixty

shâter شاطر baker

shatranj شطرنج chess

shâyad شاید may, may be, possibly

shâye' شایع prevalent, epidemic, widespread

shaye'e شایعه rumour, gossip

shâyeste شایسته worthy, deserving, appropriate

shâyestegi شایستگی merit, worth, suitability

shayyâd شیاد impostor, charlatan

shebh شبه likeness

sheddat شدت intensity, severity

shegeft angiz شگفت انگیز surprising

shegefti شگفتی wonder, surprise

shekâf شکاف split, gap, cleavage

shekâftan (shekâf) شکافتن (شکاف) to split, to rip up, to analyse

shekam شکم tummy, stomach, belly

shekamu شکمو gluttonous

shekanande شکننده fragile

shekanje شکنجه torture, torment

shekâr شکار haunting, prey, hunt, catching

shekar شکر sugar

shekârchi شکارچی hunter

shekârgâh شکارگاه haunting ground

shekast nâpazir شکست ناپذیر invincible

shekast شکست defeat, failure

shekastan (shekan) (شكستن (شكن
to break, to interrupt, to crack

shekaste band شكسته بند
bonesetter, orthopaedist

shekaste شكسته broken, sad

shekastegi شكستگی fracture,
breakdown

shekâyat شكايت complaint,
grievance, whining

shekl شكل shape, form, figure

shekve شكوه complaint, grumble

shelank شلنگ hose

shellik شليک firing an arm,
shooting

shemsh شمش bullion

shemshâd شمشاد box tree

shen شن sand, gravel

shenâ شنا swimming

shenâgar شناگر swimmer

shenâkht شناخت knowledge,
recognition

shenâkhtan (shenâs) شناختن
(شناس) to know, to recognise

shenâsâyi شناسایی exploration,
recognition

shenâsnâme شناسنامه identity card,
birth certificate

shenavande شنونده listener

shenâvar شناور floating, buoyant

shenavâyi sanji شنوایی سنجی
audiometry

shenel شنل cloak, mantle

sheni شنی sandy

shenidan (shenav) شنيدن (شنو)
to hear

shenkesh شنكش rake

shepesh شپش lice

she'r شعر poetry

sherâkat شراکت partnership

sherakt شرکت company

sherkat شرکت company, firm,
partnership

shesh شش six

sheshlul ششلول revolver

sheshsad ششصد six hundred

shetâb شتاب hurry, speed, rush,
velocity

shey' شیئی thing, object

sheyâr شیار groove, fissure, cleft

sheykh شیخ clergy, old man

sheypur شیپور trumpet, horn

sheytân شیطان Satan, devil,
naughty

sheytanat شیطنت naughtiness,
diabolism

sheytâni شیطانی satanic, diabolic,
naughtiness

shib شیب slope, slant

shi'e شیعه Shiites

shifte شیفته fascinated, fond

shihe شیهه neighing

shik شیک stylish, fashionable

shikpush شیک پوش smartly
dressed

shili شیلی Chile

shimi شیمی chemistry

shimidân شیمی دان chemist

shimiyâyi شیمیایی chemical

shir شیر lion, milk, tap

shirbahâ شیربها gift to bride's
parents

shirdân شیردان rennet stomach

shirdeh شیرده milch

shire شیره syrup, juice, extract, opium residue

shirin شیرین sweet, succulent, attractive

shirini شیرینی sweetness, candy, cookie, confectionary

shirkhârgâh شیرخوارگاه nursery

shirvâni شیروانی gable roof

shishe شیشه glass, glass bottle, wind screen

shishebor شیشه بر glazier

shishegar شیشه گر glass blower

shivan شیون mourning, moaning

shive شیوه method, style

shiyâf شیاف suppository

sho'â' شعاع ray, radius, beam

sho'âr شعار slogan, motto

sho'bade bâz شعبده باز magician, juggler

sho'bade شعبده magic

sho'be شعبه branch, section

shodan (shav) (شدن (شو to become

shodani شدنی possible, feasible

shogun شگون good omen

shohar شوهر husband

shohardâr شوهردار married woman

shohrat شهرت publicity, fame, reputation

shojâ' شجاع brave, courageous

shojâ'at شجاعت bravery, courage

shokhm شخم plough

shokolât شکلات chocolate

shokr شکر thanks (to God), appreciation

shokrgozâri شکرگذاری thanksgiving

shokufe شکوفه blossom, bud

shol شل loose, soft, lenient

sho'le شعله flame, blaze

sholuq شلوغ busy, crowded, noisy

sholuqi شلوغی noise, crowed, disturbance

shomâ شما you (plural/polite)

shomâl شمال north

shomâli شمالی northern

shomâre شماره number, digit, issue

shomâregiri شماره گیری dialling

shomâresh شمارش counting, calculation

shomordan (shomâr) شمردن (شمار) to count, to calculate

shomorde شمرده distinct, intelligible

shoq شوق keenness, desire, eagerness

shoqâl شغال jackal

shoql شغل job, employment, position

shorshor شرشر flowing noise, splashing

shoru' شروع beginning, start, outset

shosh شش lung

shostan (shur) شستن (شور) to wash, to bathe

shosteshu شستشو washing, bathing

shotor شتر camel

sho'ur شعور intelligence, common sense

shovâliye شواليه cavalier

shoyu' شيوع outbreak, prevalence

sh'r شعر poem, poetry

shukh شوخ funny, joker

shukhi شوخى joke, fun, humour, kidding

shuluq شلوغ busy, crowded

shum شوم bad omen, ominous

shur شور salty

shurâ شورا assembly, council

shurangiz شورانگيز sensational

shuravi شوروى Soviet

shure شوره dandruff, flake, saltpetre

shuresh شورش riot, revolt, uprising

shureshi شورشى rebel

shuridan (shur) شوريدن (شور) to revolt, to rise

shuse سوسه gravelled road

t

tâ تا until, fold

ta'âdol تعادل balance, equilibrium

ta'ahhod تعهد commitment, liability

ta'ahhol تاهل marriage

ta'ajjob âvar تعجب آور amazing, surprising

ta'ajjob kardan تعجب کردن to wonder, to be surprised

ta'ajjob تعجب surprise, amazement

ta'âm طعام food

ta'ammol تامل hesitation, pause

ta'ârof kardan تعارف کردن to offer

ta'ârof تعارف compliment, offer, formality

ta'asof تاسف regret, remorse

ta'assob تعصب fanaticism, prejudice

ta'âvoni تعاونی cooperative

tâb تاب curl, twist, resistance

tab تب temperature (fever)

tabâdol تبادل exchange

taba'e تبعه national, citizen

tabah kâr تبهکار criminal, convict

tabâh تباه ruined, demolished

tabahhor تبحر mastery, skill

tâbân تابان shiny, glowing, brilliant

tabâni تبانی conspiracy, compact

tabaqe طبقه class, layer, category, floor, storey

tabaqebandi طبقه بندی classification, ranking

tabar تبر axe

tabassom تبسم smile

tabbâkhi طباخی cooking

tabdil تبدیل change, exchange

tâbe' تابع dependent, follower, citizen

tâbe تابه frying pan

tâbe'iyat تابعیت citizenship, nationality

tâbesh تابش radiation

tâbestân تابستان summer

tabi'at طبیعت nature, temper

tabib طبیب doctor, physician

tab'id تبعید exile

tâbidan (tâb) تابیدن (تاب) to shine, to curl

tabi'i طبیعی natural, normal, typical

ta'bir kardan تعبیرکردن to interpret

ta'bir تعبیر interpretation, paraphrasing

tab'iz تبعیض prejudice, bias, discrimination

tabkhâl تبخال herpes

tabkhir تبخیر evaporation, steaming

tabl طبل drum

tabliq تبلیغ propaganda, advertisement

tâblo تابلو board, painting

tabrik تبریک congratulation. good wishes

tâbut تابوت coffin

tadfin تدفین burial

tadriji تدریجی gradual

tadris kardan تدریس کردن to each

tadris تدریس teaching, instruction

tafâhom تفاهم mutual agreement

tafakkor تفكر thought, deliberation
tafâvot تفاوت difference, diversity
tafraqe تفرقه division, dispersion
tafrih تفريح recreation, fun
tafsir تفسير interpretation, commentary
taftish تفتيش inspection, search
tagarg تگرگ hail
tah mande ته مانده leftover
tah neshin ته نشين sediment, deposit
tah sigâr ته سيگار cigarettes butt
tah ته bottom, base
tahâjom تهاجم attack, offensive
tahâl طحال spleen
tahammol تحمل endurance, tolerance
tahavvo' تهوع nausea, vomiting
tahavvol تحول change, transformation
tahdid تهديد threat, intimidation
tahiyye تهيه preparation, provision
tahlil تحليل analysis, exhaustion
tahmil تحميل imposition
tahniyat تهنيت congratulations
tahqiq تحقيق research, investigation
tahqir تحقير humiliation, belittling
tahrif تحريف distortion, alteration
tahrik تحريک instigation, stimulation
tahrim تحريم sanction, prohibition
tahsil تحصيل education, study
tahsin تحسين admiration
tahvil تحويل to give, to hand over

tahviye تهويه ventilation
tâj gozâri تاج گذاری crowning, coronation
tâj تاج crown, crest
tajârob تجارب experiences
tajâvoz تجاوز rape, aggression, invasion
tâjer تاجر businessman, trader
tajrobe تجربه experience
tajrobi تجربی experimental
tajviz تجويز prescription, recommendation
tajziye تجزيه analysis, decomposition
tak khâl تک خال ace
tak تک single, alone, unique
takabbor تكبر pride, vanity
takâlif تكاليف duties, responsibilities
takallom تكلم conversation, speaking
takâmol تكامل evolution
takân تكان shaking, movement, motion
tâkestân تاكستان vineyard
takfir تكفير excommunication
takhallof تخلف violation, infringement
takhassos تخصص specialty, expertise
takhayyol تخيل imagination, fantasy
takhfif تخفيف discount, reduction
ta'khir تاخير delay, pause
takhliye تخليه evacuation
takhmin تخمين estimate

takhmir تخمیر fermentation

takhrib تخریب demolition, destruction

takht تخت bed, throne

takhte nard تخته نرد backgammon, dice, die

takhte تخته board, wooden piece

takhtesiyâh تخته سیاه blackboard

takhtkhab تخت خواب bed

tâkhto tâz تاخت و تاز invasion

ta'kid kardan تاکیدکردن to emphasise

ta'kid تاکید emphasis, insistence

taklif تکلیف duty, assignment

takmil تکمیل completion, full

tâksi تاکسی taxi

taksir تکثیر multiplication, reproduction

takye تکیه reliance, leaning

takzib تکذیب denial, refusing

talâ طلا gold

tâlâb تالاب pond pool

talab طلب loan, search, claim

talabe طلبه theology student

talabidan (talab) طلبیدن (طلب) to call, to summon, to invite

talabkâr طلبکار creditor

talaf تلف waste, loss, casualty

talafât تلفات casualty, fatalities

talaffoz تلفظ pronunciation

talâfi تلافی retaliation, revenge

talâkub طلاکوب inlaid with gold

talangor تلنگر fillip

talâq طلاق divorce

tâlâr تالار auditorium, hall

talâsh تلاش effort, struggle

talayi طلایی of gold

tâle' طالع fortune, star, destiny

tâleb طالب seeker, wiling

tâlebi طالبی cantaloupe

tâle'bin طالع بین fortune-teller

ta'lif تالیف writing, composing

talkh تلخ bitter

talqin تلقین suggestion

ta'm طعم taste, flavour

tama' طمع greed

tamaddon تمدن civilization

tama'kâr طمع کار greedy

tamalloq تملق flattery, sycophancy

tamâm تمام whole, full, complete

tamannâ تمنا desire, request

tamarkoz تمرکز centralization, concentration

tamâs تماس contact, impact

tamâshâ تماشا sightseeing, watching

tamâshâchi تماشاچی spectator, viewer

tamaskhor تمسخر ridicule, mocking

tamâyol تمایل inclination, tendency

tambr تمبر stamp

tamdid تمدید extension, prolongation

tameshk تمشک raspberry

ta'mim تعمیم generalisation, extension

ta'min تامین securing, ensuring

ta'mir kardan تعمیر کردن to repair

ta'mir تعمیر repair, mend

ta'mirgâh تعمیر گاه repair shop, garage

tamiz تمیز clean, distinction

tamkin تمکین obedience, submission

tampân تمپان tampons

tamrin تمرین exercise, drill

tan تن body

tanâb طناب rope, cord

tanaffor تنفر aversion, dislike

tanaffos تنفس breathing, respiration

tanâgoz تناقض contradiction, inconsistency

tanâsob تناسب proportion, ratio, symmetry

tanâsokh تناسخ metempsychosis

tanâsoli تناسلی genital

tanâvob تناوب alternation, recurrence

tanavvo' تنوع variety, diversity

tanazzol تنزل decrease, reduction

tanbâku تنباکو tobacco

tanbal تنبل lazy, idle

tanbali تنبلی laziness

tanbih تنبیه punishment

tandis تندیس statue

tandorost تندرست healthy

ta'ne âmiz طعنه آمیز sarcastic, ironical

tane تنه trunk, body

ta'ne طعنه scoff, taunting, sarcasm

tanfiz تنفیض authorization, confirmation

tang تنگ tight, narrow

tange تنگه strait, narrow pass

tanhâ تنها alone, lonely, sole

tanhâyi تنهایی loneliness

tanin طنین echo, tone, intonation

tankhâh تنخواه capital, funds

tanparvar تن پرور self indulgent

tanqiye تنقیه enema

tanur تنور furnace, oven

tanz طنز satire, joke

tanzim تنظیم arranging, adjusting

tanznevis طنز نویس satirist

tapânche طپانچه revolver, pistol

tapesh تپش palpitation, beating

tapidan (tap) تپیدن (تپ) to beat, to pulsate

tappe تپه hill

tâq طاق arch, roof, odd

taqaddom تقدم priority, precedence

taqallâ تقلا struggle, strife

taqallob تقلب cheating, falsification

taqallobi تقلبی forged, false

tâqat طاقت power, endurance

taqâto' تقاطع intersection, junction

taqâzâ تقاضا request, demand

tâqche طاقچه mantel, rack, shelf

taqdim تقدیم presenting, offering

taqdir تقدیر destiny, fate, praise

ta'qib kardan تعقیب کردن to follow, to chase

ta'qib تعقیب pursuit, chase, following

taqlid تقلید imitation, mimicry

taqriban تقریبا approximately, almost, about

taqsim تقسیم division, distribution

taqsir تقصیر guilt, fault

taqtir تقطیر distillation

tâqut طاغوت devil

taqvâ تقوا virtue

taqvim تقویم calendar

taqviyat تقویت strengthening, fortification

taqyiyr تغییر change, alteration

taqziye تغذیه eating, feeding

târ تار cord, blurred

tar تر wet, moist, damp

taraddod تردد traffic

taraf طرف side, direction, opponent

tarafdâr طرفدار supporter, fan, follower

tarâh طراح designer, sketcher

târâj تاراج plunder

tarak ترک crack, split

tarâkhom تراخم trachoma

tarakidan (tarak) (ترک)ترکیدن to burst, to explode, to blow up, to crack

tarâkom تراکم accumulation, congestion

tarâne ترانه song

taraqqe ترقه firecracker

taraqqi ترقی progress, improvement

tarâshidan (tarâsh) تراشیدن (تراش) to shave, to scrape

tarashshoh ترشح excretion, discharge

tarâzu ترازو scale

tarbiyat badani تربیت بدنی physical training

tarbiyat تربیت training, cultivation, politeness

tard طرد rejection, expulsion

tardid تردید doubt, skepticism

tare تره leek

ta'refe تعرفه tariff, certificate

tarh طرح design, plan, sketch, project

tarhim ترحیم funeral

tarhrizi طرحریزی planning, designing

ta'rif kardan تعریف کردن to define, to praise

ta'rif تعریف praise, definition

târik khâne تاریک خانه darkroom

târik تاریک dark, gloomy

târikh تاریخ history, date

târikhche تاریخچه diary, account

târikhi تاریخی historical

târikhnevis تاریخ نویس historian

târiki تاریکی darkness

tariq طریق means, manner, via

tarjih ترجیح preference

tarjome ترجمه translation

tark ترک abandon, leaving, quitting, departing

tarkesh ترکش quiver

tarkib ترکیب form, shape, combination

tarmim ترمیم repair, amendment

tarrâhi طراحی designing, sketching

tars ترس fear, fright, panic

tarsidan (tars) ترسیدن (ترس) to be scared, to be afraid

tarsim ترسیم drawing

tarsnâk ترسناک horrible, scary

tarsu ترسو coward

tartib ترتیب order, arrangement

tarvij ترویج propaganda, promotion

tarz طرز manner, method, mode

tâs طاس bald, dice, bowl

tasâdof تصادف accident, coincidence

tasâdofan تصادفا accidentally, by chance

tasarrof تصرف occupation, seizure

tasâvi تساوی equality

tasâvir تصویر pictures

tasavvof تصوف Sufism

tasavvor تصور imagination, conception

tasbit تثبیت stabilization

tasdiq تصدیق confirmation, license

tasfiye shode تصفیه شده filtered

tasfiye تصفیه filtration, purification

tashâboh تشابه similarity, resemblance

tashakkor تشکر gratitude, thanking

tashannoj تشنج convulsion, fit

tashayyo' تشیع shiism

tashdid تشدید aggravation, intensification

tas-hih kardan تصحیح کردن correction, proof reading

tashilât تسهیلات facilities

tashkhis تشخیص distinction, diagnosis

tashkil تشکیل formation, establishment

tashkilât تشکیلات organization, institution

tashrifât تشریفات ceremonies, formalities

tashrih تشریح description, explanation

tashviq تشویق encouragement

ta'sir تاثیر influence, impression, effect

ta'sis تاسیس establishment, founding

ta'sisât تاسیسات foundations, establishments

taskhir تسخیر conquering, captivation

taskin تسکین soothing, alleviation

taslihât تسلیحات ammunitions, armaments

taslim تسلیم submission, surrender

taslis تثلیث trinity

tasliyat تسلیت condolence, sympathy

tasmim تصمیم decision, determination

tasvib تصویب approval, confirmation

tasvir تصویر picture, illustration

tatbiq تطبیق comparison, checking

ta'til تعطیل cessation, holiday

ta'tilat تعطیلات holidays, vacation

ta'tili تعطیلی holiday

tâ'un طاعون plague

tavâfoq توافق agreement, mutual consent

tavahhom تفاهم imagination, illusion

tavahhosh توحش savagery, wildness

tavajjoh توجه attention

tavakkol توکل reliance, trust

tâval تاول blister

tavallod تولد birth

tâvân تاوان indemnity, compensation

tavân توان strength, power

tavânâyi توانایی ability

tavânestan (tavân) (توان) توانستن to be able, can

tavaqqo' توقع expectancy, anticipation

tavaqqof توقف stop, pause, halt

tavarrom تورم inflation, edema

tavassol توسل resort, recourse

tavassot توسط by, via, by means of

tâve تاوه pan

tavil طویل long, lengthy

tavile طویله stable, stall

ta'viz kardan تعویض کردن to replace, to exchange

ta'viz تعویض replacement, substitution

tâvus طاووس peacock

tâyefe طایفه tribe, clan, sect

ta'yiyd تایید confirmation, verification

ta'yiyn تعیین assigning, appointing

tâyp تایپ typing

tazâd تضاد contrast, contradiction

tazâhorât تظاهرات demonstrations

tazakkor تذکر reminding, warning

tâze vâred تازه وارد new comer

tâze تازه new, fresh

tâzekâr تازه کار inexperienced, novice

tâzi تازی haunting dog

taz'if تضعیف weakening

tâziyâne تازیانه whip, lash

tazmin تضمین guarantee, warranty

tazriq تزریق injection

tazyiyn تزیین decoration, ornament

te'âtr تئاتر theatre

tebb طب medicine, medical practice

tebbi طبی medical

tebqe طبق according to

te'dâd تعداد number

tefl طفل kid, child

teflak طفلک little kid, poor thing

tehrân تهران Tehran

tejârat تجارت business, commerce

tejâri تجاری commercial

tekke تکه piece, fragment

tekrâr تکرار repetition, recurrence

tekrâri تکراری repetitious

telâvat تلاوت recital (of Koran)

telefon chi تلفن چی operator

telefon تلفن telephone

telefone hamrâh تلفن همراه mobile phone

telegerâf تلگراف telegram

teleskop تلسکوپ telescope

telesm طلسم spell, charm

televiziyon تلویزیون television

temsâh تمساح crocodile

tenis تنیس tennis

teribun تریبون lectern

terminâl ترمینال bus station

teryâk تریاک opium

teryâki تریاکی addicted to opium

teshne تشنه thirsty

test تست test

teyf طیف spectrum

teyy طی passing, crossing

tile تیله marble

tim تیم team

timârestân تیمارستان mental hospital

timsâr تیمسار high rank military officer

tinat طینت instinct, nature, disposition

tip تیپ type, brigade

tiq تیغ razor, blade

tiqe تیغه lamella, edge, ridge

tir تیر arrow, dart, shot, bullet, fourth month of Iranian calendar

tirandâzi تیراندازی shooting, gunfire

tirâzh تیراژ circulation (newspaper)

tirbârân تیرباران a shower of shots, execution

tire تیره dark, dim, dash

tishe تیشه chip-axe

tiz تیز sharp, keen

tizhush تیزهوش genius, very intelligent

to تو you (singular/familiar)

to'am توام linked, joint

tobe توبه remorse, penitence

tobikh توبیخ reproof, reprimand

tof تف spit, saliva

tofâle تفاله scum, refuse

tofang تفنگ rifle, gun

tohfe تحفه gift, souvenir

tohidast تهیدست poor, empty-handed

tohin توهین offence

tohmat تهمت accusation

tojih توجیه accounting for, justification

tojjâr تجار merchants, businessmen

tokhm ozâr تخم گذار oviparous

tokhm تخم seed, egg, sperm, testicle

tokhmak تخمک ovum

tokhmdân تخمدان ovary

tokhme morq تخم مرغ egg

tokhme تخمه roasted seeds

tolid konande تولید کننده producer

tolid تولید production, generation

tolide mesl تولید مثل reproduction

tolombe تلمبه pump

tolu' طلوع sunrise

to'me طعمه bait, prey, victim

ton تن metric ton

tonbak تنبک tambourine

tonbân تنبان loose pants

tond تند fast, spicy, hot, quick

tondar تندر thunder

toqif توقیف arrest, custody

toqyân طغیان overflowing, rebellion, outburst

tor طور manner, method, kind

torât تورات torah

tord ترد crisp, frail

tormoz ترمز brake

torob ترب radish

torsh ترش sour

torshi ترشی sourness, pickles

tose'e توسعه expansion, extension

toshak تشک mattress

tosif توصیف description

tosiye توصیه recommendation, advice

tote'e توطئه plot, conspiracy

tozi' توزیع distribution, division

tozih توضیح explanation

tozi'konande توزیع کننده distributor

tu rafte تورفته indented

tu تو inside, within, in

tubre توبره feed bag

tudamâqi تودماغی nasal

tude توده mass, heap, pile

tufân طوفان typhoon, storm

tul طول length, duration

tulâni طولانی long, lengthy

tule sag توله سگ puppy

tule توله puppy

tuli طولی longitudinal

tulu' طلوع sunrise

tumâr طومار scroll, roll

tup bâzi توپ بازی playing game

tup توپ ball, cannon, piece

tupkhâne توپخانه artillery

tur تور net

tusari توسری a blow on the head

tushe توشه provisions

tusi طوسی dark grey

tut ferangi توت فرنگی strawberry

tut توت berry

tuti طوطی parrot

tutivâr طوطی وار parrot-like

tutun توتون tobacco

tuvâlet توالت toilet

u

u او he, she

ulterâsând اولتراساند ultrasound

ulum علوم sciences

umumi عمومی general

umur امور affairs, matters

urupâ اروپا Europe

urupâyi اروپایی European

usul اصول principles

ut اوت august

utu اطو iron

utubus اتوبوس bus

utushuyi اتوشوئی dry cleaner

v

va ellâ و الا otherwise, or else

va و and

vabâ وبا cholera

vabâl وبال trouble, bother

vâbaste وابسته related, attaché, dependent, relative

vâbastegi وابستگی affiliation, connection, linkage

vâdâr وادار made, persuaded, led

va'de وعده promise, vow

va'degâh وعده گاه meeting place

vâdi وادی valley, desert

vadi'e ودیعه deposit, bond

vâ'ez واعظ preacher

vafâ وفا loyalty, fidelity

vafâdâr وفادار loyal, trusty

vafâdâri وفاداری loyalty, fidelity

vâfer وافر abundant, plentiful

vâfi وافی adequate, sufficient

vâfur وافور opium smoking pipe

vagarna وگرنه otherwise

vâgerâ واگرا divergent

vâgerâyi واگرایی divergence

vâgirdâr واگیردار contagious

vâgon واگن wagon, railway coach

vâgozâr واگذار given, transferred

vah واه oh, alas

vahdat وحدت unity, solitude, union

vâhed واحد one, single, unit, credit

vâheme واهمه fear, fright

vâhi واهی futile, vain, groundless

vahle وهله step, period, stage

vahm وهم illusion, imagination

vahsh وحش wild, wilderness

vahshat وحشت dread, fright, panic

vahshatnâk وحشتناک horrible, terrifying, frightful

vahshatzade وحشتزده frightened, terrified

vahshi وحشی savage, uncivilised, wild, fierce

vahshigari وحشیگری cruelty, barbarity, savagery

vahshiyâne وحشیانه savage, cruel

vahy وحی inspiration, revelation

vajab وجب span

vajd وجد ecstasy, excessive joy

vâjeb واجب compulsory, necessary

vâjebât واجبات religious precepts

vâjebi واجبی depilatory cream

vâjed واجد possessing, having

vajh وجه fund, money, face, reason, surface

vâkdâr واکدار voiced

vâke واکه vowel

vâkh واخ ouch

vakhim وخیم bad, critical

vakil وکیل a member of parliament, attorney, deputy

vâkonesh واکنش reaction

vâks واکس polish

vâksan واکسن vaccine

vâksi واکسی shoeblack

vâksinâsyon واکسیناسیون vaccination

vâl وال whale

vâlâ والا exalted, eminent, highness

vala' ولع voracity, greed

valadozzenâ ولدزنا bastard

vâlâhazrat والاحضرت royal highness

vâlede والده mother

vâledeyn والدین parents

vâleh واله distracted, dazzled

vâli والی governor-general

vali ولی but, guardian, parent, protector

vali'ahd ولیعهد crown prince

valikan ولیکن but, however

vallâh والله by God

valo ولو even though

vâm وام debt, loan

vâmândan (vâ mân) واماندن (وا مان) to be exhausted, to liger behind

vâmânde وامانده exhausted, helpless, worn out

vân وان bathtub

vânemud وانمود pretending, simulation

vânet وانت van

vang ونگ cry

vângahi وانگهی furthermore, besides

vânil وانیل vanilla

vâpas واپس back

vâpasin واپسین last

vâqe' واقع placed, situated, located

vâqe'an واقعا really, indeed

vâqe'e واقعه event, happening, event

vâqef واقف aware, informed, conscious

vâqe'i واقعی real, actual

vâqe'iyat واقعیت reality, truth, fact

vaqf وقف pious legacy, endowment

vaqfe وقفه standstill, pause, delay

vaqfi وقفی endowed, dedicated

vaqih وقیح impudent, shameless

vaqt koshi وقت کشی killing time, idling

vaqt وقت time, occasion

vaqti وقتی when, once, whenever

vaqtshenâs وقت شناس punctual, tactful

var âmadan (var ây) ور آمدن (ور آی) to ferment, to rise, to come off

var raftan (var rav) ور رفتن (ور رو) to tamper, to manipulate

varâ ورا behind, beyond

vâraftan (vârav) وارفتن (وارو) to loosen, to become flabby

vârafte وارفته loose, relaxed, mushy

varam ورم inflammation, swelling

varandâz kardan ورانداز کردن to measure, to look over

varaq ورق leaf, sheet, page, playing card, layer

varaqbâz ورق باز card player, gambler

varaqbâzi ورق بازی card playing, gambling

varaqe ورقه paper, sheet, coat, lamina

varaqpâre ورق پاره scrap of paper

vârasi وارسی investigation, search, inspection

vâraste وارسته free, librated

vardâshtan (var dâr) ورداشتن (وردار) to take, to pick up

vâred وارد arrived, entered, aware, expert

vâredât واردات imports

vâredâti وارداتی imported

vârede وارده received, imported, recorded

vâres وارث heir, heiress

varid ورید vein

varshekaste ورشکسته bankrupt, broke

varshekastegi ورشکستگی bankruptcy

vâru وارو reversed, upside down

vârune وارونه upside down, inside out, reverse

varzesh ورزش exercise, sport, athletics

varzeshgâh ورزشگاه stadium, sports arena

varzeshi ورزشی related to sport

varzeshkâr ورزشکار sportsman, athlete

varzide ورزیده trained, skilled

varzidegi ورزیدگی dexterity, being well trained

vasat وسط middle, centre, among, between

vasati وسطی central, middle

vâsete واسطه mediator, broker, agent, cause

vasfi وصفی explanatory, participial

vasi' وسیع large, wide, extensive

vasi وصی guardian, representative

vasile وسیله equipment, medium, means

vasiqe وثیقه deposit, bond

vasiyyat nâme وصیت نامه written will

vasiyyat وصیت will, testament

vasl وصل connecting, joining, link

vaslat وصلت matrimony, wedlock

vasle وصله patch, repair, mending

vasvâs وسواس obsession, fuss

vasvase وسوسه temptation, seduction, enticement

vasvâsi وسواسی obsessive, fussy

vatan parast وطن پرست patriot

vatan وطن motherland, native country

vatandust وطن دوست patriot

vatanparasti وطن پرستی patriotism

vâveylâ واویلا alas, woe

vây وای ah, alas, woe

vâyistâdan (vâyist) وایستادن (وایست) to stand, to wait, to stop

vaz' وضع condition, state, position

vâz وعظ preaching, sermon

vazaq وزغ frog, toad

vaz'e haml وضع حمل labour, childbirth, deliver

vâzeh واضح obvious, apparent, self-evident

vâzhe واژه word, term

vâzhegân واژگان vocabulary

vâzhegun واژگون capsized, overturned

vâzhenâme واژه نامه dictionary

vazidan (vaz) وزیدن (وز) to blow, to breeze

vazife shenâs وظیفه شناس dutiful

vazife وظیفه duty, task, obligation

vazin وزین heavy, dignified

vazir وزیر minister

vâzlin وازلین Vaseline

vazn وزن weight, tonnage, load

vazne bardâr وزنه بردار weight lifter

vazne bardâri وزنه برداری weight lifting

vazne وزنه weight, counter weight

vaz'yyat وضعیت condition, situation, position

vedâ' وداع farewell, goodbye

vefq وفق conformity, accordance

vejdân وجدان conscience

vejdânan وجدانا conscientiously, justly

vejhe وجهه popularity, esteem

vejin وجین weeding

vekâlat nâme وکالت نامه a proxy, a mandate

vekâlat وکالت proxy, attorneyship, deputyship

vekhâmat وخامت badness, critical situation

vel ول loose, free, unrestrained

velâdat ولادت birth

velarm ولرم tepid, mild

velâyat ولایت province, state, guardianship

velgard ولگرد vagabond, tramp, wanderer

velo ولو spread wide, scattered

velvele ولوله noise, brawl

veqâhat وقاحت shame, impudence

veqâr وقار dignity, poise

ver ور chatter, gabble

verâsat وراثت heredity, inheritance

verd ورد spell, incantation

verrâj وراج talkative, verbose

verrâji وراجی talkativeness, verbosity

vesâtat وساطت mediation, intervention

vesf وصف description, explanation

vesileye naqliye وسیله نقلیه means of transport, vehicle

veylân ویلان wandering, vagrant

vezârat وزارت ministry, department

vezârati وزارتی ministerial

vezâratkhâne وزارتخانه ministry, department

vezvez وز وز buzzing, humming

virân ویران destroyed, ruined

virâne ویرانه ruin

virâni ویرانی destruction, demolition

virâstâr ویراستار editor

virâyesh ویرایش edition

virus ویروس virus

vitâmin ویتامین vitamin

viyâr ویار pica, longing of a pregnant woman

viyolon ویولون violin

vizâ ویزا visa

vizhe ویژه special, specific

vizhegi ویژگی speciality

vofur وفور abundance, overflow, plenitude

vojud وجود being, entity, existence

voqu' وقوع happening, occurrence

vorud ورود entrance, arrival, entry

vorudi ورودی entrance, imported, admission fee

vos' وسع ability, capacity

vos'at وسعت breadth, extent, width

vostâ وسطا medieval, middle

vosul وصول reception, arrival, collection

vozu وضو ablution before prayer

vozuh وضوح clarity, lucidity

vul وول wiggle, tossing

y

yâ یا either, or, oh

yâbu یابو pony, nag, hack

yâd dâdan (yâd dah) (یاد دادن (یاد ده to teach, to instruct

yâd gereftan (yâd gir) یاد گرفتن (یاد گیر) to learn

yâd یاد memory, recall

yadak kesh یدک کش towboat

yadak یدک towing

yadaki یدکی spare part

yâdâv ardan (yâd âvar) یاد آوردن (یاد آور) to remember, to remind

yâdâvari یاد آوری remembrance, reminding

yâdbud یادبود memory, remembrance, memorial

yâddâsht یادداشت note, reminder

yâdgâr یادگار ma reminder, a souvenir, a keepsake

yâdgiri یادگیری learning, instruction

yâ'ese یائسه menopausic

yâ'esegi یائسگی menopause

yâftan (yâb) یافتن (یاب) to find, to obtain

yâgut یاقوت sapphire, ruby

yahud یهود Jews

yahudi یهودی Jewish

yahudiyyat یهودیت Judaism

yakh zade یخ زده frozen

yakh یخ ice

yakhchâl یخچال fridge, refrigerator

yakhdân یخدان icebox

yakhe یخه collar

yakhshekan یخ شکن ice pick, ice chopper

yâkhte یاخته cell

yâl یال mane

yaldâ یلدا the longest night of winter

ya'ni یعنی meaning, namely, it means

yaqe یقه collar

yâqi یاغی rebel, outlaw

yaqin یقین certain, positive, sure, confidence

yaqinan یقینا surely, certainly

yaqmâ یغما plunder, booty

yâr یار friend, companion, sweetheart

yarâq یراق braid, harness

yaraqân یرقان jaundice

yâri یاری help, aid, assistance

yâru یارو a guy, a chap, a fellow

ya's یاس despair, disappointment

yâs یاس jasmine

yashm یشم jasper

yâtâqân یاتاقان bearing of a car

yatim یتیم orphan

yâvar یاور helper, aid

yavâsh yavâsh یواش یواش gradually, little by little

yavâsh یواش slow, slowly, softly, gentle

yâve یاوه nonsense, absurd, vain

yâveguyi یاوه گویی talking nonsense, babbling

yâzdah یازده eleven

yâzdahom یازدهم eleventh

yazdân یزدان God

yegân یگان unit (army)

yegâne یگانه unique, only one, sole

yek bâr یکبار once, one time

yek daf'e یک دفعه suddenly, all at once

yek dar miyân یک در میان every other, alternatively

yek ho یکهو suddenly, all of a sudden

yek jânebe یک جانبه unilateral

yek navâkht یکنواخت monotonous, tedious

yek pârche یکپارچه solid, integrated

yek shabe یکشبه overnight

yek tarafe یک طرفه one way, biased

yek یک one, a, an, single

yekdande یک دنده stubborn, persistent

yekdast یکدست pure, uniform, unmixed

yekdigar یکدیگر each other

yeki یکی one, someone, somebody

yekjâ یکجا altogether, in a lump

yeksân یکسان identical, equal, similar

yeksare یکسره one way, straight

yekshanbe یکشنبه Sunday

yektâ یکتا single, unique

yeylâq ییلاق countryside, summer quarter

yeylâqi ییلاقی summer residence, villa

yobs یبس dry, constipated

yobusat یبوست constipation

yod ید iodine

yomiyye یومیه daily

yomn یمن blessing, grace, felicity

yonje یونجه alfalfa

yunân یونان Greece

yunâni یونانی Greek

yuresh یورش attack, raid, assault

yuzpalang یوزپلنگ panther

z

zâbete ضابطه standard, criterion

zabt ضبط recording, confiscation

zadan (zan) (زن) زدن to hit, to beat, to play instrument

zado khord زدوخورد fight, clash

za'f ضعف weakness, feebleness

za'ferân زعفران saffron

zâher sâzi ظاهرسازى pretending, faking

zâher ظاهر appearance, obvious, look

zâheran ظاهرا obviously, apparently

zâheri ظاهرى superficial, outward

zahr زهر poison, venom

za'if ضعيف weak

zajr زجر torment, torture

zakât زكات alms

zakhâmat ضخامت thickness, coarseness

zakhim ضخيم thick, coarse

zakhire ذخيره reserve, stock, saving

zakhm زخم injury, wound

zakhmi زخمى wounded

zâlem ظالم cruel, brutal, ruthless

zâlemâne ظالمانه unjust, ruthlessly

zalil ذليل weak, abject

zamâd ضماد plaster

zamâmdâr زمامدار ruler, governor

zamân زمان time, duration, era, tense

zamânat ضمانت guaranty, warranty, bond, bail

zâmen ضامن bail, safety bolt, bondsman

zamime ضميمه attachment, appendix, annex

zamin larze زمين لرزه earthquake

zamin shenâsi زمين شناسى geology

zamin زمين earth, ground, land, floor

zamine زمينه background, field, basis

zamir ضمير pronoun, conscience

zamzame زمزمه whispering, murmur

zan زن woman, wife

zanamu زن عمو paternal uncle's wife

zanande زننده repelling, shocking, obscene

zanâne زنانه womanly, female, feminine

zanâshuyi زناشويى marriage

zanbâbâ زن بابا stepmother

zanbaq زنبق lily

zanbâz زن باز womaniser

zanbil زنبيل basket, hamper

zanbur زنبور bee, wasp

zandâr زندار married man

zandâyi زن دايى maternal uncle's wife

zang zade زنگ زده rusty

zang زنگ bell, dial tone, rust

zanjabil زنجبيل ginger

zanjalab زن جلب cuckold

zanjir زنجير chain, shackle

zann ظن suspicion, doubt, mistrust

zânu زانو knee

zar زر gold

zarabân ضربان beating, pulse

zarâfat ظرافت delicacy, elegance, tenderness

zarar ضرر loss, harm, damage

zarb ضرب multiplication, rhythm

zarbe ضربه stroke, hit, impact, beat

zarbohmasal ضرب المثل proverb, saying

zard زرد yellow

zardâlu زردآلو apricot

zardchube زردچوبه turmeric

zarde زرده yolk

zarf shuyi ظرف شویی dish washer

zarf ظرف container, utensil

zarfiyyat ظرفیت capacity, valency

zargar زرگر goldsmith

zarib ضریب coefficient, index

zarif ظریف delicate, fine, elegant, frail

zarih ضریح shrine, tomb

zarrâfe زرافه giraffe

zarrât ذرات particles

zarre ذره particle

zarrebin ذره بین magnifying glass

zartosht زرتشت Zoroaster

zartoshti زرتشتی Zoroastrian

zarurat ضرورت need, necessity, emergency

zaruri ضروری necessary, essential

zarvaraq زرورق foil

zât ذات essence, nature

zâti ذاتی intrinsic, innate

zâtorriye ذات الریه pneumonia

zavâl زوال decline, downfall

zavvâr زوار pilgrims

zâye' ضایع spoiled, rotten, damaged

zâye'e ضایعه damage, loss, wastage

zebh ذبح slaughter

zedd ضد contrary, against, opposite

zedde yakh ضد یخ antifreeze

zegil زگیل wart

zeh زه cord, rim

zehâr زهار pubis

zehkeshi زهکشی drainage

zehn ذهن mind, memory

zekr ذکر mentioning, recital

zel' ضلع angle, side

zelânde no زلاند نو New Zealand

zellat ذلت lowliness, suffering, misery

zelzele زلزله earthquake

zelzelezade زلزله زده victim of earthquake

zemestân زمستان winter

zemn ضمن meantime, while

zemnan ضمنا by the way, meanwhile

zemni ضمنی implicitly, implied

zenâ زنا adultery

zenâkâr زناکار adulterer

zenâzâde زنازاده bustard

zendân زندان prison, jail

zendânbân زندانبان jailor

zendâni زندانی prisoner, inmate, captive
zende bâd زنده باد long live
zende زنده alive, live, lively
zendegi زندگی life, living
zerâ'at زراعت agriculture, farming
zerang زرنگ clever, smart, cunning
zereh زره armour, shielding
zerehi زرهی armoured
zerehpush زره پوش armoured
zerehshekan زره شکن armour-piercing
zereshk زرشک barberry
zeshti زشتی ugliness
zeytun زیتون olives
zibâ زیبا beautiful, nice, pretty
zibâyi زیبایی beauty, elegance
zin زین saddle
zinaf' ذینفع beneficiary
zip زیپ zipper
zir nevis زیرنویس subtitles
zir sigâri زیرسیگاری ashtray
zir زیر under, below, beneath, high pitch
zirâ زیرا because
zirbanâ زیربنا infrastructure, foundation
zirdaryâyi زیردریایی submarine
zirdast زیردست inferior, subordinate
zirpirâhan زیر پیراهن undershirt
zirpush زیرپوش underwear
zirpusti زیر پوستی subcutaneous
zirshalvâri زیرشلواری underpants

zirsigâri زیرسیگاری ashtray
zirzamin زیرزمین basement, cellar
zirzamini زیرزمینی underground
zist زیست life, living
zistshenâsi زیست شناسی biology
ziyâd زیاد many, much, plenty
ziyâderavi زیاده روی overindulgence
ziyâfat ضیافت party, reception, feast
ziyân زیان loss, harm
ziyânâvar زیان آور harmful
ziyârat زیارت کردن pilgrimage
ziyâratgâh زیارتگاه shrine
zob ذوب کردن melting, dissolution
zohr ظهر noon, mid day
zohre زهره Venus
zohur ظهور کردن appearance, outburst, advent
zoj زوج couple, pair, even number
zokâm ذکام cold, flue
zolâl زلال transparent, clear
zolf زلف lock of hair
zolm ظلم کردن injustice, cruelty
zolmat ظلمت darkness, gloom
zomorrod زمرد emeralds
zoq ذوق talent, zeal, enthusiasm
zoqâl akhte ذغال اخته dogberry
zoqâl ذغال charcoal, coal
zoqâlsang ذغال سنگ coal
zorrat ذرت corn
zud زود quick, early, soon
zudbâvar زودباور naïve, credulous
zulbiâ زولبیا a type of sweet

zur زور power, force, coercion

zurgu زورگو bully, oppressive

zurkhâne زورخانه gymnasium

zuzanaqe ذوزنقه trapezoid

zuze زوزه wailing, yelping

zh

zhâkat ژاکت jacket, pullover
zhânviye ژانویه January
zhâpon ژاپن Japan
zhâponi ژاپنی Japanese
zharf ژرف deep, profound
zhen ژن gene
zhenerâl ژنرال general
zhest زشت gesture, manner
zhimnastik ژیمناستیک gymnastics
zho'an ژوئن June
zhu'an ژوئن June
zhu'ye ژوئیه July

OTHER TITLES OF INTEREST FROM IBEX PUBLISHES

AN INTRODUCTION TO PERSIAN / W. M. THACKSTON
A comprehensive guide and grammar to the language
isbn 0-936347-29-5

HOW TO SPEAK, READ & WRITE PERSIAN / H. AMUZEGAR
A self-teaching course including book and audio cassettes.
isbn 0-936347-05-9

AN ENGLISH-PERSIAN DICTIONARY / DARIUSH B. GILANI
Includes Persian equivalents and transliteration. About 22,000 entries.
isbn 0-936347-95-3

A DICTIONARY OF COMMON PERSIAN & ENGLISH VERBS / H. AMUZEGAR
isbn 1-58814-030-x

MILLENNIUM OF CLASSICAL PERSIAN POETRY / W. THACKSTON
A guide to the reading and understanding of Persian poetry from the tenth to the twentieth century
isbn 0-936347-50-3

1001 PERSIAN-ENGLISH PROVERBS / SIMIN HABIBIAN
1001 Persian proverbs and idioms with corresponding English proverb and a literal translation in English. Illustrated.
isbn 1-58814-021-0

THE LITTLE BLACK FISH / SAMAD BEHRANGI
English translation and Persian text of mahi siah kuchulu.
isbn 0-936347-78-3

MODERN PERSIAN PROSE LITERATURE / HASSAN KAMSHAD
Classic on the subject and Hedayat with new introduction.
isbn 0-936347-72-4

PERSIAN STUDIES IN NORTH AMERICA / MEHDI MARASHI, ED.
32 articles on the state of the study of Persian literature.
isbn 0-936347-35-X

PERSIAN HANDWRITING / MEHDI MARASHI
Book and interactive CD.
isbn 1-58814-000-8

A LITERARY HISTORY OF PERSIA / EDWARD G. BROWNE
The classic history of Persian literature
isbn 0-936347-66-X

THE DIVAN-I HAFIZ / H. WILBERFORCE CLARKE TRANSLATOR
Complete literal translation of Hafez's divan with copious notes.
isbn 0-936347-80-5

THE POEMS OF HAFEZ
Translations by English literature professor of Iranian heritage.
isbn 1-58814-019-9

THE HAFEZ POEMS OF GERTRUDE BELL
isbn 0-936347-39-2

IN WINESELLER'S STREET / THOMAS RAIN CROWE, TRANS.
Renderings of Hafez by American poet.
isbn 0-936347-67-8

SELECTED POEMS FROM THE DIVAN-E SHAMS-E TABRIZI
isbn 0-936347-61-9

THE EYE OF AN ANT: PERSIAN PROVERBS & POEMS / F. AKBAR
Persian wisdom rendered into English verse along with the original
isbn 0-936347-56-2

THE LOVE POEMS OF AHMAD SHAMLU / FIROOZEH PAPAN-MATIN
On the most popular modern Persian poet
isbn 1-58814-037-7

A HISTORY OF LITERARY CRITICISM IN IRAN / IRAJ PARSINEJAD
*Literary Criticism in the Works of Akhundzadeh, Kermani, Molkom Khan, Talbof,
Maraghei, Kasravi and Hedayat*
isbn 1-58814-016-4

To order the above books or to receive
our catalog, please contact

*IBEX Publishers / Post Office Box 30087 / Bethesda, MD 20824
Phone 301-718-8188 / Fax 301-907-8707 / www.ibexpublishers.com*